GROWING UP IN RURAL
LOUISIANA

A MEMOIR
1943 - 1963

GROWING UP IN RURAL LOUISIANA

A MEMOIR
1943 - 1963

ANN MULLEN-MARTIN

Growing Up in Rural Louisiana: a Memoir
Published by Annmuma Publishing
Mesquite, Texas, U.S.A.

MULLEN-MARTIN, ANN, Author
GROWING UP IN RURAL LOUISIANA
ANN MULLEN-MARTIN

Library of Congress Control Number: 2024922911

ISBN: 979-8-9914644-4-4, 979-8-9914644-6-8 (paperback)
ISBN: 979-8-9914644-7-5 (hardcover)
ISBN: 979-8-9914644-5-1 (digital)

BIOGRAPHY & AUTOBIOGRAPHY / Women
SELF-HELP / Personal Growth / Happiness
BODY, MIND & SPIRIT / Inspiration & Personal Growth

Editing: Jennifer Christiansen (jacobswc.com/team/jennifer-christiansen)
Publishing Management: Tim Jacobs (jacobswc.com)
Publishing Consulting: Susie Schaefer (finishthebookpublishing.com)

QUANTITY PURCHASES: Schools, companies, professional groups, clubs, and other organizations may qualify for special terms when ordering quantities of this title. For information, visit annmuma-publishing.com

DEDICATION

This book is dedicated to my brother, John B, Yeager, Jr. Without John to share my growing up years, the stories in this book would not exist. He was always there, next to me, whether we were sharing a laugh or a tear. Thank you, John.

CONTENTS

INTRODUCTION

I fought my way into this world on November 11, 1943, kicking, screaming, and demanding immediate attention.

Success in getting that attention allowed nine years to pass before I learned the date commemorated something other than my birthday. Until then, the red calendar numbers belonged only to me.

My house, my clothes, my physical appearance—none of these things served to make me unique in my community. The people I lived with—the ones who loved and guided me—believed my presence alone was enough for celebration. Mama doted on me and often spoke of me as God's blessing and His challenge to her.

Every child should feel so special.

I began as a difficult pregnancy, and Mama breathed a sigh of both apprehension and relief at my appearance just short of her thirty-third birthday. Mama's survival was so in doubt that Daddy offered me to his childless sister—should Mama die while bringing me into the world. She survived, and I became Aunt Olevia's namesake instead of her daughter.

Together, Mama and I cherished every minute of the dozen or so years we were to share, and I coveted any of her time that belonged to others. A shy, bookish child, I got my library card a year before I had earned a first-grade report card. Twice a week, I clung to Mama's hand as we hiked a mile to choose books that offered windows to the rest of the world. Books and my mama became my best friends— maybe my only real friends.

With brown hair cut square, bangs across the front and the sides just below my ears, and glasses perched on my flat nose, I had a sense of invulnerableness based on complete trust in my mama's ability and desire to protect me. Despite my innocence and naivety, in my heart, I knew I could take care of myself. God built into my psyche a mix of rural simplicity and unearned worldly confidence.

Mama and Daddy brought me home from Pineville's Texada Clinic to our Tioga residence. If you looked up "rural" in the dictionary and found a picture of Tioga, Louisiana in the 1940s, 50s, or even early 60s, it would be an apt and accurate definition. Fewer than three hundred people called Tioga proper their home, and most of those were housed in frame structures—many with a dog on a short chain prominently staked in the front yard.

The Tioga area consisted of several smaller, mirror-image villages—Ball, Lee Heights, Kingsville, Paradise, and Rigolette—but none of them merited their own school district; thus, Tioga reigned as king in their midst.

The Yeager family came from Illinois and settled near Flaggon Creek and Paradise community where they bought 1,800 acres. One of the Yeager sons, Clemont, formed a company to fight in the Civil War and appointed himself sergeant. While Clemont was away at war, his brother died; when Clemont returned, he married his brother's widow. Clemont Yeager is credited with building the first sawmill in the community in 1870. Records show he bought a long steamboat boiler in Shreveport, floated it down the Red River to Alexandria, and hauled it to his home with a team of oxen.

A one-room school erected by locals in 1897 provided the podium for Miss Daisy Margaret Yeager as the first teacher. According to my dad, she held a place as a direct relative in our Yeager clan—more specifically, our cousin Yeagers, who we referred to as the "rich" Yeagers who lived nearby. Daisy was born in Rapides Parish in 1878 and died in Pineville in 1950.

In 1905, the post office's name officially became Tioga Post Office, and in 1925, the sawmill closed. The community and Tioga schools remained. In 1915, a thirty-thousand-dollar bond issue allowed Ball, Rigolette, Brasher, and Tioga schools to be consolidated under the Tioga High School name.

By the time I reached school age, the school consisted of three buildings housing grammar, junior high, and high schools, plus a large gymnasium and plenty of acreage. Locals called the complex Tioga High School. Black families across the railroad tracks shared Tioga as a living and sleeping space, but local whites did not count them in the population. Their children were bussed to schools somewhere else—I don't know where—and they attended church "with their own kind" somewhere outside of Tioga.

My Daddy said God ordained segregation as the Christian way to live. He was wrong, but he believed it.

Louisiana is synonymous with mosquitoes. As a deterrent, Daddy creosoted the entire interior of our house. The place was bug-free and had plenty of windows to pick up any breeze; even so, a dark, tarry odor often hung in the air. Most of our playtime occurred in the backyard. Three narrow, wooden steps led out the back door, and, on my every exit, Mama cautioned me to be careful.

Our three-room, shotgun house, the kind still to be seen on the back roads of Louisiana, did not give the appearance of "wind-proof" or even "rain-proof" at first glance. Still, it was well-kept and sent the message of "we'll survive whatever comes our way."

The front porch had a couple of rocking chairs, the roof held solid, and our house, without fail, sported a fresh coat of white paint. The lawn, impeccably mowed all the way out to the cattle-guard, revealed a pride of ownership. Daddy built and maintained the six-foot, white picket fence that stood between us and the gravel road. He bragged about the fence from construction to usefulness and claimed it cut down on dust.

Maybe he wanted to keep us as isolated as possible. My daddy could be like that. It makes me smile to think about it.

Tioga and its residents were typical of small, central Louisiana towns between World War II and the John F. Kennedy era. I grew up in this tight-knit, rural community and ultimately found my way to Dallas, Texas. I came to own an insurance agency, got married, and gave birth to three children. I now have five grandchildren and three great-grandchildren. I invite you to share my journey from 1943 until 1962, as I remember it, through this memoir.

— Ann Mullen-Martin

CHAPTER 1

THE TORNADO

This event originally occurred when I was five years old, but the retelling of it continued for many years. I still call it my first memory and asked Mama about it every time a tornado or any bad weather appeared in the skies. What follows here is a combination of my memory and my mother's multiple sharing of the story with me.

November 5, 1948, began like every other day. Daddy's route as a railroad engineer included the railroad tracks in front of our house. In accordance with our daily routine, John and I stood out in front to wave as he guided the engine past our driveway. Following the waves and the engine whistle in answer, we headed out back to play.

"Olevia, watch your brother! You know he can't get down those steps by himself."

"Yes, ma'am." I grinned as we neared the back door.

Despite Mama's best efforts, I tumbled out, like I did so many times—as did Johnny, my three-and-a-half-year-old brother.

"A storm's coming, you know," I said as we regained solid ground.

"Yep. I heard." Johnny shrugged as the thunder rolled and he picked himself up off the ground.

As the day unfolded, I could almost smell the storm brewing in the air. That afternoon, things seemed not quite right. Hannah, my older sister, sat in class at school, about a mile-and-a-half away. Mama put together dinner in the kitchen while the radio blared the latest country songs. Rain had threatened all day, but suddenly the storm exploded in torrents.

As the thunder continued to roll, the rain poured in thick, gray sheets, and lightning streaked through the sky. The black clouds ended in ragged white edges, the sort that drop tornados and inspire fear. John and I took refuge in the kitchen, watching Mama.

Among Roy Acuff, Hank Williams, and Ernest Tubb songs, the disc jockey warned us to take cover. Weather alerts for tornadoes were not in vogue in 1948, but it was obvious tornadoes were circling central Louisiana and western Mississippi.

Three rooms in a row with a bunch of rattling windows were not much of a storm shelter; neither was the wash house, a square one-room building behind the hedgerow out back. At least, it had only one window. Mama grabbed Johnny and me and ran to the wash house. We were there only minutes before she grabbed us up again and dashed back to the house.

Her hair hung in her eyes, and her housedress stuck to her thighs. The three of us looked like drenched chickens, and I felt like one headed to the dumpling pot. Every time we changed shelter, I cried louder, and Mama carried me closer. I hung on tight, my face buried in her shoulder to avoid the needlelike raindrops. Johnny clung to her neck and to me.

A big woman with fleshy arms and a lap to get lost in, Mama already suffered the symptoms of serious high blood pressure. The veins in her neck bulged. They stretched and stood in ridges as she struggled to catch her breath between each of our mad runs for safety.

In the main house, the radio told us where tornadoes may have touched down, what damage they were aware of, and if the school building was still standing. Mama prayed nonstop to Saint Menard, the Catholic saint recognized as the patron saint of weather, begging God's mercy and protection of life and limb for all of us.

Suddenly, the electricity went out, and we heard one of our favorite Chinaberry trees fall in the front yard. Between the thunderclaps and lightning flashes, the dark inside our house seemed almost impenetrable. For what seemed like an eternity in my mind, we just stood there and held hands.

Just as quickly as the lights had flickered off, my mom's attitude changed.

"Okay, kids. No more crying. I have a story to tell you."

She placed two coal oil lamps on the kitchen table and a quilt on the floor. As we each took our places on the pallet, we sang Hank Williams' "Move it on Over" and laughed in the darkness. After we got into the dry clothes Mama brought to us, she joined us on the floor with paper, pencils, and crayons. Just getting ready to hear her story had temporarily taken our minds off the storm's fury.

The story began, and I will use her words to the best of my memory—or at least from the multiple retellings of the story I heard.

"When I grew up in the Alexandria Catholic Orphans' home, bad weather came, and some of it came in the middle of the night," she said. "There was a rule—one I didn't like—about bad weather that came at night. Sister Grace oversaw the dormitory where I slept. At the smallest indication of bad weather, she went from bed to bed, awakening each of us. A lot of the kids were awake and frightened. I wasn't one of those kids and could have easily slept through the storm. But we all followed the same rules. All of us, the entire orphanage of children, marched down to the chapel to pray to Saint Menard. The legend is that, as a child, he was sheltered from a rainstorm by an eagle. This earned him the position as patron saint of the weather once he entered the realm of sainthood. I remember once we prayed all night. When the newspaper reported the storm damage, there was a picture of our undamaged orphanage squarely on page one. The sisters posted that picture in the cafeteria for all to see. As I got older, I promised myself I would never ever require such a ritual of my children. Yet, today, I've been Sister Grace."

John and I laughed, though neither of us really understood why.

"Isn't it better to pray, Mama?"

"Of course, it's better to pray if you are frightened or the prayer makes you feel better. And you say your prayers every night to thank God for good gifts. But it's even better to remember you're God's child—whether you're praying or not, whether you're asleep or awake, and whether you're frightened or not. God knew in 1923 there was a building full of kids in Alexandria. He didn't require any reminders from us kids—via a saint we had never heard of—in the middle of a scary storm. So, let's just bow our heads for a minute."

We did.

"Now repeat this prayer after me," Mama said. "Thank you, God, that I'm Your child, and I'm never alone. Thank You for watching over me. Amen."

We did.

"Okay. Let's draw some pictures for Daddy to see when he gets home."

"I'm drawing a picture of a tornado," I suggested.

"Well, you can't because you didn't see it!" John countered.

"Can too! Why don't you look out the window and draw a picture of the Chinaberry tree?"

Mama eased away. I don't know when she left. John and I argued as to who had the best drawing, and which one Daddy would like best.

Eventually, the lights came back on, and life went on as usual.

The post office about a mile-and-a-half from us was destroyed; the school, maybe two hundred yards from the post office, remained untouched. Many homes were severely damaged. Our Chinaberry tree, which fell on nothing of consequence, absorbed all the storm's fury at our house. I'm aware of no deaths and few injuries, though there may have been some.

A few days after the storm, several of my mom's friends gathered in our kitchen, over coffee, to discuss the experience.

One woman who had a bandana wrapped around her head and hair flying in all directions spoke very slowly, saying, "I know exactly how many bricks hit my head. There were two."

For an unknown reason (other than my age of five years), I started to giggle. It still makes me laugh as I picture the woman and hear that nasally, monotone voice. There were a few smiles around the room, but I heard no laughter. My reaction resulted in instructions from my mom to go play outside.

To this day, my mind's picture of that woman is my last memory of the tornado that hit Tioga in 1948.

Funny how a tornado still brings a smile, a remembered lesson from which I continue to benefit—a favorite memory to enjoy.

Indeed, it's one of my few memories from what we called the "little" house. My next experience will relate to our move, a few months later, to the "big" house.

CHAPTER 2

As Close to Heaven as I Ever Want to Be

Doss Taylor.

A few months after the tornado laid waste to much of our town and surrounding villages, Mama learned that the house next door was for sale. We called it "The Big House on the Hill."

The five of us had tried, unsuccessfully, to carve out individual spaces in our three-room, shotgun structure. When one of my half-brothers visited, it became even more crowded than a can of sardines. Many times, I heard Mama say, "That house on the hill is as close to heaven as I ever wanna be."

The price tag for the eight-room house on twenty acres exceeded my parent's reach. As a survivor of The Great Depression, Daddy, like most rural residents of that time, had a judicious approach to using any credit. To put it simply, if he did not have the money, we all waited until he did.

Mama remained a prisoner of her own optimistic imagination while she lived with no closets, no running water, no indoor plumbing, and little hope of changing the situation.

Eventually, her faith and optimism paid off in a most unusual way.

****

The Taylors were more than friends; they were customers who bought milk, eggs, and butter from Mom. Those purchases were typically made twice a month by Mr. Taylor. Mrs. Taylor soaked in mineral waters at Hot Wells to relieve her rheumatism on Tuesdays, the scheduled day for Mr. Taylor to knock on our door.

One day, his knock came when rain fell in sheets outside and the dark inside had the distinct odor of creosote. Johnny and I were underfoot, and our dog barked nonstop at the backdoor.

When Mr. Taylor came inside, he looked Mama up and down. Then, he said, "Mary, you look a little under the weather. Is anything wrong?"

Mama did not routinely suffer from the blues, or, if she did, she didn't show it. Mr. Taylor knew her well. That day, her smile did not come easily as she prepared the coffee.

The scene was set for the cavalry to save the day.

"I'm okay, Doss. It's just the weather."

The conversation had become interesting to me, and I glanced over and perked up my ears. I can still see the tears forming in her eyes.

"You're not okay, Mary. Tell me what's going on."

With steaming cups of coffee cn the table, that question opened the floodgates. She shared her dream of leaving the house with the creosote walls and no closets. She told him how she dreamed of the day she would move up the hill.

"I guess the rain and this whole house are bothering me today more than usual, Doss. I just found out the place up on the hill is for sale, and I realized my dream is a fancy not in the cards. I am sorry for bothering you with this."

"It's not a bother, Mary. What's on your mind?" Mr. Taylor took a long drink of his coffee and peered at Mama over the top of his glasses.

"Doss, I'm not a whiner or a complainer, but today, this rain…" she paused, took a deep breath, and continued. "John and I are trying hard to make things more comfortable in this house. We plan to add on a room as soon as we can, one for Hannah."

She stood up, reached for a napkin to wipe her eyes, and refilled their cups while she was up.

"Would you like a spoonful of this blackberry cobbler with your coffee? I made it a couple of days ago, but it's still good."

"Indeed, I would." He laughed as he spoke. "I'm not a fool! I never pass up your cobbler! Now, what were you telling me about yours and John's plans?"

"Oh, it's just a dream I've had. And when I saw that For Sale sign this morning, I suddenly realized it was only a dream. I shouldn't have brought it up."

"So, have you and John talked about buying the place on the hill?"

"Well, it has come up in conversation." Tears were gone, and the smile had returned to her eyes. "But things aren't so bad. We plan to get running water in the house next year. After that, maybe we can build a room for Hannah. She's getting too big to sleep on that cot."

I felt better with the new tone of voice and smile. I had never heard my mama sound so sad. I continued to sit on the floor with my coloring book and listen.

"It's nothing we can't handle. How's your coffee?"

"It's fine, and your cobbler, as always, is outstanding. Tell me a little more about the house next door."

"There's not much to tell. It's something that John and I have talked and dreamed about. You know, one of those one-of-these-days pie-in-the-sky goals that's nice to imagine but not to get stuck on."

"What would it take to get that place?" Doss asked.

The cavalry was almost in earshot.

"More'n we got! I shouldn't have brought it up. I'm sorry."

She sighed, and Mr. Taylor nodded.

"Really, Mary. What would it take to get that house and the land around it?"

I heard the cavalry's hoof beat in the distance.

"Five-thousand's what I heard. That house is as close to heaven as I ever wanted to be. I'm sure there'll be another one out there when we're ready."

"Well, maybe you'll get there."

"Heaven?" She laughed. "I've a better chance of getting there than I do getting that house on the hill." She stood up to clear the table and package Mr. Taylor's milk and eggs order.

He wrote a check made payable to Mama and handed it to her. He didn't often pay with a check for the butter and eggs because he knew Mama kept her butter and egg money separate to do with as she pleased—usually to buy something for one of us kids. The checking account was Daddy's territory, so a check would go through him. She folded it and put it on top of the ice box.

"Aren't you going to look at it?"

"What for? You know how much you pay for your regular order. Was I supposed to put something else in? Or leave something out this time?"

"No, my order is the usual. Still, you ought to take a look just to see if I got it right."

She got up, brought the check down, and looked at it. "Is this a joke, Doss?" she asked as she stared at the five-thousand-dollar amount.

The cavalry in the form of Doss Taylor had saved the day.

"No, it's not. It's not a gift either. It's a loan. Tell John to call me, and we'll set up some terms for paying it back."

"Doss, I'm not sure John's going to like this." Mama remained standing, seemingly hypnotized by the check she held.

"Let me take care of John. Just tell him to call me." He handed Mama her butter and egg money in cash and got up to leave.

Mama cried, but this time they were tears of joy.

I didn't hear the conversations between Mama and Daddy, and I never knew the repayment terms they worked out. I just know we got the house, and Saturday was moving day!

No one in our house slept the night before the moving adventure began.

Daddy pushed wheelbarrow load after wheelbarrow load up the hill, while the rest of us carried whatever we could. We started early and worked late; we didn't have much stuff, but it doesn't take much to fill a wheelbarrow.

Johnny sat on top of that last load, grinning from ear to ear. After the sun set and darkness settled in, he started to cry.

"Daddy, I want to go home."

"We don't live there any more, Johnny. We live in the house on the hill."

Johnny continued to sniffle until Daddy walked with us back down to the dark, empty, and smelly little house. That's when we knew the house on the hill belonged to us.

Before we went to sleep on the pallets that night, Doss Taylor's eight-by-ten glossy hung on the living room wall as a reminder of how God used an earth angel to get Mama as close to heaven as she ever wanted to be.

Tomorrow, we would claim our bedrooms, set up the furniture, and become familiar with an indoor bathroom!

CHAPTER 3
THE VASE

The Vase.

Moving day began as the sun came up and ended when it sank in the west. Daddy drove our moving vehicle, the wheelbarrow, while the rest of us carried as many items as possible.

Tired to the bone, Mom and Dad scoured the house to find every article for the final uphill climb.

Johnny and I sat on the porch, petting the dog, and continually asking, "When do we eat? Are we done yet?"

Our parents ignored our pleas, as if not heard, while they talked in the kitchen.

"Mary, what's in that towel over there?"

"That's my vase. I'll get it."

She had removed it from its customary spot on a kitchen shelf, wrapped it in a towel, and laid it to the side.

"I'll carry it, John."

"Okay. Let's go, kids," Daddy said as he placed John on the top of the wheelbarrow.

We were officially no longer living in the little house. Exhausted, Daddy left the last load in the front yard of the big house—all except Mama's vase, held firmly in her arms.

"John, I'm going to take my vase inside for safety. Is there anything else we need to carry in?"

"Nah. It'll all be sitting here in the morning. I'm done for the day." Carrying a couple of quilts, he climbed the steps, while Mama carried her vase.

Once inside, she unwrapped it with the care one would give a Ming vase and sat it on the upright Baldwin piano abandoned by the previous owner. She stepped back to admire the one decoration in an otherwise bare room—except for Doss Taylor's picture—in a bare house.

"What do you think, Olevia?" My mom spoke to me as if I were much older than my five years, but she always did.

"I like it, Mama. Where'd we get that vase?"

"That's MY vase, Olevia. James brought it to me when he came home from overseas during the big war."

James, one of my older half-brothers, like the other three, had served in World War II.

"Did he buy it for you?"

"Well, I guess so. It's an Italian vase. He brought it across the ocean. I think that's special. Don't you?"

No longer listening, I explored what seemed to me to be a huge house until Mama called me to bed. We laid down on our quilt pallets, and sleep came quickly.

The following day began with a breakfast of homemade biscuits, eggs, bacon, and coffee. Age was not a requirement for coffee drinking in our house, and, as long as I can remember, John and I both drank coffee with our parents at breakfast. As I enjoyed breakfast, I felt antsy to go outside and itchy to explore the lay of the land surrounding our new palace. I felt like a prisoner of many years who had received the governor's pardon.

"John, you want to go exploring today?"

"Yeah. Where? In the barns?"

"I wanna walk down to the pine trees. Can we go there, Mama?"

"Tell you what—you two can help in getting things put away until lunchtime. Then, if you still want to go exploring, I'll make you a picnic lunch."

"Okay!" We both quickly nodded our heads.

We spent the morning sorting out our small supply of furniture and other possessions. John and I were assigned bedrooms; mine would be shared with Hannah, and John's would be shared with Henry. Hannah quickly took control of our room.

"Olevia, that's your bed," she said as she pointed to one of the single beds with iron bedsteads.

"Okay. Are you going to put sheets on it for me?"

"This time. But you're going to learn to make your own bed."

My interest was confined to "this time," so the answer satisfied me. "What about my clothes? Do I hang them in here?" I pointed to the small closet.

"No. Your clothes should be taken to the rack in the Washer Room."

Again, no static from me. My goal to finish my assignment and go exploring loomed first and foremost in my mind.

Mama dug out a couple of crocheted scarves and chose one for the piano. She laid it carefully and sat the vase on top.

"Hey, kids, come see my vase," she called from the living room.

We admired it as if we had not seen it before. I suppose it had blended in with everything else on the shelf in the dark kitchen of the little house and had gone unnoticed. We stood staring at it for several minutes. I know now that I made my first true connection with the vase on that day.

It's a simple but elegant white vase with colorful flowers as if it is blossoming into a bloom itself. Today, they reminded me of a family tree. The flowers begin as a small bouquet expanding to fill a garden. A cherub sits at the bottom as if offering a blessing to all who take the time to view it.

"How long have we had this vase?" I asked.

"About five years. James brought it to me about the same time as you were born." She walked toward the kitchen. "I have your picnic lunch ready. Why don't you take a quilt to the side yard and have your picnic there?"

"Okay. Why can't we go to The Pines?"

"I'd rather go with you the first time you go."

We ate our peanut butter and jelly sandwiches and then wandered around the yard, looking unsuccessfully for a four-leaf clover. When I complained to Mama that I could not find one, she laughed.

"We've had more than our share of luck lately."

With everything put away, time came to take baths. John and I were first in line, and we shared the tub. Mama showed us how to adjust the water to a comfortable temperature. She cautioned us not to put more than three inches of water in the tub—a rule that never changed and one ignored completely unless Daddy was home. We had a deep well with an electric pump and a water heater utilizing propane. Maybe that expense caused the caution.

A piano, a vase, and a hot bath! To say we felt as if we were moving on up is to put it mildly. Electric lighting in the center of each room, operated by a pull-string, resembled the lighting we had at the little house, but everything appeared so much airier and more open. The walls were papered, not painted with creosote, and they reflected the sunlight shining through the many windows.

Electrical outlets were non-existent, or heating sources were limited to a fireplace in the living room, a small gas heater in the bathroom, and a stove in the kitchen. One closet in the entire house represented one more than we had before. A long rack for all other clothes to hang complemented the less-than-adequate closet space. We felt rich, and we were—in all the important ways.

We agreed the vase made the piano more special, and it sat there until the day the piano was sold—six or so years later.

When the piano left, the vase moved to the dresser in Mom and Dad's room and stayed there until the last months Mama lived. Sometimes, I sat on her bed listening to stories about the vase. She spoke about how James brought it to her on his first leave during the war and how special she believed it to be. She emphasized the need to take care of it, so someday I could tell my children about its origin.

As she described it, I imagined the day James came home.

"Olevia, he wore his dress whites. You know he is making a career of the Navy."

"Yes." I did not want to say too much but rather just listened as she recalled the day.

"He looked so handsome when he walked into the yard, and I ran out on the porch to meet him. Your Daddy was at work when James arrived. Hannah was at school, and you were a baby."

I imagined tears in the corners of her eyes as he handed her the vase.

After she died in 1956, Daddy allowed me to move the vase to the chest of drawers in my room. Many nights, I lay in bed, staring at the vase and thinking about things.

Mama felt closer to me with that vase in my room.

After I left home, Daddy moved the vase back to the mantel in the living room. During the last couple years of his life, my visits home occurred about every six weeks. I relished our talks while we each sat in a rocking chair facing what used to be the fireplace and mantel. Several times, he mentioned how Mama wanted me to have the vase someday, but he wasn't ready yet.

On the last of my routine visits, I arrived home on May 31, 1965. As I approached Daddy's house, Mrs. Curry waved and called from her front porch. When I stopped to listen, I learned my dad had died of heart failure the night before, and his body had been discovered by Mr. Curry that morning.

I sat in the living room, staring at the vase and thinking about things. I remembered the day Mama brought the vase into the house. I recalled the conversations as I watched her become weaker and weaker before her last trip to the hospital. I thought about all the times Daddy had told me how much my mom wanted me to have the vase.

I got up, wrapped the vase in a towel, and put it in the back seat of my car. Soon, the house would be full of people and all sorts of activity, and Mama's vase needed to be safe from the center of such commotion.

The vase continues to follow me, always occupying a place of honor. Today, it sits on a cabinet in my dining room, and I share its eighty-year history with my grandchildren and great-grandchildren. The value of Mama's vase lies not in its monetary significance—of which there is likely little, if any at all—but in its cohesive quality. Some things, by their mere presence, provide a connection both to the past and the future.

My own future would change in less than a month from moving into the big house. My first school day, September 6, 1949, caused equal amounts of anticipation, excitement, and dread.

CHAPTER 4

School – A Shaky Start

Me, first grade.

As Mama, Mrs. Curry, and I sat at Mrs. Curry's kitchen table, I listened and learned. Most mornings began that way now that life had changed.

"You know, Mary, it's been almost a year to the day since the tornado hit Tioga."

"Yeah. That was in November, right?" Mama stirred her coffee and reached for a piece of Mrs. Curry's cinnamon toast.

I reached for one too! I loved having next-door neighbors.

"I think that tornado made a change in all of our lives," Mama continued. "Had it not been for Doss Taylor, I would not be living on the hill. We wouldn't be sitting here together in your house. Novie, you, and Ellis have done wonders with this place. Twice the size, new paint, new plumbing, and a bathroom."

The Currys had moved into what used to be our little house. Mama and Daddy had known them for a long time as customers buying butter, eggs, and milk. Now that they were neighbors, they had become close friends and confidants for each other.

"Well, we thank Doss Taylor too. Without his money, we could not have made the change. We're all lucky that Doss, Ellis, and John share a railroad camaraderie." She laughed.

Mama arched her eyebrows in surprise. "I guess I didn't really realize that."

Mrs. Curry returned a puzzled look as Mama explained.

"I mean, I knew they worked together, but I sorta thought Doss was my personal angel." Now she laughed. "I wonder if John knows that?"

"Probably need to keep it between us. Don't you think, Mary? You know our husbands."

They both laughed at that as Mrs. Curry poured second cups of coffee. I inhaled the aroma and smiled. The scent of coffee would forever remind me of my roots.

The beginning of my education about life sprouted from these coffee sessions in Mrs. Curry's kitchen. In years to come, Mrs. Curry and her kitchen became my safe place to be me and learn who I was.

At this point, Mrs. Curry changed the course of the conversation to what I now realize to be a preordained subject that morning—me.

"Well, Olevia. Looks like you'll be a school girl soon," Mrs. Curry said.

"I guess so." I stared at the table.

"You don't sound as excited as I thought you'd be," she responded to my barely audible answer. "You know, it's only a few days away. September 6. Right, Mary?"

Mama added her remarks to the pep talk that I did not recognize as a pep talk. "Yeah, Novie. John took me and Olevia shopping last week. She looks so pretty in her brand-new outfit."

Mrs. Curry smiled. "Ooh, Olevia. That sounds nice. I can't wait to see it. Do you like it?"

"I guess so."

I did not share in the enthusiasm for school. Oh, I looked forward to reading more books, learning arithmetic, and whatever else went on there, BUT I had a challenge. The thought of leaving my mother all day, five days a week, made me nauseous. My inability to accept not having my safety net with me blinded me to all the advantages of school. School seemed like a high tightrope, and I felt safer staying grounded at home.

Mama and I went to bed together; we didn't sleep together, but she laid down with me for a little while at bedtime. We got up together in the morning and spent most of the waking hours together. Maybe it wasn't healthy, but that's the way it was. On rare occasions, we were separated for short periods; those separations were always of my own choosing. I had never been left with a babysitter unless I asked to be. If I couldn't go, my mother did not go.

Mrs. Curry shifted her position to embark on a new approach. "You like books, don't you? Mary tells me that you can already read, so won't the teacher be surprised! What was the last thing you read?"

"The *Bob and Nancy* reader." I could not avoid a bit of enthusiasm sneaking into my voice. At less than six years old, I could read well, and I enjoyed my favorite indoor pastime. When *Dick and Jane* replaced *Bob and Nancy* as the first-through-third-grade readers at school, Mama acquired a set of the outdated books.

I loved them, and we spent hours together reading the stories, talking about the stories, and connecting the pictures to the stories. I could also count and write my numbers to one hundred—a chore done only to please Mama.

Reading became a rocket ship that allowed me to travel without ever leaving the launch-pad. Learning, I craved; leaving Mama, I feared. I wanted the safety of Mom nearby. She provided me with a feeling of being safe.

Mama again joined in, saying, "Tell Mrs. Curry what you liked about Bob and Nancy."

I began to get into this conversation. They made a good tag team. "Bob and Nancy have pets—a dog named Mac and a cat named Muff. They play circus and school and lots of stuff. Mama said that the new book, *Dick and Jane,* will be like making new friends. She said there's even a workbook that goes with it."

By now I had become all smiles, eager to share the details of my school shopping trip. "Daddy bought me a Big Chief tablet, a number two pencil, a pencil box, and a sixty-four-crayon box instead of the eight on the school list. I got colored paper, a book bag, paste, scissors, and a ruler. Everything on the school list."

Mrs. Curry beamed at me. "Why don't you stay with me a little while this morning? I need help with my gardenia bush; it's loaded with dead flowers. We need to get them off so it will bloom again."

"Can I, Mama?"

"I guess so. You're getting to be such a big girl, almost a first grader."

I swelled with pride and independence, but the feeling did not transfer to full school days. I slept little the night before my school debut.

I had been the star of Labor Day. I sat on Daddy's lap and heard how much I would love school and about having my own pencils and paper and sitting at a desk. Mrs. Curry joined my mom in oohing and aahing when I modeled my new school outfit and showed off my neatly packed red and blue book bag. I felt like a princess until I got in bed, and the Boogie Man of fear stole my sleep.

Mama and I were up before daylight, and I sometimes think she shared my anxiety. Well before the 7 o'clock bus stopped at the bottom of the hill, I stood dressed in a dark plaid wool jumper, a white blouse, saddle oxfords, and ankle socks. My outfit mirrored 99% of the elementary Tioga school girls on opening day.

Louisiana Septembers do not lend themselves to wool clothing; the weather is hot and sticky, but they did mark the end of summer. We all dressed as if the weather changed, instead of the calendar. Within days, the pinafores and sandals reappeared, to be worn until late October.

Our house, being the first stop on the bus route, meant we were just over one mile from school. We had two choices as to how to get there: walking or riding the bus. On that first day, Mama went with me, and we took the bus. I fought back tears as we boarded and sat down on the first seat. Because Tioga was a twelve-grade school, by the time we reached the elementary building, an hour or so later, the bus had grown crowded with kids of all ages. As I remember, only I had an adult accompanying me. Of course, I'm certain many moms drove to school.

Until then, I had no friends or playmates, save my younger brother—no one except my mother. She occupied every corner of my whole world. My days were filled with Mama's complete approval and acceptance; I dreaded the change first grade might bring. Frightened and shaking, I stepped off the bus and into Mrs. Carpenter's first grade class.

On that first day, I did not yet know Mrs. Carpenter embodied an angel posing as a schoolteacher. My heart lodged in my throat when she showed me my desk and where to put my things. With my things stowed, I sat down for a few minutes and watched Mama and Mrs. Carpenter chat, oblivious to anything going on around them. Quietly, I walked out and headed home. I ran all the way and got there before anyone knew I had left.

I sometimes wonder what happened when someone noticed my empty desk. I do know that no one considered it a 911 situation (had 911 been established, which it wasn't until 1968).

Walking a mile down the railroad tracks did not constitute a dangerous activity. Once home, I sat in a rocking chair to wait, with the intention of explaining why I did not need to go to school. Surely, Mama could teach me everything. That plan flew right out of the window when she walked through the door.

Her calm demeanor scared me a bit, as I did expect some concern on her part. She didn't scold me for leaving or ask why. She just smiled and hugged me.

"Leaving early and coming home alone, Olevia, was okay for today. But tomorrow will be different. School's necessary, and you'll learn to love it." She then turned on the radio and went about the business of making lunch.

A lead weight felt lodged in my tummy. My first thought of *I don't believe it* did not offset my knowledge that Mama never lied to me. Thoughts danced in my head, and I had the feeling of spinning like a top with no control over my world.

Just watching Mama allowed her calmness to wrap a warm blanket of love and peace around my flailing soul. I knew everything would be okay—at least, I knew it in that minute.

CHAPTER 5

THE GOODBYE SONG

Me, Hannah, and John at the Little House.

As I stood on the piano stool singing "The Goodbye Song" to Mama, tears began to drip down my face.

"Olevia, I know you like this song. Don't cry, or you'll make me cry."

"I do like this song, Mama, but I don't want to go to school."

I heard Hannah mutter under her breath and sigh.

"Come on, Mom!" She shifted her feet with impatience. "Olevia's acting like a baby. Hurry up! I don't want to miss the bus." She gave me a hard stare and slammed her books down, but she also waited for me.

Mama took a middle road, smiling at me and saying, "Olevia, aren't you glad Hannah's going to walk you to class this morning?" Then she added for Hannah, "I'm so proud of you for taking care of your little sister."

Hannah shrugged, glared at me, and again demanded, "Hurry up!"

I felt a bit more comfortable because Hannah promised to get me safely to class.

Once at school, she deposited me on the steps outside of the first-grade wing and pointed to a window in the high school building. "Watch for me in that window, Olevia. Your teacher will be here soon."

I never saw her in that window! But my teacher did soon appear. I latched onto Mrs. Carpenter as tightly as a dying man might to a caregiver managing his pain medication.

From eight in the morning until three-thirty in the afternoon, for six weeks, I accompanied Mrs. Carpenter almost everywhere she went. When she left the room, I would call after her, "Please don't leave me."

And she wouldn't, even if a substitute teacher manned the class in her absence.

For six weeks, she hugged me, took me with her to teachers' conferences, and allowed me to run errands with her. I clung to her like Velcro. I stood hall duty beside her chair. I cleaned erasers, passed out papers, tutored the less-capable readers in the class, wrote numbers on the blackboard—any possible jobs allowing me to remain near Mrs. Carpenter.

An abrupt change came along with report cards and real grades! Mrs. Carpenter stood at the door to hand us each one as we left the classroom. The first six weeks faded to the rearview mirror.

"Class, let me have your attention, please. These report cards are important. They let your parents know how much you have learned this first six weeks of school."

My heart beat loudly, and excitement filled every pore of my being like an electrical current energizing every cell. Indeed, I felt a little compassion for some of my fellow students, knowing they were struggling in class.

Mrs. Carpenter continued, "As soon as you get home tonight, ask your mom or dad to review your report card and sign it. Then put it in your book bag, so you will not forget it tomorrow."

I wished the line would move faster. I had no doubt my report card would include only A's. I could spell and count as well as, if not better than, my classmates, and I belonged to the *Red Birds* reading group—the best readers.

Mrs. Carpenter never scolded me for talking in class, or getting out of line in the cafeteria, or any other of the routine things for which I heard her scold other children. I visualized my parents' smiles and congratulations when they could see my straight-A report card.

From first grade to graduation, all students were seated in alphabetical order by last name. I occupied the last seat in the last row. I noticed Mrs. Carpenter took a few minutes to talk to various students as she handed out the report cards. My annoyance level rose: I wanted to get home to some praise. Finally, my turn came. I grabbed the report and ripped it open as I hurried toward the bus.

At first, I didn't comprehend the B I received in behavior. That B may as well have been an F at my house. Anything less than straight-A's represented failure in my dad's eyes and was looked on with pity by my mom.

"Mrs. Carpenter," I almost sobbed as I ran back into the classroom. "Why did you give me a B on my report card?"

She put her arm around me. "I did not give you a 'B'. Olevia, you earned a B in behavior. You cry every day. You don't play on your own, and you have not attempted to make friends with your classmates."

That ended my tears! I now had a story to tell my parents, and I also had a goal. Mama stood waiting at the driveway to walk me up the hill.

"Mama, I'm sorry I got a B," I said as I got off the bus. "Mrs. Carpenter said I will get an A next time if I don't cry anymore."

"Okay. That sounds good. Daddy likes to see all A's, and I do, too. Let's see the rest of those grades."

Further tears were private ones between me and Mama in the mornings, and those soon disappeared as well.

I made a friend, Judy Deah, a girl with long, curly, dishwater-blond hair pulled back in a barrette. Her hair had a beautiful natural white-blond streak beginning at the very front and ending at the back.

She came from a military family, and they moved a lot. My family seldom traveled, much less moved, so she easily held the place of most exciting person in our class and, I thought, the prettiest girl I had ever met. We played jacks, built playhouses, jumped rope, and became fast friends. inseparable from eight until three-thirty, Monday through Friday. Then, I went to school one day to find Judy's chair empty.

"Mrs. Carpenter, is Judy sick today?"

"No, Olevia, her family moved away."

"But she was my only friend, Mrs. Carpenter!"

"You have plenty of friends, Olevia. Play with someone else."

I don't have plenty of friends. I don't have any friends now!

I did not say that out loud, but it boomed in my brain like riotous thunderclaps.

My world fell apart again, and I sat alone through recesses and lunch. As soon as I got home, I told my story to Mama, who listened and sympathized but said I hadn't tried hard enough yet.

Even as I write this now, I cannot believe my own self-centeredness. Equally difficult is understanding Mama's unending patience with me. Perhaps it had to do with her knowing she did not have that many more years to spend with us, or perhaps it was just her nature.

"Olevia, you go to school for one more day. See if anybody plays with you."

"Nobody likes me, Mama."

"Of course, they like you." Mama stroked my hair and replaced a stray strand behind my ear. "You just need to act like you want to be liked."

I heard a little edge of annoyance in her tone, but not enough to stop me from complaining.

"What if nobody plays with me? What then? Do I have to go back anymore?"

"First, you must be friendly. No crying. Olevia, you must try."

"I'll try, but it won't work because nobody likes me."

Mama just sighed and walked away.

I left for school the next morning laden with doubts but secretly hoping things would work out. I liked everything about school except recesses and lunch periods. Still, I walked onto the playground wearing my best game face.

Sharon Barton asked me to play Red Rover, Lydia Lipscomb asked me to play jacks, and Carol Nalley sat by me at lunch. Everybody wanted to be my friend that day!

Although real popularity eluded me forever, and I remained socially inept when compared to the popular girls, I discovered I could get along when I tried.

My next report card, and those for many years afterward, reflected only A's. Crying vanished, and I learned to truly enjoy school, just as Daddy had predicted on Labor Day.

Perhaps my greatest lesson from the first grade has lasted a lifetime. I learned success depended on MY attitude. Though I did not know it then, I did truly say goodbye to the fear of failing. Support surrounded me, from my parents to my teachers to my friends, but the decision to accept and treasure it depended on my disposition.

CHAPTER 6

TERE-TONE BOOGERS

With the scarcity of playmates, John created some imaginary ones of his own to fill the void. On a rare occasion, he would let me join in the games. But, for the most part, I did not share in his private, imaginary world. Tere-Tone Boogers belonged to him, and their relationship is best described in his own words.

John takes it from here:

There was a time when I had the privilege of being a small boy. A small boy is a creature few people truly understand—and an understood boy is blessed beyond belief.

A small boy is not a little man, much as a caterpillar is not a butterfly. An imaginary friend, Tere-Tone Boogers, shared my small-boy world. He played such an important part in my life that it can still be difficult for me to believe he was imaginary.

I am not certain how Tere-Tone arrived in my life. To me, it seems as if he came with me from birth. I asked Mama about it on more than one occasion, and she said I always enjoyed having some alone-playing time from the beginning. She said, at around three years old, I began to talk as if an invisible someone shared the room with me. She told me that she could recall one day asking me, "Who are you talking to?"

I answered, "Tere-Tone" or something that sounded like that. She decided to add my "friend" to our conversations. If I seemed to be lost in my own world, she might ask,

"Johnny, is your friend here today?" She reacted to my actions as if they were normal and acceptable.

Although my only memory of those conversations with my Mama is what she shared with me, it rings true. Tere-Tone became a part of who I was.

Tere-Tone Boogers had a Mrs. Tere-Tone, and together they had a pet owl kept in the pressure cooker stored in a kitchen cabinet. When the Tere-Tones came to visit, I carried the pressure cooker to the back porch and settled in for an afternoon of fantasyland adventures. I still wonder why I addressed them as Tere-Tone and Mrs. Tere-Tone, rather than Mrs. Boogers. I don't know.

Typically, my first challenge involved the owl—a Houdini at escaping his container. I chased the invisible owl from tree to tree with my fishing net, usually used for catching perch down at the trestle. Tere-Tone silently yelled instructions that I heard clearly in my mind. Eventually, the owl would be trapped in the Weeping Willow and returned to his rightful owner.

Our next adventure could be anything—chasing rabbits, perhaps. I even caught a few using Tere-Tone's suggested methods, carefully visualized as I listened to the thoughts shared with me. Other times, our chickens were saved from becoming a chicken hawk's meal. We secured every one of them in the chicken house—a chore that could take an hour or more since the frightened chickens ran in every direction.

Once the chickens were out of danger, we sat on the porch to watch the hawk until it flew away, allowing the chickens free range again. A mockingbird or a blue jay could fill in for a hawk just for practice. The possibilities were endless.

I occasionally let Olevia play with us, but far more often, the games were shared only between Tere-Tone and me in our pretend world. It was better that way. Without fail, Tere-

Tone understood and became immediately available with just one thought. Although I learned a lot, I occupied the position of the boss. In our private Twilight Zone, I made the rules. I felt invincible.

One Saturday in 1954, I hitched our mule, Kate, to the slide Daddy had built for me. Tere-Tone and I planned to take a ride-or-slide down to The Pines. Just as I finished hitching Kate and climbed on board, Olevia came running up, begging to go with us.

It wasn't so much that I didn't want her to go. It was more that I objected to her lack of respect for me and my ability to hitch and drive the mule. As soon as I said okay, she wanted to take the reins. No way! Even if she weren't a girl, I wouldn't have let her take over. This trip belonged to me and Tere-Tone.

She squalled and screamed, "I hate you!" She jumped off and went back to the house.

Tere-Tone stayed on the slide. His friendship had no limits. He always respected me, never hated me, and belonged only to me.

That's how lucky a small boy can be when he has an imaginary friend.

****

Although I remember the slide incident, until I heard this story from John, I did not know that Tere-Tone was involved. Hearing this story helped me better understand both the incident and my brother.

CHAPTER 7

SPRINGTIME

Butterflies in springtime.

Spring is my favorite time of the year. Well, unless it is the first few weeks of summer, fall, or winter. Maybe what I most love are the seasonal changes, and spring is nature's hyperbole in contrast. There is something about seeing the redbud trees peek out of the woods along East Texas Farm to Market roads that inspires and uplifts my spirits, no matter what. A flowering dogwood means Easter is right around the corner and it is time to pack away the warm jackets and winter caps.

In rural Louisiana (and in my young mind), narcissus blooms were synonymous with springtime's renewal. They were the flower our family loved most. The sweet smell wafted in the air to be enjoyed when walking up the driveway and, later, sitting on the porch, the smell of narcissus even influenced our conversations.

I recall one evening when we sat together on the porch lazily watching and enjoying the sunset. Mama took a break from cooking dinner and sat in the rocking chair, remaining silent for a few moments as she glanced over at us and tilted her head.

"John, the narcissus seems to have doubled in plants this year," Mama said in between deep inhalations of the wonderful odor the flowers provided.

"Yeah, Mary. They do multiply fast, but I think you could add some along the front fence, under the Martin houses."

"Maybe so. I could just spread them out a little. They remind me that we've survived another winter."

The smell of narcissus added bounce to Mama's step. The bouquets John and I put together brought forth oohs and aahs as she put them in a quart jar that served as a dining table vase.

The Louisiana camellias blossomed earlier, in late January—too soon to really herald spring's arrival, though they held their own charm. Camellia bushes dressed the gardens of the more well-to-do residents. Our yard was more apt to be graced with narcissus, along with a daffodil or two, wild onions, and a little purple clover for diversity.

Spring of 1951 had just begun in earnest when Aunt Minnie and her two sons, Clyde and August Lee, came for one of their rare overnight visits. Indeed, it is the only one I remember.

They lived in Houston and always seemed a bit uptown to me—a little fancy and citified. The boys were obnoxious, maybe because they were totally out of their element on a farm. Clyde, 10, and August Lee, 11, attempted to lord over both John and me—at least, that is the way it felt. John and

I took every possible opportunity to share between us any frailties we spotted in them. For instance, I considered it the height of hilarity when they would suggest we go hunt rather than gather the eggs. We rather enjoyed their fear of John's horse. Of course, they were guests, so we were careful not to advertise our dislike for them.

And their worldliness did intimidate me since I rarely left Tioga, much less Louisiana.

Mama outdid herself with fried pork chops, sweet corn (canned last year), and turnip greens flavored with both ham and bacon. The smell of hot, homemade cornbread permeated the kitchen and dining room.

The eight of us, including me, Dad, Hannah, Johnny, and our guests, sat down to dinner. That day's narcissus bouquet graced the center of the table to be admired by all. Just seeing it there made me feel a little proud, and it pleased me even more when Mama mentioned it.

"John, Minnie, did ya'll notice the flowers Olevia brought us today?"

"Yeah. Nice," Daddy murmured.

Aunt Minnie just smiled.

Daddy did not encourage a lot of mealtime conversation. Life seemed to be serious business with him, and while he and Mama might talk a little, Johnny, Hannah, and I were expected to follow the better seen, not heard rule that applied to children. I just could not be quiet that night.

"Guess what, Mama. I learned a poem at school today."

"That's good, Olevia. What's it about?"

"It's about spring. It's a really good one!"

"John, do you think maybe Olevia could recite her poem for us?"

Clyde and August Lee glanced sidewise at each other; a hint of smirk danced on both of their faces. Hannah rolled her eyes, and only Johnny appeared pleased with the prospect of my recitation.

Daddy looked a bit dubious, but he agreed to the performance. To understand the honor being bestowed on me, you would probably need to have lived with us. I guess it took little to impress an eight-year-old country kid in 1951. I immediately stood next to my chair, hands at my side, and looked straight ahead.

"The title of my poem is 'Today is Springtime.'"

Mom, Dad, Hannah, and Johnny all put down their forks and focused on me. Aunt Minnie and her boys followed suit, hands in laps, as if I were about to say grace or pledge allegiance to the flag. Me! Being the center of attention happened rarely when Daddy was part of the audience.

"Okay, this is a good poem, and I learned it from my friend, Carol Nalley. It's not very long and—"

"Olevia, recite your poem before the food gets cold," Daddy interjected.

"Okay, here it goes," I said before beginning the following verse.

The grass is riz.
The spring has sprung.
I wonder where the birdy is?
The bird is on the wing.
Oh, don't be absurd,
the wing is on the bird!

After a moment of deafening silence, everyone began to laugh. Well, everyone except for my mom and dad. Although, they did allow whispers of a smile to cross their faces. Clyde and August Lee guffawed, as I stood mortified. I felt the heat of tears forming and had no way of escaping. I sat down quickly and stared at my plate.

My dad saved the day and my dignity.

"Olevia, you did a fine job with that poem, and I appreciated hearing it. Do either of you boys know a spring poem to recite?"

The laughter ceased as they shook their heads. "No, Uncle John."

"Hannah, John, do either of you know a poem about springtime?"

Both said no.

"Well, I guess Olevia is the only one at our table tonight who knows a poem about spring. Now, eat your dinner."

The laughter ceased, and I returned—at least in my mind—to a place of honor.

I shall always be grateful to Daddy for coming to my rescue. For the last seventy-two years, that scene replays in my memory at the first sight of spring's narcissus blooms.

Springtime is a time of rebirth on so many levels.

CHAPTER 8

Easy Money Is Not Always Easy

"Olevia, what are you doing?" Ms. Whitehead, my second-grade teacher, asked.

"Nothin'," I said, barely audible.

****

In 1950, rural Louisiana grammar schools still had fifteen-minute morning and afternoon recesses, along with an hour for lunch. Physical education was of the disorganized variety, allowing kids to run, jump, play jacks, or take advantage of their classmates via a sales scheme. Apparently, one of those schemes occupied my time, on this day, though I didn't fully realize it then.

Daddy gave me my coveted one-dollar-bill allowance on Monday, and lunch for the week got paid immediately. I reduced the other fifty cents to dimes with a plan to spend one a day, every school day, at the school canteen. Most large items cost a nickel, so a candy bar and a soft drink or chips were available from the lunch ladies, who also manned the canteen at recesses.

Monday and Tuesday went well. But, at Wednesday morning recess, I found my pocket empty when I reached in for the allocated dime. My discretionary funds were lost! I sat on the school steps alone, pondering my problem and digging through my book bag in hopes of finding the lost wealth or maybe a penny or two. Leah Cryer, a fellow second grader, walked up to me.

"Wanna play house?" she asked. "You can be the sister, and I'll be the mother."

"No. I'm lookin' for my money."

She sat down beside me as I continued to dig through the book bag contents: a Big Chief tablet, a box of crayons, two number two pencils, an eraser, and four small pads of colored paper. Not even the sound of her dropping her book bag between us distracted me from my mission. I continued my search with as serious a focus as a tightrope walker. I laid the colored pads aside, and Leah picked one up.

"What's this? Can I have one?"

"It's some paper my daddy brought me from his work. He got it in Lake Charles and gave it to me to write my spelling words on."

"Can I have one?" she asked again as she examined the four-by-four-inch pads. She reminded me of crickets chanting the same refrain over and over.

"No!" I jerked it out of her hand. "These are important. Look, see all the different colors?"

"You could give me just one," Leah begged. "Gimme just one. I'm only asking for one."

A lightbulb went off in my brain. Picture a cartoon with one of those little clouds above the character's head. That's how that idea would have looked and felt if I had drawn it!

"Do you have any money?" I asked.

"I got three pennies. I'm gonna get three suckers at the canteen." She showed me the pennies in her hand.

"For two pennies, I'll give you five pages of paper, and you can pick which colors you want."

She quickly handed over the money and chose three blue, one pink, and one green sheet.

"Thank you," she said over her shoulder as she ran toward the playground, waving her prize in her hand.

I repacked my book bag, getting ready to head for the canteen, when Carol Kay Wren, another fellow second grader, approached and asked, "Olevia, do you have any more of those colored papers?"

A business venture materialized, and I began to rack up the pennies. I heard the clink and clank of coins in my head. Even before Ms. Whitehead showed up, I had an inkling this wasn't my finest hour. The paper pads were small but thick with probably fifty or more sheets each. As I remember, my daddy told me he paid a dime for all four of them. They were packaged together inside one cellophane sleeve, with the price tag still attached.

So far, my customers seemed happy, and I had replaced not only the ten cents I'd lost, but the twenty cents I'd spent earlier in the week. And I still had lots of colored paper left. Greed and the smell of a Peanut Patty stifled the voice of conscience like putting the lid on a boiling pot.

****

Ms. Whitehead's presence proved to be more difficult to ignore. She stood over me with a frown. She continued the conversation that opened this story.

"Nothing?" she asked. "That's not what it looks like to me." Her frown deepened like a tangerine sunset shifting to crimson.

"I'm selling colored paper to all my friends. They asked me—first."

Ms. Whitehead's shadow amplified that still-small voice I tried to ignore, and I thought I'd better establish a quick defense. I decided on the truth, as she continued to ask questions. Besides, I wasn't sure I'd done anything wrong. Well, maybe I was, but I didn't know exactly what.

"If someone asked you to set them on fire, would you?"

"No, ma'am!"

"Why?"

"Because I know better?"

My response sounded more like a question than an answer. I wasn't sure what she wanted to hear. It crossed my mind that maybe she would have been satisfied with some sort of don't play with matches routine.

"So, what're you doing wrong?"

Even though busted, I still had no clear idea of my crime. Tears started to form, and I hung my head. The bell rang, and my classmates passed by as I continued to endure Ms. Whitehead's grilling.

"Olevia, answer me. What did you do wrong?"

"I don't know." I sobbed. "They asked me to sell them my paper. Daddy bought that paper for me, and they wanted it."

Ms. Whitehead reached for my hand. "Come on. Let's go into class."

As we entered the door, she nodded to indicate I was to go to my desk.

"Class, today, we're going to talk about how to play fair. Winning is fun, isn't it?"

"Yes, ma'am," the class answered as one.

"Is winning always fun?"

"Yes, ma'am," everyone answered in unison.

I breathed a sigh of relief. Maybe I'd escaped any punishment. I thought perhaps my reasoning did make sense because those kids did ask to buy my paper. Just as my composure had almost returned, Ms. Whitehead brought out the big guns.

"What if you cheat to win?"

Forty-two seven-year-olds (classes were much larger in those days) sat almost unmoving as Ms. Whitehead continued.

"Oh, I'm not talking about looking at somebody else's paper for the answer or cheating when you play jump rope. We know that's wrong, don't we? Winning's not so much fun then, is it?"

We silently agreed, nodding heads.

"None of you would do that, would you?"

We collectively shook our heads 'no.'

"But what about when we know we're doing something wrong, but it really doesn't break any rules?"

Okay, now I knew I still sat in the hot seat. But thankfully, my classmates did not share in that knowledge. We all appeared puzzled, brows knit or eyes rounded. She had us in the palm of her hand.

"Let's pretend I paid a nickel for an apple, and Olevia asked me if she could have it. Let's pretend I told her I would sell it to her for one dollar. Is that fair?"

We stared without response. I honestly didn't know if it was fair or not, and I'm pretty sure neither did anyone else.

Ms. Whitehead trudged on, saying, "Let's pretend Mr. Aiken asked me for my apple, and I charged him one dollar. Is that fair?"

Still, I had no clue, but the lump in my throat told me I hadn't gotten off as scot-free as I thought.

"Class, now I'm asking you to think hard. First, let me tell you that charging Olevia a dollar for my apple would be cheating, but charging Mr. Aiken a dollar would be okay. Can you imagine any reason why that is true?"

I couldn't imagine why, but I knew instinctively it was true. No one replied as we sat there in our continued seemingly hypnotic state, staring. The sound of the wall clock echoed in my ears and seemed to amplify.

After several seconds of class silence, Ms. Whitehead answered her own question. "Olevia is a child."

I wished she would quit using me as an example. I doubt Madoff felt more guilty at his trial than I did sitting in that classroom.

Ms. Whitehead continued. "Olevia may or may not know what apples cost. Her parents may or may not have given her permission to spend her money any way she wants. She may or may not know that she could go to Merritt's Grocery and get twenty apples for one dollar. If I took her dollar and gave her my apple in return, would I be cheating?"

The whole class began to get the hang of it, but I still had a problem understanding why it would be cheating to give someone something they asked for at a price they were willing to pay. When all of us continued to sit and stare blankly at Ms. Whitehead, she answered her own question again.

She said, "I would be cheating because I took advantage of Olevia's lack of knowledge and maturity."

I heard my name again and slunk down a little deeper in my chair, as if it had turned to quicksand.

"Mr. Aiken is another story. He's an adult and knows how much apples cost. He has permission to spend his dollar, even if he spends it foolishly. Selling him an apple that cost a nickel for a dollar is not taking advantage of him. Mr. Aiken had all the facts and chose to spend his dollar on my apple. Maybe he made that choice because he didn't have time to go to the store. But whatever his reason, I did not cheat him."

Ms. Whitehead sat down at her desk and looked around the room. Our eyes connected briefly when she reached my desk—I think purposely so. Then she finished her story.

"Taking advantage of someone else is cheating. There may not be a rule against it, but you always know."

She paused for dramatic effect and then threw us a benign glance that scanned the whole room. She stopped at me for a few seconds as she added, "Just listen to your conscience."

We sat in silence for what seemed like half an hour but was more likely less than a minute. She then stood up, turned to the blackboard, picked up a piece of chalk, and began writing the multiplication tables. Over her shoulder, she said, "Okay, class, get out your arithmetic books."

****

Ethics class ended for the day, but what I learned remains with me to this day. If it doesn't feel right, it's probably not. I remain ever grateful to Ms. Whitehead. Just the thought of her makes my heart as warm as apple pie fresh from the oven.

Teachers have an opportunity to influence lives, and many influenced mine in ways that changed my future. I enjoy selling and have made my living that way for forty years. Indeed, I owned an insurance agency for over thirty-five years. I know my employees, my customers, and my companies would agree that the guiding light of our business has been and continues to be 'If it doesn't feel right, it probably isn't.'

We need more Ms. Whiteheads in our classrooms.

CHAPTER 9

LAZY DAYS OF SUMMER

"John, do you think that locust is a boy or girl?"

"I don't know, Olevia. How do you tell on a locust?"

"I think they all look alike. Let's catch a grown-up one and see."

"First, let's see where this one goes."

I don't know what other country kids did during the summer, but John and I were pretty isolated in terms of playmates. The world felt safe, and our parents gave us long leashes to explore our surroundings. We entertained ourselves, tested our limits, and remained within Mama's hollering range.

On some of those warm, sunny days, John and I watched, chased, caught, and played with bugs. We performed surgery on more than a few. We learned more about who we were than what we learned about insects.

Hot biscuits topped with watermelon-rind preserves and black, sweetened coffee let the day begin on a high note. Mama armed each of us with a quart jar with a lid for our specimen collections.

The number of bugs on a farm—to use the word loosely—is monumental. They come in all sizes, shapes, and degrees of usefulness from a kid's point of view. We called the cicadas, locusts, dragonflies were called mosquito hawks (we called real locusts by the name giant grasshoppers). These varieties along with honeybees, bumblebees, and yellow jackets were among our favorite options. Their individual lifestyles lent themselves to our imagination in various ways.

Taking advantage of the best opportunity to find locusts, we began our search early on one already warm and humid August morning.

"Hey, Olevia, look here!" John said as he circled and studied the base of our sycamore tree in hopes of catching our bug-of-the-day just emerging from the ground. No luck there.

"Over here!" I called as I looked closely at the few pin oak trees near the house. Again, no luck.

"Looks as if it's going to be The Pines today."

John eagerly joined me in moving toward the small, wooded area at the edge of our property. Once there, the hunt resumed.

"Do you think we're too early, Olevia? Maybe we should give up."

"Give up! No! Let's sit on one of these stumps and wait."

Of course, today, I know locusts (cicadas) live on a seven-to-seventeen-year cycle with most of that time spent underground. They emerge, shed their shells, sprout their wings, and have two to six weeks of loud noise, mating, and egg-laying to enjoy before they die. When the eggs hatch, the larvae burrow back into the ground to begin the journey again. At that time, their life cycle was unknown and immaterial to us because our interest in locusts began when they emerged from the ground. We did recognize August as the best month for finding one.

We waited for an hour or more—not all sitting. Periodically, one of us would wander to the fence posts, or any bush available, to catch sight of a locust climbing from his hibernation to a place in our world.

"Hey, Olevia," John shouted from a hundred yards or so away. "Come see!"

I raced over as if it were my first glance at the pot of gold at the end of a rainbow. "Whatcha got?"

"I found one!"

Success! John spotted one struggling up a small oak tree near the end of our property. Once mounted for transformation, the back of his shell split. The locust began a long, strenuous exercise, giving us ample time to do other things. We marked the spot.

We wandered around The Pines to see if we might find another one. No luck. We did see a couple of baby rabbits, but today was a bug day. We enjoyed watching them for a few minutes and moved on.

The morning had faded to early afternoon, and the heat encouraged us to go home for some cold water and a break. We took a last look at our locust to check his progress and then headed for home.

"Mama, we found a locust coming out of its shell," I shouted before we reached the back door to find Mama in the kitchen preparing lunch for us. Just as we arrived, she put a single piece of cold, fried chicken and a baked sweet potato for each of us in a bag.

"What are you doing, Mama?" John asked.

"I didn't know if ya'll would be home before lunch, so I packed one to bring to you. We could have a picnic."

"We can go back!"

"No, honey, we'll have our picnic on the back porch."

She handed each of us a lunch bag while she made a pitcher of strawberry Kool-Aid. Mama often engineered impromptu picnics. Sometimes they were in The Pines. Sometimes they were down at the trestle while we fished for crappie, and other times they were on the back porch. Cold, fried chicken was among my favorites, made better by Mama's company and conversation.

"Mama, we found a locust coming out of its shell," I repeated.

"Be sure not to touch it until the wings are dry. If you touch it, it'll never be able to fly."

"We won't touch it."

"Mama, how can you tell the difference between a girl locust and boy locust?" John had not forgotten our earlier conversation.

"Only other locusts need to know that."

John hung his head a second, looking as perplexed as a rabbit who spotted a dog nearby, but then he shrugged and smiled.

She laughed and gave us each a napkin and a glass of Kool-Aid, and then we sat on the back porch steps together, recounting the morning's adventures. She listened to every detail from flushing a flock of fee' larks, to the woodpecker chicks with their heads sticking out, and the grass snake that escaped before we could catch it.

When lunch was over, we grabbed our fruit jars and raced to The Pines to find our locust right where we left it.

The several stages of skin shedding from the crack in the back until the locust emerges and stretches its wings to dry never failed to take longer than we could stay in one place. Sometimes, we picked the creature up, put it in one of our jars, and placed it on a tree located in a more favorable location for our observation—always careful not to touch its wings.

On days when we found our locust in the late evening, we took it home and offered it a fence post for its final emerging. The locusts never appeared any worse for wear provided the relocation took place early in the metamorphosis and the wings were protected.

John wanted to help the beetle through what appeared to be a long, painful process.

"Let's get this one out."

"Remember what Mama said. You'll kill the locust if you help it. Only God can help it."

"I wonder why God makes it work so hard. I think it hurts the locust."

"John, it doesn't hurt! I think it's like a baby being born."

"You mean like a calf or a puppy?"

"Yeah, sorta like that. The calf or the puppy isn't hurt when it's born."

"It looks like the mama hurts, though. Remember, when we watched Josie have her puppies?"

"I don't know. I thought Josie just looked sad because she had so many."

We both laughed as we wandered through The Pines in search of other conversation pieces.

As the afternoon passed, we caught a couple of butterflies, picked up some pinecones, took a terrapin home to mark its shell with our crayon signature, and watched a chameleon change colors as we moved it from place to place. We continued to return to the locust so as not to miss the grand finale of his flight.

In the unlikely event we missed the flight to freedom, we would collect its shell in an Eight O'clock Coffee grounds bag to be used later when we played store in the big oak tree near the house. If one of our locusts died before completing its radical change, we mourned its passing, convinced we caused its death—and we may have.

Dragonflies, or mosquito hawks as we identified them, ate mosquitoes. That alone made them my favorite bug, from the tiny ones on wild violets near the trestle to the large ones on our clothesline or barbed-wire fence. The challenge of catching one was amplified by a mosquito hawk's speed and tendency to bite.

We chose a likely spot to sit near the clothesline to wait for one to perch. As if participating in an Olympic sport, we lunged several times toward an imaginary target to be sure the distance and angle were right. Sometimes, we were successful in capturing one or two, which we quickly deposited into our quart jars.

"Did you get stung?" John asked as he screwed down the jar lid over his.

"I did. Did you?"

"Not this time."

The jars had adequate ventilation holes, but the prisoners looked so forlorn we soon released them for fear they may die before eating their share of mosquitoes.

Strangely enough, we did not worry about the life spans of captured grasshoppers or honeybees and often decided one or more needed surgery. We anesthetized the creatures by putting an alcohol-soaked cotton ball in the jar. We began surgery as soon as they were asleep, removed something, sewed up the incision, and replaced them in the jar without the anesthetic.

Their inevitable deaths surprised us every time. I'm not sure if that surprise resulted from our being a bit dense or overly optimistic. I prefer to believe it was optimism.

The huge, utilitarian grasshoppers escaped surgery based on their ability to amuse in a different way.

John and I each chose our favorites and hitched them to penny matchboxes using sewing thread harnesses. These experiments typically occurred on the back porch during a break while waiting for our locust to complete his transformation.

"Hey, how many of the big grasshoppers do you have?" John asked.

"Right now, in my jar?"

"Yeah."

"Two pretty big ones. What about you?"

"I only have one, but he's really big. I bet he is stronger than yours."

"I bet not!"

And the game began.

Determining the weight-carrying capability of various specimens seemed important, though now I can't imagine what value that knowledge could have. First, we tested our grasshoppers' strength with just the empty matchbox. Then we upped the stakes with crushed locust shells or an actual match—and, once, with a real penny. The strongest grasshopper won the game for its owner and freedom for itself. Once a winner had been crowned, the game ended, and we moved on to an equally fascinating barn bug.

Intermittently, we would check on our locust to determine progress or sometimes just sit in one of the clover patches looking for elusive luck to be found with a four-leaf clover.

Honeybees buzzed over the clover. "Wanna catch some honeybees, John?"

I do not remember him ever saying no. Whoever captured the most in one jar without allowing any to escape won the typical prize of a clover flower chain necklace made by the loser.

Always barefoot, we were susceptible to stings from both the honeybees and the yellow jackets, but stings were not a deterrent. I removed stingers for John, and he did the same for me. We took pleasure in believing that the source creature would die having lost its stinger. I don't know if that is true or not, but believing it brought some comfort.

The barn offered its own unique bug population. Among them was the doodle bug. Our cows provided the manure attraction, and we easily located several bugs hard at work creating their own treasured manure ball. They seemed to be extra motivated as the ball became larger, twice the bug's size or more. We wagered on each bug's ability.

"I bet my bug will last longer."

"Why, Olevia?"

"Because he's got bigger pinchers. I bet a penny."

"Do you have a penny?"

"Yes, but it doesn't matter because I'm going to win."

"I bet my biggest grasshopper you don't."

And so it would go, until one of us moved a manure ball, leaving the doodle bug confused and scrambling to find his purpose for that day. We gathered several of them for our collection, and when daylight had turned to twilight, we headed home. Sometimes, we had a freshly born locust and sometimes we did not, but we always shared all the days' accomplishments with Mama.

As we related the experience of capturing each bug, and the ones still in our jars, Mama said, "Well, ya'll can't keep 'em in those jars."

"Why, Mama? There are lots of air holes in the lids."

"They'll die, Olevia. They must eat, and they need to be with their families too."

We let them all go every time. Following supper, Mama and Daddy sat on the front porch enjoying the ever so slight breeze as the sun sank in the west. John and I attempted to catch fireflies in the same jars that had housed our earlier conquests.

Once the moon made its appearance, we all went inside to prepare for bed. Daddy got out the DDT—a banned substance in today's world due to its cancer-causing ingredients and connection to the decline of the Bald Eagle population. He poured it into a hand pump cattle sprayer and sprayed it to rid the living room and bedrooms of mosquitoes before we went to bed. It did the job.

Thus, our bug research ended another day.

As I crawled into bed, I mentally reviewed our conversations, our fun, and how blessed I felt to have spent the day with my family.

I now think about how much of who John and I grew up to be originated in the times we spent playing together in our fields and the nearby woods. While wandering around the pasture, John and I talked about everything. Our brother-sister relationship went as deep as the deepest ocean and served us well for years to come.

I smile again as I read the above.

CHAPTER 10
VISITING WITH THE TAYLORS

Other than mine and John's bug days, piano lessons, and the scads of summertime activities we invented, we also participated in a couple of our parents' planned excursions. Among those events were trips to visit the Taylors.

Besides being our benefactor in obtaining the House on the Hill, Daddy worked with Mr. Taylor. They had no children—at least none I ever knew of—and they seemed to be a rung or two above us on the ladder of success. On occasion, they came to visit, drink coffee, play the fiddle, and talk about what was going on in each other's lives.

However, the trips we made to their Grant Parish home every summer stand out in my memory today. The Taylors lived about two hours northeast of us and, as a family, we made at least two visits per summer. There were so many reasons to look forward to these expeditions.

"Mama, do you think they'll have a black diamond ready for us?" I asked before we even got into the car.

"I don't know for sure, but I expect so."

Daddy interrupted, "Do not ask for anything not offered. Understand?"

"Yes, sir." I certainly hoped they had one because I could already taste it!

On each visit, a black diamond watermelon would be chilled and waiting. The thought of that iced-down watermelon may have been a deciding factor in our visits—though I doubt it. It would have been one for me!!

By some strange southern phenomena, watermelon is a treat eaten as if it is the last opportunity to do so. Mr. Taylor's black diamonds provided bragging rights, not only for the sweet pulp, but also for the rinds perfect for preserving. We never left their house without a watermelon or two and a bag of watermelon rinds which Mama would transform into preserves. A lobster tail and butter feast at the best restaurant in town could not compare to hot biscuits and watermelon rind preserves on a cold, rainy morning. Having never been to a restaurant at that time in my life, I could not make that comparison based on fact, but even now in my memory, biscuits and preserves win!

On the Friday before such a trip, Mama prepared some food to take with us and added to whatever Mrs. Taylor had prepared. My favorite menu included a pot of chicken and dumplings, a container of fried chicken, or rice pudding. The trips were huge adventures from the time we climbed into the car until we crawled out that night.

Before dawn Saturday morning, Daddy sat at the wheel, and we were loaded up. Mama said Daddy drove a car just like he drove the train, but it lacked the safety of rails to make it stay in a straight line. If he looked to the right, he turned to the right. If he looked to the left, he turned to the left. Top speed was the only way to go.

Once settled in the backseat, Mama would hand out some snacks.

"Okay, kids. It'll take about two hours to get there, so settle in with your treat bags."

These bags typically contained a piece of fruit, a sweet of some sort, and a small bottle of water or Kool-Aid. John and I immediately began negotiations.

"Johnny, can I have your lifesavers?"

"Why?" he replied. "You have some."

"But yours are butterscotch, and I like them best."

"I like butterscotch too."

Hannah usually stepped in to solve the problem. "Okay, Olevia. I'm putting all three lifesaver rolls in this bag. We have butterscotch, wild cherry, and pineapple. Do you both agree to keep the one you choose?"

We nodded simultaneously. "Who goes first?"

I raised my hand as if in school. "Me! Me! Me!"

"Is that okay with you, John?"

He nodded again. Problem solved.

****

One particularly interesting trip involved Mama falling out of the car. In today's world, falling out of a car is not likely to happen, and, if it does, serious injuries could be suffered. This memorable trip occurred when Daddy was still driving his A Model Ford. Five people filled the car to capacity, and it had no seatbelts, no locks on the doors, and no safety equipment.

Less than two miles from our house, we went around a tight curve at probably ten or fifteen miles per hour. The front passenger door opened. Mama fell out and landed in the ditch. The brakes squealed, nearly throwing us into the front seat.

Daddy backed the car up. He called out through the open door, "Mary, what'd you get out for?"

"I don't know, John," she replied, dusting herself off.

"Well, you'd better get back in, or we're going to be late getting up to Doss's. I'd like to be there by ten."

Mama climbed up the slope. She straightened her dress and returned to the front seat.

"I'm ready. When we get on the highway, remember the speed limit is fifty."

"Don't worry, Mary." He chuckled. "I'll do my best to make it."

At the time, it didn't seem strange how amazingly calm Mama remained. In retrospect, I'm impressed with her unwillingness to ruin a special day for all of us by focusing on herself. We kids remained quiet in hopes of preserving the party atmosphere. Daddy continued to drive with abandon and made every effort to avoid being passed by anyone. This two-hour trip could be made today in less than an hour.

****

Despite his flawed driving skills, Daddy consistently delivered us safely to the Taylor residence. The car barely stopped before John and I jumped out and headed to the nearby woods.

I don't know why their woods were so inviting when we practically lived in the woods. Perhaps a new place to explore attracted us. Sometimes we saw deer, and we inevitably caught glimpses of squirrels, rabbits, multicolored butterflies, and redheaded woodpeckers.

"Why don't we ever see any redheaded woodpeckers at home?" John asked.

"I don't know. Maybe we don't look in the right places. Maybe they like these trees better than pine trees?"

"Do you see that praying mantis on that oak leaf?" John asked excitedly.

I quickly ran over and peered at it. "Don't touch it. It's good luck. I wish we could bring it in for Mama to see."

"What makes it good luck?"

"The look of praying hands. A lot of people believe finding a praying mantis means that God is pleased with your life."

"Wow," John said over his shoulder as he headed to see what else he could find.

Around noon, Daddy's whistle alerted us that dinner was on. This would be followed by the melt-in-your-mouth watermelon. The men's dinner conversation routinely involved politics.

"What do think, John, about this anti-Long faction—Strom is a what—a Dixiecrat?" Mr. Taylor began the conversation.

"I don't know. He's endorsed by Jimmie Davis, and I haven't been too happy with him," Daddy replied.

"Well, he can sing," Mr. Taylor said before singing a little of Davis' campaign song *"Take Me Back and Try Me One More Time."*

Everyone laughed. Daddy continued. "He oughta go back to picking that guitar. I'm leaning toward Earl Long."

Jimmy Davis relied heavily on his music career, and it worked well for him in 1944, 1946, 1960, and 1962. He died in 2000 at the age of 101.

Mama, Mrs. Taylor, and even Hannah talked about canning and preserving. Their conversation also included what was coming in from garden, if Hannah had any sewing projects, and other women's work subjects. When it was time to clean off the table and move toward dessert, they took the dishes to the sink and brought out the watermelon.

With dessert, it seemed the men's conversation invariably turned to professional boxing. Daddy was a Joe Louis fan, and Mr. Taylor favored Jersey Joe Walcott. The women continued to talk about gardens, canning, and various other chores. John and I stayed at the table and listened until the watermelon appeared. Then, we took our slices out on the back porch where spitting seed fights were okayed.

In the late afternoon, we loaded up for the trip home. Tired and refreshed at the same time, we had plenty of topics to share during the two-hour drive home. Oftentimes, John and I fell asleep.

These getaways were special in that the only entertainment provided was what we concocted. We heard adults talk about adult things, and they interspersed that conversation with questions for us while we shared the dinner table. We ran free in the woods and used our imaginations to create memories.

There were no televisions, and I cannot ever remember the phone ringing during a visit. These times were small cocoons where everything was good. Nothing could penetrate the peace, like a snow globe rotating on its stand.

CHAPTER 11
UNCLE JAMES

Daddy and Uncle James.

I leaned on the kitchen table, grinning ear-to-ear at the sight of Uncle James unloading a bag of groceries. I loved it when he came to visit.

"Olevia, get that bag over there for me."

"This one, Uncle James? What's in it? Is this fruit or what?"

"It's a pineapple. Have you eaten a pineapple before?"

"Just out of the can. I've never seen this kind of pineapple. They grow on trees in Hawaii, don't they? What does the tree look like?"

"They don't grow on trees. They grow from a plant close to the ground."

Uncle James, Daddy's youngest brother, came to our Tioga house six or seven times. Each occurrence with my favorite uncle left me with an extraordinary memory. Always unexpected, each visit included an unusual gift— typically one for the family but also, without fail, one especially for me. He spent extra time with me, one-on-one, and seemed to enjoy it. I certainly did.

As he skillfully cut the pineapple, he continued to educate me.

"Did you know it takes two or three years to grow a pineapple?"

"No. Why is that? Isn't sugar cane like that? Have you ever seen a pineapple farm? I've seen a sugar cane farm."

"Slow down, Olevia."

His beautifully-engaging laugh made me laugh. I felt even better when he put his arm around my shoulders to give me a squeeze.

"Here," he said, "why don't you sit down beside me, and I'll tell you a little bit about pineapples.

I happily climbed into the chair he indicated. I suppose my standing practically on top of him had interfered with his pineapple peeling. I swung my legs, smiled, and waited.

"No, I have never been on a pineapple farm. Most are grown outside of the country and shipped in. Hawaii would be a good place to see a farm."

He spoke about how they were harvested and shipped. He explained how pineapple picking required perfect timing because, unlike tomatoes, they do not ripen after harvesting. He answered every question without hesitation. His explanations were such that I felt a part of the scenery he described. As if he were a hypnotist, I sat spellbound while he added a worldly aspect to my isolated existence.

Once, he showed up with T-bone steaks. We butchered our own beef and pork and had year-round access to both. But we had never grilled or cooked outside. We did not own a barbecue pit; we had wiener roasts on occasion, but those involved a stack of logs.

Our beef and pork were stored in an Alexandria meat locker. The tiny icebox freezer in our kitchen could not accommodate more than a day's supply of meat. Other than chicken, meals with meat required Daddy to drive downtown and back. Since this needed advanced planning, it didn't happen too often.

Uncle James' six fresh T-bone steaks got my attention when he took over Mama's kitchen.

"Whatcha doin', Uncle James? Can I help?" I stood close to observe his every move.

"Well, first you need to wash your hands; be sure they are clean." I followed him to the sink and carefully imitated his approach to handwashing. Once done, we each dried our hands on a clean dish towel and returned to the table where the steaks lay.

"Next, we gotta be sure the meat's tender and well-seasoned," he explained as he removed the steaks from the butcher paper and laid them on the countertop.

I felt as important as a contestant on any cooking show being instructed by the world's greatest chef. Of course, there were no cooking shows on TV then, and we didn't have a TV anyway. What I had in my uncle was a real, flesh-and-blood person who shared his time with me, and that far outweighed any other situation.

Then, he brought out a strange-looking tool—a meat tenderizer. A bit smaller than a regular hammer, it had peaks and valleys on each side of the mallet portion. Mama's cooking apparently did not require such a tool, as I had not seen one in our kitchen.

"Olevia, would you like to help me tenderize these steaks?"

I smiled, and he handed the tool to me.

"Okay, you don't have to hit'em hard, just firmly. Twice on each side of each steak."

"Okay. Like this, Uncle James?"

"That's good. Now, we need our seasonings. That's what makes the meat good tasting."

He reached into another bag and brought out three or four bottles of different spices. Although he described each one as he applied them to the steaks, I don't remember what they were.

I watched closely. "Did you use salt and pepper too?"

"Well, I saved that for you. Where are your salt and pepper shakers?"

"Right here."

"Okay, with all those other spices, we just need a little salt and pepper. Shake a little on each side of the steak."

I did as he instructed, then looked at him for approval.

"Okay." He smiled, starting for the door. "I gotta get something out of my truck. Wait here."

Other than Mr. Curry frying fish in the backyard, I'd never seen a man cook. I felt in awe. Within minutes, he returned, carrying a portable grill and a bag of charcoal.

I have never eaten a steak I enjoyed more than that one. It began with the aroma drifting through the air from the grill set up in the backyard. I watched Uncle James slice squash and prepare new potatoes to put on the grill with the meat. Daddy, home from work now, stood beside him. His hands were tucked into his overall's bib as he marveled about the meal to come.

I wish I had a picture of the two of them as they were deep in conversation about the steaks, the trimmings, and the perfect weather with the slight breeze sharing the enticing odor with everyone in the area.

John, Hannah, and Mama joined me on the back porch. We watched as Uncle James added a few marginally grilled sweet onions and sliced tomatoes to the meal. The distinctive, almost addictive fragrance served as the best appetizer ever.

I heard Daddy say, "I bet better meals than this are not served in Heaven."

They both laughed, and Daddy put his arm on his baby brother's shoulder. Indeed, we all oohed and aahed over that meal.

****

I occupied the perfect world of an eight-year-old kid when I enjoyed that day. As I grew older, I discovered Uncle James had another side that was often hidden from John and me.

Daddy and Uncle James were close, and they corresponded or phoned each other more than expected for our family. Daddy lent him money and worried about him.

Uncle James suffered from alcoholism.

In the 1950s, alcoholics were just considered drunks, and they were kept as family secrets. Every drunk had an excuse manufactured and supported by their family.

Uncle James had at least three. The first was that his mother never let him taste liquor because he was the baby in the family. This led to him not learning how to drink in moderation. The other two excuses were that his dad abused him, and his wife refused sex with him. We all accepted that Uncle James did not bear any responsibility for his behavior; his family bore all of it.

Once, he bragged that a hitchhiker friend he brought to our house could speak fluent French. He became incensed when Mama and his hitchhiker friend refused to carry on a conversation in French. Mama's limited French consisted of Cajun dialect. I don't know if Uncle James' friend could truly speak French. I did know he and Uncle James were both more drunk than sober. Daddy stepped in to calm him and avoided a fist fight between them.

On another visit, when he was disoriented (alternate word for drunk), Daddy caught him in the middle of the night urinating into a basket of just-laundered clothes. This time, Daddy yelled in anger, and Uncle James left before daylight.

A most extraordinary visit with Uncle James took place in Pasadena during our first and only family trip outside of Louisiana. Before we left, Mama spent the day frying chicken for us to eat on the way. Daddy had the car washed, the oil changed, and the tank filled. We packed our suitcases and went to bed early. I didn't sleep a wink while I watched the sky for any hint of sunrise.

Before first light, we climbed into the Henry J already packed from the day before. Daddy knew Texas lay west of Louisiana and had been told Houston could be found in a straight shot from Alexandria.

He drove to the MacArthur Drive Circle and took the west exit. Thus, the trip began. Anytime he saw a road sign for Houston, he turned in the direction indicated. Hannah, John, and I sat in the back seat eating chicken and marveling at the scenery we passed. We stopped for gas a couple of times, and Daddy inquired from the attendant about directions to Pasadena, a suburb of Houston.

"Well, sir, I've got a map here. And it's only a dime."

"Don't need a map. Just tell me what you know about getting to Pasadena."

One attendant even offered, to no avail, to *give* him a map—probably after seeing the four of us waiting in that small Henry J. But Daddy remained as stubborn as a mule.

"Son, I don't need a map. I need directions."

The young attendant continued to be patient and courteous in trying to explain the quickest route, and Daddy never realized his response had been an oxymoron. None of us did.

Well after dark, we arrived at Uncle James' house. Daddy's unorthodox method of finding our destination had stretched a five or six-hour trip into fourteen. Still, John and I had no idea it took longer than necessary. We had kept busy being fascinated by road signs, asking repeatedly what various signs meant.

I recall looking out the window and exclaiming, "Look at that! That sign reads Historical Marker. What's historical here? Is that like the sign at home for Buhlow Lake?"

Mama said, "I don't know, honey. I expect there's some historical site. Perhaps a battlefield or a famous person's house."

Pointing to another one, John asked, "That one says, Trucks Use Low Gear. Why?"

"That's a good question," Mama said. "Perhaps because of the hill?"

"Hey, this sign says that Houston is 150 miles. The last Houston sign said we only had 140 miles to go."

Mama smiled patiently. "Sometimes the Highway Department makes a mistake in where they place their signs."

A wise response, though I did not realize it at the time.

We arrived well after dark and traipsed into the two-room efficiency apartment with all our luggage. It had a kitchen and a combination living room/bedroom. That proved the perfect bachelor pad for Uncle James, but it burst at the seams when the five of us arrived with the intent of spending a couple of nights.

Mama and John got the bed, Daddy and Uncle James slept on the floor, and Hannah and I had the plastic sofa bed with a crack from one end to the other and right down the center.

I lay next to the window, eye-to-eye with a giant dog chained outside. It stood on its hind legs and barked all night. An eerie light from the street and Uncle James' cigarettes provided enough illumination to watch the cockroaches crawl across the floor.

Mama later commented on how the roaches were drunk and could not crawl in a straight line.

The whole place reeked of whiskey.

An exciting day followed the long night. Uncle James insisted on taking John and me on a trip to a toy store. He told us to choose anything we wanted from the displayed fantasyland. We walked the aisles, choosing and putting back.

A crawling doll caught my attention, and although my eyes drank it in, I felt the cost exceeded what I should expect. I carried it a little while before putting it back on the shelf. I went to the cash register with a large book of stories, much more practical. Back in Uncle James' truck, he surprised me with the crawling doll. My heart overflowed with love for him at that minute.

Daddy and Uncle James enjoyed the wrestling matches. Gorgeous George, The Baron, Bulldog Danny Fletcher, and Duke Keomuka were wrestlers who made Daddy's blood boil. He listened to the matches on the radio and became worked-up just hearing a mention of Gorgeous George or Duke Keomuka.

As special entertainment, Uncle James had tickets to a wrestling match in town that night, and The Baron headlined. We loaded ourselves into Uncle James' truck, which he insisted on driving. Quite a feat, as six of us sat in the front seat! We headed to the Sportatorium, which was in Houston, if memory serves me correctly.

A black cloud began to form when Uncle James lost a parking space while backing into it. He slammed on the brakes, jumped out of the truck, and raged at the driver as he walked away. He wanted to chase the thief down or key his car. Daddy calmed him, spotting another parking space, which we obtained with ease.

Uncle James still fumed when we entered the huge arena overflowing with loud, beer-drinking people. Spotlights above the ring magnified the experience. The smells— popcorn, beer, roasted peanuts, and cigarettes—seemed amplified too. Vendors walking up and down the aisles gave rise to a carnival atmosphere bordering on chaos.

The wrestlers stood around the ring, signing autographs, and Hannah admired one in a rhinestone outfit. She strong-armed her way to where he was standing. As she offered her program, The Baron stepped up, took the program, signed it, and returned it. He had long black hair and looked sinister just standing there. Hannah accepted the signed program without protest, though her expression showed she had hoped for a different result.

Fear buzzed through every pore in my body like a swarm of bees before the first toehold was applied. We settled into our ringside seats, and the wrestling began. Uncle James got into an argument with someone behind us. As he attempted to climb over the seat to make his point to the other inebriated fan, Daddy diverted his attention to the tag team entering the ring, thus avoiding another brawl.

Wrestler after wrestler came out. I hated it. John hated it. Mama looked uncomfortable, and Hannah seemed mildly interested. Daddy and Uncle James were having the time of their lives as they slurped beer, yelled, and threw air punches.

This was one of only two times I ever recall Daddy drinking beer. I endured the spectacle in the ring. At one point I even came close to being entertained by it until a ferocious-looking, seven-foot-tall bear followed his trainer into the ring. The announcer made a show of fake fear as he described the bear and introduced him to his opponent.

Terrible Ted—the Canadian Black Bear—apparently traveled both Canada and the United States in search of opponents. His win/loss record weighed heavily in his favor, and it counted as a special treat to have him as part of the line-up.

The bear wore a muzzle and claw protection, along with a restraining collar. Still, to me, he looked capable of inflicting considerable pain. He stood erect, waving his front paws in all directions. One claw cover fell off, and the wrestler's blood splattered from the ring onto us. The referee rushed forward with a jar of honey to draw the bear's attention. With covered faces, John and I continued to watch between our fingers.

I whispered to John, "Please promise me you'll never become a wrestler."

He whispered back, "I promise, Olevia."

Mama held both of us close until the ordeal concluded. I have determined since that the real Terrible Ted was both declawed and toothless. I also learned that various counterfeit bears stood in for him in arenas all over the South. I have no idea what bear I saw at the one and only wrestling match I ever attended.

The relief I felt upon returning to Uncle James' place made the plastic sofa seem a safe, comfortable bed. The trip back to Tioga the next day took half the time of going. I slept most of it, clutching both my crawling doll and the new book of stories.

That was the last time I remember seeing Uncle James. Sadly, sometime later, he took his own life in his truck on the side of the highway. I am not sure if months or a couple of years had passed. Time is a moving target when remembering things from childhood.

The day before his suicide, he mailed Daddy a homemade drawing of himself with squiggly lines going in every direction. On the drawing, he wrote, "This is how I am feeling today."

The next day, he pulled off the highway, blocked the exhaust pipe, and somehow re-routed the fumes into the cab of his truck. He then climbed back in and got out a pencil and paper to record what it felt like to die from carbon monoxide. His note began by saying he was eager to cross over to the other side and had no regrets about leaving.

Aunt Denie called to let us know the police had found his body. I recall Dad sitting on the front porch, rocking, with tears running down his face. When I asked what was wrong, he answered quietly, "Your Uncle James died last night."

Nothing more was said. We both stared at the sky until darkness wrapped around us like a cloak.

****

The next morning, Daddy left alone for Houston to join his brothers and sisters at Uncle James' remembrance. At the memorial service, Daddy's sister gave the suicide note to Daddy. He kept it in his trunk along with the drawing.

I learned, sometime later, that he had taken his own life. But suicide remained a taboo subject Daddy never discussed. I did not see either the note or the drawing until 1965, when Daddy died, and his trunk was opened.

Years later, when we had a TV, Saturday Night Wrestling became one of the few shows permitted in our house. As Daddy watched and threw his air punches, I sensed he relived our family trip to Houston.

A pineapple, grilled steaks, a crawling doll, and a book of stories—still on my bookcase—are precious memories of my favorite uncle.

CHAPTER 12

JOHNNY'S FIDDLE

My family: Daddy, me, Hannah, John, and
Mamma – 1952.

As I've said before, some of my most enjoyable and
outstanding memories are better related through John's eyes
and his experiences. This is one of those!

****

John's Story:
Daddy and I sat on the front porch on a late Friday
afternoon, not really talking, just communicating by being
together. He held a magazine, which he had folded back,

and his glasses had slipped down on his nose. His gaze lifted to me.

"Hey, come here. Look at this."

I got up from my perch on the steps to see his finger poised over a seed company advertisement.

Sell seeds. Win valuable prizes. All you must do is sell our assorted seeds to your neighbors, and you will win valuable prizes. When you sell 250 seed packets, this violin will belong to you.

A picture of a fiddle lay in the center of the ad. Before I could answer, Daddy had more questions.

"Son, do ya think you could sell enough seeds to win that fiddle?"

"I don't know, but I'd sure like to try."

"Okay. Tomorrow, I'll send for the seeds."

The next morning, I watched him write a note and a check and put them in an envelope. He slid the envelope into the inside pocket of his overalls.

"Son, I'm runnin' up to the post office. Be back shortly."

At eight years old, I was as happy as a hog in slop. Selling seeds sounded like a new game to me. And a fiddle? I hadn't digested that part yet.

"Mama," I said as I ran into the kitchen, "did Daddy tell you I'm getting a fiddle? All on my own, too."

"No, he didn't mention it. When's this supposed to happen?"

"I don't know. I gotta sell some seeds first."

"Seeds?"

"Yeah. I don't know ever'thing about it yet. Daddy's takin' care of it."

Mama just smiled and went about cleaning. I wandered out into the backyard to play with Waggles and share my good fortune to come with Olevia. I'm sure neither of us gave it much thought after that day.

****

About two weeks later, Daddy came in carrying a good-sized box and sat down in a rocking chair to open it.

"Come over here, son. I think we got us the makin's of a fiddle to come."

I ran over as he held up an eight-by-ten picture of a violin that lay on top of the box. Before I could appreciate that picture, I got a look at the rest of the contents. I immediately realized I had no idea how numerous 250 seed packets were until I looked in that box.

"You're gonna have to sell every one of these seed packets and, when you do, we'll get this fiddle." He held up the picture again.

Daddy grinned like a Cheshire cat, and I mumbled, "Okay."

Looking at that box filled to the brim with seed packets made me wonder if I'd even met 250 people in my whole life. I figured I might as well get started, and I reached in for a handful of seed packets. Daddy put his hand over mine.

"No, no, son. Start out slow." He handed me three packets. "Start with these three. Where're ya gonna go?"

"I'm gonna walk the Pardue Road."

"Okay. Knock on the door, and when someone answers, be sure to smile. Tell them you're working to buy a fiddle, and you need their help."

"Yessir."

I left right away and knocked on four or five doors before I reached the end of that road. I chose doors where there were no dogs (but almost everybody had dogs). I saw one pulling on its short chain as it barked and wagged its tail. I went on by that house as well.

I did smile, but I forgot the rest of the sales pitch. I didn't sell any seeds, and I knew Daddy would be waiting. He sat in a front porch rocking chair, the box of seeds next to him.

"How many did you sell, son?"

"I didn't sell a one, Daddy. I don't think folks want any seeds."

"Well, while you were gone, I got to looking through these seeds. You know, I like to keep a lot of seeds around because you never know when or where you might need some. I think I might just buy all of them from you."

That boggled my mind! What in the world could Daddy do with 250 seed packets? To me, I saw enough seeds to plant all of Tioga in vegetables and flowers. Still, I stayed quiet and hoped this was the cavalry coming to my rescue.

He went inside to his desk, got his checkbook, figured the price, and wrote a check. When he came back outside, he rummaged in the box to find the self-addressed return envelope. He put the check and the receipt copy in it before sealing it.

"I just bought all of your seeds."

If I had known he was interested, I could have saved myself from that long walk up Pardue Road. He took the box and put it in the trunk in his room before he left the house.

He raised the envelope over his shoulder as he walked to the car. "I'm taking this to the post office." He grinned.

****

About four weeks later, he brought home another box, and he called out to me before he even reached the front steps. I went running. As soon as he sat down, I wanted to rip it open.

"No, son. Don't want to damage anything. Let me get my knife out."

He cleanly cut the tape down a seam on the side and opened it as carefully as one would a pot of gold. I watched every move. A bunch of old newspapers served as packing, and he gingerly reached in to pull out the prettiest fiddle I had ever seen. Of course, I hadn't seen many fiddles. His approach in lifting the instrument out of the box reminded me of when he tried to remove an egg from a setting hen's nest. She cackled like a mad hornet ready to sting. Every move was calculated.

"This sure is a nice fiddle," he said before bringing out the bow.

"It sure is, Daddy."

I didn't know anything about fiddles or violins and felt pretty sure my daddy didn't either. Most eight-year-olds know their parents' hobbies, talents, and interests. I figured we would learn the fiddle together.

He continued to carefully remove the wrapping from the bow. "This here's a horse hair bow," he explained.

"You mean it's made out of a horse's hair?"

"Well, it's made from the tail hair of a horse. It's bleached and stretched. See, look at that." He slightly extended the hair on the bow. "You can tell it's made from horse's hair. There's even an adjustment on this."

He showed me a little knob to tighten or loosen the bow strings.

"Let me tell ya something else you gotta do before you can play your fiddle. You must resin the bow."

Resin was a new word for me, and I stumbled for an answer. "Where can we get some? Do we have to order it too?"

"You need pine resin, and it's made especially for bows. Come inside with me."

I followed him to his desk where he opened the middle drawer to remove a small, almost clear, golden block. He handed it to me.

"That's pine resin, son. I keep it for times like this."

As I handed it back, I wondered how he knew there would be a time like this. We took seats in the living room where he rubbed the resin block gently up and down the bow string. He adjusted those horse hairs. Finally, he laid the bow to the side and went back to unpacking the fiddle.

He meticulously removed each section of the newspaper before handing it to me and going on to the next one. Within a couple of minutes, he lifted the fiddle from the box. A clear plastic bag enclosed the instrument. He held it out for me.

"Son, why don't you slide the plastic off while I hold the fiddle?"

"Yessir."

I couldn't wait to get my hands on that fiddle. As soon as the protective cover was off, I reached for it.

"No, son. Not yet." He took the fiddle and plinked on each string, turning the keys at the end each time he plinked a string. Sometimes, he hit the strings with his thumb and listened.

I watched him in disbelief and admiration. He looked as comfortable with that fiddle as I imagined Tommy Jackson accompanying Hank Williams in performing 'I Saw the Light.'" When he finished plinking the strings and turning the knobs, he handed the fiddle to me.

"Play it."

I took it and sawed the bow up and down. It screeched and squawked, and I couldn't imagine how you could ever make it sound good.

He laughed as he watched me, and then he reached for the fiddle. "Let me see that, son."

He had a big smile on his face when he took the fiddle, but the smile turned upside down before the music played. He placed the fiddle under his chin, put his left hand on the neck of it, drew the bow back, and looked as if he were on the verge of tears.

When he began to play and rub that bow up and down, it sounded like angels singing. I sat staring until he finished playing.

"Boy, Daddy. That was good. I didn't know you could play the fiddle. Where'd you learn?"

His answer ignored my question. "So, you liked 'Soldier's Joy?'"

"I sure did. How'd you learn to do that?" I asked again.

"Oh, I just picked it up."

He sat for a moment, staring into the distance and rubbing his chin between his thumb and forefinger.

I waited.

Directly, he picked up the fiddle again and got that same sad look. I assumed I would hear another one of those slow numbers, but he cut down then. Soon he stopped.

"A new bow is just hard to keep resin on."

He put another layer of resin on and started up again. Boy was this a different genre! The happy sound made me happy. Once finished, he laid the fiddle in his lap with the bow beside it.

"Son, do you know the name of that one?"

I laughed. "No, but it sure was a good one."

"The name of that one is Sally's Got a Wooden Leg. Fiddlers call that type of tune a breakdown."

"I really liked it. How'd you learn that?" I asked, still hoping for a little more background.

"Just picked it up."

While we sat together, he told me about the catgut strings on the fiddle and how important it is to understand a fiddle before you play it.

"This fiddle has a brace in the neck. That means it's a pretty good fiddle. Some fiddles don't have a brace in the neck, and they bow when you tune 'em. See this little wooden piece? That's called the bridge. See how each string runs through one notch on the bridge? Did you see me turning these knobs up here? That's called tuning it. The tighter you get a string, the higher the note. A loose string makes a lower note."

This time he played another jumpy little tune—one I thought I might have heard at school. I could hardly get my head around watching my dad as a fiddler!

"Do you know what that one was?"

"No."

"That's another breakdown. It is called 'Turkey in the Straw.'"

He put a little more resin on the strings. You must get it just right so it will sound right."

"Well, how do you make it sound like certain songs?"

"You do that with your ear."

"With your ear? Daddy, how'd you learn to do that?"

"Just something I picked up."

I marveled at him with my eyes as wide as saucers. I picked up my fiddle and started to go out of doors with it.

He reached to touch my shoulder. "No. Let me keep this for you in my trunk. This is a nice fiddle, and we wanna take care of it."

He took it and handled it with a lot more care than I would have. I hadn't even thought about a fiddle until he mentioned one. He unlocked his trunk to lay the fiddle inside.

"We'll get it out, and you can play it every now and then."

We did get it out every so often, and he played it. I don't know if those were the only three songs he knew or if they were the only three he liked to play. I do know they are the only three I ever heard him play. Sometimes, he would give me a pencil and let me try to keep time on the neck of the fiddle while he played. Afterwards, he would shake his head, tussle my hair, and chuckle.

"You're just not very good at this, are you, Johnny?"

I wasn't, and my only interest in the fiddle lay in hearing him play. One Saturday, early in the morning, he made a phone call and looked over at me when he hung up.

"Doss Taylor's coming over for a while today."

I liked Mr. Taylor. He had a Santa Claus look about him, a jovial, round man with what looked like naturally white whiskers. His beard looked as though someone had rubbed soot in to create a blue tint. He kept those whiskers and matching hair perfectly coifed, and his eyes sparkled much like the Santa I saw every year on the downtown square.

Daddy described Mr. Taylor as being as good of an engineer as the best engineer who ever drove a train, maybe better. Daddy only praised people he admired, and I knew Mr. Taylor excelled as an engineer. I had a lot of respect for Mr. Taylor, too. His picture hanging on our living room wall served as tribute to his generosity.

Two hours later, I watched Mr. Taylor's pickup creeping up our hill-driveway. When he parked, I realized he was not alone. Mrs. Taylor perched there beside him.

I hated to see that. Mrs. Taylor, a large woman as broad as she was tall, radiated old. No matter how friendly an act she displayed, she seemed grouchy to me. She pretended she loved kids and, anytime I showed up, she would ask me the same question.

Today, she tilted her head and tossed her usual query. "Do you like me better than Doss?"

"I like Doss better."

"Oh no you don't." She laughed.

I tried to keep walking and avoid having to be in her presence.

Daddy walked down the steps and out to greet the Taylors at the gate, and that's when I saw the little black case Mr. Taylor carried. Daddy shooed the dog off, shook hands with Mr. Taylor, and helped Mrs. Taylor climb the porch steps.

Once inside, Mama served coffee before she and Mrs. Taylor retired to the kitchen. I loved the aroma of coffee, and the scent of freshly baked blackberry muffins mingled with it like a fragrant bouquet. Everyone automatically inhaled when Mama entered the room.

After pleasantries were out of the way—light conversation punctuated by sipping from mugs and nibbles of muffins—Mr. Taylor and Daddy began to discuss my new fiddle.

"Well, Johnny, are you ready to fiddle a little bit?"

Mr. Taylor talked to Daddy, of course, not me.

"Yes."

Daddy went to the trunk, pulled out the fiddle, and handed it to Mr. Taylor.

"Here it is, Doss. That fiddle's what this boy got for selling seeds."

He plinked it, tuned it a little, examined the bow, and seemed to give it the stamp of approval.

"Do you mind if I play it a bit?"

"You go ahead and play it, Doss." Daddy smiled and nodded.

He sawed down on that fiddle and had a look of pure ecstasy on his face. He fiddled with an ease that Daddy didn't have, and the music the fiddle made seemed heaven sent.

I stared, open mouthed. "That's pretty music."

He glanced in my direction. "Boy, you sure have a nice fiddle here. Come over here and listen."

I moved over closer to him, and he sawed down on it again playing some fast, jerky tunes. I grinned, and he handed the fiddle back to Daddy. He grabbed his black bag by the handle and opened it with caution as if a snake might slither out. He pulled out his own fiddle, and I could see resin piled up on both sides of the bridge.

"Start one, John, and I'll help you scratch it out."

Daddy played one of his three customary tunes, and they got with it. Daddy looked mournful, and Mr. Taylor beamed with joy that infused the entire room like incense. They played together for thirty or forty minutes, maybe an hour, and then, as if on cue, Daddy put more resin on his bow, got up, and started toward his trunk.

Mr. Taylor picked up his case and put his fiddle away. He handled it as if it were a Stradivarius, for which he had great respect. He snapped the case closed and took it out to his truck.

When he returned, he and Daddy sat on the porch in rocking chairs to visit. I sat on the steps to listen. In less than an hour, Mr. Taylor stood up.

"Well, Johnny, I guess I better go."

As he passed by, he reached down and tussled me on the head. "You take care of that fiddle, boy." He yelled for his wife, and she waddled out of the house and down the steps.

The truck moved deliberately toward the road while Daddy and I stood on the porch. Back then, our hill looked like a mountain to me, and we watched silently with our hands in our pockets until we could no longer see the truck.

As we turned to go into the house, I glanced at Daddy and asked, "Daddy, how come you never told me you could play a fiddle?"

"Son, it's not important what a man does, but rather what he doesn't do."

To this day, I am still wrestling with that one!

****

John and Daddy had a special relationship that I could not be part of except as a bystander, an onlooker, and I cherished watching the two of them. Indeed, I learned a lot about my dad, my brother, and human nature in general by observing their interactions. On this day, I got to hear some fiddle music too!

CHAPTER 13

THE CIRCUS

"Olevia, get your things together. You need to go with your dad right now," Mrs. Bamber said, gazing at me.

My dad and brother, now a first grader, were standing in front of my third-grade classroom. My heart raced, beating so hard, I could hear it; I could not hear the conversation between my teacher and Dad.

John looked surprised and sad all at once; his eyes grew wide, but no smile accompanied them. My dad looked serious, his brows knitted, and I felt something must be terribly wrong on that Friday afternoon.

John and I rarely missed a day of school. If either of us were sick—running a fever or obviously physically impaired—we stayed home in bed with alphabet soup and Coca-Cola. Otherwise, we were in school where, to quote Daddy, "The learnin' takes place."

Mrs. Bamber continued to speak as she handed me a piece of paper. "This is the homework you're to complete over the weekend and turn in on Monday."

I glanced down at it as if it were a life preserver. I will be back at school on Monday. The list covered only what the class would be doing the rest of that day—some reading, associated workbook pages, and one page of arithmetic.

Still, I felt tense. I had the life preserver, but how cold would the water be? Daddy approached life seriously with little frivolity. Oh, he might play the fiddle or Jew's harp for us, but those times were more like performer and audience scenes with applause, which he deemed more appropriate than laughter or any real interaction.

Events involving my dad were special to me but not necessarily fun. We did not attend movies, play any silly childhood games, or even horse around. Daddy laughed— but not usually when he dealt with me.

Mama bore the responsibility for those things—talking, playing games, taking us swimming, picnicking, singing with us, and doing the things mothers did in the 1940s and '50s. Dad worked to support the family and to remind us that life should not be taken lightly.

With obvious trepidation, John and I marched down the hall, carrying our books and glancing up at a man who had a half-smile on his face. Our questions tumbled out in quick succession.

"Where are we going, Daddy? Is something wrong?" John asked.

"Where's Mama?" I asked. "Are we going home?"

"Does Mama know we aren't in school? Where are we going, Daddy?" John added.

Daddy said not a word. He kept that sly grin on his face while we followed him to the car, growing more apprehensive by the minute. In the car, our questions and his silence continued. Our tension subsided as we realized a smiling Daddy could not forebode anything too bad.

About ten minutes into our ride, Daddy began to question us.

"Have you kids ever seen an elephant?"

Quick to answer, I said, "I've seen elephants in my *Dumbo* book. I've seen elephants in my reader at school."

John added, "In our *Dick and Jane* reader, they have a circus come to town. Then they play circus. I think there were elephants in that story."

"I'm talking about a real elephant. Have you ever seen a real elephant or maybe a lion?"

We answered in unison, "No!"

I added, "We've never seen anything like that. Well, maybe at the zoo, but I don't remember for sure."

"Well, I'm not sure, but I think you might see something today that you've never seen before."

We had already seen that—Daddy picking us up from school unannounced and smiling! We weren't going home, and wherever we were going, only Daddy would be with us. At first, I thought we were going to Alexandria, but he didn't turn on Upper Third, so I felt lost again. John and I stopped our questioning to concentrate on watching, listening, and answering Daddy's continued inquiries.

"Do you know what cotton candy is?"

"No, sir," John replied.

"Do you like peanuts?"

"Yes, sir." John sat up straighter in his seat and looked eager, his eyes wide. "Are we going to have peanuts today?"

"Well, it's possible. We'll see."

"Where's Mama?" I asked. "Is she going to come with us?"

"Mama's busy at home."

"Are we going to see an elephant?" I asked.

"We might."

The twelve miles Daddy drove to MacArthur Drive felt like three hours. Daddy prided himself on negotiating The Circle—a much discussed round-about on the south end of Alexandria—like a pro.

The Circle included four outlets: MacArthur Drive, Bolton Avenue, Highway 71, and Highway 1. MacArthur Drive led to the ritzy section of town on the left, with the poverty-stricken areas diametrically opposed to it. Years later, my friends and I would drive through the ritzy area in the summertime with our windows rolled up to give the appearance of an air-conditioned car. *Teenagers!*

Within a few blocks, huge canvas tents came into view. I immediately assumed a church revival meeting occupied the area. Those were common in Tioga, typically complete with loud music, faith healing, and shouting. A traveling Pentecostal preacher usually ran the show.

I knew Daddy would not take us out of school to go to a revival meeting. Nothing made sense to me! We parked near the tents and the milling crowd. Being a school day, there were few kids our age to be seen. A strategically placed Ringling Brothers Circus sign caught my attention.

"Is this a circus, Daddy? Have you taken us to the circus?" I glanced around and smiled. "Are we going to see a circus?"

People lined up for tickets. Clowns in colorful costumes were milling about and stopping to speak to children. The reactions were faces either flinched in fear or lit up with joy when handed balloons twisted into shapes. I remember one that looked like an apple, and another took the shape of a dog.

"Hey, John, look at that clown over there! The one standing next to that little bitty car! I wonder if he's going to drive it?"

"I don't think he could fit in it." John glanced around and sniffed the air. "Everything smells good here. I wonder if Daddy would get us one of those waffles with powdered sugar."

"Where?"

"At that concession stand over there. I've never seen that before."

We were barely out of the car, but already the excitement bubbled out. We were eager to move in closer to the scene playing out in front of us.

"Now, hold on!" Daddy spoke up. "We've got plenty of time to buy our tickets and get our seats. You two, wait right here."

As Daddy left to buy the tickets, a clown wandered in the crowd, his oversized shoes flopping like a hound's ears. John hid behind me for fear he may come our way. I hoped so! He didn't.

The electricity in the air was palpable even in the parking lot, but we had not yet seen any animals.

"I wonder where the elephants are?"

"Right now, I want one of those waffles with powdered sugar," I replied. "Look, there's Daddy coming our way."

He motioned for us to join him. We followed him into the tent and to our seats. Busy trying to look in every direction at once, I stumbled several times as we climbed the steps to our seats. The crowd noise, the flash of all the cameras, and the sweet smell of cotton candy made my spine tingle in anticipation and eagerness. The three rings of activity competed for our attention.

"Look, there come the elephants!" John shouted.

"See the baby one holding on to his mama's tail!" I laughed and pointed.

"Oh, look over there—way over there—at the acrobats."

They were in the third ring and were scary to watch, making it more difficult to take my eyes off them. The glittering costumes made flying through the air all the more exciting.

Daddy called our attention to the seemingly endless exit of clowns from a small car. Men in striped uniforms ambled amongst the audience, hawking cotton candy, peanuts, and drinks. We started to pepper Daddy with questions while we tried to keep up with happenings in front of us.

"Daddy, that pink stuff is cotton candy, isn't it? Hey, look! There's some that's blue! Can I have a blue one?"

John punched me in the shoulder. "That guy over there is selling peanuts. I hope he comes to our row. Daddy, can I have some peanuts?"

Daddy bought cotton candy, peanuts, and drinks—one of which John managed to spill on me as he tried to see the finale setting up in the center arena. This was not a day to be annoyed or to scold.

Daddy smiled as he commented, "Watch out there, boy! We're close enough to see it all."

The three-ring finale seemed almost indescribable in its smorgasbord of activities.

The lions paraded around one ring and then into a barred enclosure with the lion tamer. He stood, cracking his whip and holding a chair, as the big cats formed a pyramid. The ring next door filled with clowns who walked on stilts, rode unicycles, honked horns, and sprayed each other with water guns. The clown car continued to circle in and out of the ring, sometimes driving directly in front of where we were sitting-though we were a tier or two up the arena seating.

We collectively held our breaths watching the high wire walkers in the final ring. Each one carried a long bar for balancing on the thin wire. When a performer leaned from side to side, I covered my eyes to avoid seeing the fall I feared would come.

When the final act left the stage and most of the audience had departed, we headed to the car for the trip home. We climbed into the backseat—cotton-candy-sticky and spilled-drink-wet—and talked nonstop about what we had seen. On the way home, we relived everything we had seen and done that day.

That evening as we gathered on the front porch, Daddy sat quietly while we shared with Mama every event from getting out of the car to getting back in. I remember Daddy saying only one thing as we prepared to go inside for the night.

"And that's why they call it the greatest show on earth."

The most memorable event of that day involved Daddy and the opportunity of a glimpse of his softer side—more often than not hidden under the minutia of life.

CHAPTER 14

THE TRUTH ABOUT SANTA

John, me, and our bikes.

I had just turned eight when I learned the truth about Santa—another proof that I've always been lucky. Some people never know the truth, at least not the truth as I learned it to be. Let me tell you about that day.

December 19, 1951 was a Wednesday in Mrs. Lily Bamber's third-grade class of thirty-one students, which was about average in the early 1950s. All the grammar school classes had from thirty to forty students, and, to the best of my memory, we all got the attention we needed.

Mrs. Bamber divided her class into the Redbirds, Bluebirds, and Yellow Birds based on our reading ability; this division applied to all our studies except math (arithmetic back then) where we were evaluated according to our math skills.

For the rest of the studies, our reading prowess determined our seating order. The Bluebirds were the average readers, the Redbirds excelled, and the Yellow Birds needed a little extra help. Mrs. Bamber bridged this gap by pairing Redbird students with Yellow Bird students. I don't know how she chose a partner for each of us but, generally speaking, the partnerships were successful. Ralph Beeson and I were assigned to each other.

Ralph was the only son of a family I considered to be a step or two higher on the economic ladder than mine. His parents were older, more like grandparents, and they doted on him. He had the fastest bike, the nicest book bag, and a box of sixty-four crayons when the teacher required only a sixteen-pack. Sometimes he wore a V-neck sweater over a sports shirt. He had a leather jacket, and a crew cut—at eight years old, he already had the look of a 'bad boy.'

His behavior included bullying other students— although such tags were not assigned to third graders in that day and age. I did not like him much. When Mrs. Bamber called my name as the Redbird helper for Ralph, I swallowed hard.

Sometimes he made fun of my flat nose or square haircut. Other times, he called me a baby because I feared taking the chances he took. I didn't want to be his partner, but I took assignments seriously; I didn't complain.

We quickly formed an uneasy truce. He still made fun of me sometimes and often mocked me when I would correct his reading. As a crybaby, I personified the perfect target for Ralph and the arrows he frequently sailed in my direction.

When Mrs. Bamber noticed waterworks flowing, she checked on us.

"Olevia, what's wrong with you?"

"Nothing."

"It's not nothing. Why are you crying?"

"I don't know, Mrs. Bamber. I'm sorry."

"If there's nothing wrong, then stop crying. You're a big girl."

Geez, it would have been easy to get him in trouble. I could have if I wanted to be labeled a tattletale, but I did not want that tag. I wanted him to treat me nicer. But, more than that, I didn't want to admit his domination over me. At eight years old, I didn't consider the reasons why. I basically followed my instincts in trying to earn his friendship. The pricks of his barbs were becoming less frequent, and the ensuing tears were slower to flow.

By mid-December, the entire class buzzed with talk of Christmas. The conversation extended through lunch. Ralph and I both ate in the lunch room in separate groups. We met back in Mrs. Bamber's room for tutoring during the lunch-free period.

On December 19, I ran late from lunch and found Ralph busy drawing on the blackboard when I dashed in.

"I'm sorry I'm late. What's that, Ralph?"

"It's a lady having a baby."

"What?"

"I bet you don't even know where babies come from."

"Yes, I do. I've seen it."

Now, he had my full attention as I stared in disbelief. Ralph had finally hit on a subject in which I could be an able adversary, ready to go toe-to-toe with him. He looked a bit disappointed.

Of course, my knowledge of giving birth had been acquired by watching numerous farm animals produce babies. When the family collie had pups, we all stood by like midwives to assist in cleaning and sorting puppies. Waggles usually had at least ten pups. One year, she had so many that she buried two, not able to accommodate all of them. We saw her do it, so we rescued them and raised both with tiny doll bottles.

"Well, do ya know there's no Santa Claus?"

"No Santa Claus!" I almost yelled.

"It's your mama and daddy buying presents."

"There is too a Santa Claus. I know there is."

"How do you know? Have you ever seen him?"

"The real one—or his official helper—is on The Square in Alex for two days before Christmas Eve. I've talked to him before."

"I guess you think he comes down the chimney, too?" Ralph laughed at me. "You're such a baby, Olevia. Everybody knows there's no Santa Claus."

Waterworks! Tears were flowing when Mrs. Bamber stopped in to check on us.

"What are you two up to? Who drew the picture?"

Ralph quickly erased the drawing and, with my back to her, I reached for our reader as he answered, "We're studying."

"Okay. Make sure you're studying and not playing," Mrs. Bamber warned with a strict frown.

Ralph and I reviewed the lesson together, but my heart and mind were occupied elsewhere. I needed to be home. My mom never lied to me, ever, and I knew I would hear the truth about Santa. The afternoon dragged on. I kept glancing at the clock, which seemed to move slower than usual, but three-thirty finally arrived.

Bus students were assigned to either the early or late bus, and even though my name appeared on the first bus list, I did not wait the ten or fifteen minutes necessary to board. I only lived a mile from school. I ran most of the way and panted as I flung open the front screen door.

Mama stood in the living room, wide-eyed in surprise. She happened to be about to go sit on the porch to watch for me getting off my bus.

"What are you doing home? What happened?"

"Mama, is there a Santa Claus? A *real* Santa Claus?"

"Get yourself a drink of water, Olevia. Settle down."

Easier said than done! I grabbed a glass of water from the kitchen and dashed back to the living room.

I stood there, panting, as Mama instructed, "Now, sit down and let's talk."

I immediately sat in a rocking chair, staring at Mama, almost afraid of the answer.

"Why are you asking about Santa? Christmas is still a week away." She smiled as she moved to sit down in the rocking chair beside me.

"Because Ralph Beeson says there's not. He said you and Daddy buy presents and pretend there's a Santa. And there's not a Santa!" I huffed then peered at her. "Do you do that?" I asked with an incredulous tilt of my head.

"So, Ralph doesn't believe in Santa?"

"No, Mama, and I'm so scared."

"What are you afraid of?"

"You told me there is Santa. Is it only a story?"

At my house, a lie was considered a semi-ugly word and rarely used by the kids. We said story when we meant lie.

"I think there's a cold baked sweet potato in there on the stove," Mama said as she got up to move toward the kitchen. "Why don't you get it, and let's sit at the table."

I now realize she was stalling for time while she got her story straight. Then, it simply seemed safer and calmer to be eating a cold sweet potato while Mama explained.

"I feel so sorry for Ralph, Olevia. He must be a sad little boy."

"Well, he don't act like it! He's always pickin' on me."

"Sometimes that's how you can tell when somebody's sad."

"Mama, please tell me about Santa Claus!" I did not feel sorry for Ralph, and my patience ebbed as my anxiety increased.

"Well, if you mean is there a man dressed up in a red suit that delivers presents on Christmas Eve, then there's not one."

"What? You said—"

Mama held up her hand. "Just a minute. Don't you want to hear the whole story?"

I nodded.

She continued, "If you mean what we call the spirit of giving and the fantasy of Christmas, then yes, there is a Santa. We all know Christmas is the day chosen to celebrate Jesus' birthday, and we know the wise men brought gifts to Jesus. They were honoring him as the Savior of the world. When we give presents, we are merely reminding people that we love them."

Mama paused for a few seconds as I hung on every word. Then she continued, "In many families – like ours - to make it more special, we all become part of a fairytale. Santa Claus is what we call the feeling that makes us want to share with others. I wasn't storying when I told you about Santa. I only made you a part of a big fairytale where everything is good."

"So, there is a Santa?"

Mama laughed and gave me a big hug. "Yes, Olevia, there is a Santa, as long as we believe there is."

The subject of Santa Claus never came up with Ralph again. But, from that day forward, I always felt a little superior to Ralph and maybe a little sorry for him. I saw him with new eyes. His teasing ceased to make me cry, and our relationship began to morph into something we could both understand and accept. We were never best friends or anything close, but I had a new soft spot in my heart for him.

Ralph, at age twenty-one, was killed in an argument at the Pelican Club in Marksville, Louisiana. He played the trumpet there on weekends, and I don't know what happened that night. My guess is that he probably tried to prove he was right about something because he was afraid to be wrong.

My mom's statement rings true: *Ralph Beeson was a sad young man.*

To this day, Mama's answer to "Does Santa exist?" is the kindest I've ever heard and—for our family—an accurate response. He does exist—as a concept of kindness, generosity, compassion, and joy! Sharing that truth with my own kids and grandkids has been, and continues to be, my goal.

CHAPTER 15

WHAT'S WRONG WITH THIS BOY?

Johnny, 1952.

On a hot July night, we all sat around the dinner table. Daddy had been home from work less than a half-hour, and it was just the four of us: Mama, Daddy, Johnny, and me. Johnny and I were quietly eating dinner when he suddenly became the center of attention.

"Mary, what's wrong with this boy?" Daddy peered at him intently.

"I don't know, John." Mama followed suit, and their faces made it clear they knew something was amiss, but they couldn't quite place it.

****

In 1952, conversations served as our primary source of entertainment, whether listening or participating. Almost daily, our parents sat on the front porch to talk. John and I sat there to listen and participate when invited. Our private conversations were relegated to the back porch. The troubles we got into while mimicking our parents were more nonsensical than consequential. Those led to some of my most treasured memories.

The topics holding our imagination included such weighty subjects as:

- Why do dung beetles like to play in dung?
- Do mosquito hawks eat mosquitoes?
- Is the devil really beating his wife when it rains while the sun shines?
- How big would a grasshopper need to be to fly if we hitched it to a penny matchbox containing a penny?

We had strong opinions about these ponderous subjects and many others. We often found ourselves in contests and arguments to prove one theory or another.

On a summer Saturday early afternoon, Mr. Nettles' name found its way into our back-porch discourse. He had visited our house earlier that day to buy milk, butter, and eggs from Mama. In his coat and tie attire, Mr. Nettles breathed "important person," and not many of those came our way, so we took close note of him. When we knew his arrival time, we generally sat under the front porch to make sure we had a clear view from his parking the car to exiting it.

A large man, weighing probably three-hundred pounds or more, driving a tiny, two-door car reminded us of circus clowns. As he climbed out, his body seemed to expand, much like a sponge when dipped in water. He never failed to lean back in to get his suit jacket from the back seat. Air-conditioned cars were rare, and he did not drive one; his shirt revealed full moons of moisture under each armpit as he retrieved his jacket. A short, fat cigar hung from the corner of his mouth to complete what we visualized as a top executive resembling President William Howard Taft.

When he walked up on our porch, he knitted his bushy eyebrows, pushed one hand through his hair, and threw the cigar butt off the side of the porch. Then he called out, "I'm here, Mrs. Yeager."

We recognized that as John's signal to grab the cigar butt and take it out back as a prop in whatever game of the day materialized.

Playing businessman that day brought up the subject of eyebrows. John stuck the cigar in the corner of his mouth, frowned to produce the bushy eyebrow effect, and practiced calling out, "I'm here, Mrs. Yeager."

As I studied John's face from eyebrows to chin, I had a whimsical vision. "I bet a man would look more businesslike if he had no eyebrows at all."

John replied, "That's silly! Have you ever seen anybody without eyebrows?"

"I don't think cousin Vanner Claunch has eyebrows, and he looks important when he's preaching."

"Brother Vanner's bald, Olevia. That's different."

"I don't see why. Hair would make it even better."

"You're a girl, and you don't know anything."

"Well, I know more than you do. I'm right, and I can prove it!" I smiled, turning away to emphasize how my knowledge eliminated my need to argue.

"Yeah, how?"

"If you really want to know, we'll have to remove your eyebrows."

"What?" He sounded hesitant and maybe a little apprehensive.

"Eyebrows grow so quickly that they'll be back before you know it. You can wear a cap or something for a day or two, but I don't think anyone will even notice—unless you decide to keep them off."

It is still amazing to me how pliable a seven-year-old can be and how a crafty nine-year-old can use that malleable quality for whatever reason she cares to. The more we talked, the more excited we both became. We got Daddy's straight razor, lathered up John's eyebrows, and he stuck that cigar back in his mouth.

"You already look impressive!" I said encouragingly. "No eyebrows will make it even better."

He began to get a little fidgety. "Hurry up! I want to see."

I shaved off one eyebrow. Almost immediately, I had an inkling maybe we had not thought this subject completely through. But once you jump off the bridge, you're bound to get wet. I shaved off the remaining eyebrow.

Until that very moment, I didn't know what a wide-eyed look a person has without eyebrows; it's sort of a perpetual look of surprise. John could not wait to see himself in the mirror. As eager as a hound is to tree a raccoon, he threw the cigar butt down and ran to the bathroom to get a look. I ran behind him. That first glance caused his bottom lip to quiver.

"Don't worry, Johnny. I have an idea. Eyebrows grow really fast, so we only need a couple days. If we glue something on, Daddy and Mama will never notice. Mostly, we need to get through supper tonight. Otherwise, you can just wear your cap."

As we explored our options, John perked up.

"What about Waggles? Can't we just cut a little of her hair and soak it in glue?"

"She's a white collie! I'm not sure white eyebrows would improve your look a great deal."

"What about from the cow's tail? That's brown."

I shot that idea down as well. "It's too wiry. I don't think we can make it look natural."

And thus, it went, from the horse to the neighbor's dog to possibly catching a rabbit. As each idea died, one-by-one, John's anxiety grew.

"I've got it, John! We'll use doll-hair!"

We checked each of my dolls against John's hair before choosing my favorite doll, Susie, with dirty-blond nylon hair. The color was not perfect, and the texture wasn't too great, but we thought we could pull it off. Besides, time was running out. Next, we needed some way of adhering the disguised hair to John's forehead.

Daddy sometimes left a bottle of mucilage on top of his desk. So, if it was there, we would be home safe. An absent mucilage bottle turned up the heat. We had almost overcome our fear of opening Daddy's desk drawer when we noticed a bottle of white school paste with a brush in the center of the lid. It sat right there in the open, ready for the taking.

With John lying down on the back porch, I applied a layer of paste where his eyebrows used to be. Then I pressed Susie's hair into the paste. Standing up allowed the excess hair to fall, and what remained failed to adequately cover the paste base. But the time to consider an alternate plan had expired. We heard Daddy's footsteps on the porch.

"Mary, I'm home."

Maybe it was the absence of doorbells or door knockers or because the door always stood open that caused people to announce themselves as soon as they stepped onto our porch. Whatever the reason, anyone entering our house automatically called an advisement to Mama (in this case, also a warning to us). I attempted to calm John as time had run out.

"Do you think Daddy will notice, Olevia?" The squeak in his voice amplified his apprehension. I could tell there might be tears nearby.

"No. You look natural." I used my most calming tone.

"Really?"

I could not stifle a giggle, and John's tears edged close again. "Don't cry, John. Just look at your plate and eat. It's not like Daddy's going to be looking at you."

We headed to the kitchen. Daddy expected supper on the table when he walked in the door, so only minutes passed before Mama called us to the table. As we bowed our heads to return thanks, my prayers involved a subject other than food.

With the blessing done, John barely lifted his head as the food was passed around. He stared at his plate and ate quickly. As a matter of course, conversation ensued at our table, mostly limited to our parents; we kids joined in only if spoken to. Daddy's intense and serious persona did not lend itself to kids' nonsense.

Daddy glanced at John. I looked at Daddy. At first, his eyes had just crossed over John. Then, almost as in the movies, his fork stopped in mid-air, his head jerked back, and he stared.

"Boy, what's wrong with you?"

"Nothing." John spoke barely above a whisper.

"Look at me!"

John looked up and right back at his plate.

"Mary, what's wrong with this boy?"

"I don't know, John," Mama answered as she joined Daddy in observing John.

I may as well have been James Stewart's invisible rabbit, Harvey. John held their attention as if hypnotized, and I freely studied their faces.

Daddy stared at John, who stared at his plate for what seemed to be eons. He finally said, "Go wash your face, boy."

John did as ask and returned to the table, sans eyebrows. Daddy stared at him. Mama stared at him. John continued to keep his head bowed as he ate. No one said another word until Daddy broke the silence.

"Mary, I don't know what's wrong with that boy. You need to watch him more."

"I will, John."

That was it. John didn't say, "My sister did it." Mama didn't ask any questions, and their conversation turned to normal, mundane things.

We finished dinner, John's eyebrows grew back, and we moved on to our next adventure.

Just an average day in the lives of country kids in the 1950s. It makes a marvelous mental video to be taken out many times over the years to re-enjoy.

CHAPTER 16

Porch Time

Just before the curtain dropped on another day, the actors (our family) began the final scene. Mama's deliciously prepared supper graced our table at five o'clock, and by 5:30 we were expressing our appreciation.

"Mama, you do the best pot roast!" I said as I set the dishes in the sink.

"Let's go sit on the porch, Mary," Daddy said, throwing her a soft smile.

"I'll get us some coffee," Mama answered as Daddy headed for the front porch.

In a few moments, they occupied two rocking chairs and sipped their coffee, gazing out at nature as daylight waned.

"Hey, Johnny!" I tilted my head in the direction of the door. "Wanna go outside?"

He sat on the floor playing with plastic army men, but I knew he preferred sitting on the porch with our parents. As expected, he got up immediately. "I'm ready. I'll pick these up when we come back in."

The absence of television, cell phones, computers, and today's twenty-four-hour imagined need to share every thought via social media allowed us to enjoy family time. We could think, ruminate on a subject, and communicate with each other directly. I enjoyed those moments immensely, and just thinking about them warms my heart with gratitude.

John and I scampered to our usual seats on the porch steps.

Over time, our unassigned seats had morphed into our specific spots. Daddy's rocking chair sat nearest the left porch edge; Mama's occupied a spot near the door, just in case Daddy needed something from inside the house. That's conjecture on my part, but it felt that way.

John and I perched on the steps. I have no memory of Hannah as part of our porch group. My first porch-sitting memories began after our move to the big house in 1948. Being eight years older than me and a teenager, she may have opted not to take part in our evenings. I don't know.

We immersed ourselves in the quiet surrounding us, feeling the peace of watching the sun as it slowly approached the top of the tallest pine trees. The fireflies—which we called lightning bugs—blinked as dusk fell, augmenting the silence in our minds even as the cacophony of waking locusts began.

Then, as if the script required it, Daddy initiated the first subject of the evening. On this night, the local birds proved to be front and center. "Did you know that a single purple martin can eat two thousand mosquitos in one night?"

He said this to no one in particular, but we all listened as we watched the acrobatics of dozens of purple martins chasing and eating mosquitos as the sun sank behind the pines. The birds provided fascinating and captivating aerial escapades around the six martin houses Daddy had painted a bright white and strategically placed along our front fence line.

The goal was twofold: to attract martins in late February or early March and to encourage them to stay through the fledging of their final clutch, typically mid-to-late August.

Mosquitos are the bane of Louisiana, both outdoors and indoors.

Mama commented, "Louisiana mosquitos come in two sizes, those small enough to squeeze through screen doors and those large enough to open them."

John and I laughed. A smile crossed Daddy's face, but jokes—other than his own—were not especially encouraged during this family time.

Daddy returned the attention to himself, exclaiming, "Look at those birds! Two thousand mosquitoes a night. What is that? Six birds around that one house? How many mosquitoes will not be here tomorrow?"

To get a little attention of my own, I raised my hand as if in school. Then, I almost shouted, "That's twelve thousand mosquitoes eaten by our martins!"

Years later, I discovered there was no basis to the tale of two thousand mosquitos in a single night. But I believed the myth back then, and the lack of evidence has had little effect on what I think today.

Talk of the purple martins led Daddy to more talk about birds. "John, I saw you out in the field today. Did you see any fee' larks?"

"No sir."

"Well, you need to watch when you're out there with Kate. Fee'larks have nests on the ground, and you don't want to step on one."

John often rode Kate, our favored Jinny, when exploring. Other times, he hitched her to a slide. And sometimes we savored the experience together.

"Yessir, I'll be careful." He answered and excitedly exclaimed, "Look over there! That looks like a baby snake hanging from the barbed wire!" He gasped as he pointed. "What's that?"

"That's a snake," Daddy replied. "A small grass snake hung there by a butcherbird for a later snack. They eat all sorts of small reptiles, like lizards or tiny frogs. I've even seen a crawfish stuck on a thornbush before."

Mama would join the conversation occasionally. That night she added, "I saw a chicken hawk out near the chicken house. We need to watch the baby chicks."

Daddy laughed. "Mary, how're you going to watch those chicks? It's nature. The hen'll watch what she can and, if one's lost, it's okay. Hawks only eat when they're hungry. Those little chicken hawks probably only eat every three or four days."

About that time, we heard a whippoorwill call. Daddy mimicked back. "Chip-cut-down-the-white-oak."

After a short silence, the bird answered, "Chip-cut-down-the-white-oak."

This communication continued for a few minutes, and then Daddy repeated another widely held myth about whippoorwills.

The unsettling story held that hearing the call of a whippoorwill before the sun completed its trip beyond the horizon foretold someone's death. Once the sun set, the whippoorwill calls increased, and Daddy's response followed each one until they faded into the night.

I suppose one of those nights first ignited my interest and love of birding. I've learned the fee'larks were Eastern Meadowlarks, and the butcherbird is rightly named Loggerhead Shrike. Based on the call and Daddy's answer, the whippoorwill sounded like a chuck-will's-widow. And that chicken hawks (probably a sharp-shinned hawk) prefer a diet of small birds which are unlikely to include chickens. The correct bird identification carried no weight in our discussion and is not the point of this story.

Our evenings' subjects varied from birds to politics to what was going on in town. Sometimes, we talked about the skies or the stars, and I never failed to be amazed by the number of falling stars we saw—almost on any given night. We called them shooting stars.

Being unfamiliar with the term meteor shower made the events no less bewitching and spellbinding. Looking back, I know we watched the Perseids and the Bootid meteor showers, but again, the specifics were not the goal of our evenings.

Typically, Daddy chose the primary subject, and Mama might mention Bible School for us. Or maybe she'd comment on a cow ready to calve or someone in the neighborhood who died. Her subjects tended to be more practical and mundane in my opinion. One could call Mama's stories an opening act, but the main attraction came when Daddy's tales lifted the curtain to begin the main attraction.

We learned about unions on the night he explained featherbedding and the threat of a railroad engineers' strike to support the firemen. For my entire childhood, Daddy talked about impending union strikes, but he never experienced one in my lifetime at home.

Talks about politics always included the Longs of Louisiana, from Huey to Earl. He idolized Huey Long and talked about his assassination in 1936. One night, he told the story of Earl Long coming to Tioga to campaign from the back of a battered pickup truck.

"You should've seen him," he said with a chuckle. "He got out of his truck wearing unkempt overalls, a pocket-watch clearly displayed in his upper overalls' pocket, and high-topped shoes most often worn by the railroad men. Earl Long checked that watch two or three times while he sat on the tailgate of his truck." Daddy laughed again. "But he didn't try to put anything over on us. He showed the crowd the suit he had inside his truck and told us he preferred to look like his audience because he was one of us."

Daddy then shared with us the saying of the day. "The Longs take four dollars from every citizen. They build a bridge with one dollar, they build a charity hospital with one dollar, they provide free school lunches with one dollar, and they put one dollar in their pockets."

That story brought another round of laughter, as did whatever finale story occurred each night.

"Okay, kids, we need to get inside. It's getting dark, and the sun comes up early."

Sorry to see the porch time over, but already looking forward to the next day, we entered the house.

Porch time is one of the places where we learned to enjoy the simplest things and the most important ones—who we were, and that character and honesty can't be faked.

The evening's theme and the details' accuracy were inconsequential. What stands out in my memory is the setting and the scene's actors—us growing up. The conversation created the peace of that day, the connection, the hope, and the belief in a better tomorrow. It's not what we heard, whether trivial or important, but the listening that made the difference in our lives.

As I climbed into my bed, I sighed inside, relishing yet another porch time providing another chapter in discovering *Life is Good*. The peace enclosed me like a warm sleeping bag on a very cold night.

CHAPTER 17

PIANO LESSONS

The upright Baldwin piano inherited from the previous owners of the big house served as a blessing for Hannah. She had taken piano lessons for a few years without a piano on which to practice. In lieu of a piano, she used a large cardboard keyboard replica placed on the kitchen table to perfect her skill. Her progress grew much improved by playing a real piano.

"Hannah, play us one more hymn before you go to bed," Mama said.

"How about 'The Old Rugged Cross?'"

"Yeah, that's a good one."

Mama took pride in Hannah's playing, and Hannah enjoyed performing for her. The upright Baldwin came as an answer to everyone's prayers.

Every good Baptist has a pilfered hymnal somewhere in their house, and we were no exception. Ours was proudly displayed on the face of the piano. Hannah sometimes played for our Kingsville Baptist church services, and her past performances had consisted of hymns played dirge-like with little regard for the director's or the music's tempo instructions. She and the choir resembled an eerie, out-of-sync puppet act.

All breathed an audible sigh at the end of the song service, and the tense congregation sought solace in Brother Curtis' predictable preaching cadence.

Our church services closed with "Just as I Am," a hymn made for Hannah's plodding approach, but even it became tedious by the fourth stanza. Lord, we were all thankful

Hannah now had a piano at her disposal as her playing had improved by leaps and bounds.

"Hannah!" one of the deacons called out. "You certainly did well in accompanying Violet's solo this morning."

"Thank you."

"Have you been taking more lessons?"

"No, sir. We have a piano now, and I practice the hymns every day. Hearing myself play helps."

"It sure does." The deacon laughed and walked on.

Our piano had also found a fan in Mrs. Richey, a neighbor who lived within walking distance of our house. She fancied herself a piano virtuoso. On her bi-weekly visits, she plopped on our front porch steps to catch her breath, panting and sweating as if she had just completed a marathon. Her two-hundred-pound body confined to a five-foot frame presented a square appearance.

"Can I have a drink of cold water, Mary?" she gasped.

"We got plenty of good cool water. I'll let it run a few minutes."

She gulped down a full glass, nonstop, and topped it off with a loud burp.

"Nothing like a good glass of water when you're thirsty. How you been, Mary? Brother Curtis says you've been feeling poorly."

"Nothing serious. It's this heat. I don't take it well, not like I used to. Saps all my energy, and I've got two bushels of corn to can. Why don't you take home a bag? It's really sweet this year."

"Chester would like that. How can I pay you? How about a song or two on the piano? Come on. I got just the tune to cheer you up. Come on, kids. Ya'll might know the words."

We didn't know the words, and I wondered if she knew more than one song. They all sounded alike, and all finished with a flourish and the same announcement. "Well, what do you think of the St. Louis Blues or The Boogie-Woogie Blues?" It was always something similar.

I guess, truth be told, I admired her ability—and Hannah's as well. A twinge of jealousy for the attention they got also played a part. But jealousy didn't mean I wanted to follow in their footsteps. I simply wanted Mama to be a little less impressed with them.

Mama had other ideas, and she signed me up for piano lessons. Daddy said the whole thing was a waste of money and time, but Mama controlled her butter and egg income to spend as she liked, so he didn't put his foot down.

I have a clear memory of the first day I showed up for class: optimism started the day, and disappointment ended it. I am amazed as to how quickly one can go from the mountaintop to the valley with, perhaps, a misinterpretation of a few words.

Mrs. White had five students waiting for lessons in her house, counting me. At seven years old, I was the youngest of the group and felt much like Gretel being led by the wicked cannibal witch to her house of bread, cake, and sugar. In private, I referred to her as Mrs. Witch!

"Come in, Olevia." She smiled and opened the door leading to a small room with a couch and a piano.

"Do you know any of these young ladies?"

I glanced at the other three girls, and they glared back at me like a pack of wolves. In retrospect, I imagine it's highly unlikely any actual glaring occurred anywhere except in my mind.

"No ma'am."

"What grade are you in?"

"Second. Mrs. Whitehead's class."

"These girls are a bit older than you. I'm sure you'll all get along fine."

"Girls, have a seat on the couch. We're going to let Olevia go first today."

I wanted to shout that I did not want to be first, but I obediently sat down on the piano bench.

"Here's your beginner book. Notice the first piece in the book is *Off We Go to Music Land*. That's where you are headed today, Olevia, beginning your trip into the wonderland of music." She sat down beside me. "Listen."

She played "*Off We Go to Music Land*," a tune played with only the right hand. At the time, I did not know playing with one hand would turn out to be my forte!

Mrs. White pointed out what piano keys related to the score in front of me. She instructed me in the skills necessary to practice the scales.

After the first hour, she said I should be able to play the scales without looking at my hands. She added, "Your assignment for this week is to learn to play Off We Go to Music Land. Be sure to practice so I can see what our next step should be." With that, she indicated that my time had expired, and I could go outside to wait for Hannah to pick me up.

Already, I started to gain respect for Hannah and Mrs. Richey. Maybe neither had the skills of Liberace, but their ability far outranked mine. Although Mama wanted me to take the lessons and learn to play the piano well, she never insisted I do anything not absolutely necessary to my wellbeing. She might say, in passing, some reference to my piano classes, but I felt no urgency.

"Are you supposed to be practicing what you learned last week?" she asked at breakfast one morning.

"I don't know." I shrugged. "I will, after a while."

"What did you learn last week?"

"Mrs. White said I needed to practice the scales this week. I don't think I've learned anything yet."

She would let me slide. The next time I looked at that beginner book, I sat at Mrs. White's piano. She referred to the class room as The Piano Salon. I thought of it more as a torture chamber. Mrs. White looked as if she may faint when I made mistakes playing the scales. That look of astonishment turned to horror as the class went on, as if I had grown horns or something. She belittled me, treating me like a village idiot and a complete waste of her efforts.

"Olevia, you have come to class unprepared today. Did you practice?"

"No, ma'am."

"Maybe you'll benefit from listening to how well your classmates are doing."

Because I was unprepared, she had me sit on the couch while other students played. My job was to listen to them excel in pleasing her. To be honest, their expertise did impress me and made me wonder if they were first-year students. I never found out.

At the end of the session, she assigned a new song to me, "*The Traffic Cop*," which required both hands to play. As we left class, I heard my classmates whisper about my lack of ability and failure to follow instructions.

"Did you hear Olevia? She can't even play *Off We Go to Music Land*. Mrs. White's mad at her."

"I'm glad I practiced last week. Olevia should practice, then she wouldn't get in trouble."

"Mrs. White always likes my playing. I practice every day. I might even be a piano teacher when I grow up."

"I wonder if Mrs. White will let Olevia come back next week?"

I silently determined to do better and practiced "*Off We Go to Music Land*" and the scales every day for a week. Mama sat and listened to the repeated playing of both; she smiled and complimented me as if I had won a prize in piano playing. I perfected those two exercises before I visited The Piano Salon again.

I had not tackled *"The Traffic Cop,"* but it didn't occur to me this would be a problem. I guess I thought Mrs. White would be so awed by my achievement that nothing else would matter. Boy was I wrong! I took my place at the piano and began to play *"Off We Go to Music Land."*

Mrs. White reacted as if she had been stabbed in the back or stuck her finger into an electrical outlet.

"What are you doing, Olevia? That's last week's lesson. This week, you were to practice *'The Traffic Cop.'*"

"I didn't practice that song. I thought I needed to learn the first one, no?"

"Well, you were wrong. You needed to learn them both. What you are supposed to do is follow instructions and keep up with the class. See what you can do with this week's song."

She insisted I only play the piece I did not know—again and again. The lesson learned that day may not have been the one she intended to teach, but it became permanent.

I realized I had no talent for playing the piano and found it physically impossible for my right hand or left hand to move independently of the other. I lost the little interest I had in learning to play the piano. I left the class demoralized and resolved that all piano-related activities would be limited to those required in Mrs. White's presence. I would not squander another summer hour at a piano trying to do something I could not and did not want to do.

Warm, wonderful summertime weeks continued with only short, agonizing breaks listening to Mrs. White wonder aloud at my lack of ability, lack of discipline, and lack of character.

"Trying to teach you is a waste of my time and your parents' money. Why don't you practice?"

"I don't have time for practicing."

"What do you do instead of practicing?"

"I catch bugs with my brother. We make matchbox wagons for them. Sometimes, we operate on them...."

"Olevia," she interrupted me, "does your mother know you don't practice?"

"I guess so."

My objective had mutated into survival only, and I am not sure whether my classmates admired my moxie or just felt sorry for me. At any rate, they stopped laughing.

Finally, the six weeks came to an end and recital pieces were assigned. I received *"The Swan Song,"* the name of which turned out to be appropriate to my piano lessons.

Just looking at the page bewildered me. I had barely mastered the simplest two-handed piece, so one with sharps and flats far exceeded my talent. Mrs. White played the recital scores to let us know how they should sound. I had no ear for music and knew only my rendition of *"The Swan Song"* would be unrecognizable.

I imagined Mrs. White's admonition about our parents' possible rewards, according to our abilities, to be a threat. For just a moment, my heart quivered. But my lack of practice had not escaped my mother, so she could not be expecting much. That week, I spent an hour or two at the piano, which proved too little effort made far too late.

Recital day came, and I prepared to go. Mama and I walked out the door, down the steps, and toward the gate. Within inches of opening it, I stopped in my tracks. I don't know if the fear of being humiliated or a determination not to let Mrs. White win caused the abrupt paralysis. Whatever the cause, it ended my piano playing career!

"What's wrong, Olevia?"

"I don't want to go."

"Why?"

"I can't play the piano, and I hate trying."

"Okay." She waved to Hannah waiting in the car to drive us to the auditorium. "We're not going," she yelled.

We went back into the house, and Mama never mentioned piano lessons for me again.

In the summer of 1950, I learned a lot of things. I learned about Tom Sawyer and Huck Finn; I enjoyed Augustus' books. I learned to multiply and divide. I knew how to walk to the library and check out a book by myself. I learned how to sneak up on a dragonfly and not to touch a locust when it is emerging from its winter shell. I learned honeybees and grasshoppers do not recover from surgery, and I learned my mama could be trusted with my worst shortcomings.

I did not learn to play the piano.

Years later, after Hannah left home, Mama died, and Mrs. Richey went to a nursing home. Daddy sold the piano for fifty dollars. As I watched it leave in the back of a pickup truck, my thoughts drifted to the good times it represented as well as my failure as a pianist.

I shed no tears at its departure.

CHAPTER 18

TURKEYS CAN BE A NUISANCE

As I have said before, sometimes I must give the pen to John because his memories, those so special to me, are better shared from his point of view. Such is the case with the story of the turkeys.

****

John's Story:

Daddy, an opinionated man, had an uncommon way of making things specific to him. At least, that's how it appeared to me. He said most folks got into jams because they failed to reason. The conversation below occurred in 1953 when I was an eight-year-old boy.

"John, your underwear? Why didn't you put them in the dirty clothes?"

"I don't know, Daddy. In a hurry."

"Is that your reason or is that your excuse?"

"I don't know. I was in a hurry."

"John, if you don't learn to reason, you're going to have a hard life."

Daddy was a unique man. Now, I know most kids (maybe even adults) think their parents are or were unique, but my papa really was. I didn't know it so much then, but I know it now.

I've seen a lot of parents. And, to this day, I've not seen a parent like my pop. He turned fifty years old just a couple of months before I arrived as his fifth son; some might think his age would cause him to be more of a best friend or grandfather kind of dad. Not so. We did not go fishing, throw a ball around, or do any kid stuff. Sometimes I felt more like a project than a kid.

That underwear conversation continued something like this:

He had sat down on the side of the bathtub as I stood inside so we would be eye to eye. Being eye-level with my papa usually meant trouble for me.

"John, I think you left your underwear on the floor because you thought your mama would pick 'em up. You thought I would never know. Is that what you thought, son?"

"I don't know, Daddy. I was in a hurry."

"Not very good reasoning? Folks get into jams because they don't reason."

With that, he walked out, leaving me confused. I knew I had been punished, but I wasn't sure how. Years later, after Mama died, I left my underwear lying beside my bed one night. I put a note on Daddy's desk to be seen when he got home from work near midnight.

It read: Daddy, my underwear is on the floor. I will pick them up in the morning. Love, Johnny.

I still have that note because I found it among Daddy's things when he passed away. As I said, my daddy had an unusual air about him—not strange, just one of a kind.

One day, he sat on the front porch in his rocking chair. He wore his striped railroad overalls and had his hands sort of holding on to the bib. One of his tall railroad caps and the watch chain hanging from the vest pocket topped off his typical outfit. He chewed a matchstick, crossed his legs, and stared out over the field in front of him. I sat on the steps, minding my manners. Daddy's rule of 'children should be seen often but rarely heard' echoed in my head. Without any warning, he spoke.

"Know what, son? I spotted some dappled turkeys the other day. The old man that has 'em wants to sell a gobbler and some hens. I'm thinkin' 'bout gettin' some."

Of course, I immediately grew excited. Daddy liked animals, and he knew I liked animals. The mention of getting some new kind of animal caused visions to appear in my mind as to what it might be like.

"Dappled turkeys? What's a dappled turkey? Have I ever seen one? When? Are we going to get 'em today? Where does the man live? Can you call him? What's his name?"

"Slow down, son. Before you get anything like that, you gotta think a while. Then, after you think, you'll know whether to get 'em or not. You need to know if they'll suit ya."

When my papa said something like that, I absolutely went along with it. I didn't usually understand what he meant, and I knew if I asked a question, I still wouldn't understand. We both sat there as the evening light faded. As the warm, moist Louisiana breeze blew and fireflies winked, vague turkey visions danced in my head.

Eventually, he said, "Time to go in and sleep on it."

I agreed and went in, but I spent a good part of my night dreaming about dappled turkeys in various colors. I still had no idea as to the description of dappled, but I knew what a turkey looked like.

Turkeys were not part of any conversation for the next several weeks, and I dared not bring it up. I knew he hadn't forgotten it; letting a subject simmer for days or weeks added to the mystery and was typical of Daddy's approach to any changes.

Unexpectedly, one afternoon, he came in carrying two tow sacks. As he climbed out of our salmon-colored Henry J, I raced out to meet him. I mention that color only because I never saw another one like it! Certainly, no other railroad guy rode around in a pink car. Daddy bought it new and liked to brag that no one else drove one like it. I always smiled and chuckled under my breath when I heard him say that. But, that day, I had turkeys on my mind!

"What's in the sacks, Daddy? Did you buy us something? Did you get some turkeys? Am I going to see a dappled turkey?"

He never said a word as he walked toward the porch carrying those two tow sacks with a solemn look on his face. It's strange to say, but true: I wondered if Aladdin felt this way before rubbing his lamp. I knew something special would appear shortly, but I had no clear picture of what. I circled around, ran in front and behind him, and finally settled down on the front steps.

Daddy stopped right at the steps.

Out of one bag, he pulled a turkey gobbler. The bird had white feathers with little gold and black spots all over its body. His tail feathers ended in black spots with gold centers. Daddy sat him on the ground and reached into the other bag. He released two turkey hens with similar markings but not as colorful.

My excitement emanated from every cell in my body, and I grinned from ear to ear. A dappled turkey represented a new experience, and I could not wait to share it with Daddy. Despite his silence, his pleasure in the moment escaped via his smile and gestures. His chuckles and antics proved he knew we shared our enthusiasm.

While the turkeys explored our front yard, he sat in his rocking chair. I occupied the steps. Neither of us said a word for a good while. We stared at those turkeys. The gobbler strutted, and his head turned a bright red. He circled, stomped his feet, and gobbled.

Daddy laughed. "Look at him, son. Listen to him brag to those hens." He chuckled and repeated, "Listen to him brag." As the evenings went by, the turkeys entertained us. I looked forward to meeting Daddy on the front porch every afternoon at about four-thirty or so. The gobbler and the hens behaved as if they were actors there for a show, and they provided it.

"You know what he said just then, son?"

"No. What?"

"He told those hens how pretty he is. Look how red his head is. He's courtin' those hens."

Daddy's laugh sounded like water rippling through a brook—happy, light, and peaceful.

I enjoyed hearing him interpret for the turkeys. Together, we admired their coloring and the gobbler's fanned tail as he strutted around the hens. It became an every-night affair to watch the turkeys for an hour or so before Mama came out on the porch.

"I've never seen a turkey that color!"

"I know." He grinned. "They're rare. A cross between a white turkey and probably a Royal Palm turkey."

"A what? Is that another kind of turkey?"

"Yes, it is. They started in Florida, but they're everywhere now. We call them dappled turkeys."

I don't know if Daddy made that up, but I believed every word. To this day, I have never seen turkeys that look like the ones in my memory. I wish we had taken pictures.

Then, one day, Daddy's mood changed. We were out at the barn, merely walking around and not really doing anything, when he dropped a bombshell.

"Son, those turkeys are becoming a nuisance."

"A nuisance? How can they be a nuisance? Don't you like watching them?"

"Well, I do, but they're getting in the way."

"In the way?" Now confusion set in, and my anxiety rose to the level of a long-tailed cat in a room full of rocking chairs.

He explained, "Every time I go out to feed the cows, the turkeys get in the feed. They jump up into the cows' trough. What they don't eat, they mess in. I try to keep 'em scared out. Then I throw a few chops to the chickens, and that big gobbler beats the chickens off." He sighed and kicked his foot. "The chickens can't get enough food."

"Well, what are we gonna do, Daddy? Can we put them in a cage?"

"Looks like we might have to get rid of 'em. They're a nuisance."

We walked toward the house with me wracking my brain for an argument in favor of those turkeys. I liked them, and I thought Daddy did too. Those turkeys made me proud. I had described them to all my friends at school, and they had seemed jealous. We had the only dappled turkeys in Tioga. Being the center of attention with my friends did not happen often, and I hated the thought of losing that position or the turkeys.

I tossed and turned that night, unable to sleep. Daddy's attitude change seemed like a flip of a switch to me. *How could he not like them anymore?* After he got them, he told me about the thinking and reasoning that had gone into his turkey buying. With that thought, I formed my plea and practiced it all the next day.

****

When Daddy got out of the car on Friday afternoon, I stood waiting on the porch steps. I saved my presentation until he had his coffee and sat on the porch.

"Do you still think those turkeys are a nuisance?"

"Yeah, son, I do."

"Well, you told me you reasoned it out before you got them. I figure you must have decided they wouldn't be a nuisance, or you would never have brought 'em home. Are you sure they're a nuisance?"

He stared into the distance for several minutes like he looked for an answer in the sky or somewhere far away. He rolled his cheek between his forefinger and his thumb, a sign his answer would be well thought out.

Finally, he said, "That's right. I reasoned it out before I brought those turkey's home. From the beginning, I knew there would be a degree of nuisance. Son, there are different degrees of nuisance. The only way to know what degree of nuisance is associated with owning turkeys is to experiment."

"So, if you already knew turkeys were going to be a nuisance, why do you want to get rid of 'em now?"

Again, time passed as slow as molasses while he considered his answer with more cheek-rolling, staring into the distance, and sipping his coffee.

"Johnny, I hoped owning turkeys would have a low degree of nuisance, but it turned out that turkeys have a very high degree of nuisance. Sometimes the only way a man can learn something is to experiment. We've tried out the turkeys, and we learned we don't need turkeys. Their nuisance degree is way too high."

I knew arguing or begging would not help. The turkey conversation ended with a sense of finality. I now understood my dappled turkeys would be gone soon.

****

Sure enough, a couple of days later, Daddy brought out the two tow sacks. We hemmed up the turkeys, and Daddy left with them in the back seat of the Henry J.

I didn't want them to go, but more than that, I dreaded the next time my friends asked me about them. If I hadn't bragged so much about them being special and different, the pill would have been easier to swallow. I ducked my friends for a couple of days, but that solution wore out quickly. I found myself in a spot of no escape as I got off the school bus one morning.

One of the boys waved and called over to me. "Hey, Johnny, how's your turkeys?"

I looked up and answered as cheerfully as possible. "We got rid of them."

"Got rid of them? Why? Did your daddy make you get rid of them?"

"Nah. Me and Daddy ran an experiment."

"An experiment?"

I squared my eight-year-old shoulders, stuck my thumbs in the waistband of my pants, and took a deep breath. "Well, we knew those turkeys were going to be a nuisance, but we had to find out what degree of nuisance they would be. Turkeys carry a high degree of nuisance."

Then, doing my best daddy impression, I walked away from my pals and headed into school. They just stood there, looking at me. The turkey experiment concluded, as did any conversation concerning the turkeys.

Sometimes, my reasoning came down to mostly imitating my daddy.

CHAPTER 19

A MEETING OF THE HEARTS

Texada Clinic, located less than ten miles from our house in downtown Pineville, also housed Mama's doctor, Dr. Miller. My Aunt Olevia relayed this story to me so many times that it almost feels like my own memory.

Daddy and Aunt Olevia sat in the patient family waiting room as the orderly wheeled Mama to the delivery room section. Daddy kept fidgeting, shifting his position over and over like a nervous rabbit. It was 1943 and about to be the beginning of my life's adventures.

As Dr. Miller came in the door, both Daddy and Aunt Olevia stood, concerned that the doctor's face telegraphed the possibility of bad news.

"Mr. Yeager, I'm concerned about Mary. Her blood pressure is off the charts, and I want you to know there's a chance she won't make it."

"Doc, she's only thirty-three and healthy as a horse! You must be mistaken!"

"This baby's breech. The blood pressure's way too high, and there's a chance her kidneys will shut down. It's not looking good. I'll keep you posted."

Dr. Miller turned on his heel as he returned to care for Mama. Aunt Olevia and Daddy sat back down.

"Leevee, if Mary dies, you can have this baby if you want it." He said this solemnly and in all seriousness.

"John, don't say that. Mary's going to be fine."

"Well, I hope so. But, if that's not in the cards, I don't think I can raise another child. Hannah and I'll be okay. Would you take the baby?"

"Of course, I would, John. But Mary's going to be fine. Let's make a deal. You can name this baby after me if it's a girl."

Thus, my birth certificate reads Olevia Ann Yeager, and Aunt Olevia remained childless.

****

Being born on June 13 in 1895, over a century ago now, says a lot about who my dad was. Geronimo had recently been transferred to Fort Sill, Oklahoma; the United States of America consisted of thirty-eight states; and remnants of the Civil War remained a clear picture in his father's mind.

Daddy married young, and by age twenty-eight, he was a widower with four sons—the oldest was an eight-year-old and the youngest, only three. The Masonic Orphans Home helped him to rear those boys—my half-brothers. I've heard he had some stormy times over the twelve years between the boys' mom and mine, including a short-lived marriage or two—to the same woman. Then, in 1935, Mary Katherine Williams, my mom, came to his rescue and married him.

I didn't meet him until eight years later when I became his second daughter. My older sister, Hannah, had pretty much filled the bill with what he wanted in a daughter—mostly, just *a* daughter. My spot could be best described as more of an extra on the scene. Mom experienced a difficult pregnancy, and Daddy had lost his first wife during childbirth.

The result: he felt frustrated with me before my first cry.

Mama and Daddy's child-naming pact, made years earlier, provided for him to choose first names, giving Mama the right to choose the middle names. Daddy had named all of his sons: Johnson Hugh, James Hickman, Noah Webster, and Henry Ford. Mama said he liked important-sounding names, and when his first baby girl came on the scene, he assumed he would continue as "namer" of his children.

"Mary, I've decided on a name for our baby girl."

"You've decided? What?"

"I'm naming her for my mother."

"Hannah? I like that. What about her middle name?"

"I'm giving her my mother's full name: Hannah MoHattieBelle Yeager. I like the way that sounds, don't you?"

"John, this baby cannot be saddled with MoHattieBelle! What else do you like?"

I'm sure she hoped he was kidding.

"Nothing. MoHattieBelle suited my mother fine. If it was good enough for my mother, it's good enough for my daughter. This baby is Hannah MoHattieBelle Yeager."

Mama didn't give up easily. She continued to negotiate as if her input was being seriously considered. I suppose it was.

"What about 'Mary' for me and your sister, Mary? 'Hannah Mary.' I like that. Your mother, God rest her soul, would like it too. What do you think?"

After several more minutes—so I'm told—they agreed. Mama knew how to manage Daddy, so she solidified the deal, saying, "If we ever have more children, you can choose the first names, and I'll choose the middle names."

Daddy agreed, though he probably did not think it through; it was merely expedient to close that conversation. Now, some eight years later, Daddy kept his word. He chose Olevia and Mama chose Ann—just because she liked it.

From the beginning, Daddy and I rarely talked. When we did, it typically involved more listening on my part than talking.

We had a distance between us—not an estrangement, simply a distance because of who we were—more of a palisade separation. We could clearly see and hear each other, but touching hearts presented more of a challenge. I loved my dad intensely, and I knew we shared the feeling. Still, he felt like a stranger to me for years.

The times we lived in, his age, and his history played their part in creating a schism between us. My independence, loner personality, and Mama's tendency to protect me perhaps provided the rest of the wall. A better description is more like a picket fence we could see through, but finding the gate took time.

Years later, on a visit home with my baby son, Ray, Daddy shared a story with me as the three of us sat on the front porch. Daddy enjoyed babies and fell in love with Ray. He rocked him as he shared some thoughts with me.

"Olevia, I don't know if you realize it or not, but you're the most stubborn child I have."

"What do you mean?" I said incredulously with some attitude easily heard in my voice.

"You have never listened to me. Always, always, you've had to learn on your own."

"That's not true!" I began to get annoyed, but I held my tongue.

Daddy laughed. "Things haven't changed, have they?"

"Daddy, I'm an adult now. I have my own family, but when I was a kid, you ruled the house. Nobody, not even Mama, ever really challenged you."

"You did, Olevia. And I know you remember lots of those times."

Now, my tone sounded much as if he were a young child having difficulty understanding the real world. Through all of this, Daddy remained calm with no apparent concern for my building annoyance.

"Well, maybe as a teenager, but that's different."

He hugged Ray a little closer, laughed again, and continued to speak. "I remember a time when you were barely a year old, just walking. Your mama and I were sitting on the front porch down at the little house. Hannah sat on the steps, and you were in your mama's lap. You started to squirm, wanting down."

"So?" The story interested me, but I could not keep the irritation from my voice.

"So, your mama wanted to go back into the house with you. As I recall, the scene went something like this:

'John, I'm going to take Olevia back inside so she can play.'

'Just put her down, Mary. She'll be fine right here on the porch.'

'I'm afraid she'll fall off.'

'No, she won't. Hand her here.'

I put you down on the porch, told you not to go near the edge, and before your mama could catch you, you were laying in the yard."

"Daddy, I was a baby! Did I get hurt?" I threw up my hands in exasperation and shook my head.

"Not enough to learn anything. I picked you up and sat you back on the porch. I told you again not to go near the edge. I thought you would be afraid to. Not you. Before I got back into my chair, you were laying in the yard squalling. That time, your mama picked you up and took you in the house."

"I can't believe you would just let me fall off the porch like that!"

Daddy continued to smile at the memory. "Olevia, you were stubborn when you were born, and you never changed. Maybe that's a good thing. It helped you get through some tough years."

In an instant, my attitude changed. I suddenly understood what he said and how he felt.

"Daddy, sometimes I think I'm like you in that sense. I learned more than you can imagine by watching and listening to you. You have been an amazing teacher by being yourself."

Daddy smiled, hugged Ray closer, and stared with moist eyes into the distance as if looking through mist for some of those old times.

I leaned back in my chair with a satisfied mind.

****

That's maybe the closest my dad ever came to saying he was proud of me. Oh, I knew he was, and saying it out loud suddenly became unnecessary. We found the gate and shared a meeting of the hearts that had escaped us for so many years.

CHAPTER 20

TEN TO TWELVE YEARS

In early fall of 1945, Mama saw Dr. Miller for a routine checkup following John's birth in August.

"Mrs. Yeager, your blood pressure's too high. We cannot manage your congenital heart valve problem with medication only. It's okay now, but when menopause arrives, hypertension will increase. Mrs. Yeager, you cannot live without a heart valve replacement."

"I'll only be thirty-five in December. I can't be in that bad of a shape!" She raised her eyebrows incredulously.

She later told me that knew she had a blood pressure problem, and it had recently been harder to breathe. Still, she had a new baby, a two-year-old, and a ten-year-old. Naturally, she was tired and sometimes had to sit for few minutes, but "cannot live without a valve replacement" sounded a bit over the top. As anyone would, she began to negotiate.

"I've been off my diet. I'll do better—watch the salt, forget the bacon. I'll do better. I know I need to lose some weight." To lighten the conversation a little, she added, "I think I exercise enough, chasing a two-year-old." She attempted a smile, which was not returned by Dr. Miller.

Knowing her well, he put his hand on her shoulder. "Mary, this is not an easy fix, and you need to think about it. Heart valve replacement is new, but it's getting more common. You are young and a good candidate."

Mama turned serious again, a frown darkening her brow like a thick cloud obscuring the sun. In her typical matter-of-fact manner, she inquired, "What are my chances? With the surgery?"

"My guess, based on your health and where we are, I would say at least fifty-fifty. But without it, they are zero outside of ten or twelve years." He gave her a consoling smile. "That's honest, Mary. We've known each other a long time, and I know you want the truth."

Although Mama did not completely believe the dire circumstance, she answered, "Dr. Miller, I've got three kids and now with a pretty solid promise of ten to twelve years with them compared to a fifty-fifty chance of none—" She paused for dramatic effect. "I'm taking the ten to twelve."

"Of course, it's your decision, but I encourage you to give it some real thought. You do not have a lot of time to change your mind. Your hypertension's getting less treatable every day. The kidney damage must be considered. Be sure you're making the decision you can live with."

"I'm taking the ten to twelve." She left that office with a made-up mind.

****

She spent the next eleven years giving us kids the tools to live in a world without her. In the last year of her life, she shared with me her death-sentence conversation in one of the many life-without-mama sessions we alone shared.

I don't know what my decision would have been, but I'm grateful for the one she made. Having almost thirteen years of physically being with my mom has been the greatest blessing of my life. Without a doubt, it led to the multitude of others I've experienced because she helped me become me.

CHAPTER 21

ALL UNDER ONE ROOF

The rain slowed to a pleasant drizzle as we ate the last biscuit and headed for the porch. Saturdays were always a special exploring day for John and me, and the rain had already stolen part of our day.

"Mama, we'll be back in a little while," I said over my shoulder as the screen door slammed behind me.

"You kids be careful in this rain. I don't want you around the trestle today. It's too full."

I smiled. Mama always cautioned us about something; today, the trestle took first place.

We promised to be careful. As we were poised to go down the steps, a car pulled into our driveway—a city-looking car, long and black with four doors and a big grill.

"Hey," I called out to Mama and Daddy. "We have company."

We retreated to the porch, and both Mama and Daddy soon stood next to us.

"Who could that be?" Daddy murmured as the car eased up the driveway and finally stopped at the front yard gate. The man and woman got out and gathered a few things before they started toward the house. Little did I know, I would soon meet my first real Yankee relative.

The woman picked her way through freshly made mud puddles to struggle with opening the gate. Wearing three-inch heels, accompanied by a trying-to-be-brave smile, she carried her purse and a suitcase. She looked more like a cornered rabbit just before panic set in. I felt a little sorry for her friend, but he didn't seem daunted at all.

Daddy suddenly started for the gate.

"Noah? I didn't know you were coming."

"We decided at the last minute." He gestured toward the woman. "This is my wife, Marie."

Noah, the second oldest of my four half-brothers, lived in Maryland. I did not actually know him, as he was well over twenty years older than me. I had seen him maybe two or three times, and I had heard Daddy complain that he had married a New York Yankee.

With all of us now on the porch after lots of hugging and welcoming, I grew intrigued by the thought of meeting a sister-in-law. At eight years old, it seemed funny to me to have a sister-in-law. I did know my oldest half-brother, Johnson, and his wife, Viola, quite well. They lived in Louisiana and visited often, but I never thought of her as my sister-in-law. I don't know why.

Once we were all dry and situated, Marie mentioned their dog to Mama. "Mrs. Yeager, we have a dog in car. He's a small dog and well trained. Shall I bring him in?"

Daddy overheard and answered, "Marie, I don't allow dogs in the house. If you're afraid he'll run away, Noah can chain him out there."

"Oh no, Mr. Yeager. My dog's not used to being outside, much less in the rain! He's slept beside my bed since I got him as a puppy. He's never been on a chain, and I don't want him tied up."

"Well, I hope a coyote don't get him or anything, but he ain't coming in this house."

Daddy now spoke to Noah. "Noah, you know only riffraff allows a dog to stay in the house. We ain't riffraff. That dog stays outside. I don't want hair in and on everything."

Marie made one last plea. "Please, Mr. Yeager, just for one night?"

Daddy stood his ground while Marie put her dog on a leash to take a walk now that a slight sprinkle had replaced the downpour. We had two collies, both of which were kept in what we called the dog yard, a twelve-by-twelve fenced-in area within our very large fenced-in yard surrounding our house. The dog yard included a couple of doghouses. As Marie and her pooch passed it, our collies, Waggles and King, ran to the fence, barking.

Scruffy responded by barking. Soon, the three were licking, whining, and trying to get together. All three seemed happy to see each other and wanted to play. Ultimately, Marie decided to let Scruffy into the dog yard for some off-leash and much-enjoyed exercise.

The thing about living in the country is that life goes on, no matter what else might be happening in the world. Marie received no special slack in the day's chores, as we simply added her to the work force.

On the first day, she helped to feed the chickens, gave the calf a bottle, and took an interest in getting the cows milked. By nightfall, Marie had earned my admiration—at least, a tad of admiration. Her method of getting her own way with Daddy proved her to be streetwise (or maybe that should be womanly wise.) She won a battle, and Daddy didn't even know he had lost.

Once Daddy left for work or was otherwise out of the house for an extended time, the small, black, long-haired Scruffy found his way inside. Later, Mama referred to Marie as a gutsy little Yankee. She hadn't made a scene, but her dog curled up beside her that night (and every other night they spent at our house).

By the evening of the second day, Marie called "Soo…ooo…ee cow" almost as well as Mama. She laughed loudest when the setting hen pecked its disapproval at her groping hand, and she did not hesitate when I asked her to help me pick the cutworms off the tomato plants. I didn't know how long they would be staying, but I hoped it would be a while.

On the third day of their visit, we had another surprise— at least, a surprise to me, but apparently Mom and Dad were expecting James and Mary to come.

James, the third of the four boys, and his wife arrived in a cab. I had seen him a few times. On an earlier visit, he brought my mom a vase from Italy, purchased while he served in the Navy; that vase occupied a place of honor in the living room, on the piano.

While stationed in Florida, he got married. And we were about to get our first glance at his wife.

"Guys, this is Mary."

Again, there were hugs all around.

Mary was another Brooklyn Yankee—I don't know how she happened to be in Florida—but without the adaptability of Marie. She looked fragile. She suffered from a combination of chronic illnesses—including multiple sclerosis—and a natural clinginess James had barely gotten her settled into a rocking chair when Noah looked out the door.

"Hey, Dad. Isn't that Johnson and Viola? I thought they weren't coming until the weekend?"

Daddy rushed over to look out as well.

"It's your brother, son, and he has Henry with him."

****

Thus, we began one of the most interesting weeks of my childhood days. All five of my brothers, the three wives, my sister, me, and my parents were together. That had not happened before and never happened again while I lived at home. This once-in-a-lifetime visit provided a unique learning experience for everyone involved.

As marry-ins, the three wives hung around with Mama in the kitchen, commiserating over the difficulties of living with a Yeager. Mary whined, demanded, and pouted—requiring too much attention from James to suit Daddy. Viola and Marie fit in, so to speak, doing whatever chore Mama might be involved in—from cooking to milking to caring for the chickens. Hannah stood around the fringes of whatever the women were doing.

Daddy and his boys talked nonstop while they drove around, sat on the porch, or built a fence. Johnny stayed on their heels, and even at the tender age of six, his presence seemed to be encouraged by the group. Being a Yeager male had its advantages.

I tended to hang around the edges of both worlds, helping with Mama's chores and observing Daddy and his sons.

Daddy built fences—some that were needed and others entirely to satisfy his urge to isolate. John and I called him The Super Fencer.

On the second day of the visit, all the brothers gathered to help Dad build a fence. I perched in a nearby tree with my nose in a book. But my attention focused on their banter.

"Noah, get that posthole digger over there. Didn't anybody ever teach you how to build a fence?"

"To tell you the truth, Dad, I've not missed having that skill."

All the brothers laughed; Daddy did not.

"Johnson, hold up one of those fence posts so your brother can see how deep the hole needs to be. You remember, the depth must be about a third of the height of the pole."

Johnny sat on a stump watching. Henry had just completed digging a hole. All the poles were about ten feet tall.

"Hey, Daddy, look at this one " Henry motioned Daddy over.

Daddy walked in that direction and glanced at Johnny. "Hey, John, come see."

Johnny ran over to peer down the hole as if he might find something of interest in it. Daddy picked him up and lowered him into the hole. It came up to just below his shoulders.

"Look over here, boys. This is how deep each of these holes need to be."

They glanced in the direction of Johnny's giggles and joined in the fun. Johnny became the yardstick to measure most of the holes. Once the posts were packed, they were aligned straight within a quarter inch, verified by Daddy's folding ruler and level.

Setting the corner posts—often railroad crossties with braces and cross wires to avoid sag—involved the steady use of Mr. Jeansonne's Come-Along.

"Johnson, come help me with this Come-Along."

"Be right there." He settled at one end of the pulley and Daddy at the other. "Okay, let me know when you're ready."

I figured this would go on for the whole afternoon, so I went inside for a cool drink and to see what was going on in there. When I returned, I saw that not only did they use it on the fence they were building, but they also checked all corner posts of the completed fences. Together, they made certain the fences were sturdy and designed to last forever.

When I came back outside, Daddy occupied one end of the winch, and the boys alternated at the other.

"James, you look so strong, but you sure don't know your way around a Come-Along. Don't get soft. We must do something about your lack of fence-building know-how. What are you going to do if you ever need a fence built?" He cocked his head and teased.

"Don't know, Dad. Can I call you?"

Laughs all around.

Every completed fence on our property stood six to seven feet high with hog wire topped by barbed wire. It reminded me of some sort of encampment!

Tired of pretending to read, I clambered down from my branch and headed inside, chuckling about how amusing the boy team proved to be.

****

I recall spending time watching the fencing fiasco for at least two of the four days all four were at home. Noah took dozens of pictures of Johnny grinning while standing in postholes up to his underarms. When I look at those images now, it conjures up my memories of those days in vivid detail.

I still marvel at how Mama, along with the other wives, spent their days cooking for hungry men who would not be coming in before the sun began to sink. They managed to work in doing the cooking around performing the everyday chores of a rural farm.

****

After those four days, everyone left except Noah and Marie. Noah doted on me and Johnny whenever Dad didn't occupy all his time. Over the kitchen sink, he washed, cut, and combed my hair into a new style. With Johnny, he rode the jacks and jinnys and taught him little things he had not yet discovered, such as mounting his ride from the porch.

Noah joined us in eating potted meat sandwiches, drinking Kool-Aid, and fishing at the trestle. We had the added pleasure of listening to stories of his childhood as he grew up in the orphanage. And, I guess, in our minds, he became a contemporary. As such, he also became a target of our practical jokes.

Noah's eyesight required thick glasses to get around without stumbling, and John and I made the most of this situation. We'd hide his glasses and watch his frantic search. He reminded us of a doodle bug who had lost his ball of manure. We found it amusing, and I'm pretty sure he was on to us in that he exaggerated his frenzied search to increase our amusement. He never reported our behavior to Mama until one day's particularly egregious act.

With the sun at its brightest, we asked him to gather eggs with us. He walked into the windowless chicken house like a sheep to slaughter. In an automatic reflex, he removed his glasses and placed them on a nest near the door. Immediately, Johnny picked them up as we backed out quietly, locked the door, and ran for the house.

Noah, soon engulfed in total darkness, took a minute or so to realize what had happened. By the time he did, we had raced through the kitchen and dining room, stopping only long enough to tell Mama we had finished our chores. Then we settled into the living room rocking chairs. Noah's glasses were on the piano. Mama and Marie sat at the dining room table peeling peaches for canning when we began to hear Noah yelling, "Mary, Marie, I need help."

Mama and Marie continued to peel and talk, unaware of the shouting. I suppose John and I heard him first because we expected it.

Another yell, louder this time, sliced the silence. "Marie, Mary, I'm trapped."

At this, Mama and Marie stopped, mime-like. Their knives were poised over the peaches in hand and their heads were slightly eschewed.

"Did you hear something, Mrs. Yeager?" Marie asked, tilting her head.

"I don't know. Sounded sort of like someone hollering, didn't it? Olevia, John, did ya'll hear anything?"

"No ma'am."

"Where's Noah?"

"I think he's out gathering eggs, Mama."

"Maybe he's calling up one of the cows or something."

Then, as if electric power returned, their hands worked robotic-like again, and they resumed peeling the peaches. My lungs were about to erupt, but I managed to survive by grinning and rocking harder. Then came a blood-curdling scream that eliminated any doubt from whence it came or the seriousness of the caller. For the first time, I considered that John and I might be in real trouble.

*"**Get me out of this chicken house!**"*

Mama and Marie bolted from the dining room like a fire alarm had gone off. They dashed through the kitchen and all the way out to the chicken house. We trailed behind. The closed and fastened door provided immediate proof that this was not a self-inflicted situation. Mama jerked it open, nearly removing it from its hinges.

Noah stood motionless inside—watermelon red, sweat rolling down his face, and with a look that could kill. John and I were reprimanded on the spot.

In time, all was forgiven at our house. Our parents told and retold this story with chuckles all around. But on a visit to Noah and Marie's Maryland home some twenty years later, I discovered he still failed to see the humor, even from the vantage point of looking back.

****

Hannah starred in perhaps the most memorable event of Noah and Marie's visit. They announced on Tuesday that they wanted her to go with them on Friday to dinner at the Hotel Bentley.

Our family never went out to dinner—*ever*—and, if we had, the Hotel Bentley would not have been chosen. We considered it for upper crust city folks only—certainly not us. Hannah's evening out became a family adventure, from planning it to reliving it.

Mama and Hannah agonized over the dress she would wear. Would she get a new one? Was her Sunday pink suit appropriate? Should she go over to Mrs. Rice's to get her hair done? What about shoes—flats or heels?

In the end, she chose a new dress and shoes while on a Noah-and-Marie-sponsored shopping outing, but she did her own hair. I thought she looked beautiful that night, and we snapped a twenty-four-roll of film of her in various poses: standing on the porch between Noah and Marie, alone, with Mama and Daddy, with Johnny and me, etc. Not only did Hannah's eyes and smile broadcast the fairyland atmosphere in our house that night, but we shared, at least vicariously, in every moment.

I asked Noah, "Why are you taking only Hannah?"

"Well, this is a grown-up place, and Hannah's sixteen."

"Will I get to go when I'm sixteen?" I tilted my head.

"I'm sure you will." He smiled.

"Will you come back to take me?"

"I'll certainly try." His smile grew wider.

Knowing my turn lay somewhere in the future felt almost as good as a treat that very day.

We waved from the porch until they were out of sight. I glanced over at my parents. Mama had tears in her eyes, and Daddy laughed.

"What's wrong, Mary? You look like you're about to cry."

"John, Hannah looked like a woman when she left here."

"That wasn't her husband, Mary. That was her brother! I think she'll be here a few more years."

"I guess so."

****

Everybody except Daddy stayed up until they came home—after dark. On an ordinary day, we climbed into bed as daylight turned to night, and anything after dark happened too late for us.

We stood at the gate when Noah stopped the car, and we shifted to immediately outside its back door by the time it opened. Johnny and I peppered Hannah with questions, while Noah and Marie stood by smiling. The scene reminds me now of a celebrity leaving an event and being mobbed by reporters. Hannah easily slipped into the I'm-important category!

"What did you have to eat, Hannah?" I asked.

"Baked chicken."

"A whole chicken?" My eyes grew round.

"No, Olevia, just a chicken breast, new potatoes, and those little green English peas."

"What did you drink? Sweet tea? Or what?" John asked.

"We all had sweet tea."

"What did the hotel look like?" I grabbed her arm, eager to hear more.

"Well, we didn't really go into the hotel part, but I could see the lobby. A big chandelier hung there, and some couches were occupied by people who seemed to be just sitting there. A couple of employees stood behind a long counter, and the red carpet looked soft and luxurious."

"Who asked you what you wanted to eat? A man or a woman?" Why I thought that might be important is beyond me, but my curiosity extended to every detail.

"We had a dressed-up waitress, not like the ones at Billips. She wore a rose-colored dress with a white apron and had a little cap on her head. After we told her what we wanted to eat, other people served our plates and filled our glasses and everything. The first waitress just came by later to ask if everything was okay."

"So, she merely took your order? Nothing else?" John asked.

"Yes."

"Wow! Sounds like an easy job. I could do that someday."

Hannah continued, "We ate off a white tablecloth, and the silverware looked real. The plates were so thin I could see through them, and they were covered with pink roses. Our glasses were those fancy kind with a little stem at the bottom."

I thought it all sounded magical and longed for a time I could experience such an event. It's a memory that doesn't fade over time. I smile again now, remembering how my sister, brother, and Marie were truly celebrities in our family that night. Maybe fittingly, that is my only remembered visit with Noah and Marie coming to our house.

****

I first ate at the Hotel Bentley in 1987. And, although I ate alone, I shared the meal with a lot of good memories.

CHAPTER 22

THE BLUES IN MY TUMMY

Mama and Aunt Grace.

"Mama, I've got the blues in my stomach," I said as I approached Mama on a peaceful, hot—and a little muggy—Louisiana afternoon.

Mama sat on the back porch, shelling peas (what we called butterbeans, and I'm not sure what they were). Late June usually found her canning something from our small garden harvest. I loved our garden and everything that grew in it, from the early-ripening bell peppers and onions right through the July watermelons—usually the oblong, striped variety.

I started recalling fond memories of previous summers. One year, Daddy planted an entire quarter acre in sugar cane. Of course, that can take up to a year and a half or more to mature and develop that wonderful, sweet taste. The harvest did not yield enough to sell or really to even make cane syrup. It served as a treat anytime John and I wanted to chew some. We would cut a stalk at the bottom and then sever it into however many sections were easily shown on the stalk. From there, we peeled each section and chopped the pulp into small bites.

At this point, we typically took it to Mama to wash and provide any additional cleaning. Sometimes, she put it in the refrigerator and suggested we come back when it chilled a little. Once in our hands, we simply chewed it to get the juice and threw away the pulp. Ooh, what a sweet memory!

On this June day, school had closed, and summer vacation had set in. As a newly promoted second-grader, summer and excitement went hand in hand. There was nothing special planned—just life. Some days, we'd walk over to Aunt Grace's to pick plums.

On other days, Mrs. Laird would pick us all up in her car for a trip to the city swimming pool with a picnic. I had no idea where the Lairds lived and still do not know. The only time we saw that family followed a phone conversation between Mrs. Laird and Mama. Mrs. Laird had a daughter, Sarah, who was Hannah's age. She also had a son, Porter Vine, who was my age. Those trips to the pool were especially fun excursions, though Mama typically sat outside the fence warning me to stay out of the deep end. I did. I had an extreme fear of water deeper than my waist, but I loved egg salad sandwiches and Kool-Aid.

During summer, we might even take a trip to Alexandria to visit the zoo, but the possibility of that leaned in the direction of nil and I doubt it. Daddy worked a lot of overtime in the late 1940s and early 1950s. Many times, he got stuck overnight in Little Rock, Arkansas, or he had a sleepover in Lake Charles if his union time as a railroad engineer ran too long.

Because my mother did not drive after she and Daddy married, we spent most of our time at home enjoying each other. Oftentimes, John and I would merely sit on the back porch watching Mama work and listening to her stories.

But this day was different. I had the blues.

"Blues in your tummy? What's wrong?" Mama asked.

"I don't know. I'm just sad. The sun even makes me cry."

I had been laying on a quilt in the side yard, reading a book and looking at the clouds. I had no good reason to be sad, but I suddenly felt desperately alone.

A tear rolled down my cheek, and Mama squeezed me with a hug. "Do you still have your Big Chief tablet from school?"

"Yeah."

"Well, I want you to go get it and sit at Daddy's desk. I'll be there in a minute."

Though it sounded silly to me, I did it.

In a few minutes, Mama walked in. "You know, Olevia, I don't know why you get so sad. You have everything to be happy about."

"I don't know either, Mama. I just don't even want to be here." Tears fell in earnest, and Mama gave me a huge hug.

"Well, maybe we can find out what the problem is today. We're going to talk about what makes you sad."

This was not Mama's first run-in with my sad sessions. But, to my memory, the Big Chief tablet first became a tool on that day.

I suppose if it had not been in the late 1940s, and if I had not lived in rural Central Louisiana, I would have been into counseling somewhere. I found out, years later, that Mrs. Carpenter had mentioned to Mama that I seemed more depressed than a child my age should be. Mama chalked up my teacher's comments to my not wanting to be away from her. Although Mama suffered from illness most of her life that I remember, her good days far outnumbered her bad ones.

At seven years old, I was unaware that I had less than six years left to be with her. Besides, seven years represented an entire lifetime to me, so it would not have mattered if I had known. It would have seemed like forever.

"Okay, Olevia. Open up your tablet."

I did. "And what?" I studied the page and looked up at her. This new approach got my attention a bit. Maybe it would be interesting.

"At the very top of your page, I want you to write down something that makes you happy."

"Nothing makes me happy! You promised we would talk about what makes me sad." And the tears turned into a flood, generating another hug from Mama.

"I know, baby. And we will. But first, I hoped I might get just a little smile. Can you think of anything that would make you smile right this minute?"

"An ice cream cone, especially strawberry."

I started to grin between sniffles, and even Mama smiled a little.

"Well, let's write that down. It makes me smile too. What else do you have?"

"Nothing! Mama, I'm sad!" I became frustrated and threw her a deep frown.

Mama calmly continued, "Okay, let's see if I can do one for you. What about 'Grunt?' Does he make you smile?"

Grunt was my dog. He earned his name by how he, from a puppy, would grunt while he slept. The story circulated that the source of his sleeping habit involved Mama having given him doll bottles filled with hot toddies. Apparently, as a puppy. he whined and cried a lot, and hot toddies helped him sleep. I don't know if that's true or not, but I believed it.

Grunt became my outside partner when John played with Tere-Tone or was otherwise occupied. Grunt fetched. He loved belly rubs. He liked just sleeping beside me while I watched the clouds. Once, I almost choked him by putting a rubber band around his neck as a collar. Fortunately for Grunt and me, Mama noticed it in time to prevent any permanent damage.

"Yeah, I guess Grunt can make me smile." And I smiled as I thought of him.

"Okay, I must blanch those beans and put them into the pressure cooker. Can you work on this list until I get through with that? Then I want to talk about what makes you sad."

"Okay, Mama, but you promise we'll talk about being sad?"

"I promise if you promise to really list as many things as you can that make you smile."

I don't know how much time passed before she returned. I simply knew I could not lie to my mama—I had to list everything that made me happy, and I did. When she came back, I had the entire front page of that Big Chief tablet filled with happy thoughts.

The nausea in my tummy had eased a lot.

"Okay, Olevia, let's see what we have here." Mama took the tablet and began to read off my list.

"Well, I see that you like going to Mrs. Curry's when I have coffee. That's interesting. Why do you like that?"

I went into detail about how Mrs. Curry always fixed me a cup of coffee too and how Mama and Mrs. Curry said funny things about Mr. Curry and Daddy. Mama never interrupted. She let me talk and appeared interested in what I had to say. The desperate terror of feeling alone abated somewhat.

When I finished that entry, she picked another one. "I see you like *Tom Sawyer*. What does that mean?"

"Hannah has been reading it to me at nights. I love it when she does Aunt Polly's voice. She's so funny!"

I attempted to duplicate my sister's voice imitating Aunt Polly. We both laughed as the sadness began to seep away. Mama read every entry on the front side of that Big Chief tablet page and encouraged me to amplify each one. I did, and by the time we finished the page, we had moved to a rocking chair with me safely secured on Mama's lap.

When we reached the bottom of the page, I started to get up.

"Wait a minute. We need to talk about what makes you sad. Let's turn this page over so you can write down those things."

"I don't want to!"

"Why not? I want to know, so we can talk about them."

"I am not sad, Mama. I want to go play store with Johnny. I think he has something under the sycamore tree."

I no longer felt nauseous; there were no blues in my stomach or tears in my eyes.

"Well, okay. If you're sure. You know, you can tell me anything?"

"I know," I said as I climbed down. Before closing the door behind me, I called out, "Can we go to the library tomorrow? I want Hannah to read to me the *Pippi Longstocking* books."

That first encounter with The Big Chief tablet turned out to be the first of many—and maybe not even the most memorable of the two sessions clearest in my memory. The second indelible impression occurred when I was in the fifth or sixth grade.

This time, I knew why the sadness engulfed my very soul, but I don't recall any particulars of the day. Had there been a doctor's appointment? Did Mama have a bad day? Did anything out of the ordinary occur? I don't even recall for sure what season we were in or if I was ten or eleven years old. My memory begins with sitting in the living room alone with Mama.

"Mama, I feel sad in my stomach."

"What's the matter?"

"I don't want you to be sick. Why doesn't God make you well? I pray and I beg, but nothing happens. I try to be good. Why doesn't God care?"

"Olevia, God loves you, and He loves me, and He cares."

"I don't believe you. If God loved us, He would make you well. I'm sick to my stomach."

"I tell you what. Why don't you get your Big Chief tablet?"

Oh, how I hated to hear those words!! I knew the drill. "I don't want a Big Chief tablet! I want you to be well. I want to be happy." I threw my hands in the air and made a loud sigh.

As usual, Mama's reactions to my theatrics were low key. She got the tablet and handed it to me, along with a sharpened pencil. I stared at her, not moving.

"Okay, Olevia. Pick a page and write down everything you can think of to be happy about."

"I really don't want to do this. I want to hear your answers to my questions."

I tried to stare her down, but Mama hardly noticed as she continued to talk.

"And you will. I promise we will talk about it today when you feel better."

By the time I reached this age, I knew my mother would not live to see me grow up. Indeed, Mama made sure I knew it. She felt it important that I be prepared to face my teenage years without her, so she spent time talking to me about what that would be like. She never told the story as something macabre or something to dread but rather as an example of how life can be.

On this day, it seemed as if darkness surrounded me, and I feared the future with a dread like I never had before. Imagine going from hearing about a tornado miles away to being in the center of that tornado as it destroyed everything you loved. It was that and a hundred times worse. The reality of life without my mom seemed impossible and useless, indeed a life not worth living. Still my mom persevered, and the most expedient way to move on to a discussion involved the Big Chief tablet.

I took the offered tablet and pencil.

"Okay, pick a page. Today, let's write together everything you think can make you happy."

Well, until now, I had not experienced that approach, but I was too deep in the well to immediately accept the lifesaving rope.

"I'm really too sad today. I don't feel like writing anything." The tablet and pencil lay limp in my hands like a wilting piece of lettuce.

Mama plowed on. "What about watermelons? Were you happy we had a midnight snack in the watermelon patch last week?"

My dad had this weird rule about not eating the pulp of a warm watermelon; we could only drink the juice when eating a non-chilled melon in his presence. Mama believed that rule a bit silly, and she found a delightful way to break it.

Our entire family went to bed with the chickens—i.e. when the sun went down, we crawled into bed. In July, without warning, she would wake me and John in the middle of night; sometimes, Hannah joined the fun. Together, we sneaked out the back door into the night like thieves, carrying a knife and a flashlight, heading for the watermelon patch. We shopped together there in the moonlight; John and I took turns guiding the flashlight, while Mama thumped melon after melon. Eventually, she would choose the perfect one, crack it open, and we'd eat the heart of it. All the time we were eating, Mama would be telling us some story about her childhood life.

These nighttime adventures were major treats, and remembering one never failed to lighten my mood.

"Yeah, that was fun."

"What about when we went to Grandpa's for Easter, and you got to fight eggs with Grandpa? Remember, he sneaked in those Guinea eggs? And, at the end, he gave you all the eggs?"

"Okay, I remember that." My mood lightened as I recalled Mama watching the egg fighting and laughing with Grandpa as every one of mine cracked first.

"Okay, I'm going to give you one more, and then it's your turn. What about when Daddy must stay in Little Rock, and we go to sleep together telling stories or playing *I Spy* games?"

"That's a really good one! And I have one too. What about when we have picnics in The Pines?"

"Oh, yes I like that!" She grinned.

I don't remember how long we sat there, and I noted every story on the Big Chief tablet. While the filled page brightened my mood, it did not remove questions from my mind. Neither did they leave my mom's thoughts.

"Okay, Olevia. Now that's done. Let's talk about why you're sad today."

"I'm not so sad anymore, but I want you to get well."

"So do I, baby, and maybe I will. But, if I don't, that just happens not to be the road you and I are on. We must walk the paths chosen for us. But I promise you wherever those paths go, they will be filled with good things that can't be found on anybody else's path. They are special for us, for you and me."

"But everybody's mamas are not dying. It's not fair."

"Well, maybe if I had gotten a long path to walk, you wouldn't be my little girl. I wouldn't like that. Would you?"

"No!"

"Then I guess we're pretty lucky, aren't we?" She chuckled and gave me a little squeeze. "We still have a lot of living to do and a lot more fun to have. I need to get a pot of coffee started now. Do you want to grind it for me?"

I did. I loved spending time with my Mama and her precious wisdom.

****

Mama's gift lessened, and still does lessen, my struggle to overcome the sadness that remains a built-in part of my psyche. I did not completely unwrap this most valuable gift during those childhood sessions. As life would have it, paths have chuck holes. I mentally brought out, and still do bring out, the Big Chief tablet when sadness starts to cloud my sunny days. It continues to comfort me as I explore more and more layers of this most cherished and precious gift.

I continue to discover how blessed I am to be on my chosen path. It is indeed one filled with infinitely more happiness than sadness. Remembering to think about the good stuff began with the Big Chief tablet.

I often utter a silent "Thank you, Mama" as I continue to learn from the lessons begun so long ago. She's been on the other side since 1956, but she's never far from my heart and will always play a part in my life in all the important ways.

CHAPTER 23

Dog Stories

Bandit.

John's knocking on my mental door again with a story that is more his than mine. My memory is from the outside looking in, so I'm handing him my pen now.

****

The turkeys hadn't been gone long when my ninth birthday rolled around in August of 1954. I couldn't recall any birthday for any one of us resulting in birthday cakes or expensive gifts. As far as I could tell, this birthday would follow precedent birthdays.

I got up about the same time as usual and headed for the kitchen and coffee. I loved the smell of hot coffee in the morning. It seemed to waft through the whole house, along with biscuits browning in the oven and bacon frying. Mama and Daddy sat at the table.

"Morning, son. I guess this is sorta a special day."

"A special day?"

Mama chimed in with a laugh. "Your birthday, Johnny. You didn't forget, did ya?"

I sat, still confused.

Daddy continued, "Nine years old is a big birthday. You are getting older and should be more responsible. Fourth grade, next year, right?"

"Yessir."

The conversation ended. The aroma of Mama's biscuits encouraged buttering a couple and smearing them with homemade blackberry jam. I'm not sure there is any better beginning to a good day. I finished off two and left the table to see if Olevia had gotten up. As I walked through the living room, I noticed a gun against the wall beside the fireplace. I immediately stopped and went over to check it out.

Daddy kept his twenty-two-rifle in the back room (Henry's room) on the top of a six-foot tall, black cabinet. We referred to it as The Black Thing. My BB gun could also be found there. A gun laying in the living room or up against the wall did not compute in my brain.

I approached near enough to see a tag on it.

To: Johnny. From: Daddy.

I let out a whoop, grabbed the gun, and ran to Daddy in the kitchen.

"What's this, Daddy?"

Daddy laughed. "Well, son, I think you can see what it is. It's a 410 shotgun. Just the thing for huntin' rabbits and stuff. I think you've outgrown that BB gun of yours."

Mama cautioned, "You must be very careful with a gun this powerful, and don't just carry it everywhere you go."

"Thank you, Daddy." I hugged him as hard as I could, and then I looked over at Mama. "Don't worry, Mama. All my friends have 410s. We're careful."

Mama's wrinkled forehead and lack of enthusiasm presented a clear indication that she wasn't too happy about this turn of events. She said nothing else. Carrying my gun, I ran to the porch to sit and study it from end to end.

A rifle, open spaces, and a country boy depicted the norm in my community, and most of my friends had gotten a 410 for Christmas. Now I fit in with my fellow fourth graders—except for one thing. Hunting required a hound, and I didn't have one.

We had plenty of dogs, cats, rabbits, cows, and donkeys, and I didn't figure Daddy would take kindly to me asking for a hound dog, so I didn't. What happened next proves my Daddy knew me from the inside out and communication does not always require oral conversation.

Daddy brought her in that afternoon. She was black and tan, all ears, skinny, shivering, and shaking with little bitty eyes floating in a pool of red. She looked as if she had just come off a long drunk. I shook with excitement and couldn't wait to hold her. He handed her to me.

"She's a good-un, son."

Good for what, I didn't know. You see, Daddy had never had hounds before and didn't really know much about them. Maybe he meant good-un to stir a young boy's heart. I rubbed her slick, shiny ears that felt like satin. She licked my hand while Daddy looked on.

"What you gonna name her, son?"

The weather steamed July-hot in Louisiana. So, I said, "July" (except I pronounced it 'Ju-lee').

I sat her down, her pencil tail tucked between her legs. To me, it seemed she wanted to be accepted and feared she wouldn't be. I could tell she tried hard to please. When I touched her, she licked my hand again.

"Can I keep her inside, Daddy?"

"Naw. This is an outside dog."

I didn't understand the reason for an outside dog and still don't today. Before long, I started taking the dog inside because it's the best way to enjoy them. I haven't changed since then, and as soon as Daddy went to work, she came inside. And when I went out, she went with me. If I sat on the front porch in a rocking chair, she sat beside me.

Only at night, when Daddy came home, was she banished to the dog yard. She cocked her head as if we had an understanding about that. She knew the decision occurred outside of my hands and that she would return to her rightful spot beside me as soon as Daddy went to work.

In my mind and heart, Jack London's *White Fang* did not hold a candle to her. I read about the hounds in Mr. Curry's old *Field and Stream* magazines; then, July and I would take a fantasy trip. In our shared imagination, we would tree bears, cougars, wild hogs, and, of course, coons. In the real world, we settled for chasing rabbits in our field.

Her bawl shook the acorns from the trees, and my heart raced. I became the great Hound Man chasing dangerous game. We didn't catch many rabbits. Sometimes, she would chase one into the hay dock blocks by the barn, and I would take them down to get to it. Then I would try to make a pet out of the rabbit, which never worked. Wild rabbits must be brought in as babies to get to know their captor and establish a relationship. My rabbits always ran at the first chance they got. And, if I tried to hold one, it bit me.

****

July and I grew closer and closer over the years. She never lost her love of chasing rabbits. It used to make me chuckle a whole bunch, watching her.

Sadly, a speeding car killed July as she chased one of those dangerous rabbits. I shot my 410 toward that car, but the driver didn't stop. July was dead. I lost a good friend that day—probably the best one I ever had.

I've had a lot of hounds since July and even named some of them after her. Although I've never recaptured those boyhood fantasy feelings, I continue to try like a junkie looking for the perfect high one more time.

****

Three-plus years had passed since July was killed; it was now 1957. Things had been normalizing slowly since Mama died in late 1956. Daddy had been unusually tolerant of the dogs, pups, cats, kittens, snakes, and sundry other animals I added to our menagerie.

We had an unofficial dump on a rural road about a half mile from our house. For some weird reason, city folks believe country folks love throw-away animals. On almost any day of the week, there would be animals abandoned at the dump. Sometimes it was a mama dog with some pups. Other times, it might be a cat and some kittens or maybe only a singular dog. I found it impossible to leave all of them and would bring home the most pitiful of the finds. When one too many mouths showed up to be fed, a moving tow sack would be in his hand when Daddy drove off to work. In a few days, he would mention some specific dog.

"Have you seen that little brown and white pup lately?"

"You mean Nookie?"

"Yeah, that's the one."

"No."

He smiled, saying he hadn't either, and the subject ceased to be. I've often wondered where he took those dogs, but I never asked. And I never knew.

Daddy hadn't added anything to our collection since the turkeys and July. I had almost forgotten the way it worked, though the process never changed. He began about two or three weeks in advance, making a new animal sound as good as Christmas. One evening, right after school began, Daddy and I were sitting on the porch just talking about nothing and everything. Out of the blue, he asked me if I knew what a Catahoula Hog Dog was. I had heard some of the woodsier boys talking about them at school. I told him that, but I had never seen one.

Well, he had.

"Son, there's some Choctaw Indians over in Flats who have some. I've talked to 'em, and they know a lot about 'em."

I was all ears. "Like what, Daddy?"

"Well, you know, white men discovered these dogs living with Indians in Catahoula Parish, and they were scared of 'em. They have white eyes, a strange brindled color, and are smarter than most dogs."

"What can they do?"

"They hunt, but not like most hounds. Indians use 'em to catch big and little stuff like rabbits. They are natural born tree dogs, and what makes them special is huntin' wild hogs. That's why the Indians call them Catahoula Hog Dogs. Not many people outside of Louisiana have even heard of 'em. These dogs are extraordinary. They make good guard dogs too. And, on top of all that, they sure are pretty. Their eyes are glassy, and they have webbed feet and a spotted coat. Plus, they're smart."

"Reckon we got any chance of getting one?"

"Well, we might, but don't go getting your hopes up."

Over the next two or three weeks, Daddy remembered little tidbits he had forgotten to tell me. There was a tale about one of the dogs that caught a bull by the nose and threw him. Then another would surface even more attractive, such as one saving his master from a wild mother sow at the cost of his own life.

Every little bit of information Daddy shared increased my prayers for the chance to own a Catahoula Hog Dog. Then Daddy quit talking about dogs, so I started asking him what our chances were. He grunted and said he would check it out, or he still considered it, or something equally non-committal.

This went on for a week or ten days before I believed we would not be getting a Catahoula Hog Dog after all. I stopped bringing it up. Though disappointed, I accepted it just as we accept inclement weather even if we don't like it. It simply is what it is.

So, on that shivery February Saturday morning when Daddy drank his coffee and walked out of the door without a word, I wondered what was up. But nothing about a Catahoula Hog Dog crossed my mind.

At about ten-thirty, the dogs barked as the two-toned Willys crept up the muddy hill. Daddy climbed out in a cold, drizzling rain. He carried a cardboard box under his arm. I met him on the porch, trying without success to get a peek into the box. I followed him to the living room where he set the box in front of the fireplace. He pulled back the top as I peered in.

The pup peering back at me exuded ugly—lopped ears, a head that looked as if it belonged to a full-grown pit bull, eyes glowing like clear glass, and a light brown Joseph's coat crisscrossed with dark brown and black stripes covering him from top to bottom.

A big potbelly dwarfed his rear end, which looked about an inch wide. Though I knew it, I had to hear Daddy say it to believe it.

"What kind of dog is that, Daddy?"

Daddy took off his glasses and looked proud. "A Catahoula Hog Dog, son."

Pretty did not come to mind as a word I would have used to describe that mournful-looking pup. What Daddy and a tribe of Indians saw pretty in this dog is still a mystery to me. I lifted him out of the box to find he couldn't stand. His back end fell first, and then his front drooped down as if in slow motion. Daddy watched this pitiful sight for a while.

"You know that dog might die!" He spoke as if the puppy's condition came as a complete surprise to him.

"I would surely hate that, Daddy, now that we have him and all. Can't we do something for him?"

"Well, he's probably wormy. You ought to take him to the vet on your scooter."

That's when I knew Daddy cared about this dog! He usually hesitated about me getting out in a cold rain, especially on my scooter, because I might catch the sniffles and cost him money. I grabbed the dog and ran out of the house, bee-lining to my scooter.

"I'm going right now," I shouted over my shoulder. "I think I should hurry."

"Take it easy, son. You don't want to have any wrecks and hurt yourself or that dog."

"Yessir!"

I headed to an old veterinarian in Pineville that Daddy referred to as "good with dogs." Money never entered my mind, but Daddy must have called the vet after I left, as they seemed to be expecting me when I arrived. It didn't take long to reach the office about six or eight miles away. When

I skidded to a stop and ran in, a kind, soft-spoken, and grandfatherly sort of person met me right inside the door.

Icy water dripped from my hair and clothes, and my shoes made squishy noises. Holding the box together had been largely unsuccessful, and the pup under my coat suffered from uncontrolled shivering. Doc put the pup on the table and seemed tickled to see that dismal-looking animal. I wanted to cry.

"What kind of dog is this, son?"

"It's a full-blooded Catahoula Hog Dog, sir."

The vet feigned a serious countenance and said he would save him if he could. After examining the pup and giving him a shot and a big pill, he outfitted me with a dry box and another huge pill with precise directions as to how to administer it the next day. At the end of the step-by-step procedures, I recited the directions back to the vet.

"He needs to take this pill first thing in the morning," I echoed.

"That's right." He nodded.

"He should take the pill before I give him anything to eat."

"That's right."

"I should hold his head up with his mouth closed and rub on his neck to help him swallow."

"That's right."

"I should give him this pill even if he is feeling better in the morning?"

"That's right."

"Okay. I can do that. How much do I owe you?"

"How much do you have?"

"A dollar."

"You owe me fifty cents."

I always called Daddy a dollar man—he believed a boy should always have a dollar in his pocket but never more than a dollar. I paid the vet and bolted for the door.

"Hey, wait a minute, son. If that dog is dead in the morning, don't give him the other pill."

The vet smiled as I solemnly assured him I would not. At home, I recounted to Daddy everything the vet had said.

"Well, son, let's wait until Sunday evening to name him. No use naming him if he's gonna die."

The dog lived, and Daddy named him Spike. He got big, but he never seemed beautiful to anyone other than me, Daddy, and (I guess) those Indians. He never did anything heroic. He licked my face when I was lonely, he loved me when I was not very lovable, and he missed me when I was gone.

Come to think of it, I guess he was a hero.

****

In 1979, the Catahoula Hog Dog was renamed the Catahoula Leopard Dog and selected as the Louisiana State Dog. The selection seems fitting to me. Louisiana is filled with colorful and unique people, so it's well represented by this colorful and unique dog. Spike certainly provided a memorable chapter in my growing-up years.

CHAPTER 24

THE FLYING SQUIRRELS

Daddy, Jacks, Jennys.

"Gimme the box, John," I said as we stared at the animals flattened on a tree branch. I'll hold it while you catch the squirrels."

"What if they bite me?"

"Don't be a baby! They're just babies. They won't bite."

"Well, they scratch. Besides, where's their mother?"

"John, are you scared of those tiny babies?"

He frowned. "I'm not scared. I'm careful."

John's voice had that I-might-cry sound to it, so I backed off quickly. After all, I didn't want to touch the squirrels myself.

While we had pets of all sorts and the usual farm animals, we derived the most fun from the less cooperating kind—the wild kind—such as rabbits, opossums, raccoons and, on this day, Sugar Gliders, more commonly known as Flying Squirrels.

Late February is comfortably cool in Louisiana. Baby owls fledge, young squirrels emerge from their nests, and tiny rabbits are glimpsed scampering in the weeds. Once, we even brought in an opossum. On another occasion, a fiercely fighting raccoon remained free—all we had to show for our efforts were some scratches, but we grew considerably wiser with that encounter!

For the most part, Mama ignored our newfound pets until the end of the day. Nightfall meant freedom for the pet-of-the-day and an opportunity to return to its own family. Concern in our household that we might be bitten or catch some dreaded disease from wild animal encounters didn't really exist. At least, I can't ever remember being cautioned about those possible consequences.

Of course, obvious damage required alcohol—or more likely, a cleaning with Dr. Tichenor's. And, if we had stepped on a nail or some other object, we typically soaked the injured foot in coal oil to make up for any expired tetanus shot.

Daddy did not get involved in our day-to-day activities. He wasn't given to the levity of life, and I thought of him as part of another, more ancient, world. He rarely laughed and did not appreciate practical jokes. Life weighed heavily in the air when Daddy stood in the room; he projected the feeling one might have when the weatherman says, "Tornado Watch." The advisement may advance to a tornado warning and sometimes an order to get to your safe place. That's the exception, not the rule. The rule was simply to be prepared.

His somberness did not infringe on John's and my ability to have fun. Many times, Daddy increased our fun by virtue of his presence. Without his knowledge, he became the straight man, the Dean Martin to our Jerry Lewis.

He unknowingly played that part in this our Flying Squirrels story.

"Hey, look, John. Why don't you take off your shirt and use it for a shirt-net?"

"What?"

"Here, gimme the box and take off your shirt. I'll show you how you can catch the squirrels."

John carried a saltine box that we planned to use as a temporary home for whatever that day's catch might be. Wandering around The Pines, I saw something fly down from one branch to another.

As the oldest, I tried—not always successfully—to be the leader. I punched John in the shoulder and pointed to the tree. Sure enough, another one glided down. We tiptoed closer to get a better look at the two young flying squirrels lying flat on the branch. The sun shone brightly, the birds were active, and the cows were headed home for the morning milking. Being nocturnal, the Sugar Babies were settling in for their day of rest along with the possums, the raccoons, and the other nighttime creatures.

John took off his shirt, put his hands in the sleeves and scooped up the babies in his shirt without even touching them. Then he put both his shirt and the Sugar Gliders in the box.

My mind had already wandered into a world of fantasy filled with trained squirrels dressed in fancy clothing and an admiring crowd watching their performances. John sat down beside me so we could dream together of our good fortune.

"You know, there might be an easy way to train these squirrels. When they learn their names, I bet they'll come when we call them," John suggested.

"I don't know if squirrels can even learn names. I've never seen anyone with a pet squirrel."

John admitted he hadn't either, but that didn't mean we couldn't be the first. That fact made the thought even more attractive.

"I know we could train them to use those little wheel things like we've seen at Grant's Pet Store."

He asked, "What wheel things? I didn't see any there."

"That's because you always want to play with the puppies."

When our collie had puppies, the pet store became a destination when they reached eight weeks old. They were purebred collies, and they usually found homes via our veterinarian, Dr. Paige. If we needed another source of placing them, Grant's was available. My dad did not believe in selling dogs. I'm not sure why, but he said it was Biblical. However, he bought dogs!

"Am not! We've only been there twice. What wheels?"

"We've been there three times! Remember when Grandpa bought us the parakeet?"

I described the exercise wheels available for guinea pigs, white rats, and hamsters. We discussed what to feed them and how to train them for the Sugar Babies' first performance.

By the time we started home, we knew these animals had found their new forever home. We also knew secrecy and subterfuge would be required to succeed in making them permanent members of our family. We figured once they were trained, our parents would be so impressed by our new pets that the subject of letting them go wouldn't even be broached.

We headed straight for the house and talked all the way. We discussed where we would keep the squirrels and exactly how the kidnapping and re-homing would be executed without a hint to our parents. The squirrels proved to be more agile and agitated than we had expected.

We slipped through the back door and into John's bedroom. Let me take a minute here to explain the layout of our house, as it contributes greatly to the adventure in this story.

We had a front porch where we sat on the steps and listened to our parents talk. Through the front door one entered the living room with no entryway, foyer, or anything of that sort. To the left our parents' bedroom was located. Through the bedroom door and to the other side and the other door was my bedroom.

Our hallway and bathroom were located to the right of that. John shared a bedroom with Henry down the hall on the left, and a utility room opened directly across from it.

The utility room housed our washing machine among other things including a rack that ran the entire length of the room. On that rack hung our family's wardrobe including coats, Daddy's suit, Mama's Sunday dress, and our everyday clothes. One extra-special military issue coat could also be found there.

My brother, James, a Navy guy, brought it to my mother. According to him, this coat was certified as safe from the cold down to fifty below. I suppose he meant fifty below zero Fahrenheit, but the phrase used was always just "fifty below."

He suggested Mama wear it when she milked the cows on cold mornings. She never did—the coat weighed about forty pounds, and we lived in Louisiana. *Fifty below* had not been experienced or even imagined. Still, the coat hung proudly to be admired as some sort of trophy. Daddy regularly called visitors' attention to it.

Once, Mr. Pardue, a deacon in our church stopped by to chat. He had barely gotten seated when Daddy stood up.

"I want ya' to look at a coat I've got."

Mr. Pardue dutifully followed him into the utility room where Daddy reached for the coat as if it were the queen's crown.

"This here coat is certified to fifty below. My son gave me that." He handed it to Mr. Pardue.

"Well, it certainly looks like it would be a warm one."

"It is indeed. The military use these at the North Pole."

Mr. Pardue had little interest in the subject, and, to me, he resembled a bug caught in a spider's web. No way out could be seen, but the struggle went on.

"This is a nice coat, John, but I'm on a short leash this morning. Several stops left. You know how it is. Gotta visit with everyone on the homebound list. How's Mary feeling?"

"Oh, she's doing well. Yeah, I know how it is with the clock ticking." Daddy took the coat to re-hang. "I guess you better get going."

He escorted Mr. Pardue to the door and relaxed back in his chair before the deacon could catch his breath or knew what had happened.

****

Oops! I ran down one of those rabbit holes again! Let me get back to squirrels!

To continue, a 360-degree route through our house was created by each room's two doors, one on each side. When all doors were open, a complete and unimpeded circular path ran through our home. Johnny's room occupied a corner in the house, and not a part of the circle.

Daddy and Mama might sometimes close their bedroom doors, but we kids were not allowed to close ours. If we did, someone knocked to ask, "What's goin' on in there?"

Safety and privacy were more available with the door open. Indeed, we could have built a bomb in an open-doored bedroom, and no one would have looked in.

John and I sat on the floor of his bedroom with the door wide open and our two squirrels in the saltine box. We discussed names for our new pets. We wondered if they were girl squirrels or boy squirrels and pondered exactly how one might be able to tell the gender difference between flying squirrels.

"John, let's look at them to see if we've got girl or boy squirrels."

"I bet they are a brother and sister, just like us."

"Maybe. Then we could call them Olevia and John."

We dissolved into laughter as we lifted the shirt out of the box. Although our plan seemed perfect, the squirrels' desire to escape overcame our best efforts. They seemed to fly through the door, across the hall, and out of sight. We ran after them, but they disappeared into thin air. We were distraught, not only at the loss of our pets, but also about the possibility of our parents finding them first. We knew they were not likely to see the value of our new pets and might even be angry at their escape into the house. We moped around all afternoon, looking and watching for the squirrels to come out.

They didn't.

Sundown brought bedtime. Daddy explained the foolishness of burning electricity to stay up. I suppose we could have stayed up in the dark, but we didn't. Early to bed, early to rise was the motto in our house. Sundown found us in bed or getting ready to be there. And, at daybreak, we got up.

As this evening came on, we worried our lost pets would starve, or worse, eat whatever they could find in the kitchen.

"What do you think the squirrels usually eat, Olevia?"

"Acorns? Pinecones? I don't know."

"What about chicken-scratch?"

"Hey, I bet they'll eat that."

We headed to the barn to get a two-gallon syrup bucket full of chicken-scratch, still talking about the adventure we were on.

"We can keep this bucket under your bed. I don't think Mama will find it there."

"Okay." John nodded. "How are we going to feed our squirrels?"

"I don't know."

"They were headed for the utility room when they disappeared. I wonder if that would be a good place?" John suggested.

"Yeah, probably. They'll wander around the house looking for somethin' to eat, and that's the most open area."

It was settled. That night, we poured a little mound of chicken scratch in the middle of the utility room.

Sure enough, the next morning, where we left the grain looked like the remains of something a mouse had been chewing. When Mama found it, she immediately feared we had mice in the house. Field mice getting in the house happened in the winter, but at the end of February, it was not likely. By that time, the weather warmed, and mice found ample food outside and in the barns. Mice-in-the-house ordinarily cropped up as a December-January problem.

Mama cleaned up the leftover grain and set a baited mousetrap right there. That night, we unset the trap and poured another small pile of grain. The next morning, the grain had disappeared, and a sprang trap remained. Mama mentioned it to Daddy.

"John, I think we might have a couple of mice in the house."

"You need to set a trap."

"I did. That's what I'm telling you. The trap had gone off this morning, but the bait's there. Something that looked like chewed up chicken feed surrounded the trap."

"Probably young mice. Set two traps about a foot apart. That'll catch 'em."

The subject closed for the day, and Mama used the two-trap approach that night. We followed our same routine for the next several nights—unset the traps and put out the grain. We were thinking about how we might catch our pets before they came to harm, but nothing came to mind. Of course, the problem only crossed our minds near bedtime. Then one moonless night we were in bed almost asleep.

Suddenly, something sounding like a herd of little mice running brought the peaceful night to an end. We heard them coming through the dining room, through the living room, and into Mama's and Daddy's room. Daddy leaped from bed in his long johns and yelled, "Mary, a bunch of rats just ran through this room."

Mama didn't make much of an effort to reply, but my ears and John's perked up. We heard them coming again. Daddy jumped up and turned on the lights. The flying squirrels disappeared.

The next night, a similar experience occurred.

Daddy screamed again, "Mary, those are the biggest rats I've ever seen, and there are two of them."

Daddy now became involved in the rat-killing contest. The action he took first included telling Mama she didn't know how to catch a rat, but he would teach her. He went to Merritt's

General Store and brought home five huge rattraps that were about ten inches long and four inches wide. Until that day, I had never seen a rattrap of those dimensions, and I don't think I've seen one since.

At bedtime, he lined the doorway between my room and his room with rattraps. We were required to look at his handiwork while he pointed out that a man must *think* to outsmart an animal.

He related stories about how rats the size of those in our house could chew off an arm while we slept, or how they might kill a dog and even carry all sorts of dreaded diseases. He said he had been foolish to have left this problem up to Mama, but now everything would be okay because he knew what to do. Those rats would die before morning.

My heart leaped to my throat as I considered the fate of our beautiful baby squirrels. John and I felt sad and responsible for their fate. He even suggested that we fess up.

"Let's just tell 'em they ain't rats."

"No. We'll get in trouble if we do that, and I don't think Daddy's going to care what they are."

"Well, we can't let 'em die."

"Let's pray for them."

We climbed in bed, prayed, and waited. We were still awake when we heard the rumble of our squirrels making their nightly run. I'm not sure any human has ever enjoyed the intensity of the prayers offered for those two sugar gliders. John and I begged God to save them, and it is possible Daddy prayed as potently for their capture. I think Mama leaned in our direction because she seemed a little put out with Daddy's big speech including her incompetence at rat killing.

When the squirrels came to the traps, John and I held our collective breath as they sailed over them like a horse jumping a fence. Daddy jumped out of bed and ran for a broom. By the time he had one, the squirrels had disappeared.

All was quiet except for a few giggles coming from John and me. We didn't forget to say, "Thank you, God."

But our problem wasn't solved, just postponed, and we knew it.

The next night, the traps were set again. This time, Daddy got into bed with a broom and a flashlight under the covers next to him. We waited and prayed. At about nine or so, a rumble came. John and I pumped up the prayers, and Daddy eased up on the side of his bed with the flashlight in hand and the broom lifted.

The squirrels raced by and over the traps, and Daddy didn't move a muscle. He waited for their next turn through. As they approached his door, he turned on the flashlight. For just a moment, their beady, little eyes met his before he jumped up with the broom. They moved like greased lightning with Daddy right behind them. He slammed the broom to the floor, shined the flashlight, and stepped on the rattraps. John and I could not contain our giggles as the squirrels disappeared. Daddy looked frantic and perplexed at the same time. He also seemed near the end of his rope with these rats.

"That's it. I'm gettin' some rat poison tomorrow."

Mama protested because she did not like rat poison around us, but her protests fell on deaf ears.

"I'm tellin' you, Mary, those rats are more dangerous than any rat poison. We've got to get rid of 'em."

Daddy stood near the planned execution site, looking like a weird Wizard of Oz scarecrow in his long johns with the broom and flashlight still in his hands. Traps were scattered around his feet. I wish I had a video as clear as the memory in my mind.

John and I didn't sleep much that night. To the squirrels' good fortune, we were coming up on a weekend. So, we could devote the next couple of days to solving the problem. At first light Saturday, we began talking, worrying, and planning when it occurred to us that the squirrels always disappeared in the utility room where there were only so many places to hide.

Immediately after breakfast, we dashed in to conduct a thorough search. We looked under the washing machine, under and in a couple of boxes, among cleaning materials, and even under the mattress on the cot. We found nothing, not even any evidence that the squirrels had ever been there.

We sat on the floor feeling desperate and guilty. As a last resort, we reviewed every item in the room.

"I don't know where else to look!" I felt defeated.

"Well, there are lots more places. We have only checked this room."

"Yeah, let's look in my room. Maybe they found a place there."

"Wouldn't you have seen if they stopped in your room?" John offered.

"I guess maybe you are right. How about the dining room?"

"Okay, we've already looked once, and there's not many places they could have hidden there."

"I didn't look under the refrigerator. Did you?"

"No." John was already on his feet and headed in that direction.

Another dry well—no squirrels. Feeling defeated, we returned to the utility room and sat on the cot. Our eyes scanned the room as if an answer awaited us, if only we could find it.

Again, we checked the obvious spots with no luck. Then, something seemed to occur to both of us at once.

"We didn't check clothes rack!" John exclaimed.

"I'm not sure why we would. That rack is disturbed every day when Mama and Daddy change clothes or hang clothes." I said this in my most superior voice.

John appeared unimpressed. "Yeah, but I think only one end of the rack is used daily."

He hadn't finished the sentence before we were back on our feet, both walking toward the end that held the less-used items.

"Shhhh...be careful and quiet." I held my arm in front of John as if to slow him down.

Together, we began to look at the rarely disturbed clothes. The Antarctic, fifty-below coat hung at the very end of the rack. Lo and behold, we saw our squirrels in the pocket of that coat—quiet, asleep, and resting up for the night's run.

John and I immediately closed the pocket, took the coat, and headed outside. We released the squirrels before we cleaned out the pocket the best we could and re-hung the coat. That night, we didn't put out any grain. We also skipped the evening prayers except to say "Thank you, God" that Daddy had not had occasion to show off the fifty-below garment in the last several weeks.

That night, he put out rat poison around the squirrel feeding area, set his traps, and went to bed with the broom and flashlight nestled next to him. Nothing happened. He did the same thing every night for about a week. Finally, the traps disappeared, the rat poison vanished, the broom stayed in the closet, and the flashlight went back in the utility room.

My dad told this story many, many times. But his telling had quite a different ending than mine. He talked about the time the largest rats he had ever seen infested our house, and how he proved rats understand what people say. His story always ended the same.

"If you want to use rat poison, be sure to whisper—or don't mention it at all—because I know those rats heard me and left the house that very night."

CHAPTER 25

My First Sleepover

"Wow. Mama, I'm so excited! Mrs. Urban will be here in an hour to pick me up. I'm spending the night with Charlene!" I repeated for the umpteenth time. Winnie the Pooh's Piglet laying in a field of daffodils could not have been happier than me. I literally smelled the good time coming!

At eleven years old, I had never experienced a night spent away from home—not with a relative, not with a friend, not with anyone unless my mom was there. As the ultimate Mama's girl, I enjoyed being home—or anywhere—with her. I knew we had limited time, and that made separation a momentous decision, though I don't think I thought about that at the time.

This was an important day!

My friend, Charlene Urban, stood out as one of the most popular girls in our sixth-grade class. As I remember, she won Class Favorite in a landslide for four years in a row. Her mother, an excellent seamstress, guaranteed Charlene wore beautiful clothes every day—and not just from the Simplicity patterns that many of our moms could manage. Some of her dresses came from McCall, Vogue, or even Butterick with more intricate and difficult patterns. Sometimes, Mrs. Urban designed and created her own styles.

The Urbans—Charlene, her mom, her dad, and her sister Annette—lived in what I considered an upscale house on the Monroe Highway. Her two-story, white-framed home nestled under the pine trees and a couple of magnolias. Camelia and gardenia bushes surrounded it. In the spring, yellow daffodils and white narcissus filled the flowerbeds. The setting, though small, gave one the feel of *Gone with the Wind.*

When visiting there many years later, I discovered an average home—well-cared for but far from being elaborate. In 1954, it occupied a spot well outside of my normal setting with light switches on the walls, closets, lamps, and more. The list seemed endless in comparison to my home.

"Well, Olevia, I'm letting you go because I know Mrs. Urban; you'll be supervised. Besides, Charlene has visited you many times, so it's fair you get to go. Still, don't forget your manners, and let me know what's happening when you have access to a phone."

It sounded to me as if Mama hadn't completely gotten on board with the idea and still worked to convince herself.

"Mama. Don't be sad. I'll be fine, and we're going to a movie today."

"What movie? I'm not sure Mrs. Urban mentioned that when she called."

"*Seven Brides for Seven Brothers!* Can you believe it? I can't wait!"

Seven Brides for Seven Brothers held center stage in most sixth-grade girls' movie discussions. As I think back, I don't know why eleven and twelve-year-olds would be drawn to the film. Maybe we just heard our older sisters talking about Howard Keel or Jane Powell. The going-to-the-movies idea excited me, no matter what the film.

To further increase the excitement, our movie of choice played at the Paramount Theater, the nicest one in downtown Alexandria. I felt like a princess going to the ball; Cinderella had nothing on me! In our family, only my sister went to movies with any regularity, and very seldom did she take me with her. As a family, we went to two movies I remember, including one my father chose. I don't remember the name of it, but I do recall it as a Bible picture of some sort, something about Moses. That summed up most of my movie experience until this most important day.

"There's their car, Mama. Mrs. Urban's about to turn into our driveway."

Once across the cattle guard, she had to negotiate another 150 yards or so up our gravel driveway to the front gate. I grabbed my bag and started to leave the porch.

"Hold on, honey." Mama touched my shoulder. "I want to talk to Mrs. Urban for a moment before you go."

"Mama, please don't make me look like a baby. I'm eleven years old!" I said indignantly, my hands on my hips.

Mama chuckled a little, gave me squeeze, and urged me on. "Okay, sweetie, take off. Behave, and make me proud of you."

I ran to the gate and got there just as Mrs. Urban pulled up.

"Hey, Olevia. Hop in the car with Charlene. I want to say hello to your mom." She started for the porch.

I thought, *Why don't you just wave, and let's go?* Of course, I said nothing. And, once in the car, it didn't matter anyway. Charlene and I had lots to talk about.

"I brought my new pajamas. Do you sleep in the same room with Annette?"

"No. Annette's room is sorta across the hall at the top of the stairs. You'll see when we get home. Mama's going to drop us off at the theater, and then she'll pick us up out front after the movie. Did you bring any snack money?"

"Yes. Mama gave me two dollars. The movie's a quarter, right?"

"I think so, but sometimes the special movies are thirty-five or forty cents. Popcorn and a Coke totaled thirty cents. So, you have plenty of money."

"Do they have a pay phone at the theater?"

"I don't know. Why?"

We were still in the driveway, and I already began to worry about leaving my mom. "No reason, really. Just wanted to know."

Mrs. Urban had climbed back into the car by now, and we were on our way. "Okay, girls, have you got your purses? Did you put a nickel in your shoe?"

"Yes, ma'am," we answered in unison and giggled.

We learned early in life that all girls carried a nickel in one of their shoes as a safety measure. Pay phones were plentiful and cost a nickel. We made certain we were able to make a phone call no matter what. Even though I did not completely understand the reasoning behind it, I never left home without a nickel in my shoe.

We enjoyed the movie, and we agreed Howard Keel was probably the most attractive old man we had ever seen. Russ Tamblyn, who played the youngest brother, seemed more our type (as if we had a type). We swooned over what heaven it would be to be married and live in Oregon someday. We also agreed that kidnapping seemed romantic but scary. We relished playing grown-up for a couple of hours, but I had called my Mama twice from the lobby when I went for snacks.

Once the movie, the cartoon, and the five minutes of World News that accompanied every movie terminated, we took our time getting outside. I relished the aroma of freshly popped corn and the bright lights and colorful décor. I glanced around as if trying to memorize a dream.

"What was your favorite part?" Charlene asked.

"The last scene! The shotgun wedding when everybody got married. What was yours?"

"Probably at the very beginning when Adam first gets to Oregon, starts singing, and then sees Milly. I don't know though—maybe just all of it."

We threw our popcorn boxes in the trash on the way out of the theater.

Mrs. Urban had parked directly in front of the theater. We climbed in, and soon we were on our way to Charlene's. Idle chit-chat made the forty-minute drive pass very quickly, and we swiftly arrived at their home. I had my bag in hand as we walked in through the kitchen. Mr. Urban sat at the table. When we ran up the stairs to her room, Charlene called out to him, "Hey, Dad, this is Olevia. She's spending the night."

"Hello, Mr. Urban." I turned my head in his direction and waved.

He just smiled and waved a hand. I barely noticed even that. The house had all my attention as my eyes scanned in every direction. It turned out not to be a two-story house, but rather a one-story with a converted attic. The stairs went from the first floor to the attic to two separate A-frame rooms—one for Charlene and one for Annette. Each room had a window on one side and a closet on the other. Charlene's bed immediately captured my attention.

"I love the comforter on your bed. It looks like strawberry ice cream and is as soft as whipped cream! The pillows could be the cherries on top."

We both laughed.

I glanced over at Annette's side of the room to see one decorated completely different from Charlene's.

Charlene seemed eager to add some details about her room. "Mama made the curtains, but she bought the bedspread." Her eyes scanned around. "Those curtains are made from pink chiffon. I think she's working on a quilt for me. She's already finished Annette's."

"Your curtains look like cotton candy."

Again, we laughed together.

But before I could investigate everything, I asked, "Do you have an upstairs phone?"

"Yes. Right there on the table between our rooms."

"Can I use it? I just want to call my mom really quick. She likes to know when I get home."

"Sure."

That night is still a blur in my mind. I remember playing canasta with Mr. and Mrs. Urban. I remember whispering in bed about everything and everybody. I remember their dog, Yuma—so named because they got her in Yuma, Arizona. I remember looking out the window, each of us wishing upon a star, swearing never to reveal our wish to anyone and then telling each other later. I don't remember the wish, but I do remember calling my mom once more just before going to bed.

Breakfast was magical!

"Are these waffles?" I asked. I had certainly heard of them but had never eaten one.

"Yes, they are, Olevia. Do you like them?" Mrs. Urban added a bowl of fresh strawberries and whipped cream to the table. It looked more like dessert to me than breakfast, and they smelled scrumptious.

"Is it okay, Mrs. Urban, if I call Mama to tell her I am eating waffles?"

"Sure. Why?"

"It's my first time to ever eat them. We usually have biscuits with grits or eggs or bacon or something for breakfast. Sometimes, we might have a pancake. I want to tell her about these waffles."

"Go ahead." Mrs. Urban chuckled under her breath.

Home by noon, I had been out of the house less than twenty-four hours, but it seemed much longer. When Mrs.

Urban's car entered our driveway, I could see Mama in a rocking chair on the front porch. Once the car stopped, I made a quick exit.

"Thanks so much, Mrs. Urban, for having me over. I had a really good time. See you at school, Charlene."

I almost ran from the car to hug my mama.

"Mama, I'm glad I'm home."

"Me too, honey. Did you have a good time?"

"Yes, ma'am, but I don't think I want to do it again very soon."

Mama smiled and gave me a hug. I felt much as a three-week old blind puppy must feel when he's lost track of his mom and finally finds suckle again. A warm comforter of safety and familiarity engulfed me.

"Come on. Let's get your overnight bag unpacked, and you can tell me everything."

With her arm around my shoulders, we shared every detail of the time of our separation. Mama even promised to get a waffle iron so we could have waffles at home.

It would be three years before I spent another night away from home alone again, and there was never another one as clear a memory as this one.

CHAPTER 26

HANNAH LEAVES HOME

Hannah, Robert, Peg, and Suse.

"Hannah, have you got everything packed?" Mama called from the kitchen as I watched her pack a lunch for Hannah's trip.

"Yes, ma'am. I'm ready," she replied. "Mr. Smith should be here any minute."

"Honey, are you sure this is something you want to do?"

Mama wandered into the living room carrying the brown bag with two fried chicken drumsticks, a thigh, and a breast. The smell was almost good enough to taste. Mama made the best fried chicken in the South. That opinion was shared by anyone ever lucky enough to taste a piece!

"Here, Hannah, there's enough here to share with Bert."

Bert Smith, our school bus driver and good friend, had volunteered to drive Hannah to begin her next adventure. Her time saving money while working part-time in high school and full-time after graduation paid off. Hannah personified the *Little Engine that Could*. With a little help from Daddy, she personally signed the contract to pay her own way.

"Baton Rouge is a long way, and you've never been away from home. You can still change your mind?" Mama's voice held a bit of fear and resignation, as if she had already lost the battle but needed to fire one more shot.

"No, Mama! I'm eighteen years old, and I won't be gone but nine months!" Hannah frowned, frustrated with Mama's attitude and determined to be accepted as an adult.

"I'm going to Draughn's Business College, and I'll be home most weekends. I'm not even staying in their dorm. I don't know if I'll like that family *you* chose for me. I'm an adult." Her voice had an edge to it—not a disrespectful edge, but a tone that said, 'I make my own decisions.'

Mama fussed around some more, tears falling as she warned Hannah of all the pitfalls facing a young woman on her own in a big city in 1954. She looked so forlorn that, for a minute, I felt a bit sad. But I quickly recovered, reminding myself of the benefits Hannah's absence would bring to me.

I eagerly watched the taillights of Mr. Smith's car taking Hannah out of my day-to-day life. I would soon have control of my very own closet! Our eight-room house had only one tiny closet, located in Hannah's room and belonging exclusively to Hannah. I slept in that room, but Hannah, being eight years older, made and enforced *her* rules.

The small closet was two feet deep and six feet long. It had a bar across the top for hanging clothes, a rail at the bottom for shoes, and a three-foot opening. There was no door.

Only Hannah's clothes and Hannah's shoes occupied that sacred place. Her secrets lay in a box with a tape lock around it on the floor in the corner. I wondered if her Rainbow Girls book was hidden there. *Checking that out is first on my agenda!*

All day, I stayed next to my mom in hopes she would lighten up a bit. She didn't, but my anticipated prize drowned out Mama's plight. When the car was out of sight, I ran to my closet.

Funny how when you get what you want, it is not always as sweet as you imagined.

I coveted that closet and visualized my own things in that special place. At long last, I moved up the chain of command. I loved my sister, but I craved to be the sole occupant in the room where I had been a visitor for the last six years. Hannah exercised her friend privileges, allowing her to banish me from the room when she had company. Her clothes hung in the closet. She created the radio rules and, if she chose *Inner Sanctum*—a scary radio drama—in the middle of the night in total darkness, she did so despite my pleas. I could hear those conversations replayed in my mind.

"Lay still."

"I'm still."

"You moved."

"No. I didn't!"

"Please!"

"I'll be still."

My sister and I shared that, or a similar, conversation on many 1950's Saturday nights. Our twin beds, separated by Hannah's radio, were close enough for a location change in a single bound. Most nights, it did not matter.

But the sound of the creaking door in *Inner Sanctum* motivated my limited athletic ability. Hannah's bed-sharing rules—no touching, lay flat, and don't move—were strictly enforced. Any infraction meant expulsion.

The onset of the final Carters' Little Liver Pills commercial signaled the end of the episode and my misery!

Those memories had me champing at the bit for the fresh air of autonomy. It wasn't as if Hannah would be gone for good; she had enrolled in a secretarial course at Draughan's Business College in Baton Rouge and would live with a family near the campus. She would spend most weekends at home and complete her course in nine short months. Still, a chance at having my own space had the allure of a drug to an addict—and perhaps the same reward of diminishing returns.

That afternoon, I took possession of MY ROOM with visions of peace and importance. I was already thinking of what school friend I might invite to spend the night.

Mama cried off and on all evening. And, when it was time for bed, my own reality set in. I felt so lonesome I could cry, paraphrasing a Hank Williams song. My heart hurt as if there were a tiny hole created by a missing connection. The security, the belonging established by the pecking order, and the things that translate into a safe family cocoon were rocked to the foundation.

An era had ended, and I felt a cold wind, foreboding for the future. I teetered on the edge of security and the chasm of the unknown.

In Hannah's absence, we focused more on her presence than we did before she left. She and her expected visits were the center of everyday activities When would she come home? What would we have to eat when she came home? Where does she sleep at school? Would we ever get to visit her?

Mama orchestrated a letter-writing time, every other day, to keep the family fabric tightly sewn. Our letters chronicled the smallest of details from whether we had turned on the radio that day, to who might be coming to the house, to what John and I had discovered in the barn. We shared our lives as if she had never left—maybe more than when she had been with us. I still have many of those letters today. As I reviewed them before writing this story, two caught my attention and brought a smile. The first one John wrote:

Dear Hannah. We miss you. I found a worm having a baby in the barn today. I think. Love, your brother, John.

Mine:

Dear Hannah. Mama cried almost all day today. Daddy said if she didn't stop crying, he would drive to Baton Rouge to pick you up. Please write to Mama more. Love, Olevia.

She came home most weekends, bumming rides from friends at school. Mama worried when a guy drove her because it was too many hours in the car alone; she worried when a girlfriend was at the wheel because girls shouldn't be on the road alone.

A no-win situation existed for Mama and perhaps for Hannah as well.

Every Saturday, Mama guessed where Hannah might be in route, from early morning until she walked through the door. When she arrived, Mama ran to greet her as if she had been gone for many months.

"Are you okay? You look like you've lost weight? Do you get plenty to eat? Are you sleeping?" Mama's rapid-fire questions accompanied multiple hugs.

"Mama, don't squeeze me so hard!" Hannah laughed.

We all settled down in the living room to hear the details of Hannah's adventure. I don't have a clear memory of those conversations, probably because the adventure I experienced bore little resemblance to hers. The adventure that occupied my mind every day was learning the new pecking order in the family.

Hannah never really came to live full-time at home again, although she completed the nine-month course in six and moved back to the house for almost a year. During that time, she was the visitor, and I was the resident. She no longer carried the title of boss but more like that of a live-in tenant.

Soon after Hannah returned to Tioga, she began to date Robert Breneman again. They had spent time together in high school before he enlisted in the military. While stationed in Guam, his correspondence with Hannah turned serious, and she looked forward to his return.

During the day, she worked at Life of Georgia Insurance Company. At night, she labored over a notebook, planning the wedding of her dreams. She chose songs, bridesmaids, a bridal gown, and attendants' dresses, meticulously crafting every inch of the affair. She didn't count on Robert's constitution, though I don't know why.

While still in high school, he came to our house for one infamous dinner still discussed with humor. In high school, Robert was an excitable sort of guy with a weak stomach to boot. After he and Hannah attended a few movies together, Mama called Mrs. Breneman suggesting Robert come for supper and hot chocolate afterward.

On the following Saturday evening, a nervous sixteen-year-old Robert—with a brand-new driver's license—maneuvered his dad's Hudson up our hill. He wore a suit and tie and looked uncomfortable before Daddy even said hello.

Hannah paced the floor in the kitchen while, in the living room, Daddy interrogated Robert. My mouth stayed closed, but my ears were wide open as I listened from just inside Daddy's bedroom.

"Your dad's in the Army, ain't he?"

"No, sir, he's in the Air Force."

"Career man, is he? I don't reckon I'd like the service much. Someone always telling you what you can or can't do."

"Yes, sir. He's career. He's been in for over twenty years already."

"Lot of traveling in the service. You like that kind of thing? How do you know where home is? A man needs roots, don't you think?"

At that point, Hannah rushed in to save Robert and announce that supper sat on the table. We gathered around to enjoy the fragrance and taste of Mama's roast beef with all the trimmings. If fried chicken had not been her specialty, roast beef would have been. The aroma drew your attention anywhere you might be in the house. Rarely did we have to be called to a roast beef dinner.

As food passed from person to person, Daddy continued to harass Robert.

"Son, you didn't take much beef. Beef's good for a man. Here, have a little more."

"Yes, sir. I like beef, but my stomach's a little queasy tonight."

"What's the matter? Something you ate?"

"I don't know, sir."

"Here, take some beets, son. Mary makes good, pickled beets. One time, she tried to poison me with them though. She used rubbing alcohol 'stead of vinegar to pickle them," Daddy commented without a hint of smile.

"John, you know that was a mistake!" Mama smiled, trying to save the situation. "Robert, are you feelin' okay? You look a little peaked."

"No, ma'am. I think I need to lay down."

Mama helped Robert into bed. Hannah got a cool washcloth for his head, and Daddy called Mr. Breneman to come get him. Johnny and I continued to eat and giggle right through Mr. Breneman's arrival and quick departure.

During the three-year-plus interval since that visit, Hannah and Robert had been together, broken up, gone their separate ways, and now were together again. He was home on leave, and their relationship turned serious. They decided to get married in January 1956.

Robert felt it was his obligation to talk to Daddy to get his permission for the union, as was the custom in the 1950s. I'm not sure that permission carries much weight anymore.

Mama and Hannah forewarned Daddy as to the purpose of this Sunday afternoon visit and begged him to behave. His agreement to do so did not settle any nerves. Wearing his overalls, Daddy sat on the front porch staring off into the distance when Robert arrived. He mounted the steps slowly but appeared confident when he stuck out his hand to Daddy.

"Hello, Mr. Yeager."

Daddy nodded his head in recognition of Robert's presence and indicated a rocking chair.

"Sit down, son. Hannah says you got somethin' to say."

"Yes, sir. Hannah and I have known each other for some time now, and—"

"Ya'll went to school together for a while, didn't you?"

"Yes sir. What I'm trying to say is—"

"Just a minute, son. Let me get my glasses."

"Yes, sir."

Daddy went into the house, got his glasses, came back, and sat back down in the rocking chair.

"What were you saying, son?"

"Mr. Yeager, Hannah and I are—"

Daddy leaped from his chair. "Look at that, son. What's he doing?"

With that, Daddy ran down the steps, out the gate, and all the way down the driveway to the cattle gap. Mama and Hannah hurried out to investigate the commotion and found Robert sitting in stunned silence. John and I stared from our hiding place under the porch, stifling our giggles.

Hannah had tears in her voice when she said, "What is Daddy doing, Mama? Why does he have to be like this? Everything's ruined."

"Everything's not ruined, honey. Your daddy will be back in a minute. Robert, would you like a glass of sweet tea?"

"No, ma'am. What do you think happened to him, Mrs. Yeager?"

"I don't know, son. Let's just wait and see."

She put her arm around Hannah as they went back inside. By this time, Daddy was making his way back up the hill to the house with no obvious urgency. He chatted with Mr. Curry, who stood on his side of the fence. Then he petted Queenie the mule and called out to Grunt, my dog, to get on home.

As he climbed the steps, he seemed ready to continue the conversation. "Now what were you saying, son?" He nodded and sat down. "I left my jacket down there on the fence. Looked like someone was stealing it. It's a good jacket. Wouldn't want to lose it."

Daddy wasn't carrying a jacket, and I'd never known him to leave one hanging on the fence. I figured if someone had been trying to steal something, Daddy wouldn't be home yet. He would have chased them all the way to Alexandria if that was what it took to get it back.

In one breath, Robert got to the point of his visit by rushing to say, "Mr. Yeager, Hannah and I want to get married, and I'm asking for your permission to take her hand in marriage."

"Son, she can't cook, and she can't clean, but she's pretty book smart. If you take her hand, you get all of her. I hope you know what you're in for. Now, let's go eat. I think Mary's got supper on the table."

The next morning, January 23, 1956, Hannah and Robert drove Mr. Breneman's car to Mississippi to get married. On their second stop in the state, they were successful. Once the I do's were done, they returned the same night to the Trailer Courts—the motel/cottage complex in Lee Heights where his parents lived when stationed in Louisiana.

Tuesday, they came by the house to let us know the deed was done.

Hannah leaned on the counter and said, "Mama, we're going to Missouri to live. Robert's stationed there now, and we're leaving this weekend."

Mama nodded slowly, looking like she just heard about someone who died. She began to cry, and I cried because she cried. Hannah hugged us both and assured us it was not the end of the world.

Meanwhile, Daddy and Robert talked on the front porch. I could faintly hear snippets of their conversation between our tears.

"Son, how are ya'll gonna get to Missouri? Have you thought about that? Is your daddy selling you, his car?"

"No, sir. I guess we can go on a bus. I have my travel pay."

"What are you gonna do when you get there? How're you gonna get around?"

"I don't know, sir. We'll try to live on base, I guess."

"Why don't you look for a used car? If you find something you like, you can take it up to Rush McCarty's to be sure the engine's good."

"I don't want to go into debt, sir, and I don't even know if I have any credit."

"Well, that's a good thing, son, but you can't walk everywhere." He chuckled under his breath as he got up to go into the house. His posture and pace indicated pride in his own wise humor.

****

In a day or two, Robert and Hannah drove a black 1952 Ford in our driveway.

Daddy went out to meet them. "Looks like a pretty good car, son."

"Yes, sir." Robert grinned. "We haven't signed the papers yet. Hannah wanted you to see it first."

"How much is it?"

"Two hundred dollars."

"Do you have two hundred dollars?"

Robert continued to walk around the car while Hannah spoke up. "Daddy, maybe you could help us with that. We'll pay you back with interest. You could draw up a loan paper or something." She tilted her head and made her eyes wide. "Do you think you could help us out?"

"Well, Hannah, I don't know. Why don't Robert and I take a ride in it? Son, you get in over there. I'll drive."

Hannah stood in the driveway wringing her hands until they came back. Without a word, Daddy walked into the house, sat down at his desk, and wrote out a check for two hundred dollars. He handed it to Hannah as she and Robert came through the door.

"I expect to be paid back."

"Yes, sir. You will be."

That Saturday, January 28, 1956, we all stood on the porch waving goodbye while a cold rain fell on the black 1952 Ford taking my not-yet-twenty-year-old sister to a new life in a new place.

Her closet was completely empty and had become MY CLOSET at long last.

Somehow, the jubilation I anticipated did not materialize.

CHAPTER 27

A TOUCH OF CASH

After Thanksgiving in 1955, a new Christmas tradition formed in our family.

We didn't have our Christmas tree up yet, as that tradition required a live tree that was cut, erected, and decorated on the nearest Saturday to December 10. I have no idea how that became the chosen day; it just was. And, as an adult, I continued the custom in my home for over forty years.

But tree decorating has little to do with this story, other than as a custom on which this newly born event, seemingly spur-of-the-moment, became a tradition and changed every Christmas to come.

John and I wandered onto the front porch with no particular destination in mind.

"Where are ya'll going?" Daddy asked.

"Down to The Pines. Might see a good Christmas tree," I called over my shoulder as we headed for the front gate.

I am not sure why Daddy sat in a rocking chair, drinking coffee, on a Monday. He often worked six days a week, sometimes choosing to work weekends. He rarely took a Monday off.

"Hey. Hold up there, Olevia!"

"What's up, Daddy?"

"I want ya'll to take a little ride with me."

"A ride? Where?"

John and I were on Christmas break from school. From Thanksgiving to Christmas, we spent long hours talking about Christmas morning, about Christmas Eve, about what we hoped to get for Christmas, and about what we had gotten the last year.

This year, we had even more to discuss: Hannah was about to be married and move to Missouri with her Air Force husband. 1955 would be the last year the five of us gathered around the Christmas tree. Mama's health declined, and though we didn't really believe this would be our final Christmas together, it still felt more special than usual. We hoped the Currys would come up for eggnog because they brought a sense of celebration by telling jokes that made everyone laugh.

The subjects were endless, and it seemed John and I never tired of talking. That was more or less our plan for the day, but we stopped in our tracks at Daddy's mention of a ride. A ride with Daddy certainly came out of left field.

"Where are we going, Daddy?" I asked again.

We went places as a family, and Daddy might take Johnny with him on some errand, but Daddy's reputation did not lend itself to anyone expecting him to take two kids on a joy ride.

He got up from his chair. "Never mind where. Just tell your mama ya'll be back in an hour or so."

I ran in and told Mama, who seemed as surprised as I, but said nothing other than the usual warning for riding with Daddy.

"You kids ride in the backseat, sit back, and be still."

"We will," I replied on behalf of both of us.

Within minutes, Johnny and I were in the back seat of Daddy's 1953 Henry J. Daddy was at the wheel.

Driving a car well was not among Daddy's many talents. Due to a trait Mama indicated as common among railroad engineers, Daddy drove at top speed and tended to turn in the direction he looked.

John leaned over the seat. "Daddy, where are we going?"

Daddy's brief glance in his direction and re-focus on the road ahead provided the expected redeposit of Johnny against the backseat.

"Don't get ahead of yourself, boy. You'll know where we are going when we get there!"

That reply quieted both of us. We looked at each other and out the windows but said nothing as we traveled the eight miles to downtown Alexandria.

Daddy pulled into the Rapides Parish Bank parking lot, turned off the motor, and stepped out of the car. Before we could get out, he leaned back into the open window. "Wait here, kids. I won't be long."

And he wasn't. He exited the bank, sliding what looked like two white envelopes into the pocket of his overalls.

"Did you get something, Daddy?" John asked.

Not a word—just that half-smile he did when he knew something that we didn't.

I chimed in. "Is this where we were going?"

Out of character, Daddy laughed. "No. It's where we have been," he said as he backed the car out of the parking space.

John and I again glanced at each other, and we both shrugged our shoulders. As we headed toward Tioga, my thoughts drifted between *I wonder what the surprise is?* to *I wonder if there is one?*

Then we approached the intersection of the Kingsville Cutoff and Highway 71. Daddy chose the Shreveport Highway rather than the most direct route home.

"Daddy, are we going home?" John asked and received no response.

I could see the envelopes in his pocket, and it occurred to me we might be going to the post office. Before I could share my suspicions with John, Daddy took a sharp right turn toward Tioga. By the time John and I recovered from the turn, he took another one, this time into the Merritt's General Store parking lot. We were still righting ourselves when Daddy opened the driver's side door, stepped out, and leaned the seat forward.

"Get out over here," he instructed.

We crawled out and stood expectantly as Daddy rolled his cheek between his thumb and forefinger and stared off into the space behind us. After what seemed a lifetime, he spoke again.

"Do ya'll know what a Christmas Fund is?"

"I think I do, Daddy," I answered before John had a chance. "At the beginning of school every year, the teacher asks us if we want to sign up for a Christmas Savings Account. Anyone who signs up can bring their money each week to the teacher for a deposit, or their parents can do it. You said you didn't want us being a part of that."

"And I don't, Olevia. We don't need no teachers telling you kids what to do with our money. But your mama wanted something special for you this year, with your sister about to leave and everything."

With that, he reached into his lapel pocket and withdrew the two envelopes. He handed one to each of us.

"This is your Christmas Cash. Take it in the store, and Mr. Belgard will cash it for you. You can spend it on anything you want to. Take your time. I'm going on home. Ya'll can walk. It's a nice day."

He settled back into the car and drove off before John or I even spoke. We tore open our envelopes and pulled out ten-dollar checks. For some seconds, we were the ones who now stared—not off into space, but at our checks.

Our finances usually went like this: Daddy gave us each one dollar every Sunday night or Monday morning. Fifty cents paid for a week of hot school lunches. The other fifty cents made up our discretionary funds, typically spent at the school canteen. Mama gave us money for the occasional movie, school event, or whatever might be needed, but Daddy did not. To have him hand us ten dollars to spend felt like the world turned upside down, easily compared to expecting a hamburger when steak is served.

"What are you going to buy?" John asked.

"I don't know."

We rushed up the steps and immediately separated once inside the store. John ran to the toy area, while I went to the more adult Christmas displays. There were vases, dishes, and dish towels—all bearing some holiday decoration. Of course, the usual perfumes, body powder, and bubble bath occupied their own area along with the shaving creams, razors, and wallets. The list seemed endless.

Indeed, on none of my visits to Merritt's had I ever taken note of the displays, decorations, and opportunities to shop for anything other than groceries.

"Hey, John," I called out.

He came running over. "Yeah?"

"Did you see this electric train?" I asked as I wandered into the toy area. "I didn't even know Merritt's had those."

"I saw it. I didn't know they had a lot of this stuff. Maybe they only have it for Christmas or something."

"Probably. Have you picked any gifts yet?"

"Just one." He said as he opened his bag to lift out a bottle of Old Spice shaving cologne. "Do you think Daddy will like this?"

"Yeah. You don't have to buy each thing one at a time," I said as I showed him my carry-cart.

"Where did you get that?"

"Right there at the end of the aisle."

"Okay. I'm getting one and going to keep shopping."

"Be careful not to pick up more stuff than you can pay for."

John had already moved on and likely didn't even hear my warning. We felt rich!

When we left the store, some hours later, we each had a bag to carry on the one mile walk home. I remember only one item I purchased—a leaf-shaped candy dish edged in gold. I bought it for Mama, and it turned out to be the last gift I ever gave her. Other than another knickknack I got for her at the Shreveport Fair, that candy dish is the only gift I recall having given to her.

The feeling of an unexpected windfall of cash—my first Christmas bonus, so to speak—never left me. Life has blessed me with opportunities to share the experience, every year, with some unsuspecting person. Sometimes, it is a Walmart shopper standing in the layaway line. Sometimes, it's a friend that I know to be down on their luck. Sometimes it is a family our office staff chooses to benefit, and other times it is a homeless person. The abundance of choices can make it difficult to choose, but each time I remember my own Touch of Cash, and the blessing is multiplied.

Mama died the following year on October 26. I do not have the candy dish today. I am not sure it still exists and, if so, where. I do know one place it will always be—vividly etched in my memory of that most special day.

I am forever grateful for December of 1955.

CHAPTER 28

January 1955 – July 1956

The year 1955 began just as every year in my life had begun. Mama seemed a little sicker than before, but she had been sick almost as long as I could remember. I did not accept that her death could be imminent, despite her efforts to prepare me. I turned twelve in November, and her upcoming forty-fifth birthday fell in December. From where I stood, that seemed old anyway. Her hair was gray with a thinness not before evident. She seemed a shadow of her former self. I imagined most elders talked about dying, or maybe that was just how I could cope with it.

However, not every day was a bad day. Mama made extreme efforts to create and maintain a pleasant household. Indeed, 1955 included a lot of life-changing activities for me, and it ended on a high note.

John and I returned to school the day after Labor Day with the same attitudes, fears, and confidences as in the past. As a fifth grader, he continued in grammar school, and I, as a seventh grader, attended classes in the junior high building.

Changing classes, attending Mrs. Henderson's hygiene sessions, and shaving my legs were among the dozens of things new to me. Classes taught by men were a first as well—as was fantasizing about boys who didn't know I existed.

Moving to the junior high building seemed to be a peek into the grown-up world. Multiple classes in different rooms with different teachers were not a challenge, but they added a teenage feeling to the day.

"Hey, Charlene!" I called out to a friend who shared Mrs. Henderson's homeroom. She leaned against the wall studying the schedule received that morning.

"What's your next class?"

"That's what I'm trying to figure out!"

We laughed together as we compared our schedules.

"Looks like you have World History. That would be Mr. Till's class. I think he's in the last room, down near the bathrooms."

She looked relieved and asked, "And where are you going?"

"Mrs. Collins. I've got Pre-Algebra. I think her room's next door to Mr. Till's."

We walked together down the hall and talked as our gathered skirts with petticoats galore rustled next to each other.

Charlene mentioned the older class first, saying, "I saw an eighth grader this morning in the bathroom. She had on a straight skirt and was busy drawing lips to fill in with lipstick. Annette's done that before. I haven't. Have you?"

"No. I don't even wear lipstick!" We laughed again. "Will your mama let you wear straight skirts?"

"Annette does, and Mama has a lot of patterns. So, I guess so."

Annette, Charlene's older sister, was already in high school. She often served as a barometer to us when we talked girl-stuff.

We reached our destinations and parted ways. I met Mrs. Collins for the first time. A large, tall (likely approaching six-foot) lady, I think she was of German or Austrian heritage but without an accent. I'm sure she lived in the area. Daddy did not have kind feelings toward anything German—perhaps a hangover from World War II—even though he himself claimed German heritage with a family tree back to the 1700s.

Based on her looks and Daddy's influence, I felt a little frightened when I first entered her classroom. I found a seat near the front, not the row or seat closest to her desk. Mrs. Collins appeared to be a no-nonsense woman, and I felt a little distance might be warranted. Once she had solicited our names via roll call, the room immediately transformed into a serious classroom.

"Class, I expect your undivided attention when I'm talking, and homework is to be turned in on time. Any late assignment will not be given a passing grade."

She glanced around the room. A little chit-chat could be heard going on between a couple of boys, seemingly ignored by Mrs. Collins who proceeded to teach.

"Does anyone here know what invert means?"

I think we all knew, but no one wanted to be the center of attention. So, hands were not raised, and the two boys continued to quietly whisper.

She explained, "Invert means to turn upside down." She wrote a fraction on the blackboard: one-fourth is 1/4. "When we invert that fraction, it becomes four divided by 1 or 4/1. Invert will be used a lot in our pre-algebra class."

She stood there quietly for ten or fifteen seconds before turning to face the class. "Larry, can you tell me what invert means?"

Larry Brady, one of the whispering boys, also stood out as one of the most popular in class. He had been voted Class Favorite multiple times during our grammar school years. He had a short stature, but he breathed "handsome" and Mr. Personality in the opinion of most girls. I'm sure those facts did not escape Mrs. Collins' knowledge and likely played a large part in her choice of which whispering boy to call attention to. I cannot even remember who the other boy was!

A dozen pins dropping would have been heard in the absolute silence of our class while we awaited Larry's answer.

"No, ma'am," he answered without hesitation.

"Larry, please come to the front of the class."

Larry stood and walked confidently—maybe even a little cocky—to stand facing Mrs. Collins.

What happened next is burned into my memory. It's as if I didn't really see it happen, I only saw the result. Mrs. Collins bent down and grabbed Larry by the ankles. And, suddenly, he was suspended in the air. Coins, pencils, a wallet, some keys, and even his protractor and compass fell from his pockets. The look of surprise on his face probably matched our own as we watched and listened.

Mrs. Collins went on. "Class, this is what invert looks like when applied to a young man who was not listening to my explanation."

She carefully lowered Larry to the floor, where he sheepishly picked up his things and returned to his seat with a lot less bounce in his step.

I had never seen such a thing, and that image became my first real, in-person, experience of how different junior high could be.

A second incident exposing the extent to which life could change quickly began a week later. We settled into the everyday routine that had become almost normal. That is, until the next bombshell.

Mrs. Henderson, my homeroom teacher, announced that the half hour of free time following lunch would now be devoted to hygiene classes. The girls stayed in her classroom, and the boys went to the gym to meet with the physical education teacher. It sounded ordinary-like and certainly nothing special … until the first class.

Mrs. Henderson placed a towel over the eight-by-eight-inch opening in the classroom door and explained why access for boys to peek in should be avoided.

"This is a girls' only time. We are going to learn about our bodies and how we should behave when we are with boys."

What? I felt entirely familiar with my body and unconcerned about how to behave with boys. Still, it did pique my interest a little bit.

She began with some drawings on the blackboard and some posters. She explained what being female meant from a physical standpoint. That exhausted our first half-hour meeting. I now knew what my insides looked like, and I wondered if the boys learned anything about our physical make-up; we learned nothing of theirs. We were told they could be pushy.

In a couple of days, she directed the lesson toward our responsibility in managing relationships with boys. Making ourselves attractive to boys without looking trampy (to quote Mrs. Henderson) took skill and the right attitude.

She detailed the application of make-up, emphasizing it should be a thin layer not detectable except in the result of it looking natural. She demonstrated so we could see her goal.

"Sharon, please come forward. Take a seat."

Sharon's nervousness revealed itself in her blushed face and shaky smile.

"Have a seat here, honey." Mrs. Henderson pointed to a chair next to her desk. She then picked up a wet washcloth from a bowl on her desk.

"Okay. First, we need to remove any oils that might be on her face," she explained as she wiped Sharon's face carefully from top to bottom.

Sharon sat straight up in the chair and seemed to relax as the demonstration continued. Mrs. Henderson provided a blow-by-blow interpretation of exactly what she wanted us to see.

"Notice, girls, I will make up one side of Sharon's face as it should be done. Only a thin layer of make-up is needed to enhance the natural beauty of her skin. We'll add a slight touch of blush and a minimum of eyeliner. At this point, we'll avoid eye shadow and mascara." All the while, she made up one side of Sharon's face using the technique she advocated.

"Now, can you girls see how beautiful Sharon looks?"

She had Sharon sit at an angle where only the made-up side was clearly visible. Personally, I didn't see much difference, except maybe the blush. Apparently, others did because the oohing and aahing filled the room as if the wicked witch's face had been transformed into the fairy godmothers.

Mrs. Henderson then performed the same procedure on the other side of Sharon's face. This time, she used a heavy layer of what appeared to me to be a much darker make-up. On top of that, she added a heavy blush, eyeliner, eye shadow, and mascara. The wicked witch who had disappeared now reappeared on the left side of Sharon's face—no doubt to show the advantages of a light make-up approach.

Now, everyone laughed and made various comments. I felt a little sorry for Sharon, but she joined in the fun when Mrs. Henderson handed her a mirror.

Class was then dismissed, and Sharon washed her face in the bathroom.

Clothes took up the following class. Skirts must not cup our bottoms. Bras must be worn. Dresses must not be too short—the mini-skirt had not yet even become a figment of our generation's imaginations! Mrs. Henderson talked about penny loafers and how they were useful in storing that emergency nickel we must always carry. These classes were beginning to hold my interest. Maybe I did have something to learn.

"Girls, you have reached the age where boys will become a part of your social life."

We all looked at each other, and I'm fairly sure we all were thinking the same thing—*I'm not allowed to date until I'm sixteen!* And that birthday was years away. As it turned out, some of my friends did begin dating in the eighth grade. I did not belong to the dating group, and neither did most of my other peers.

Of all her teaching, the how-to-say-no session rated highest with all of us, but I do not have a clear memory of specific examples of the instructions. I remember the physical tools we had, as listed earlier. I also have a vague recollection of the need to smile and to let the guy feel in charge but never, ever lose control. I understood there was a clearly outlined goal, but reaching that goal seemed complicated and outside my ability.

As a late bloomer, my female plight had not yet occurred to me. The objective seemed to be inviting the boys to look. However, that goal included guard rails, and the entire game was lost if the boys looked too much or not at all. Getting the attention of boys and then rebuffing that attention in a way that further encouraged them seemed like walking a tightrope. Still, I now had the tools to at least wear the proper attire should I wish to begin the balancing act.

In October, our entire seventh grade class had an opportunity to attend the Shreveport State Fair. My girlfriends and I spent hours talking about Shreveport, as if the city name substituted for the trip and the activities—the entire event.

"Hey, Olevia, are you ready for Shreveport?"

"I don't know what I'm going to wear. I'm trying to get Mama to take me shopping for pedal pushers. What are you wearing?"

Another of the girls chimed in. "My mother's making my outfit: black, lined, wool pants with a V-neck top. It's a Simplicity pattern."

"We have a sewing machine, but my mama doesn't sew anymore. I wish she'd take me to Wellans to shop," I responded.

In fact, my mama had never sewn much beyond replacing a missing button or putting a patch on John's blue jeans. The machine had been bought for Hannah and, unless Hannah used it, the Singer treadle machine collected dust while it waited for the next user.

"Wellans? Do you shop there?"

She knew I didn't. Everybody knew shopping at Wellans did not fall among my activities. Wellans could be described as the Neiman Marcus of Alexandria's department stores, and it was a step or two above my spending level—and most of theirs as well.

"Not really. It's usually Pennys, but Wellans has a gorgeous blue pedal pusher set in the window. I saw it when Daddy took me to town to get school shoes. He thinks I shouldn't want to wear pants, but I do."

And so, the talk began. First, about what we should wear, and later, with whom we should sit on the bus. That conversation gave us an opportunity to sound grown-up. We play-acted situations where implementing Mrs. Henderson's boy-attracting techniques could prove useful.

Although on the fringe of the popular group of girls—the outside fringe—I was still a member. Fortunately, good grades offered a way in, albeit a back door and lower rung. Thus, I met the qualifications to belong, despite a continued inept approach to social activities.

On the third Saturday of October, I boarded a school bus in the pre-dawn hours. I was armed with ten dollars for spending, a free ticket to get in, and a sack lunch. The teachers prepared the seating arrangements on the way to Shreveport: girls sat with girls, boys sat with boys, and the chaperones sat in the front of the bus. The only exceptions were couples going steady, and none of my group qualified.

The two-and-a-half-hour bus trip was filled with talk of where we wanted to sit on the way home and with whom. During the day, we would be sizing up the boys to determine who appeared to be either the most attractive and/or the most approachable. My seat partner, Valda Ingram, and I began our pursuit of the perfect conquest almost before we were off the bus.

"Hey! Ya'll wanna get snow cones with us?" We approached a couple of likely candidates. Valda and I both smiled and attempted some sort of come-hither look.

The guys' response let us know the look may not have totally failed—or maybe, they were simply being polite. "Nah. We're about to get on the roller coaster. Are ya'll going to ride it?"

"Yeah." Valda turned to me. "Let's ride the roller coaster before we get a snow cone. Want to?"

"I've never ridden a roller coaster. I'm not sure I want to. Why don't we shop for souvenirs? I haven't spent any of my money yet."

"No." In a whisper, she added, "We might get to sit with them if we ride the roller coaster. Don't be a baby."

"I'm not going. It looks too scary. I'm shopping."

Valda wasted no time in choosing the boys' company over mine, and the three of them climbed on the roller coaster. No one missed me.

Despite my ruined chances for snagging a prized seat partner, I had a good time that day. I shopped and bought a gold pillbox—a one-inch square engraved with my name. With careful budgeting, I also bought a shell heart pin crisscrossed with my name in gold and a small candy dish for Mama. Sitting alone at a picnic table, I enjoyed Mama's fried chicken and white bread. With Mama's chicken, no additional sides were needed. Talking about it now makes my mouth water…

The ride home, after dark and with no prior seat assignments, had no effect on Valda and me, as we continued to sit together. Apparently, the roller coaster approach did not work out. Chaperones sat amongst us instead of up front, reducing all ardors from a fire to an ember. That first kiss sneaked in the back of the bus eluded not only me, but most of us.

Halloween and Thanksgiving created little fanfare at our house. Trick-or-treating required that we be driven to town, a treat not apt to happen in my family. Indeed, to this day, I've never been trick-or-treating except to accompany one of my own kids. Nevertheless, I have one vivid Halloween memory.

As I put away some towels Mama and I had folded, I noticed what appeared to be some sort of costume in the bathroom closet. It was all white and looked like a full-length robe with a pointed hood.

"Hey, Mama, I saw a Halloween costume in the closet. Whose is it?"

"We don't have any Halloween costumes. What are you talking about?"

I ran back, grabbed the outfit, and returned. "This, Mama." I held it up for her to see.

She immediately went pale. "Give that to me. That belongs to your daddy. It's not exactly a Halloween costume, and it's nothing you need to be concerned with. I thought John had this stored in his locked trunk."

She seemed almost afraid as she took the clothing back to the linen closet and placed it on the very top shelf. "I'll remind John to put it away when he gets home."

As weird as her actions were, I let it drop. I had no facts or basis of knowledge to know what I had seen. I know now it was a Ku Klux Klan outfit. I had no knowledge of The Klan, and certainly, no one mentioned it within my hearing until a year or so later when civil unrest hit our area.

A couple of years later, The Klan was well-known. Even my biology teacher, Mr. Brister, announced himself as a KKK member to our class. It all sounded like some sort of weird game with its invisible empire, Grand Wizard, knights, secret handshakes, and code words.

On the surface, it also reminded me of the Masons, of which my dad was a member. There was a similar sense of secrecy with a cloak-and-dagger approach to the membership. Mama belonged to the Eastern Stars by default. But, to my knowledge, she never attended a meeting. Hannah became a devoted Rainbow Girl with all its secrecy. I looked forward to joining that organization and did so. Within a few months, however, I lost interest due to the secrecy, inside and outside doorkeepers, secret passwords, privately known greetings between members when meeting in public, and a myriad of other peculiar activities. It all seemed so superficial and silly. It had little to no effect in real life outside of playing some sort of illogical game.

****

Thanksgiving arrived with more attention than any preceding holiday that year. We had a small celebration, just the five of us, rather than going to my grandfather's which was usually attended by dozens. Daddy was not in the mood for turkey. He said the meat lacked moisture, and Mama did not feel up to par. We enjoyed a roasted hen with dressing and all the trimmings. That baked chicken tasted delicious from the noon serving through a very late evening when Mama, Hannah, and I sat at the table stripping and eating the final morsels still attached to the skeleton. Delicious!

Christmas turned out to be exciting as my dad surprised us with ten-dollar Christmas Savings Club checks to be used to buy family gifts at Merritt's Store. We slept through New Year's Eve. Without any effort on our part, 1956 dawned bright and sunny with no hint of the upheaval destined to come our way.

In January, Hannah married and, a week later, she and her new husband moved to Missouri.

The spring school trip highlighted the second school semester. It occurred early in 1956—in February, the best I recall. Sixth, seventh, and eighth-grade students were all eligible to vote and go on the ultimately chosen trip. We had three destinations to choose from: Jackson, Mississippi, Avery Island Salt Domes, and New Orleans. I hoped for and voted for New Orleans. With a stroke of luck, more votes were cast for it than the other two combined.

Two Trailways buses arrived at five in the morning, and ten teachers stood at the doors as we boarded. This time, neither seating arrangements nor boys crossed my mind. I have no clear memory of who I sat with going or coming. My most vivid memory occurred in Baton Rouge.

At seven forty-five, we arrived in Baton Rouge for a state capitol tour. In the rotunda, I examined the chained-off area marking the 1935 assassination of Huey P. Long; his statue stood next to the spot where he was shot by an assassin or unintentionally by his guards. That discrepancy has never been resolved. At our house, Huey P. Long "The Kingfish" served as a hero, and Daddy told me to remember everything I saw there that day.

He, like most Louisianans, believed Mr. Long held the solution to the poor people's problems. Because of his radical populist approach and sponsored government reforms that endeared him to the rural poor, we listened to his ideals long after his death.

His objectives included Social Security money originating from wealth redistribution. He proposed reforms such as heavy taxes on the wealthy, limited incomes, and inheritances to provide a guaranteed income for every American. Huey Long built bridges, paved roads, provided free school lunches and textbooks, and built VA hospitals.

To get Daddy's vote, one only needed to have Long as a surname.

Earl K. Long stepped out of his brother's shadow after Huey's death to follow in the set path. His last election as governor occurred in 1956, and his last visit to Tioga had a significant impact on my feelings toward politics and politicians. The gist of his in-the-back-of-his-pickup speech consisted of the following.

"How ya'll doin' today?"

"We're good."

"Got enough to eat?"

"Yes, sir!"

"Your kids getting free lunches?"

"Yes, sir!"

"Remember why they get those lunches. It's your vote for me."

His speeches consisted of a great deal more, and the things I remember may be unique to me. His ability to allow everybody to hear what they wanted to hear composed a huge part of his political talent. In truth, Earl Long was a womanizer and a narcissist. He also spent time in a mental hospital.

The influence on me came less from what Earl Long said and more from what my dad said about him. Maybe if your name was Long, your family's history overshadowed any personal deficiencies, or maybe they just enhanced any political talents.

I memorized the Huey P. Long memorial for my Daddy.

At eleven thirty, we began our New Orleans discovery with a tour of Canal Street. I bought souvenirs and several stalks of sugar cane to enjoy later I used my camera to take several rolls of one ten film of the Cabildo, St Louis Cathedral, Old French Market, and Pirates Alley.

The trip climaxed with a boat ride in Audubon Park where we ate our sack lunches on the grounds. It seems strange to me to say I remember nothing of with whom I shared lunch or my beignet or even what I ate for lunch. I have nothing more than the most limited recall when it comes to what I did that day except for the capitol building and visiting the Huey Long memorial.

Daddy picked me up at the schoolyard during the wee hours of the morning, and he peppered me with questions all the way home.

"Did you actually see The Kingfish's statue?"

"Yes, sir. I even touched it."

"Did you learn anything about him?"

"Yes, sir. His family had no money when he was born. He wanted to go to college, so he had to go to work when he was sixteen. Do you think that's why he cared so much about poor people?"

"I'm sure that had something to do with it. You said, 'no college?' I thought he attended the University of Oklahoma studying law?"

"You know what, Daddy, I think the display material did say something about that and maybe that he also attended Tulane University at some time."

"Well, I'm sure you heard a lot to remember."

"I did, and I brought home brochures for you. You might know all that stuff anyway."

"No, I doubt it. I'll look at them."

"Did you know he had a Share the Wealth program where he promised every family five thousand dollars?"

"I don't know everything. I'll look at the brochures."

By this time, we were pulling into our driveway, and the feeling I had from a conversation with my dad seemed almost overwhelming. It felt good, like a prisoner who met with an understanding judge!

****

In March, Mama, though hospitalized a couple of times, made it home. She had some tough days following each hospital stay, including days when she was tired to the point of being almost unable to get up and about. But she had some good days too. On those days, she talked about going to Missouri to visit Hannah.

Daddy kissed her when he walked through the door on the day she brought it up.

"How are you feeling today, Mary?" He smiled at her.

"I'm feeling pretty good today. Coffee's made. I'll get you some."

"I just wanna half a cup. I'll get it myself."

The two of them sat on the front porch for a little while, Daddy telling her about his day.

"There's still talk of a strike. I can't see it myself. But, if they call it, I won't be workin' for a while."

"I know we'll make it; we always do."

"Jeansonne was my fireman today. He said he and his wife are comin' over this weekend. Have you talked to her lately?"

Mama laughed. "All I know is what Novie has heard on her party line! I did hear one of the girls, Lorraine, I think, blinded herself in one eye."

"Pshaw! How?"

"She had a case knife, trying to cut a string. When the string broke, the knife went into her eye."

Small talk lasted for a half an hour or so before Daddy needed to check out the chickens, the barn, the cows, or the garden. Mama moved back inside to rest a bit.

****

Every day unfolded with the same routine.

Then, suddenly, in May, she made a surprising decision and shared it with Daddy during one of those chats.

"John, I'm feelin' good. The weather's good, and I think it's helpin' me get a little energy."

"Glad to hear it. You probably need to talk to Dr. Miller about it next time you see him."

The whole atmosphere perked up, and I had a sudden burst of hope. Then she unwrapped a totally surprise bomb.

"I wanna go to Missouri."

"What!" Daddy's eyes grew wide like he didn't believe his ears.

"I'm not leaving this earth until I know Hannah's okay. She's pregnant with my grandbaby and living in an upstairs apartment. I'm worried about her carryin' laundry baskets up and down those stairs."

Daddy prepared to put his foot down. "Mary, it's not a good time for you to go right now. Whatcha gonna do with the kids?"

"They're going with me. They can help me on the train and everything."

"It's not a good idea."

Mama sighed. "All I'm asking, John, is for you to get us a pass for the train. We'll only be gone a week."

That conversation ended for the day, but she was again waiting on the front porch when Daddy came home the next day.

"Did you get that pass for me today, John?"

"No. It's not the right time for you to be running off to Missouri. Maybe we'll go sometime soon."

The conversation wandered off in another direction. The same conversation opener repeated every day with small variations.

****

It seemed as if Mama truly felt better. Mrs. Curry had been coming up for visits, and the laughter I heard while listening to Mama and Mrs. Curry felt like manna from heaven. It fed my soul and increased my hopes.

Mama saw the funny side of life. She seemed to be amused by my daddy and his peculiarities, and Mrs. Curry told funny stories about Mr. Curry's drinking. I enjoyed listening, and not just the stories drew me to them. The atmosphere was clothed in joy, peace, and life—a great place to escape from fear and sickness.

That next day, Mrs. Curry began a conversation saying, "I saw John mowin' the lawn yesterday. Looked as if he was walkin' fast. What's up?"

A grin appeared, and Mama's bright face showed her spirits lifted at the mental picture in her mind. "Novie, for the life of me, sometimes I can't figure out that man. Would you believe he was mad at Kate? Mad at a mule! When plowing, he left her standing there while he went to do something else. She moved, and he became so furious that he couldn't see straight. He yelled, screamed, and jerked her around. Sometimes I think Kate has more sense than John."

"It looked like he was talking to himself when he was mowin'. Was he?"

"Yeah, you know how when he gets mad, he talks to himself. If he is mowin', he has to talk really loudly to be able to hear."

More laughter, then Mrs. Curry told a story of her own about her son, George Edwin. She leaned forward and said, "Last weekend, Ellis and George Edwin went to Little River fishin'. When they came in, I could tell Ellis had had a few nips. He knows that gets my dander up."

"I thought I smelled fish frying down at your house."

"Yeah, they caught a passle of crappie. They had 'em all cleaned and in an ice chest. I asked 'em what they were gonna to do with that many fish. You know, I have that tiny little freezer in my icebox, and it was stuffed already."

"What did they do with them—other than the mess George brought us?"

"Well, Ellis started talkin' about his fishin' buddies comin' over for a fish fry and how we're gonna have all this company. It's Sunday afternoon, mind you, and he's invited this boatload of drinkers over for a big fish fry in my backyard. I couldn't believe it."

"Did they come?"

"No, they didn't come! I told Ellis I had a migraine and, if he had company comin' over, he'd better start cookin' more than fish 'cause I wasn't cookin' anything. I went to bed. I don't know if he called 'em or what. He cooked up all that fish, put it in the car, and left for about an hour. When he got home, he didn't say another word about a fish fry, and neither did I."

"I think men are the Lord's way of teaching women patience, and we have two good teachers!" Mama replied.

Another laugh followed, and then all felt right with the world. The days Mrs. Curry came to visit were days I could step out of worrying about Mama and into a wonderland where everything decorated with sugar plums and fairies. I cherished those days like precious coins to be taken out and polished often.

The afternoon conversations continued for close to a month. On one of Mama's good days, Daddy came home to another surprise. I didn't even know about it, although I had seen one of the railroad men come by. He didn't stay long, and I didn't know why he was there.

Daddy came in, kissed Mama, and the usual conversation commenced.

"How are you feeling today, Mary?"

"I feel good. I got passes today for me and the kids to go to Missouri."

"You what?"

"I got a pass for Olevia, Johnny, and me to go to Missouri to see Hannah."

"I told you we could go later! Who got you a pass?"

"That doesn't matter, John. I must go. Hannah's gonna have a baby, and I must see her. I must see her. I gotta know she's okay. I'm goin'. Will you take us to the train?"

"When do you leave?"

"Sunday morning."

All the air went out of his sails. He sighed and walked to the kitchen, his back slumped and his posture dropping. I guess he resigned to our going, as he knew he could not stop her once she set her mind to it so strongly. After he got his coffee and sat down again in the chair beside Mama, he answered, "I'll take you."

Well, this was a lightning strike!

Going to Missouri on the train! Mama must be feeling good. *Maybe things are going to be okay after all,* I thought as I sat down to join them. If we could go all the way to Missouri on the train by ourselves, things had to be looking up.

CHAPTER 29

A VISIT TO MISSOURI

I missed my sister and Robert, but mostly I simply wanted to take a trip. A train ride all the way to Missouri sounded exciting. My experience riding a train consisted of the few times Daddy stopped his locomotive engine in front of our house to pick up Johnny and me for a short ride up to the post office turn. He would then drop us off on his way back to Alex. A trip to Warrensburg, Missouri would be the trip of our lifetimes.

I heard Mama on the phone, talking to Hannah. "Guess what, honey! I'm bringing the kids up for a short visit. Have you got room for us?"

A pause while Hannah talked on the other end.

"Sunday," Mama said. "I'm not sure when we'll get there, but I'll let know."

Another moment of silence while Hannah responded.

"Okay. I love you. Take care of yourself."

I heard only Mama's side of the conversation, but it was easy to imagine Hannah's responses and her excitement. We packed our suitcases that very day and waited for Sunday. As promised, Daddy drove us to the station.

"Mary, there's still time to change your mind. This trip is not a good thing." His voice carried concern as well as annoyance.

"I must go. It's right for me. I need to see that Hannah's okay and settled in."

"Olevia, watch your mama. Ask for help if you need it. There'll be a conductor on the train, and he's there to take care of the passengers."

Mama responded, "Don't worry about us. We'll be okay."

At the station, Daddy guided us into the passenger area and got Mama seated.

"Olevia, you come with me," Daddy said as he led me over to buy tickets. At the check-in counter, I listened as he turned in our passes and got the tickets.

"My wife and kids are taking this train all the way to Missouri." Daddy nodded toward where Mama sat. "My wife's not in good health, and she might need some help along way."

The woman at the counter showed little interest in our plight and, to the best of my memory, responded with an unconcerned nod. We returned to where Mama and John were waiting.

"Okay. This is it. Here's your tickets." He leaned in closer and whispered to Mama, "Last chance to change your mind."

She just smiled.

Daddy handed her the tickets, kissed her on the forehead, and walked out. Suddenly, I felt a cold shiver of dread, but I blew it off as I heard "All aboard" from the conductor.

Seeing our struggle with the luggage, a guy came over to help. I don't know if he was a railroad employee or not, but he didn't appear to be, based on his clothes. He guided us through the boarding process into the car assigned to us—no Pullman car, just regular seats. We settled into the front four seats, two facing another two.

Mama and I sat beside each other, and I got the window. Johnny sat opposite me. Mama brought us some snacks to eat on the way while we stared out the window, mesmerized by the passing landscape. I had never seen so many new sights all at once. They hypnotized me to the point I don't even remember what snacks filled our goody bags. I sat there, stuffing my mouth, and staring out the window as if I were in a theater watching the best movie ever.

John seemed preoccupied with a different fascination. He discovered that if he lay down, he could see through a crack and into the bathroom. He went to sleep counting toilet disbursements onto the tracks.

At our first stop in Little Rock, Arkansas, it became apparent this trip may become arduous. An eleven-hour layover and a change of trains proved to be a challenge. Mama's difficulty breathing prevented her from walking the length of the depot in one attempt. By default, John and I became restricted regarding where we could go.

Exhausted by a forty-five-minute struggle, she first sat on a bench near a souvenir shop.

John and I checked it out while she rested. It had several things we had never seen before but quickly caught our eyes.

"Hey, Olevia! Look at the keychain. It has a train engine attached."

"That's neat, but don't forget our spending money needs to last for the entire trip."

"I know. I was just showing it to you!" The annoyance in John's voice enhanced his frown, and he made a quick turn to something else of interest.

****

Several rest-stops later, the three of us ate hamburgers at a station café. I loved observing the variety of customers surrounding us. Back home in our local café, Billips, we usually saw people who looked like and sounded like us. Things were different here, and both John and I carefully studied the people surrounding us. Indeed, they became main characters in stories we shared to pass the time as we waited.

After lunch, we found our way to the next train. Once seated in the boarding area, Mama allowed us to explore with the restriction that we stay within seeing distance.

John and I entertained ourselves by creating stories about the people sharing the depot. Some were families, and others looked almost lost and alone. But the best basis for our stories were the ones in the shops.

We watched what purchases they made, from newspapers to souvenirs. We designated some as businessmen based on the suits they wore and what newspapers they read. Others we labeled as housewives, and we chose to characterize one particular woman as on her first train trip. She seemed as baffled as we were as to where she should be and what souvenir should be purchased.

"John, did you see that lady in the gift shop?"

"Which one? There were several ladies in several gift shops!"

"The young-looking one wearing the pedal pushers. The shop we were in earlier today."

"The one eating popcorn and picking up every souvenir and putting it back down?"

"Yeah." I laughed, suddenly realizing John might have been watching closer than I. "What do you think her story is?"

"Well, I don't know. She looked uncomfortable by herself, as if she couldn't make any decisions."

"Maybe this is her first trip away from her husband? I think she had on a wedding ring," I replied.

"I didn't notice. Maybe she had a fight with him and decided to leave."

"What??? Where did you come up with that? If she was running away, she wouldn't take a train. Maybe she's just going to visit her family."

"Whatever. I liked that old guy in the wheelchair looking alone," John answered.

"Yeah. I didn't see anyone with him, but I did wish there was a way to borrow his wheelchair for Mama."

We both laughed at this, though the laugh was hollow.

Probably the most interesting characters were two little girls. Maybe seven or eight years old, they looked like twins in their matching outfits. We even named them Ella and Ester. We gave them rich parents because they were allowed to choose anything in the gift shop but could not make up their minds. One minute, they chose barrettes made in the shape of a railroad engine. Then, just before reaching the cashier, they turned almost in unison. Without a word to each other, they headed in the direction of a stack of jigsaw puzzles. It looked almost prearranged. But, of course, it wasn't. I don't recall what they ultimately purchased.

Funny stories and sad stories—both helped to pass the time.

****

At long last, eleven hours elapsed, and we boarded the next train. Same set-up as the first one, providing identical seating for us. We felt glad to settle in. Mama, who had one side of the facing seats to herself, asked for a pillow. She lay down as completely as possible and fell asleep quickly. Her labored breathing seemed to ease a bit.

Johnny and I sat together, talked, looked out the window, and counted telephone poles.

"Hey, do you remember how many telephone poles Daddy said are in one mile?" Johnny asked.

"What? I'm not sure I've heard Daddy say," I replied.

"Yes, you have. Remember when he and Mr. Jeansonne were arguing about it on the front porch? One of them said twenty, and the other said twenty-one."

"Which one said which?"

"That's what I can't remember! Maybe we could ask the conductor."

"Let's just count them. There are mile markers along the tracks."

"Okay."

We never found out. We kept either losing count due to the speed of the train or by being tantalized by the panoramic view of a new world just outside the window.

I marveled at how each passing scene differed from the next as we moved northward. I wondered about the lives of the people living in those houses. Did they mirror ours? Or were they somehow different? It occurred to me that the basic needs and goals of most people are likely the same for all people.

The distance between Little Rock and St. Louis evaporated quicker than I expected. The conductor's loudspeaker voice chimed in, saying, "Ladies and gentlemen, we're approaching our St. Louis stop. If you are not in your seat, please return to it now."

A few people moved. We didn't, but we did awaken Mama to listen with us.

"This stop includes a twelve-hour layover."

Mama murmured under her breath, "I should have checked those passes. I wonder why John didn't get us an upgrade to a Pullman car."

Until then, I didn't know a choice existed, and I wondered too. The reason probably lay somewhere between being annoyed with Mama's going without his blessing and his desire to prove himself right.

The twelve-hour layover following the eleven hours in Little Rock grew to be a frightening prospect. It became more so when we were given our transfer slips upon arrival. Our train was scheduled to leave from the other side of a depot much larger than the one in Little Rock.

Our twelve-hour layover gave us no place to go and nothing to do but figure out how Mama could make the long walk. No wheelchairs were in sight, and nobody offered to help us.

Mama struggled to reach the other side of the depot, and I feared she might die on the way. Her breathing became more labored, and the veins in her neck bulged. She had to sit every ten minutes or less and rest at fifteen-foot intervals. Maybe an apt comparison would be a wheelchair-bound person trying to negotiate the streets without today's improvements, including ramps created by the ADA. But my memory pictures an even more horrifying scene.

"Mama, should we ask someone to find a wheelchair?"

"Honey, I don't see any wheelchairs anywhere. I don't think they are available. Let's just go slow."

"Okay. If you want to sit on a bench for a little while, I can get you something to drink."

"No. Let's keep moving forward as much as we can. We can rest at the other end."

I wanted to cry, but crying would only make it worse, so I prayed instead. Internally, I questioned the wisdom of taking this trip, while Mama fought to reach the other side. John stood on one side with me on the other. Little conversation took place, just whispered appeals to God to get us there. We made it six hours later. But we made it! John and I were exhausted, and we all lay down on benches to sleep until our connecting train arrived.

Surprisingly, we fell asleep so soundly that a kind passenger had to awaken us when it was time to board. An older woman tapped me on the shoulder. I sat up immediately.

"Honey, where are you going?"

"We're going to see my sister in Warrensburg, Missouri."

"Well, I think this is your train. Let me look at your transfer pass."

I handed it over, and she confirmed we were to board shortly. I woke Mama and John. We all needed to go to the bathroom, but we weren't sure where it was. We decided we could manage until we got on the train. The kind lady stayed with us.

"Let's see if we can get you guys to the front of the line. I'm sure the conductor will be calling 'All aboard' shortly."

"My mama can't walk very fast."

"I know. I will help her."

Those words felt like peace incarnate; she sounded like an angel. I gave her a grateful half-smile.

She stayed with us, guiding us to the front of the line and installing us as first boarders precisely as the conductor appeared. We were able to take advantage of the same seating arrangement we had on the last two trains.

We settled in as our Angel waved goodbye.

"Honey, you watch your mom closely. If you need anything, just pull that string, and the conductor will come. I've got to find my cousin. She's on this train, and we're traveling together."

I nodded as she smiled and disappeared down the aisle. At this point, I became aware of something I had not noticed since leaving Alexandria: there were a lot of black people on this train, even riding in our car. Until this point, I had only seen white people.

John, Mama, and I were all alert and sitting up after our six-hour nap.

"Where are all of these people going?" I asked Mama.

"Well, I guess they might be going to visit a relative just like we are."

"The black people too? Do only St. Louis Negroes ride the train?"

"No."

"There weren't any Louisiana or Arkansas Negroes on our train."

"Yes, there were."

"Where? I didn't see any, not even in the depot."

"They rode in separate cars, Olevia. People are segregated in Louisiana and Arkansas, so Negroes ride in their own cars, and white people ride with white people."

"Oh."

By the time this conversation concluded, Johnny had gone to find the bathroom, and a red-haired black lady carrying a tiny baby sat down where he had been sitting. Remember, this was the Jim Crow era, and I had never seen a red-haired Negro. I stared.

Mama broke the ice. "How old is your baby? She's so cute."

"Four months."

"Where are you going?"

"To Massachusetts to introduce my mama to her first grandchild."

The baby whimpered and fidgeted, so the mother got out a bottle for her. She asked the conductor to have it filled with milk.

"Does she drink regular milk already?" Mama asked.

"Yes, ma'am."

When the conductor returned, the mother took the bottle of cold milk and began feeding her baby.

Mama immediately spoke up. "You shouldn't give her cold milk. She'll get a stomachache."

"Well, I usually warm it a little at home, but this is okay."

"No, it isn't okay." Mama tossed her an adamant frown. "That baby's milk needs to be warmed."

The woman nodded and looked down as she said, "I don't want to cause no trouble."

Mama called the conductor back and told him to have the bottle warmed. He took it without a word and brought it back without a word. He didn't look happy, but he said nothing.

The mother seemed so grateful, and I beamed with pride for my Mama.

The lady asked me, "Wanna feed my baby?"

"Yes, ma'am."

By this time, John had returned from the bathroom and stood at the seat's edge.

"Oh, I didn't know anyone was sitting here." She quickly started to move.

Mama put her hand up. "No. Stay. Johnny's gonna sit beside me, and Olevia can sit beside you while she feeds your baby."

I moved, Johnny sat down beside Mama, and the lady handed her baby to me, along with the bottle. It felt surreal.

I had never touched a black baby. As I close my eyes today, I can clearly see what she looked like. She had that baby smell and a tiny bow sort of taped to her head, and she smiled when I made faces at her. She made us laugh and brought a bit of joy to our small section in that car. She was a bit of blue sky on a cloudy day.

"Is it a girl?"

"Yes."

"What's her name?"

"Maleika. Do you know what that means?"

"No, ma'am."

"It means 'Angel.' What's your name?"

"Olevia. It means I was named after my aunt."

Both Mama and the lady laughed, so I laughed too.

I thought about the baby we would soon have around—a new baby in my family. I didn't know when, but I knew my sister would soon have a baby—maybe in November and maybe on my birthday. I hoped it would be a girl.

When the bottle emptied, the mom took her baby back and gently rocked her until she fell asleep. Mama had me move over and share the seat with Johnny to give more room for the sleeping baby.

Pretty soon, we started getting off the train in Warrensburg, Missouri. As we exited, we immediately saw Hannah smiling, waving, and hurrying in our direction. We took it slow so Mama could breathe better. Hannah's smile turned to concern when she saw how tired Mama looked. She didn't realize how much Mama had gone downhill since January.

"Why didn't Daddy get you a Pullman car?" Hannah's brows knitted, and her face grew red.

"Honey, you know your daddy. I'm okay. How are you?"

"I'm just fine, Mama. You didn't tell me how sick you are. Why didn't you tell me?"

"I'm no sicker than I have been. I'm just tired."

"Well, you should have had a Pullman car. What was Daddy thinking, just letting you get on a train like that? Did you have to sit up all the way? Have you slept at all? You look dead tired."

"Hannah, just let it go, honey. I'm okay. We're here, aren't we? Olevia and Johnny are eager to see everything. Is your apartment very far from here?"

"No, it's not far. I just can't believe Daddy didn't see how sick you are. Are you going to be able to make it to the car?"

"Of course, I am. We'll just take it slow. I might have to rest a couple of times."

I spoke up to see if I couldn't improve the vibe of the exchange. "Mama walked all the way across the depot in St. Louis. It took us a long time, but we did it. Didn't we, Mama?"

"Yes, we did, honey. And I'm going to be okay here, too."

I continued to interject into the conversation, hoping to shift the emotional gears.

"Did you know the Negroes ride in the same train cars with white people in St. Louis but not in Arkansas and Louisiana?"

She looked straight at me to reply. "I'm not concerned with where the Negroes ride on trains. I'm worried about Mama."

Sweat poured from Mama's brow as she fought her way to Hannah's car, and I didn't like the turn the trip was taking.

I wanted Hannah to be glad we were there and to stop fussing at Mama. She fussed all the way to her apartment. For the second time on this trip, I felt like crying, but I did not. Johnny seemed to simply follow along, almost invisible and totally quiet. Remember Harvey and Elwood (James Stewart) in the movie *Harvey* that was popular in the 1950s? Johnny's presence seemed like a scene out of that movie—you knew he stood beside you, but not always visibly.

The three of us went immediately to bed when we got to the apartment, and we slept until Robert came home from work. Hannah unpacked our suitcases and hung stuff in a closet. She set up a rollaway bed as well as a small cot.

Hannah had supper ready when we woke up. An excellent cook, she provided food that was mouthwatering from smell to taste. As I recall, she covered the spaghetti with a rich, homemade hamburger sauce and served it with a colorful salad and hot, buttered rolls. When helping to set the table, I got a peek at half of a Black Diamond watermelon in the refrigerator. If Mama began to have some of her good days, it occurred to me we might have some fun.

During the meal, I couldn't get the image of that juicy watermelon out of my mind. After supper, I asked, "Are we having watermelon for dessert?"

"Not tonight. We ate too late. Robert gets up early, and he goes to bed at nine."

I wanted to say, "So what?" But I didn't. I sat down in front of the TV, which she promptly turned off at nine, and we all went to bed. Not a spectacular ending to the first day, but then, it was *only* the first day. This trip had become a bit of a roller coaster!

Mama and I were assigned to the rollaway, an acceptably comfortable double bed. Still, Mama gasped for breath all night and spent most of it sitting up. When the morning came, she looked as if she had not been to bed yet. She put on a brave face, sitting at the kitchen table as the three of us had coffee. Robert and Hannah had already left for work. John and I felt antsy to get outside. We took turns making our case.

"Can we go exploring?"

"Not today, honey."

"Why not today?" I walked toward the window. "Come see."

"Let's wait one more day—until I feel better. Then I'll go with you."

"Really, Mama, come see," John added.

Hannah's downtown apartment included windows where we could see everything—the shops, the grocery store, department stores, and people bustling in the street.

"We'll stay where you can see us. We promise," John offered on our behalf.

Mama made her way to the window. As she observed a downtown that appeared huge in comparison to Tioga or even to Pineville, she noticed some doctors' offices.

"Olevia, come over here."

I had already given up on our chances of escaping for the day. I sat checking out the TV, flipping around the channels. At her request, I put the remote down and rushed over.

"What, Mama?"

"That building over there looks like a medical building. Can you read the sign?"

I leaned as close as possible to the window.

"Yes, ma'am. It says, 'Warrensburg Chiropractic Clinic.'"

"Okay. I'm gonna get dressed, and we'll walk over there."

Sometimes, Mama would go to a chiropractic clinic at home, though Dr. Miller told her it was useless and a waste of money. Daddy agreed, so Grandpa often drove her there.

Chiropractors were illegal in Louisiana. And, to the best of my memory, Louisiana became the last state to legalize chiropractic treatment in 1974. Nevertheless, one could always be found, even in the 1950s.

While Mama got dressed, I thought about previous visits to a chiropractor. Grandpa knew one who operated in the Piney Woods, east of Alexandria. On her visits there, Mama would have Grandpa transport her in his truck—a tiny vehicle into which we crammed the four of us into the cab. What an adventure! The always-packed office meant John, Grandpa, and I sat on the long front porch, waiting and watching folks go in and out. The patients offered a variety of people from those appearing to be wealthy to the ones barely making it. Grandpa knew a lot of them and always spoke to them. I recalled one conversation from those times:

"Hey, Evans. Is that back bothering you again?"

"It is, A.C. I don't know how long I can take it."

"Well, you oughta get some relief today."

Evans nodded and went on into the doctor's office.

Grandpa liked to share some tidbits about each person. On that day, he said, "Evans worked for the Highway Department with me some years ago. He strained his back when we were building a blacktop road down near Abbeville."

After traveling down the rabbit hole of memory, my mind drifted back to being in Warrensburg. Seeing the clinic from Hannah's window seemed to inspire Mama. After we dressed, we headed over. It turned out to be a walk-in clinic, but they probably would have made time for Mama anyway.

With no elevator in Hannah's apartment house and the clinic less than a block away, negotiating a flight of stairs and the street exhausted Mama. She looked on the verge of passing out. By the time we entered the clinic, I had begun to worry about how John and I would get her back to Hannah's apartment.

Immediately upon entering the waiting room, an attendant rushed over with a wheelchair, which Mama gratefully accepted.

"I'm Adrian." The attendant introduced herself with a kind smile. "Please, kids, have a seat. Is this your grandmother?"

That was how old my mom looked! Her gray hair tended to blend with her gray face.

I answered, "No, it's our mom."

"What's her name?"

Mama answered, "Mary. I'm okay. I wanted to see if I could get an adjustment today?"

"Yes. Kids, you can stay right here. We'll be back." Adrian spoke as she attached an oxygen mask to Mom. Until then, I had not noticed the portable tank that hung on the side of the wheelchair. Mama immediately began to breathe easier as Adrian pushed her toward the door.

The chiropractic treatment helped, even if only on a psychological level and I think the oxygen helped. We got home with less effort than it took to get to the clinic, although the stairs were definitely a challenge, with many rest stops on the way up.

****

Mama slept better that night, and John and I bounced out of bed the next day. Mama had one of her good days, but she never left Hannah's apartment again until it was time to go home. The watermelon half still lay in the refrigerator like a flower bouquet wilting in a forgotten foyer.

The next two days mirrored the first day—without the chiropractic visit and with a little more neighborhood exploration. A limeade stand within a block of Hannah's apartment house grabbed John's attention, as we'd never seen one.

"Ma'am, could I have a limeade?"

"A what?"

"A limeade, ma'am." He turned toward the seller. "How much is a small limeade?"

"Where are you from, boy? Hey, Lillian, come over here. Listen to this kid."

"I'm from Louisiana, and I wanna limeade, ma'am."

"Would you say it just one more time? Tell Ruby to come over here and listen to this kid."

By this time, I hardly recognized John; he had become so Southern! He grinned and blushed, loving the attention. He sipped that limeade feeling like a star.

The watermelon half still lay untouched in the refrigerator by the time Friday arrived—one more night before we boarded a train for home. The image of it never left my mind for a day, so I was glad when Mama asked, "Hannah, why don't you let the kids have that watermelon today? They've waited a long time."

She agreed, but the watermelon had turned out to be spoiled and soured. We threw it away.

****

The straight-through pass Daddy had sent provided an easier and faster trip home. The train stopped in both St. Louis and Little Rock, but we stayed on board. Negroes disappeared in Little Rock just as quickly as they had appeared in St. Louis on the way up. I experienced the Jim Crow laws from a white perspective without knowing they existed.

Daddy met us at the train, looking worried. Hannah had apparently made her concerns and displeasure clear on the phone. He hurried over as Mama stepped off with the help of a conductor.

"Mary are you okay?" he asked.

I saw tears in his eyes.

"Yes. I'm fine. Hannah's doing good, and I'm looking forward to sleeping in my own bed tonight."

After that, things were never the same. We didn't know it yet, but she only had about ninety days left on this side of the grave.

She could no longer really do anything around the house. Oftentimes, she stayed in bed until an hour or so before Daddy came in from work. At that point, she called Johnny and me in to help her get out of bed and into and out of the bathtub. We helped her put on a clean, starched, and ironed dress and get seated in the living room.

A dab of lipstick and a puff of face powder were part of the ritual. Some days, I would rub a little "Nair" on her upper lip to be sure no trace of a mustache remained, and every day she put on her good shoes. Oftentimes, she needed to rest between the bath and actually getting dressed, but she never failed to make it to a rocking chair in the living room before Daddy walked in the door.

Sometimes, this whole routine annoys me.

One day, I said, "Mama, Daddy knows how sick you are! Why pretend? Why do you try so hard? Why can't you tell him to make his own coffee? You never tell him you don't feel good. Why?"

"I'm not pretending. It's important to remember when you stop looking good enough to come home to, your husband will stop coming home." She chuckled and gave me a squeeze. "Help me get my hair combed and then go put on the coffee."

After combing her hair, I headed toward the kitchen feeling inspired by the selfless effort she made for my father.

****

Over the years, I've never forgotten that lesson, and I've learned a lot from all the nuances that go with it. It's not about the looking so much as the feeling of home that keeps one coming. My mom created a positive, pleasant, and desirable atmosphere as well as she could. It felt good to be in her presence.

We had a wall coffee grinder. We ground together one-half dark roast and one-half light roast Eight O'clock coffee beans to get exactly the blend Daddy liked. Before I put it in the drip-o-later, the coffee had to pass her inspection. I thought it silly for her to put out all that effort when Daddy didn't seem to even notice how hard it was for her or for us.

Daddy arrived home and smiled at Mama. "Hey, Mary. You look good today." He gave her a quick kiss.

"I'm feeling pretty good. Want some coffee? I can get it."

"Nah, you sit right there. I'll get us both a cup, and maybe we can sit out on the porch a little bit. There's a breeze blowing."

"Sounds good."

Daddy strode to the kitchen, not looking back, as I helped my mom out of the chair and onto the porch and the hot Louisiana afternoon. Daddy bragged that because we lived on a hill a breeze always blew. I rarely felt it, but I never doubted its existence.

Mama settled into a rocking chair on the front porch, caught her breath a bit, and waited for Daddy to bring the coffee. As usual, I joined them, sitting on the top step to listen as they chatted. Even at that young age, I marveled at how Mama blossomed when Daddy talked with her. They discussed politics, the neighbors, the railroad, the cows, the chickens, whether they should put in a fall garden, and the next possible labor strike (which always seemed to be looming on the horizon).

In an hour or so, Mama began to sink a bit. Without missing a beat, Daddy took his cue.

"Mary, I'm going to put these coffee cups up. I'm a little tired today, and I think I'll lie down for a spell if you don't mind. Wanna join me?"

"That sounds good. I think I will."

Daddy rose from his chair and went into the house without a glance over his shoulder. I helped Mama up and into the house. She made it to their bedroom about the same time Daddy arrived.

"Here, let me get that bedspread turned down. It's too hot for any covers. Let's just lay a spell on top of the sheets."

After she settled, I closed the door behind me as I left the room, rejoicing in Daddy's kindness to Mama. My heart felt warm and grateful despite the looming tragedy of Mama's eventual departure.

****

By late September, Mama entered the hospital for the last time, and she died on October 26. Many times, over the last sixty-eight years, I've pondered those summer afternoons and pictured the two of them rocking, talking, and sipping coffee from wartime coffee cups. I've come to recognize Daddy's courage and love in allowing Mama to keep her dignity even at the lowest point in her life. He treated her, not as an invalid, but as his beloved, cherished partner.

He allowed her the joy of being his wife until she couldn't be anymore. At the time, as much as I appreciated his kindness, I didn't realize how difficult that must have been. I do now, and I admire him even more for it.

Many nights, Mama could not breathe lying down, so she sat on the front porch trying to get enough air to stay alive. Sometimes, Daddy would take her for a ride in the car with the windows rolled down. We hoped the air would force itself into her lungs and she would be okay. John and I went on these rides, and I prayed they would work. More than one prayer left that car. On most nights, she said she felt better after the ride. As I think about it now, I wonder why Dr. Miller had not prescribed a portable oxygen tank for her.

Mama would often lay down with me until I went to sleep. Then, she'd get into bed with Daddy. But on those bad nights, she slept in the other bed in my room. Every night after she crawled into her bed and I thought she had gone to sleep, I got up to feel her chest and make sure her heart continued to beat. I held my hand over her mouth to feel her breath. I prayed God would heal her.

Toward the end, I prayed for her healing or her death before her birthday, as it hurt to watch her suffer. It felt like wrestling a porcupine whenever she winced or moaned.

I welcomed Labor Day and the beginning of the eighth grade.

CHAPTER 30
SEPTEMBER 1 TO OCTOBER 23, 1956

Life went on. Mama's health grew worse, but the world did not stop. The day after Labor Day, John and I showed up at school. On one level, I looked forward to life in that coveted eighth grade my friends and I had discussed so much. On another, I realized every day that passed shortened the time available to spend with Mama.

My solution: I put that knowledge in a separate compartment and to visit it as seldom as possible.

Our first day of school choices of outfit material had not changed much from first grade; we still had wool skirts, though now topped with a sweater instead of a blouse. The big eye-opener was that *many of the skirts were straight!* The girls who did not have straight skirts wore pleated or gathered, without the petticoats. Although most of the girls were outfitted with penny loafers, a few wore shoes with slight heels, and others wore saddle-oxfords.

We all felt superior to the new set of seventh graders, even though we were them just a few months prior.

"Charlene, did you see that girl who left the bathroom a second ago?" I poked her in the arm as we examined our make-up in the mirror, combed our hair a dozen times, and carefully inspected our skirts to make certain they did not cup our bottoms.

"No. What?"

"She had on make-up, and it must have been an inch thick. Mrs. Henderson's not going to put up with that."

We both laughed and adjusted our posture with shoulders straight, feeling superior in our new status.

Mr. Till, now both my homeroom and history teacher, had eighth-grade girls looking at him. He, probably in his late thirties or early forties, had wavy brown hair, blue eyes, and a chiseled chin. Suddenly, we noticed his good looks, and I had not had the opportunity to be in his seventh-grade class. I felt fortunate to have two classes under his direction that year.

The homeroom period did not offer much outside of roll call, a few questions, and some conversation as to life in the eighth grade. However, on the very first day in his history class, I learned that good looks do not necessarily imply an easygoing personality. We filed in and sat down, and he introduced himself to any students he had not yet met.

The roll was called, and the teaching began.

"Class, does everyone have a history textbook?" He raised his copy in the air.

"Yes, sir," we answered in unison.

"Okay. Open it to page five and silently read pages five through eight. When you finish with that, close your book and put your hands on your desk. As soon as everyone has finished, I will have some questions about what you read."

He sat down at his desk to make some notes. We read the assigned pages, closed our books, and waited. In a short time, he stood up from his desk.

"It looks like everyone is finished. Did everyone bring a notebook with them?"

The class chorused, "Yes."

"Open it to the first clean page. Write your name and today's date. I encourage you to use this notebook exclusively for this class. Then notes don't get lost."

We did as he instructed.

"I'm going to write three questions on the board, and I want you to write the answers in your notebook."

A palpable silence ensued as we watched Mr. Till list the questions on the blackboard.

Out of nowhere, there came a snore—a sound that could not be mistaken for anything other than a snore. Mr. Till immediately turned around, as we all did. His eyes searched the room for the source of the disruption.

I peered at his expressive face. His scowl caused his eyebrows to knit, and they ran together, reminding me of a caterpillar running across his forehead. A side of Mr. Till I had not seen before and did not expect to see was about to be exposed. Charlene had a class with him in the seventh grade, and she never mentioned he might turn into Frankenstein's monster. A more appropriate description would be The Incredible Hulk, but he had not yet been created. I marveled at how quickly one's appearance can change.

Mr. Till stood, and his muscles seemed to bulge against his shirt as he slowly turned his head until his eyes stopped at Greasy Griffin. Greasy's name was Vernon, but we called him Greasy due to his lightning speed on the basketball court.

Without a word and almost in slow motion, Mr. Till put down the chalk, returned the eraser to the shelf, and walked toward Greasy's desk. The rest of us stared as if we were suspended in time and unable to look away.

Our wing of classrooms occupied one side of a hallway, and the other side consisted of a glass wall with doors leading to the outside.

Mr. Till picked up Greasy, carried him to an outside door, and dumped him on the ground. Greasy, not yet completely awake, landed with a thud. He immediately jumped up to get his bearings as if awakening from a nightmare. He stood sort of wringing his hands, looking around, totally confused.

Mr. Till returned to class and picked up Greasy's desk with one hand; it met the same fate as the startled Greasy. The two of them, Mr. Till and Greasy, stared at each other for a moment or two before our teacher strolled purposely to the classroom. Greasy followed close behind, still not having said a word.

As Mr. Till reached the open door, he turned to face Greasy one more time and spoke in a voice we were all guaranteed to hear. "From now on, if you intend to sleep in my class, get your desk and sit outside."

"Yes, sir."

Sleeping in Mr. Till's class became a non-issue.

****

Before my Mama's passing, I had the opportunity to share one more once-in-a-lifetime experience—my first date (using the word "date" very loosely).

Clarence Bruce, a good-looking and popular classmate, who had become a polio paraplegic from our town's 1950 epidemic, was a close friend. His crutches did not impair his popularity, and his interest in me came as a surprise.

On the Monday of the second week in September, he asked me to go to a Saturday movie with his mom as chauffeur. I did not expect my Mama to agree, but she did—after her phone call to Mrs. Bruce.

When Saturday came, Mama insisted that Clarence must come to the door to get me.

"Mama, he's on crutches!"

"That's not the point, honey. Girls who run out to cars are not respected."

"Geez! His mother's driving us." I rolled my eyes, unable to believe my ears.

Nevertheless, I found myself pacing the living floor behind a closed door. I peeked out the window to watch Clarence's arrival. He got out of the car, managed the gate, avoided the dog, and came up four narrow steps to the porch to knock on the door. I opened it immediately.

"Hey. Let me tell Mama bye, and I'm ready." I did not have to go far; she stood directly behind me. I practically bumped into her when I turned.

Mama stepped forward. "Hello, Clarence. It's good to see you. How're your parents?" She actually put out her hand to shake hands with him. I felt mortified.

"Fine. My mom's in the car."

"Then we better go," I interjected.

But Mama plowed on as if I had not said a word. "What time do you think you'll have Olevia home?"

Again, I interjected. "Mom! It's the middle of the afternoon, and his mom is driving!"

Clarence continued to be polite even as I tried to escape. "I don't know, Mrs. Yeager." He turned and adjusted his crutches. "As soon as Mom—"

"We have to go now," I interrupted, "or we'll be late for the movie." I headed for the door.

Even in her very ill state, Mama managed to get there first! She opened the door for us and whispered to me, "Mind your manners!"

I scooted around her and headed out.

As we reached the bottom step of the porch, Mom called out, "Ya'll be good."

We answered, "Yes, ma'am," and kept walking.

Mrs. Bruce dropped us by the Paramount Theater to see *Tomahawk*. Even though it was a Western movie, I had asked to see it. The *Alexandria Daily Town Talk* had a brief review in the one-page movie section. The story indicated the picture was not only based on a true story but believed to be the first movie made with any empathy for the Indians' viewpoint.

We settled into our seats with popcorn and a drink. As soon as the lights lowered, Clarence began playing with a rubber doll transformed into a squirt gun to hit unsuspecting movie watchers. Although not caught, he was the recipient of threatening looks. He missed most of the movie while he played. I found myself wishing John and I were watching this movie so we could talk about it.

I felt mortified and disappointed! In addition to wanting to see the movie, I expected opportunities to use all of Mrs. Henderson's how-to-say-no techniques. Instead, I used my innocent looks to avoid being removed from the theater by an unhappy moviegoer. I welcomed getting out of the car at home.

"How was the movie?" Mama asked. She lay in her bed and didn't look at all well, but she still perked up when I walked into the room.

"Okay."

"Clarence is such a sweet, little boy. Did ya'll have fun?"

"He did."

"What?"

"Yes, ma'am. We had fun, but I don't want to go anymore."

"Why?"

"He acts silly sometimes."

"Oh." She smiled and closed her eyes; she appeared to fall asleep.

****

The humdrum of school served as a balm to my worrying about Mama. Sometimes, I felt no fears—just the joy of being an eighth grader. I got caught up in the latest girl gossip about who was the cutest boy, the latest McCall pattern Charlene's mom had, or some other piece of nonsense. Sometimes, without warning, in the middle of laughing at some funny situation, I would suddenly be lost in a hole of darkness. At that moment, it felt as if a thunderbolt hit, and a storm began.

Mama's pain became mine as I visualized sharing my stories with her. I could hear her attempts at breathing normally—or not breathing at all. I could see the hurt in her eyes—perhaps colored by a little fear, but I think it was more the regret at knowing we were reaching the end of those special times. When I fell into one of those chasms with the blues in my tummy, I mentally reached for my Big Chief tablet to climb out.

September melted into October, and Mama went into the hospital for the last time. As all my friends prepared for the Shreveport Fair, I prepared for a life that would be changed forever. I thought I might drown in my fear and felt thankful to have Johnny there to face it with me.

On October 23, three days before Mama crossed over, my brother James walked into my math class. James was a good-looking guy, and his uniform—Navy dress whites—accentuated those good looks. My emotions ran the gamut of what news could be so bad that he came here to get me to how proud his visit made me feel.

Mama had sent for us to come to the Baptist Hospital, and that ride seemed to be the longest I'd ever taken.

As I wrote this chapter, it became clear to me that Mama never stopped being a mom. Even at the end of her life in this physical world, she continued to love and teach me. Those lessons enabled me to not only survive but flourish. I depended on them then, and I depend on them now. I am thankful she clothed me in her web of wisdom.

CHAPTER 31

WE SAY GOODBYE

Mom and John.

Before John and I entered Mama's room, Daddy cautioned us not to argue if she told us she was dying. For the first time, I realized he had been oblivious to all the talks and time Mama had spent preparing us for this day.

Aunt Grace, my mother's sister, accompanied us into the room. Nurse Parker stood next to her bed. Tubes were everywhere, and an oxygen tent covered half of her body.

To me, Mama seemed alert when she asked Nurse Parker her name.

"Annette Parker." The nurse smiled.

"Oh, you live behind us, don't you? On the Pardue Road? You're so sweet to come down here."

"No. I'm your nurse."

"Come give me a hug." She held up her arms then looked at Aunt Grace. "This is my neighbor, Grace."

"Mary, she's not your neighbor; she's your nurse."

We did have a neighbor named Parker, and I felt angered when Aunt Grace and the nurse said Mama was hallucinating. They talked about her as if she were not in the room.

Mama looked over at John and me.

"Hello, Mama," we said simultaneously as if we had become one person.

"Hello, babies. Come here, both of you. Give me a hug."

We started to cry.

"I don't want ya'll cryin', you hear? I'm going to Heaven, and I'll never hurt again. I'll never be sick again. I don't want you to cry. I'll breathe again. I'll be pain free. Don't cry for me. Your tears will be for yourselves. I'm going to be okay."

"I don't want you to die, Mama." John sniffled.

"Well, I don't want to leave you either, but I must go. I don't know why God gave me a job to do and not enough time to finish it, but I've seen the seven candles. I must go now."

I assume the seven candles had something to do with her earlier Catholicism. The only Biblical reference of which I am aware involves seven churches mentioned in Revelation, and I could never make that connection. I also knew that seven is a symbol of completion. Candles are a symbol of love and everlasting life, and that's enough for me. I felt consoled that she had seen them and felt ready to go, even as my heart shrank and skipped beats at the thought of never seeing her again.

"I don't want you to go," John repeated as I stood there as if an observer of some weird scene in a horror movie.

Even with all the tubes in her arms and legs, a catheter, and a blood pressure monitor, Mama lifted the plastic cover from the oxygen apparatus covering her. She put it behind her as she spoke. The nurse started to replace it, but Aunt Grace touched her shoulder and shook her head 'no.'

Mama continued, "Listen to me, both of you. I don't want you two cryin' at my funeral. When your Daddy comes to tell you I'm gone, I don't want you to cry. Watch TV, walk in The Pines, do the stuff you do every day, and know I'm watchin' you. Johnny, I'm not worried about you. I know you'll be all right. But, Olevia, I do worry about you. I have dreams of you runnin' the halls wearing nothing but your panties."

"I'll be good. I promise." I reassured her with a smile as well as I could. Beaming my love at her, I tried to stop my tears.

"I know you will, but sometimes you might get lonely. Or you might simply want to talk to me. Look up at the sky and know I'm there with you. Grace, do you have a piece of paper and a pencil?"

"No, Mary, just this matchbook." She handed it, along with a pencil, to Mama.

On the matchbook, Mama wrote "Be good" and placed three dots after the words. She handed the matchbook to me as she explained, "I'm getting tired. Those dots mean 'Love, Mama.' Carry that note with you to remind you I'm with you all the time."

Her breath had become shallow and more labored.

"Now, both of you need to go home. Don't come back here anymore to see me like this. Just remember I won't be cryin'. I'll be watchin' and lovin' you."

Tears had formed in her eyes as well. We hugged her again and said goodbye as the nurse replaced the oxygen tent.

That was the last time we saw her alive.

****

I cannot imagine the strength it took for Mama to continue to be a parent until almost her last breath. It's a type of courage I doubt I have and pray I never need to find out.

That night, I cried until I thought my heart would burst. I didn't know how I could live without Mama. She was my cocoon, my place of safety where I had the freedom to be me. I thought about silly things such as who would put my hair in a ponytail, who would tell me to make up my bed, or who would go with me to Mrs. Curry's for coffee. I now know that my daddy and John were hurting too, but that night my own loss consumed my being.

The next morning, John and I made a pact to always take care of each other no matter what and to make Mama proud. Our cow had twin calves on October 25; that had not happened before. I interpreted it as a sign that life would go on and still be good. I took a picture of John holding those calves, and I still have it today. I feel sure he has one as well.

****

We survived the ten-day ordeal leading up to Mama's funeral. Mama's sisters, with one exception, were all

Catholic; they had concerns—particularly Aunt Lillian. She had first spoken about it to Daddy the night before Mama died.

"John, have you gotten a priest to see Mary?"

"No. She belongs to the Baptist Church. I don't see a reason for a priest."

"I want her to receive Last Rites before she dies. She was raised Catholic."

"I don't know a priest, and I ain't lookin' for one." His voice was firm, his jaw set.

A bit more back and forth occurred before Aunt Lillian left in her car. I thought she had given up. I found out later she had not. She went to the only Catholic Church in Tioga and explained her plight. A priest agreed to visit Mama hours before she died. I'm glad she had success in her need to see Mama off after Last Rites were administered. I believe Aunt Lillian and her siblings all felt a peace they had not had before.

****

Three days following our last visit with Mama, at three in the morning on October 26, 1956, Daddy woke me first. Together, we woke Johnny, whose first words were, "Don't cry, Daddy."

We got up, sat around a while, and went back to bed— but not to sleep. As soon as we got up again and had coffee, John and I walked together in The Pines. Aunt Denie, Daddy's sister who had come to stay with us for a while, did not want us to go. She said it looked unseemly, but we had to say things to each other—private things—and we went. We talked about Mama's funeral and how she wanted us to behave; we talked about her watching us forever and how we must try not to be sad.

****

Once the body arrived at Hixson Brothers Funeral Home, preparation began for an open casket viewing. I had no say in choosing the casket, the hair arrangement, or any other item—except for the dress. Daddy chose a pink dress that sort of looked like a nightgown, and he asked for my approval. I agreed with a slow nod. She appeared to be in a dreamless sleep and an inexplicable calm surrounded her body.

When her sisters were getting things ready for the funeral, I overheard some of the conversations.

"It's a shame Hannah won't be able to come, but that baby's due anytime now," Aunt Lillian mentioned.

Aunt Minnie replied, "John said it should be born after the first of November."

"Olevia's birthday is in November, isn't it?" Aunt Lessie joined in.

"Yeah, I think so. Maybe it will give her something to think about."

I needed something besides death and pain to think about, and I latched onto this impending birth. This new baby would be special. I dreamed my sister had a little girl born on my birthday and they moved back home. But, for right then, my goal was to survive the next couple of days.

I remember seeing her obituary in the *Daily Town Talk*. It was headed: *Mrs. Mary Yeager Expires at Age 45* as if she had run out of shelf life, reached her expiration date, and the time had come to replace her. I am sure the intention was not unkind, but I hated it. I still have a copy of it in an album, and it still makes me cringe.

Viewing began on October 26 at seven o'clock at night and lasted until nine. For the next two days, viewing hours were from one in the afternoon until nine at night. My family believed that the soul did not leave the body until the third day. Thus, Daddy, Johnny, and I sat with Mama's body for every hour from the first day it arrived at Hixson Brothers until it left in a hearse transporting it to the church.

So many people came to express their condolences and to hug us all. Though I have not looked at it in many years, I have the guest book. I remember it as packed with names, but I never counted them. I just remember the hundreds of faces I saw.

At night, when the lights went dark, John and I lay on the benches to sleep. Most of the time, Daddy just sat and cried. I know we must have eaten and bathed, but I remember only leaving that room once. That short reprieve happened just before the place closed on the last night of our vigil when Aunt Doris Sue showed up.

Doris Sue, Mama's half-sister, had a bit of baggage, based on what I had heard from Daddy. She was considered a tad loose and maybe even trampy by Daddy's standards. She smoked and had a problem with the truth, according to her reputation. But I was happy to see her and to hear her talk.

"John, how ya' doin'?" She gave him a half-smile.

Daddy answered in monosyllables. "Okay."

She chattered on for a few minutes and then said the most wonderful thing I had heard in days. "Do you mind if I take these kids next door to the bus station for a Coke?"

"No."

The thought of leaving this atmosphere for just a few minutes felt like a life preserver thrown to a drowning man just before he went down for the last time.

Johnny felt differently. "I don't wanna go. I'll stay with Daddy."

I immediately chimed in, "I wanna go!"

"Come on, Olevia. Let's take a walk and have a Coke."

I jumped up to join her walking out. When we got to the entrance of the funeral home, she explained to the attendant that I would be back in a half hour or so, and she asked if someone could let me back in. They assured her that presented no problem.

We walked over to the Trailways bus station and sat in a booth.

"Are you hungry?" Aunt Doris peered at me.

"No."

"How about a Coke?"

"Okay."

"How are you doin'? Is your Aunt Denie still at your house?"

"Yes, ma'am."

"Well, that's good."

"When's Mary's funeral? Tomorrow?"

"Yes. Saturday. This is the last night we spend at the funeral home."

"I bet you're tired!"

Our miscellaneous chit-chat continued for about half an hour. I even ate some French fries after a while. Doris Sue provided a ray of sunshine on a very dark day, and I am forever grateful for her kindness.

The next morning, we went home to get ready for the funeral scheduled for two that afternoon.

Aunt Denie had our clothes laid out, and we all bathed and washed our hair. Aunt Denie helped me fix my ponytail, get into my black wool skirt, and put on my black sweater.

****

The funeral service took place at Kingsville Baptist Church on October 29. The pallbearers carried the coffin and placed it at the front of the church. I don't recall the names of all the pallbearers, but I do remember five of them clearly—three of my half-brothers and Mama's two brothers, J.T. and Uncle Son. As a family, we followed directly behind the coffin and then individually stopped to look at her body one last time. I remember Grandpa leaned in, tried to lift her, and managed to give her a kiss.

As I briefly scanned the crowd, I initially saw no classmates and did not expect any. Being Saturday and the weekend of the Shreveport Fair, eighth graders were otherwise engaged! Then, my eyes fell on my friend, Sara Terrell, and my heart did a little jump. Her presence reminded me of life outside of the hell in which we had lived for the last week. She brought comfort through her presence, and I've never forgotten it. Indeed, I am forever grateful.

John and I did not cry at Mama's funeral, and I heard people say we didn't realize the real situation. They were wrong. Standing in six feet of snow with a blowing wind on a summer day could be more easily imaginable than losing our port of safety.

Vanner Claunch, one of Daddy's cousins, gave the official eulogy, and the church's pastor also officiated. The church brimmed with people, so many that a large group stood outside. I felt glad that so many people cared about my Mama. She lit up my life so immensely, and it touched me to see her light had touched others as well.

Once the church service concluded, we were directed to a family car following the hearse to Forest Lawn on the Monroe Highway, not far from the church or our house. Mama's plot occupied a spot at the back of the cemetery and, as we parked and got out, cars were still coming through the entrance. It improved the atmosphere to know so many people cared. John and I held hands as we stood beside the casket.

I whispered to him. "Look at the cars coming!"

"Are they coming here? To Mama's grave?"

"Yes, I think everybody loved Mama."

Eventually, we sat in a row of chairs along the edge of the grave with Mama's casket on a lift above it. Brother Bazor provided the brief graveside service. I don't remember what he said. Her coffin was lowered. It seems as if I remember each of us dropping a flower in, but I'm not sure. Things are blurry, but I do know we went home after that. Many cars followed us and stopped for a visit. Our kitchen overflowed with food brought in by friends. My aunts stayed busy putting stuff on the table, and everyone seemed to eat heartily. They told stories and laughed. I frowned. *Did they not know our world had ended?* I found it odd to hear them laughing as if it was all some kind of weird joke. John and I went to the back porch to be by ourselves. We needed to find our center of calmness within each other.

John tilted his head and said, "I wonder how long these people are going to stay."

"I don't know. I didn't know they were coming."

"Me neither. I wish they would go home now!"

"Me too," I responded. "I even heard Viola say to Aunt Denie, 'I wonder if the kids would like to go the zoo tomorrow?'"

"What did Aunt Denie say?"

"I don't know, but I'm not going. I can't believe Viola would ask."

Viola and Johnson lived in Rayne, about a hundred miles away, but her parents lived at the edge of Tioga. Apparently, she planned to stay in town for a couple of days.

"What are you gonna do tomorrow?"

I thought a minute before I replied, "I don't know. I'm going to school on Monday."

We talked about what that would be like. We talked about the new calves. We talked about anything and everything until Aunt Denie showed up at the door. I felt grateful that our conversation began to fill the holes in my heart. I believe it did for John as well.

"Kids, people are going home now. You need to come in and say goodbye."

We followed her back inside, hoping this was the first step towards a return to normal.

My mother understood me when there was no reason to understand. She rarely even raised her voice to me, but I could see in her eyes when my behavior disappointed her. The hurt I saw was powerful and broke my heart. I knew how much she expected of me, how special she saw me. The truth is that stubbornness, willfulness, and making my own decisions are part of my DNA, but Mama understood.

I inhabited a world—then and now—where I felt loved beyond anything I earned, and Mama was the root of that world. Indeed, my family was made better, for generations forward, because she lived. I shall never forget the last words she said to me: "Just remember I won't be cryin'. I'll be watchin' and lovin' you."

She continues to do just that!

CHAPTER 32

JOHN REMEMBERS

John and I shared our motherless world, but on some levels, we faced things alone. John experienced a profound, immediate, and perhaps more difficult recovery from Mama's passing. Some years ago, he wrote the following narrative from his perspective.

****

On October 25, 1956, our cow had twin black calves. Daddy said I could have them, and I named them Amos and Andy. I put a rope on them the day they were born, and Olevia took my picture standing between them. Those calves were pretty, and it was a happy day for me. When I closed my eyes to sleep in youthful anticipation of the next day with my calves, I did not imagine the pain that waited for me before sunup.

At three o'clock in the morning on October 26, Daddy woke me. Olevia stood beside him. His only words were "Mama died."

Fuzzy with sleep, I didn't comprehend what he said. I instinctively got up, without putting on my clothes, to sit in our old rocking chair.

Fruit was special in our house. And, perhaps for that reason, Daddy brought me a big, red apple from the kitchen. I believed it symbolized comfort, and I sat there eating that apple when an arrow hit my heart.

"You know you killed her, son. She got high blood pressure the day you were born."

Those words split my heart. I knew Daddy was hurting too and needed to share his grief. The apple turned to cotton, and I choked as the tears fell down my face and dripped from my chin—those were the only ones I shed at Mama's death.

I got up later to find company already in our living room. Johnson and Viola were there, and people were talking about the good things Mama had done. I listened, feeling a bit amazed to hear Mama described as such an outstanding person because life with Daddy had given me the impression Mama didn't really fit into the major scheme of things.

Her job was to take care of us, and she did, as expected, not special. Every now and then, someone would grab me, hug me, and say how terrible it was for Mama to have to leave such young children. I got the feeling they were grieving for me and not my Mama. I even heard some of them say, "At least she didn't suffer." It's not as if they knew anything about her life or mine. I wished they would go home and let us be alone.

Olevia and I went to The Pines. We needed to talk to be sure we remembered what Mama had told us about this day. We promised each other we would not cry. Later that same day, Johnson and Viola took Olevia and me to the funeral home where we had to look at Mama in the coffin. She had on a pink dress that looked like a fancy nightgown, and even her cheeks looked rosy.

People milled around, speaking in hushed tones. Being there prolonged and intensified my agony. I began to feel as bitter as the bitter weed we pulled from our field to prevent our cows from eating them. I began to resent everyone around me. All that night and the next day, we sat at the funeral home. Olevia and I slept on a bench.

At the funeral service held in Kingsville Baptist Church, Brother Bazor offered solace to the family and the mourners. His church had standing room only, probably the only such day in its history. He spoke long and impassionedly, but more about the living than about Mama.

I just sat and stared and wished it were over.

Once Brother Bazor finished his talk, we walked by Mama's coffin to look at her one more time. Grandpa bent to kiss her as tears ran down his cheeks, but he made not a sound. Grandma was crying out loud—almost hysterically—and, I thought, hypocritically. She was Mama's stepmother, and they were never close, and she behaved as if she had lost a favored daughter?

Of the eight men carrying the coffin, three were my brothers (Henry, James, and Johnson) and two were her brothers (J. T. and Uncle Son). We were in the first car following the hearse to Forest Lawn and, even though her burial plot lay at the back, cars lined the highway to enter the front as we walked to the graveside. Later, I heard people say the procession spanned almost a mile, and the flowers had taken up two rooms in the funeral parlor.

As the coffin slowly descended into the grave, I felt (more than heard) the sobs, groans, and moaning. But none of them came from Olevia or me. I didn't even look around but sat and stared at that coffin as it disappeared.

Back at home, a lot of fine food waited, and people showed up and it sounded like a party scene. An adult cousin, Merle, led me out under the oak tree to share a can of beer. I drank it—my first. I was eleven years old.

Late that afternoon, Viola wanted to take her kids and us to Alexandria City Park to take our minds off things—as if that were possible. I wanted everyone to go home, but we agreed to take a ride. On the way home, Viola stopped at a

Bolton Avenue ice cream shop and bought me a green ice cream cone—my first.

My childhood ended that day, and I knew it—just two months to the day since my eleventh birthday in August.

John wrote this piece years ago, and I have provided little editing, other than some punctuation and spelling. He remembers some things a bit differently than I, and he is entitled to his own memories.

CHAPTER 33

WORKING MY WAY BACK TO NORMAL

Merilyn.

Getting dressed for school the Monday after Mama's funeral seemed surreal. The morning unfolded pleasantly enough weather-wise, but my nerves were tingling. A bit of fear marked that day like a white line separating traffic on a dark road. I couldn't imagine talking and laughing with friends I hadn't seen in days; indeed, the thought of seeing them gave me the heebie-jeebies.

My friend, Sara Terrell, had been the only classmate to be present during the awfulness in which I nearly drowned. Every other eighth grader I knew spent Saturday at the annual Shreveport State Fair. Over the years, Sara and I have talked about that day as the beginning of a close and uniquely different relationship (not enjoyed with anyone else). It is as if we can talk without words. We remain close friends today, though she lives in North Carolina, and I'm in Texas.

But on this Monday morning, I had a problem even visualizing walking back into a school atmosphere as if nothing happened. Imagining the sound of everybody talking about their exciting weekend was as frightening to me as being dropped into another country where no one spoke English. I didn't envy their joy or the carefree attitude they had. I simply could not be a part of it, and I felt different.

As I prepared to leave the house, I became angrier than I'd ever been—maybe with God, maybe with everyone. It's hard to put those feelings into words. I inhabited a place like the Twilight Zone show where the images were distorted, the thoughts were deranged, and the actions were unacceptable. My world morphed into a topsy-turvy, scary place without the comfort of my mom's presence in my corner. I wanted the world to know how unfair it felt to go on with everyday life as if I had not lost a vital piece of me. My world turned upside down, and it would never be as it was before.

Daddy worked the seven-to-three shift at Alexandria's railroad roundhouse, and he left early that morning. I disregarded the note he had scribbled on pink paper and left lying across the telephone. I didn't care if he came home or not—or even if he ever spoke to me again. The last words I could remember him saying directly to me were, "Your mama's dead. We need to tell Johnny."

Aunt Denie planned to stay with us for a week or so to help us settle into a new routine. I ignored her calls from the kitchen and the sympathy in her voice.

As I opened the front door to leave, she called once more, "Olevia. Come get a biscuit and bacon before you go."

I let the slam of the screen door be my response as I started down the hill to the bus stop. John caught up with me before I reached the cattle gap at the end of our driveway.

"Why are you being so mean?" He handed me the biscuit and bacon Aunt Denie sent.

"I am not being mean. I just don't want that stupid biscuit." The leave me alone in my voice could be heard clearly.

"Did you get your lunch money? Daddy left it on the desk next to the telephone."

"No. I don't want it."

"How are you going to eat lunch if you don't have any money?"

"I have lunch money left from last week. And quit asking me so many questions!"

I spoke so cruelly that John flinched at my answer, but he continued to walk with me to the bus stop. We climbed on the school bus where I sat and stared straight ahead. Some of the kids tried to be nice but, in my opinion, failed miserably. Either they wanted to talk about the State Fair, or they wanted to express some sort of secondhand condolence. I simply stared at them as if we lived in different realms. Their attempts at comfort fell on deaf ears.

Meanwhile, John moved to the back of the bus, talking and laughing like everything was okay. I wanted to be annoyed with him as well, except I knew that was only the "outside" Johnny, not what he felt in his heart. He had a talent for stepping into a pretend world and becoming one with that world. At one point, the scene reminded me vaguely of his old playtime with his imaginary friend, Tere-Tone Boogers.

Now a sad cocoon surrounded my anger, making each emotion more intense. The thirty-five-minute bus ride felt like hours. Once at school, the morning dragged on, but fortunately, it dragged by in a perfunctory manner. Other than the teachers being too nice to me and none of my friends knowing what to say or do, it seemed to be just another day at school. At lunchtime, I grabbed my history book and headed over to the cafeteria. I carried my filled plate to an empty table and sat alone, somewhat separated from the rest of the eighth graders. I made my best impression of someone fascinated by a history book in which I had no interest.

"Hey, can I sit here?"

I looked up to see a girl with orange-red hair—a natural color I don't believe I'd seen before or since. Her densely freckled face included solid freckle splotches under her eyes. A friendliness and caring seemed to flow automatically in her voice.

I answered as nonchalantly as possible. "I guess so. Don't see anybody else in the chair. Who are you?"

"Merilyn Haydel. This is my first day here. We moved from Pineville over the weekend. I had hoped to go the fair this weekend, but I didn't get to."

A new girl—well that aroused my curiosity and diverted my attention from me at least momentarily. We didn't get many of those in Tioga, and I decided to continue the conversation. "So, where do you live?"

"My daddy got us a new Jim Walter's home. It's pretty close to Tioga Baptist Church. We are finishing it inside ourselves. Your name is Olevia, right?"

"Yeah. How do you know that?"

"Everybody's talking about you. Your mama just died, didn't she? Was she sick a long time?" Merilyn took on an empathic look—and not one I wanted to encourage.

"Sorta sick, I guess. I don't want to talk about it anymore." I felt tears behind my eyes and had no intention of sharing my grief with this girl I had met minutes ago.

With the ease of turning a page, Merilyn smiled and changed the subject. "Who is that good-looking boy over there?"

"David Rice. His mom's a beautician. She gave me a permanent in my ponytail. Are you going to go to Tioga Baptist Church?"

Merilyn's warmth and acceptance began to feel like a new path through my despair. I heard a bit of optimism in my voice without truly feeling it yet. Her presence had the effect of sunshine peeking out after a rainstorm. It's still cloudy and misty, but you know a sunny day is coming.

"I don't know. Does David go there?" she answered.

We both exploded in teenage giggles—my first real laugh in what seemed like years.

Merilyn instantly became my best friend, and we shared so many teenage experiences. Several years later, we moved together to Dallas, setting out to find our places in life.

The day I met my new best friend is the day I remembered every life is filled with ups and downs, and I had no corner on the market for either. This new friendship offered a way up and out of the deepest hell.

That was the day the fog began to lift, the clouds parted ever so briefly, and I saw the blue sky. I can almost swear I heard my mom's voice in my heart saying: *Olevia, you are a survivor, but it's up to you to accept the olive branches and compassion offered.*

Just one of the thousands of times I've felt her presence as if she never left. In my heart, I know she did not and never will.

Our household settled back into a routine quicker than I expected. A Trailways bus took Aunt Denie back to Pasadena within a week or so, and Daddy changed his work shift to evenings from three to eleven. Too many evenings alone were apparently more than he could bear.

When at home, he sat in a rocking chair on the porch with a tear-wet face. Johnny and I benefited from his choice to be home when we weren't. For nearly a year, Daddy's oral communication with us proved to be more limited than usual and typically only at his direction.

Notes on pink paper attached to the telephone on his desk provided our primary communication. If we wanted permission to do something, we wrote a note before we went to bed and checked for an answer the next morning. If he wanted us to perform some chore, he wrote a note before he went to work, and we read it when we came in from school.

Once John left his underwear lying on the floor in the living room and, requiring more time than necessary to pick them up, he wrote a note telling Daddy he planned to pick them up in the morning. Maybe he craved the conversation or maybe that was just him being an eleven-year-old boy.

I hadn't yet gotten the hang of cooking, so typically, lunch at school provided our only daily meal. But some nights Daddy woke us at midnight with Billips burgers and fries. They were delicious. If he picked them up but didn't feel like waking us, the burgers were left on the desk to be eaten for breakfast.

It wasn't perfect or normal yet, but we were headed in the right direction; every day we grew a bit more comfortable living in our skin.

****

I devoted the first week of November 1956 to contacting Hannah almost every day in hopes of hearing our baby was on the way. On my birthday, Robert called to report Hannah had finally been transported to the military base hospital.

"I knew you would want to know Hannah's in labor, and we expect a little one soon." He said shortly after I answered phone—and for that week, I could usually get to the phone before the second ring.

I eagerly replied, "What time?"

Robert laughed. "The baby will decide that."

"You think it will be before midnight? Tell Hannah I really, really want to share my birthday with my new niece or nephew!"

Christmas coming—that year or any year—did not hold a candle to my anticipation of this baby's birth. I needed something or someone to help fill a little of the void left by Mama's death. Something about my birthday made the pain a little sharper, and the thought of my new baby created a pain reliever for a migraine in my chest!

In response to my repeated pleas for speed, Robert replied, "Well, I'll give you a call as soon as the baby's born."

I hung up the phone in a state of bliss, convinced being an aunt was among the most treasured titles. And I must say, with my sister's and brother's children, I still feel that way.

I stayed up until midnight waiting for the call that didn't come.

Peggy Eileen Breneman was born at five-thirty on the morning of November 12, 1956. It was a Monday and the day after my birthday. I blamed Hannah for the late arrival. At thirteen, I certainly knew she did not command the situation—a fact immaterial to my reasoning or lack thereof.

Once I recovered from the misplaced annoyance, my letter campaign for a visit began. Daddy said the phone calls were an unnecessary expense. So, books of stamps and a ream of paper made their way to Hannah. One page at a time, I made my best case for her to move back to Louisiana as quickly as possible. I remembered a dream I had some weeks earlier, and I took it as some sort of prediction of the future. In lieu of a move, I requested a visit. That visit finally occurred in early February. Indeed, three-month-old Peggy looked, smelled, and sounded like the answer to a prayer; our lifelong bond began the instant I saw her.

That hands-on visit lay in the future. On that November 12, I had to get up and go to school the next day.

****

Merilyn and I were now fast friends and talked endlessly on the phone. Her mother made a rule: "Visit, don't phone." A three-minute egg timer beside her phone alerted Merilyn to hang up. If she didn't, I heard a dial tone when her mom hung up for her.

Three miles separated our houses, and we spent a lot of shoe leather to be together. Overnights were at her house more often than mine. Her mother disliked the lack of supervision at my house, and I preferred the family feel of hers.

Much to Daddy's chagrin, I moved my church membership to Tioga Baptist to be part of my new friend's world. Daddy did not go to church at all and, at thirteen, I began my term in the teenage jail of disrespect.

"Olevia, why aren't you going to Kingsville church anymore?"

"I like Tioga better."

"Your sister went to Kingsville."

"So."

"So, you should too. Do you know Johnny's quit going to church because of you?"

"He can go to Tioga, Daddy." I sounded annoyed because I was.

"Olevia, you need to be careful. You know, you're responsible for your little brother. He looks up to you."

"I don't want to be responsible for him. I don't want to be responsible for anybody."

Daddy sighed and walked away.

Thanksgiving, November 22, approached with little fanfare. We went to my grandpa's house, and the atmosphere felt funereal more than thankful. Among the crowd there, to the best of my memory, I first met Grandpa's sister, my Great Aunt Mary, for whom my mother was named. She bore an uncanny physical resemblance to my mother, but she sounded a great deal more Cajun when she spoke. I understood little of what she said, but she smiled when she said it, so I smiled back.

The day's highlights in my mind remain in the experience surrounding some guy who showed up in a truck with an out-of-state license plate. I am not one hundred percent certain of his name, but I do remember with some clarity several of the events surrounding his visit. It began with Grandpa seeing the truck coming up the long driveway. He sat in a straight chair balanced against the wall on the front porch as if holding court. He had a pipe in his mouth, and his hands moved as he controlled the conversation. Suddenly, he looked up.

"Who's that coming up the hill?"

No one could see who was in the truck or, for that matter, the entire truck. That didn't stop everyone from answering.

Uncle Son responded first. "Ain't that Rod, Grace's husband?"

Uncle Rod drove a similar truck.

Daddy answered directly to Uncle Son. "Rod's in the backyard, Son."

Daddy typically treated Uncle Son as if he were just a tad to the right of mental acuity. He talked fast and had a heavy south Louisiana accent. He lived in Jennings, Louisiana and laughed a lot. That, in and of itself, made him a little suspect in Daddy's mind. But that didn't tell the entire story.

Uncle Son was listed as missing during most of World War II and eventually declared dead. Uncle Son's paratroop division had jumped in behind enemy lines in error. He, along with everyone else in his group, spent the war in a German prison camp. He even lost two fingers during one of his unsuccessful attempts to escape. Near the end of the war, he became a part of a prisoner release. Daddy said no one could spend that length of time in a German prison and not be a little unhinged. Not everyone agreed with Daddy's assessment, including Grandpa and my mother.

At any rate, Uncle Rod did not occupy the truck in the driveway. As it got a little closer, someone suggested it had out-of-state tags that looked like Alabama.

By this time, Grandpa stood on the edge of the porch with his hands on his hips, staring out at the truck. As soon as it stopped and its driver opened his door to get out, Grandpa ran down the steps and all the way out to the gate. Everyone at the gathering stood facing the action.

"What happened to your Daddy?" Grandma asked Aunt Grace.

"I don't know. He seems to know that person in the truck."

Aunt Grace barely had that out of her mouth when Aunt Mary ran toward the gate. The rest of us stood motionless and staring.

Grandma yelled down to Grandpa. "Papa, bring your company up here. We're just getting the food out, and there's plenty of chairs in the yard." She went back into the house.

Grandpa and Aunt Mary walked on either side of the stranger, obviously known to them. The man turned out to be some cousin who had lived in south Louisiana and had come for a family meal years ago. After the meal, he took his wife home, said he was going out for a little while, and never came back. At some point, everyone decided he must dead or at the very least permanently missing from the family.

"Come on, Boudreaux, bring that chair over here. Let's talk," Grandpa suggested.

Grandma interrupted—still not having inquired as to who the new guest was. "Everybody, before you sit down, make a plate and get some iced tea."

Someone gave thanks. Then, we all filled our plates and sat in sort of a semi-circle around Boudreaux's chair.

He looked like a celebrity in front of an audience! The entire event could be favorably compared to the prodigal son come home. Grandpa first explained who he was and shared the story I mentioned earlier. The balance of the day became something of a forum—the audience asked him questions and hung on to every answer.

On that Thanksgiving, I relished this totally unprepared and unexpected sideshow. It lightened everyone's mood and transformed the atmosphere from crying over a death to celebrating a rebirth. I began to realize that in the darkest moments, there are always rays of light if you look for them.

Perhaps the most interesting part of the play did not reveal itself until sometime later. When Boudreaux drove off that afternoon, no one knew where he went. To my knowledge, no family members ever saw him again. However, after that day, the above story grew in detail when shared at future Williams family gatherings. Someone always said, "Wonder if Boudreaux's coming?" A laugh followed that inquiry, as well as a retold version as Grandpa remembered.

I perceived getting through Thanksgiving as another step in climbing the mountain to normalcy. Christmas lay right around the corner and would present its own challenges as well as lessons to learn.

Life must come one day at a time.

CHAPTER 34

THIS YEAR WAS DIFFERENT

It was December 22, 1956, just three days until Christmas. School was on holiday break, and time lay heavily on our hands. Christmastime, in past years, usually shined bright for both Johnny and me, but this year was different. It reminded me of a saying my Mama had when things went wrong. "Well, that fell as flat as a flitter!"

The thought of hearing Mama's voice as we worked toward coming to terms with a new Christmas provided a brief image of a treasured time.

No celebrations planned, no gifts to put under the tree, and no tree, even if we had gifts. My dad gave us each the traditional ten-dollar savings check to spend—but on what? The checks remained uncashed because this year was different.

It seemed as if all the joy of Christmas had died along with Mama. Thanksgiving came and went with little to no feeling of thankfulness—at least on my part—except for surviving it.

Despite our best efforts at normalcy, on some days, our lives—Johnny's and mine—occupied a dark place where we got up in the morning, made it through the day, and went to bed at night. We lived on the edge of real life, almost in the shadows, and did our best to keep our secret from everyone. Not every day, just some days—and it appeared as if Christmas faced that fate.

As we sat on the front porch, we talked about Christmases past.

"Remember the year you got your bicycle?" Johnny asked.

"I do. I went outside immediately to ride it."

"Yeah, and you fell before you got to the driveway. That was funny!" He grinned.

"Maybe to you; not to me." I laughed. "Know what I like best about Christmas? Kumquats."

"Kumquats. Why?"

"For one thing, I think they're only available at Christmas, and we get some in our stockings every year. I like the sweet rind and the tart insides."

"Oh," John responded unenthusiastically with his shoulders slumped and his gaze fixed on the wooden porch boards, as if studying them would give him answers.

We continued to sit on the porch and reminisce about what we enjoyed most on prior Christmas mornings.

Suddenly, Johnny exclaimed, "We could have a Christmas tree."

"How? Daddy always brings the tree home. I don't think he's getting one this year." I wanted John to avoid any additional sadness brought on by trying to make Christmas normal. The attempt itself created more pain.

"But I know where he gets them. Down in the woods by the trestle. We could do that."

"I don't know. Do you know how to cut down a tree? We have never cut down a tree."

John's excitement seemed only to grow despite my throwing cold water on his hot idea. "Come on, Olevia. Let's do it."

He already stood on the steps, so my choice became inevitable. I certainly could not let him go by himself.

We found a hatchet in the barn and took the half mile walk to the creek to wander among the pine trees. Following an hour or more of searching, we found one we liked and took turns swinging the axe. Eventually, it fell. We went through the motions, but the atmosphere remained solemn. No frivolity. It felt more like completing an assigned chore.

Despite this year being different, a tiny voice inside required us to make the effort, perhaps because Mama would be pleased.

"Well, we have a tree, Johnny, and it's a pretty one. Mama would like it." I spoke with the same enthusiasm as saying, 'We've washed the dishes, and now we have to put them away.'

We spent a few minutes looking at our tree and discussing how best to get it home. In time, Johnny grabbed one side, and I took the other.

We dragged it down the railroad tracks for the entire half-mile home, stopping only to change sides, as our arms ached. We reached our driveway and, ultimately, the front yard where we sat down to catch our breath from climbing the final hill—really, the only hill.

Talk of getting the tree set up began.

Properly placing our tree in the corner of the living room routinely involved a group effort. As my older sister turned the tree, Mama chose the best side to place against the wall. John and I sorted decorations and offered opinions. Hannah, now a new mom, living in Missouri and Mama lived in our hearts and memories only.

Everything kept pointing to how this year was different.

We talked about the decorations and how Mama helped us in making some of them.

"I wonder how this tree will look covered in bulbs, tinsel, and lights." It was more of a comment to me than to John.

He did not immediately respond. Just a faint shrug.

I added, "How about popcorn? Are we going to do popcorn this year?"

"I hope so, but I don't know if we can string it."

"Geez, Johnny. Didn't you ever watch Mama? She just sewed it together. Let's ask Daddy to bring some home to pop. I'm ready to set the tree up. How about you?" An edge of enthusiasm began to grow in my attitude toward the idea.

"I'll get the stand, and you get the corner ready," John replied.

We met again in the front yard in just minutes.

"Let's put it in the stand before we take it in the house. Daddy will be surprised when he comes home tonight."

"Okay. We can stand it up to see which side is best."

We each immediately grabbed one side of the tree as we stood it up. At first, I felt tears welling up, and then I looked at Johnny through the branches remaining on the tree. His surprise look included the beginning of a grin. I took a second glance at the tree, and tears dried as I continued to watch John's reaction. Our tree was completely flat on one side, with all branches eliminated by the railroad ties and rocks when we dragged it home.

With a gleam in his eye, Johnny said, "I don't think we need that corner. We can put it up flat against any wall."

Grins and chuckles turned into roaring laughter, and the stored-up sadness softened as it melted into a manageable emotion. The release of both laughter and tears can produce the same relief, it seems.

"Hey, before we decorate it, let's get our savings checks and walk up to Merritt's store. If we have a tree, we need presents—especially for this tree," I said between giggles.

Johnny dropped the tree, and the spirit of Christmas began to recover in our hearts as we went inside to get our checks.

We had a decorated tree, gifts surrounding it, and stockings hung. Daddy even joined us Christmas morning to drink coffee. Among the best surprises, for me, came from seeing the filled stockings. As every other year, Daddy filled them with fruit—including kumquats!

Maybe that year was not so different after all because Christmas is always Christmas. It is up to us to find and experience the joy waiting there. A part of that joy comes in mentally reliving memories of Christmases past while adding new ones.

Chapter 35

PEGGY EILEEN BRENEMAN

Peg.

Some people show up in your life at exactly the right time to provide a basis for an eternal friendship. That happens rarely, and yet this special blessing began for me on November 12, 1956. My niece, Peggy Eileen Breneman, was born in Warrensburg, Missouri.

The January before, Peggy's mom (my sister Hannah) had married and moved to Missouri with her Air Force husband, Robert. Mama, even though in the last months of her life, insisted on visiting her pregnant daughter to see for herself that she was okay. So, technically, I met Peg in utero in the summer of 1956 following an exhausting and perilous train trip to Missouri.

In a way, it was love at first sight without sight!

Mama crossed to the other side on October 26, 1956, and my new focus became Peg's impending birth. My dream transformed into a desire for a niece or nephew born on my birthday, November 11. Multiple phone calls to Robert resulted in his promise to call us as soon as the baby arrived. He notified us that Hannah had entered the hospital on my birthday, and I began a vigil of sitting near the phone.

Like a helium balloon losing its gas, I went to sleep with a deflated dream, but I woke up to a new universe on November 12. My niece arrived five and a half hours too late to share my birthday. We now had two birthdays to share, and though I did not realize it then, that would prove to be double the pleasure.

I longed to see and touch this baby. Success followed an almost two-month-long letter campaign when Hannah and her firstborn showed up at our house in February of 1957.

Like a cool balm on a sweaty brow, peace settled over my entire being. In my spirit, I believed Peggy answered a prayer and filled my desperate need for somebody to love as well as someone who would love me unconditionally. Our lifelong bond began in my mind long before I met her, and it cemented there when I first saw her.

In a way, looking at her felt like a *Back to the Future* moment, as if I looked in a mirror and saw myself with a new beginning in a world where love never dies. I can't really explain the hope and peace I felt, except to say, I knew my Mama stood by me and shared my experience. Her presence in my mind provided all I needed to completely realize that we live forever, somewhere, and the connection is permanent.

In my naivety, I expected Hannah being at home would feel like old times; it didn't. Not fully recovered from giving birth, plus a whole set of mommy rules governed her every move—and she limited all access to Peg. She called Robert every day to say when she and Peg would be coming home to Missouri.

Peggy slept in a cardboard box on top of Daddy's chest of drawers. Hannah allowed us to remove her only at the hours Hannah designated on an attached chart. Hoping the routine was all for show and not what she truly expected, I challenged every rule listed.

"Hannah, can I hold Peggy?"

"I told you I'll let you feed her at two o'clock, her next scheduled bottle."

I whined, "That's only ten minutes, and she's already awake. Can't I pick her up now?"

"No. I will not allow you or anyone else to spoil my child. You'll have to wait."

I begged, "She's crying now, and it's not too early. Can I change her diaper, and then it'll be two o'clock?"

"If you keep asking, I'm not going to let you feed her at all."

At night, Daddy took Peggy out of the box and slept with her. Instead of Peggy, he called her Rusty, a name my mom had chosen for her.

"Dad. I don't want her to be confused. Please call her by her name."

"Lighten up, Hannah," Daddy replied. "You'll be a mom a lot longer than I'll enjoy this child as a grandfather."

Hannah frowned. "Daddy, it's not that I don't want you to have a relationship with her, but there are rules. I'm not going to have a spoiled brat for a child."

Daddy chuckled and walked away, carrying Peggy to the front porch and his rocking chair. Hannah did not intervene, and that made me feel a bit braver.

That night, after everyone settled into bed and I thought they were asleep, I crept into Daddy's room and carefully removed Peggy from his grip. Hannah found me rocking her baby on the front porch. We lashed out at each other.

While the week she visited included many good times, I did not regret seeing her board a Trailways bus back to Missouri.

I often think of how I behaved during that visit and regret my lack of empathy. Trapped in my own temporary solitary confinement of grief, I ignored or didn't see Hannah's plight. She not only dealt with losing her mom, but she also faced the perils of being a mom herself. Add to that the hassle of traveling on a bus with a three-month-old infant from Missouri to Louisiana. In retrospect, I admire her rather pugnacious behavior exhibited by her attempt to remain in control.

The next time I saw Peg, I also met Susan, her younger sister born eighteen months later. Robert's parents lived in Lee Heights, a nearby town, and, to the best of my memory, the babies were brought down for introduction to more grandparents. Although a complete family affair this time, the visit only lasted a few days. Spending time with Peggy and Suse served as a well-needed respite from life as usual for us and for Daddy.

During a visit at the Breneman's, Daddy asked Robert to come by our house to talk—an invitation that probably aggravated Robert's nervous stomach syndrome. Nevertheless, he showed up with Hannah and the girls. Before they even got up the steps, Daddy stood, put out his hand, and indicated Robert was to sit in the vacant rocking chair.

"Hannah, hand me Rusty. Why don't you and the baby go in the house with Olevia?"

I smiled at the name he still insisted on attaching to Peg. I had arrived at the screen door and opened it for them.

Daddy turned his attention to me. "Olevia, put on a pot of coffee."

"Yes, sir."

Hannah, carrying Suse, obediently followed me into the living room as Daddy, with Peg in his lap, settled in on the front porch with Robert. I hastily put on the coffee and hurried back to the living room where Hannah still stood.

"Hey, do you know what Daddy wants to talk to Robert about?" she asked just above a whisper.

"Sorta. Let's sit close to the screen door, and we can probably hear." We each pulled up a chair. "Can I hold Suse for a little while?"

She quietly shushed me and readily handed over Suse just as the conversation outside began in earnest.

"Son, I'm not gonna beat around the bush. Hannah needs to be home. These kids need her, and she'd be better off here."

"What do you mean, Mr. Yeager?" I heard confidence in Robert's voice for the first time when speaking to Daddy. "She's my wife, and we're happy in Massachusetts."

Massachusetts is where they were transferred shortly before Susan's birth.

"Well, son, you think you are, and maybe YOU are, but what about Hannah and her orphaned siblings?"

Daddy laid it on thick. Normally, he did not refer to us as orphans, and I'm pretty sure our welfare did not appear very high on the list of why he wanted Hannah to move home. As his first daughter and apple of his eye, he missed her, especially as he adjusted to being alone. I'm not sure what he thought would happen if she moved home, but it appeared he only wanted to rebuild his environment as close as possible to what it used to be.

Watching and listening to the two of them reminded me of watching a Western movie when you knew the good guys would win the battle, but you weren't sure how.

Visibly uncomfortable, Robert ran his fingers through his hair and petted the dog, now curled up at his feet. Then, he cautioned Peggy to be still. I could not see her from where I sat inside, but I certainly hadn't heard any complaints. Hannah, sensing a needed break in the conversation, murmured, "Give me Susan, and get some coffee out there."

I moved quickly and now felt a conspiratorial bond with my sister. I first handed Robert a cup, which he quickly took, although I'm not even sure he drank coffee. Then I turned to Daddy.

"Here's yours, Daddy. Just like you like it. Half of a cup, so it doesn't get cold." He took the cup.

I reached for Peggy. "Come with me, Peg. We might take a walk out to see the chickens and maybe find some eggs." At nearing two years old, she didn't walk—she ran. She hopped out of Daddy's lap and grabbed my hand as she headed for the steps.

"Wait." I picked her up, laughing. "Let's go into the house first, and then we'll look for eggs in a little while."

The conversation resumed outside with Daddy's next volley. "So, you say you were transferred to Massachusetts, right?"

Robert leaned back in his chair, smiling as he responded, "Yes, sir. You know, being a military family, we're at the beck and call of the government. They put us where they want us." He sounded a great deal more relaxed, obviously thinking he was ahead of the game.

He did not realize what a formidable opponent he faced, and the game had only begun. The conversation slightly changed tone, allowing Robert to score several points. More accurately, Daddy threw some softballs to set up the strike out.

"Your parents are in the military, aren't they?"

"Yes, sir. They were until Dad retired a couple of years ago."

"They live around here now, don't they? I mean, I know we went to their place over at Seventy-one Courts, the other day. Is that where they live now?"

"Yes, sir. They like it here. Dad's hitch at the England Air Force Base in Alexandria was a long one. Mom made a lot of church friends, and she wanted to retire here, at least for little while."

"That's good. I'm glad your dad could make her happy. I'm sure it's a lot different when you're on active duty."

"Oh, yes, sir! It's totally different. We just pick up and go wherever we are assigned."

"Huh. Does anyone ever have an opportunity to influence the placement?"

"Not really."

Daddy stared at him questioningly but said nothing.

Robert expanded on his answer, "Well, I guess there are hardship transfers."

From our quiet spot in the background, Hannah and I looked at each other. By this time, we each held a sleeping child as the rocking chairs worked their magic. With a big smile on my face, I mouthed the words to Hannah, "You're coming home."

She shook her head no emphatically; I just continued to grin as we listened to Daddy's response.

"What kind of things are called hardships?"

As Robert explained various hardship situations, Hannah mouthed to me, "We're coming home." Her smile didn't seem as enthusiastic as I would have liked, but it's always one step at a time. Peg began to stir in my lap, and I quit listening to the conversation outside—the game was over anyway.

Peg and I took a walk to find some eggs.

****

Almost a year passed before the hardship transfer came through. I truly believe the elapsed time allowed both Daddy and Robert some taste of a win.

They moved into a house less than a mile from ours. I immediately became the babysitter-on-call, and I loved it. John had a motor scooter, and, for only a quarter, he would drive me over at the drop of a hat. After Hannah got a full-time job at Rapides Bank, I became a live-in babysitter for the summer.

The situation of my dreams did not last long enough to suit me. Robert was shipped TDY overseas, and Hannah drove across the country, moving to California to wait for their next destination to be determined. By this time, a son named Bill had joined their family.

In addition to the three kids, John accompanied her on the trip to California. Having lost interest in high school, he wanted to enlist in the military. Not old enough to do so, even with Daddy's signature, he chose a trip to California and never came back home to live.

The Breneman family's next destination was Japan, and quite a few years passed before we were united in the flesh. To the best of my memory, they were stationed in Louisiana for a while, and their last stateside destination was Abilene, Texas. They were in Abilene when Peggy's father suddenly died of a brain aneurysm, just months before he could retire at forty years old.

Hannah had his body transported to Pineville, Louisiana for burial. During the memorial service, I stood next to a sixteen-year-old Peg, squeezed her hand, and shared her grief as only one who has lost a parent early can.

****

Within six months, Hannah and the kids were living in Mesquite, Texas, just a few miles from me. My title of Aunt Olevia became AO during the many afternoons spent together.

"AO, get your cigarette and pour a Coke for us."

"What's up, Peg?"

"Nothin's up. Everything's down."

Thus, the afternoon began with a smile lifting the gloom from whatever teenage crisis had occurred. Parental disagreements, boyfriend problems, college aspirations, or anything and everything else became the topic of the day. I relived the days spent in Mrs. Curry's kitchen pouring my heart out to someone who understood. This time, I was blessed with Mrs. Curry's role, and I saw my teenaged self in Peg.

We've supported each other through her stint in the Air Force, the birth of her two children, a divorce, a remarriage, her graduation from Texas Women's University, the deaths of my two husbands, the death of her mom, and more. Every event in our lives, great or small, is made better because we share it.

Today, Peg and her husband, Matthew, live in Denton, about thirty miles from me. Over the years, a lot has happened in both of our lives, but our bond has only been strengthened. Not mucilage, but the super glue of shared experiences morphed our relationship into something unique.

I instinctively know Mama is proud of her first granddaughter and the woman she is today. I like to believe Mama shared our afternoon conversations just as she sat at the table with Mrs. Curry and me.

CHAPTER 36

MRS. CURRY

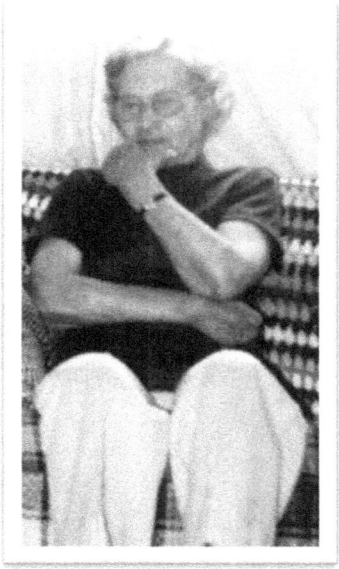

Mrs. Curry, late 1970s.

Mrs. Curry's influence became a huge part of my life during my teenage years. Though she passed away many years ago, her impact remains today. When I think about those motherless years, I find it strange that John and I lived in the same house and had diametrically opposite experiences—not in the day-to-day home life, but in what we did with our time apart.

As John did what he needed to do to face his new life, I was busy building a pretend family. I adopted whatever rules my friends had as to curfews, allowed activities, and more.

Then, I attributed them to my dad when talking to anyone else. In truth, he knew little about what I was doing or where I was doing it. Mrs. Curry provided the rails I needed on a day-to-day basis.

As things settled down in our lives, Mrs. Curry's guidance began in earnest. She became my stand-in mom, and I spent a part of every day at her house. We shared coffee (and sometimes biscuits with homemade Mayhaw jelly) before I caught the morning bus. I finished my day in front of her TV while we played Rook, Hearts, or Five Hundred Rummy.

I resented every vacation she took and pouted until she returned.

On some mornings, she awoke to my knock on her bedroom window.

"Are you up yet?" Of course, I knew she wasn't. It was not yet six-thirty in the morning. I knocked again and could see her sitting up in bed. "Oh good, is the front door locked?" I called through the screened window.

"No. Come on in," she said as she crawled out of bed and headed for the kitchen, where I soon stood next to her. "What's going on this morning? Isn't it a bit early?"

"Not really. It's already almost seven o'clock," I said, exaggerating the lateness of the hour. "The school bus will be here soon. I need to talk to you about something."

By this time, the coffee was dripping, and the cups were on the table.

"Okay. Have a seat." She smiled and yawned at the same time. Still, the welcome in her voice filled the room. She poured the coffee and then spent the next thirty to forty minutes listening to whatever teenage situation I had that needed advice.

In short, she guided me through my triumphs and disappointments, and she never complained about my clinginess. No matter what happened, I knew there would be a soft landing in Mrs. Curry's safety net.

As a kitchen table observer in the past, I saw her as a thin woman with a tendency toward having the blues and migraines. On a bad day, she signaled her desperation by playing country songs at top volume on the radio or the Victrola. Then, she'd lie prone on the cool linoleum floor with the window shades drawn and a wet washcloth on her forehead.

While Mama lived, she answered Mrs. Curry's cries for companionship. When Mama died, Mrs. Curry returned the favor to me. Now, I sat at the kitchen table—not as an observer but as a teenager trying to find my way. As I drank coffee, instead of listening, I talked.

****

Before the Currys moved into the little house, they bought butter and eggs from Mama. During Mrs. Curry's visits, they dreamed together—both wanting something better. As our neighbors, they made a lot of improvements to the little house: an added bathroom, three more bedrooms, and a screened-in back porch.

Pasquali, their carpenter, was the only Mexican (indeed the only Hispanic) I met while growing up in Tioga. It is quite possible that his name was not Pasquali, but that's what we called him.

He completed the renovation with sporadic help from one or two other guys. He did the plumbing, the electrical work, the roofing, and all the construction. We marveled at his abilities and willingness to work, often arriving at sunrise and leaving at sunset. Mrs. Curry provided him with lunch and kept a jug of iced sweet tea readily available to stave off the heat of the Louisiana summers.

Mrs. Curry was a non-church-going Christian who might sing a hymn while trimming the hedge. She kept her Bible prominently displayed, but, to my knowledge, she rarely opened it. Not only did she take food to any sick neighbor, but after the loss of my mama, she spent hours mothering her friend's orphaned children. She wore pants or shorts, putting on a dress only for the most special occasions such as a revival meeting Mama once talked her into attending or a dance, she and Mr. Curry occasionally enjoyed on a Saturday night.

She loved her hair, considered it her best feature. She bragged that it lay in waves and required little care, just a wash and comb push-up. She enjoyed singing and believed her soprano voice to be above average; it wasn't. She sang based on how she heard herself, not how others did. At the church revival that she attended with us, her strong (her word) soprano stood out among the congregation. She smoked Pall Malls, made her own clothes, had a garden, and talked often about growing up in Fort Smith, Arkansas.

She instinctively knew I needed her, and she began her quest to achieve my trust in early 1957. I initially tried establishing a relationship with Aunt Grace, but that didn't work out. She experienced her own grief, and daily interruptions by a lost thirteen-year-old just exacerbated her wounds. She had suggested to Daddy that I not come every day. He relayed the message, and the visits stopped.

On weekends, I could usually be found at Merilyn's house, but school-day visits were not encouraged by her mom. Both her mom and stepdad had jobs, there were four kids in the family, and her grandparents lived next door. In the winter, when the sun set a lot earlier, someone had to drive me home. My presence upset their routine on school days.

For a week or so after being banned from Aunt Grace's, I came straight home, did my homework, and watched TV until eleven o'clock at night when our one-channel *Window to the World* television station signed off. Unless Johnny was at home and awake, I sat immobilized by an unexplainable fear until I heard Daddy's car door slam, assuring his arrival home. I then ran for bed to prevent him from knowing I was up so late.

Those miserable evenings ceased on the day Mrs. Curry met me at the gate between our driveway and her place. I noticed her standing there when I stepped off the bus and wondered the reason why.

Out of courtesy, I spoke when I approached her. "Hello, Mrs. Curry. How are you?"

"I'm just fine. It's a little chilly today, and I thought we could enjoy a hot cup of coffee together before you go home?"

"At your house?" I asked incredulously.

She laughed. "Yeah. Billips is too far for me to walk!"

I didn't acknowledge her joke and only half heard it. I waffled emotionally between excitement at a new avenue toward normalcy and fear of being disappointed again. The indecision mummified me, and I stood there staring.

She spoke again. "Well, coming in or not?" Her voice had a kind sound and a smile to accompany it.

"I guess so."

She put her arm around me as we walked toward her house. Our relationship evolved from monosyllable answers that day to pouring out my heart every day and asking for comments, advice, and empathy. No subject was off the table while she taught me to cook, to sew, and to take care of myself.

****

One Saturday, I arose early with the intent of making a straight skirt for myself. Straight skirts were all the rage, and I had only the black wool one I wore to my mother's funeral. On the surface, making a straight skirt looked easy enough, but I had not yet had a home economics class.

I first made certain our treadle Singer machine had been threaded properly and the bobbin correctly inserted. I sewed a few stitches on a material scrap and then began gathering what I thought to be the needed materials to make a straight skirt.

I removed the waistband from one of my gathered skirts and cut the material approximately the size of the waistband. I ran a seam down the side and replaced the waistband. Of course, my efforts resulted in a ruined gathered skirt and no new skirt. Crying over spilt milk (which seemed to have become my lot in life too often), I headed to Mrs. Curry's with both skirts in hand.

That ill-planned activity culminated into one of the best days of my life.

Not even slowing down to knock, I ran through the kitchen door where I saw Mrs. Curry, still wearing her nightgown and standing near the stove.

"Mrs. Curry. I made a mess out of my skirt!" I exclaimed through sobs.

"Well, good morning, Olevia!" Mrs. Curry calmly turned toward me. "Whatever the problem, it can't be as bad as you think."

"It is! I need a straight skirt for Monday. All my friends and I plan to wear one, and I don't have any except that horrible black one." My tears were now just tears, not sobs, as the peace of Mrs. Curry's kitchen settled in.

"I just put on a pot of coffee, Olevia," she said. She continued to stand near the stove, but now her back was toward me. "I'm getting a later start than usual this morning, and George and Ellis left a few minutes ago to go fishing. We have some time to talk. Whatta you say? Wanna a cup?"

"Yes, please." I tossed her a grateful smile. "And what's smelling so good?" I asked eagerly. Tears were no longer flowing, and I knew Mrs. Curry would somehow solve my problem.

"That's banana bread I'm toasting in the oven. I baked the bread yesterday, but I like it best buttered and toasted in the morning with coffee. Want some?"

I nodded yes as I settled in at the table, and we shared coffee and banana bread toast.

"Now, tell me. What's wrong?" she asked.

The more I told the story, the more uncontrolled Mrs. Curry's laughter became. I soon joined her as she joked about the figure required to wear my new skirt. She imitated the walk necessary to move in it if I could have gotten into it. I joined her, adding my own imagined walk. Before long, we both shed tears of laughter.

That event in early 1957 marked the beginning of our souls recognizing each other.

She taught me to truly laugh again. Merilyn and I laughed with each other, but as much as we enjoyed our friendship, it mirrored every best friend's teenage relationship. We were equals in knowledge, age, and experience. The room for learning from each other was minimal—we learned together. My relationship with Mrs. Curry resembled a mother/daughter connection with an extra cup of just plain friendship.

We finished breakfast, and the anticipation of more fun had replaced all feelings of defeat. She took a dress from her closet, removed the skirt, and proceeded to teach me how to make a pattern.

"Okay, Olevia. This won't be a McCall's pattern. In fact, it's simpler than a Simplicity." She smiled at her recognition between the complex and the basic as she cleaned off the table and covered it with a newspaper, pencils, and scissors. I watched closely.

"Come over here, and let's get some measurements."

She measured my waist, my hips, and the length from my waist to my knees. Using that data, she drew a pattern on a page of the *Alexandria Daily Town Talk*. She asked me to cut it out as she explained how darts decreased the size from hips to waist and the need for a zipper to allow room to put the skirt on.

Once it had been cut out, she instructed me how to pin it to the dress material that had now replaced the newspaper.

"Be sure to place the pattern pieces in such a way as to use the minimum amount of material and still keep the correct fabric directions."

"Fabric directions? What do you mean?"

"Well, for instance, in this particular case, you want to make certain all stripes go from top to bottom. You need to pin the pattern to the fabric in a grain and cross-grain fashion."

"What? Nothing here looks like a grain to me!"

Mrs. Curry chuckled and sort of scratched her head. "Why don't I just show you what I mean?" She took the pattern and the box of pins.

"That sounds good to me!" Her patience applied to my lack of knowledge allowed me to not feel stupid, just uneducated. We worked through to the point that the skirt was ready to be assembled.

"Do you want to try sewing it on the machine?"

"I do, but I want you to go first and let me watch."

Hours later, I had that skirt on, and I wore it to school on Monday. In fact, I may have done a little bragging about having made it myself.

More of the smothering fog lifted, allowing the sunshine to break through and optimism to glimmer. Mrs. Curry always stood in the background cheering me on.

****

One more special story of the dozens available—a slumber party—illustrates Mrs. Curry's compassion and love for me and my mama. At sixteen, I wanted to have a slumber party. The idea first occurred to me while Merilyn and I sat on my bed discussing things to do.

"Merilyn, I'm thinking about having a slumber party. I'm going to see if Daddy'll let me take him to work, and I'll keep the car. Maybe we could all go to the drive-in. What do you think?"

"I don't know. I think my mom will let me come; she's gotten to know your dad a bit better. Have you asked anyone else yet?"

I had become so comfortable in my new life that it did not occur to me that supervision might be a problem with my friends' parents.

"No. I want to invite you, Charlene, Sara, Delores, Sally, Sharon, and Valda." I headed immediately for the phone.

"Hello, Charlene, this is Olevia. I'm having a slumber party and want you to come."

"Where's the party going to be?"

"At my house."

"Is your dad going to be home?"

"Yes, after midnight, he will be."

"I don't think my mom will let me come. I'll ask her and let you know."

Every other conversation ended in a similar fashion, and I ultimately got a no from each person. Merilyn and I headed to Mrs. Curry's together to see if she had any ideas. She listened carefully, wrinkling her forehead as if in deep thought.

"Let me think a minute." She ran her fingers through her hair. "I don't think Ellis would be too pleased with eight girls running around this house."

My heart dropped because I fully expected a solution from her. Merilyn pledged we would be quiet, which even made her smile at such a flimsy suggestion.

Suddenly, Mrs. Curry brightened up. "I have an idea! What about the washhouse? If we had it out there, it would officially still be at my house and disturb no one. I think your friends' parents would be okay with that."

"The washhouse? Could we have a party there? It looks filled with boxes and stuff."

"You know, I'm thinking if I had a couple of girls to help, I could get it ready," Mrs. Curry suggested with a smile.

She barely finished her sentence before Merilyn volunteered us both, saying, "We can do that, can't we Olevia?"

I immediately jumped on the bandwagon. "Let me call my friends to make sure they can come."

I gathered all the yeses, and the three of us set about cleaning and decorating the washhouse. It amazed me how many decorations Mrs. Curry created out of nothing. I brought over my record player and the few vinyl forty-fives I had at home. She loaned me her records, and Merilyn brought all she had. Mrs. Curry had tinsel, wrapping paper, glue, sequins, a string of white lights, candles, and all sorts of stuff—and the result looked like a fantasyland. I felt like Cinderella—and I didn't want to lose that golden slipper.

She furnished the snacks, paper cups, plates, and plastic ware. To top it off, Daddy did let me keep the car that night.

That magical night proved to me that I had been assigned a guardian angel. As with every miracle along the way, I took a minute to touch my mom's matchbook instructions (always in my pocket) and look toward the sky. All was right with the world, at least temporarily.

We ate snacks, played rock 'n' roll as loudly as possible, danced (using the word loosely), and went to Pines Drive-in Movie. When we got home, we stayed up all night, playing cards and talking about boys. Once everyone except Merilyn left the next morning, we eagerly shared every moment with Mrs. Curry as she helped us clean up.

"Guess what? We sneaked Delores into the drive-in last night."

"Why did you do that?"

I replied, "I don't know. To see if we could, I guess. And, besides, we added her dollar to the snack fund."

"How did you get her in? I hope you didn't put her in the trunk."

That brought laughter.

Merilyn remarked, "Gosh, we didn't think of that!"

I explained, "She laid on the back floorboard with a blanket over her. Everybody put their feet on the blanket. After we got inside, she sat up. During the movie, we sat on the benches down in front of the big screen."

Mrs. Curry pursed her lips but didn't comment. Merilyn changed the subject.

"*Midnight Lace* was playing—that Doris Day movie."

I added, "It was so scary. I'm glad I didn't see it by myself. I'd stay awake for days!"

"Who else was in it?" Mrs. Curry asked.

"Rex Harrison and John Gavin," Merilyn volunteered. "Oh, Mrs. Curry, you should have seen Doris Day! She was so beautiful."

And so, it went from subject to subject; it was so easy to share life with someone who cared. Even as the dirt from everything we cleaned became a part of our attire, I still felt like a princess.

So many things in my pretend family made my life a joy and almost as normal as it had been under Mama's care—and I could almost feel her hand resting on my shoulder.

CHAPTER 37
SUMMER OF 1957

Johnson.

I had completed the eighth grade, and so much had changed. I now had a one-on-one relationship with Mrs. Curry, including our private coffee breaks. I met my niece, Peggy. The change in my school status loomed large in my mind. Technically, I was now a high schooler.

Two important learning experiences during the summer of '57 proved life changing. One of them provided a lesson that continues to benefit me in all areas of my life. The day the lesson began is easily visualized and enjoyed repeatedly in my mind.

****

The air conditioning—to use the phrase loosely—in our house consisted of opening the windows. More than one visitor and every family member had suggested to Daddy that we needed a ceiling fan. The Currys had one, and it worked wonderfully at night to bring in whatever cool air might be available.

In lieu of a ceiling fan, we suggested a stand-up fan, a window fan, a box fan—any fan. Aunt Denie's home in Houston had air conditioning, and she visited us often and did some particularly vocal begging—all to no positive response. We settled for the old-fashioned hand-fan, usually pilfered from some church service.

And then, in mid-May of 1957, my Aunt Olevia came to visit from her Atlanta, Georgia home. As my dad's oldest sister, she held a place of authority in Daddy's family. Her visit's purpose involved checking on Daddy to see for herself that he continued to thrive after Mama's death.

A hot Louisiana day is comparable to spending too long in a sauna. The air is wet and sticky, and it clings to every pore in your body. Forgetting make-up and preparing to perspire indefinitely becomes the order of the day. Even for those of us who were as acclimated as possible, the heat took a toll on our activities.

After the first night spent in the back bedroom, Aunt Olevia not only prepared breakfast for all of us, but she also had a breakfast message for Daddy.

"John, I want you to pick up a box fan today."

"Lee-vee, we live on a hill. There's always a breeze when you live on a hill like we do. You don't need a fan. Just open a window."

Aunt Olevia frowned, and Daddy attempted to change the subject. "You did a great job with these pancakes this morning."

Aunt Olevia smiled, acknowledged the compliment, and joined in a bit of chit-chat.

"I see your tomatoes are getting ripe."

"Yeah. It's still early. Mary usually had a whole row. I just didn't feel like it this year, but those three plants are really doing good. I even put in two cucumber vines. They hit peak early this year and are about gone now."

"Are you still milking your cows? Mary made such good butter and buttermilk."

"Nah. That morning and evening milking just didn't fit my work schedule, and the kids aren't big enough to do it. I got bull calves to put on the cows, and we buy milk."

Then, without any change in conversational tone, she said, "What are you doing around two-thirty this afternoon?"

"I don't know. Why, Lee-vee?" Daddy answered with the confidence of a baby brother who thought he had won another battle with his older sister.

"Because my bus leaves Alexandria at three-thirty, and I don't want to miss it."

Daddy said nothing else during breakfast and left the house shortly after. He came home with a rotating fan on a stand—the only one that ever existed in our house. Not only did he set up the fan, but he also bragged about the three speeds, the way it rotated, and the safety grill. He went on as if the whole thing had been his idea.

Meanwhile, Aunt Olevia joined in praising his great idea and choice.

"This fan is so much nicer than I visualized! You know about this stuff. Don't ya, John?"

"Yeah, Lee-vee. If you gonna buy something, a little research helps. I've been checking out fans."

"Oh, I see. You were always good at not acting on impulse. I agree with you. The best decisions are made after thorough thought," Aunt Olevia offered.

Daddy grinned. Happy now, he expanded on his reasoning. "If I had gotten the window fan Denie mentioned, it would only cool one room. If I'd bought a box fan, it could not circulate the air in a large area."

"Oh, yes. You made the right decision. I've always been proud of you."

Daddy beamed like a teenager while John and I stared in disbelief. It felt a bit like watching a play that would surely come to an end shortly. It didn't—it just moved on to various other acts during Aunt Olevia's week-long stay.

Using her wiles and suggestions clothed in opportunities for Daddy to shine, several changes occurred in our household. Nothing big, just subtle improvements. The dog food was moved from the barn to the pump house, much closer and more convenient. John and I benefited from her pleasure at staying up a bit later at night to study the skies, and Daddy enjoyed the opportunity to explain them. Storage of an extra roll of toilet tissue in the bathroom closet became the norm. No more having to requisition one from Daddy's locked truck.

They were trivial things to improve day-to-day life, but they made a difference. One might be able to swim across a channel, but it's easier to get to the other side in a boat.

I learned a lot from Aunt Olevia about solving problems and managing people. I learned ways of meeting challenges and winning without anyone losing. No raised voices or arguments. And both parties made the decision they chose and got the result they ultimately wanted. Aunt Olevia's pearls of wisdom served me well on many occasions during my teenage years with my dad. I did not always come out on top, but often, I did.

The trick to winning is ego management and learning that the adversary need not admit they lost, and indeed they did not. The only person who needs to know you won is you. Creating an atmosphere where your adversary is excited about your win because you cede the results and give them credit requires practice. It is not always easy. That lesson has been basic to my life as a salesperson, as well as a business owner and good citizen.

****

The next time I remember Aunt Olevia visiting Tioga occurred at my dad's funeral in 1965. This time, we were both visitors to my childhood home. I remember her sitting in a rocking chair wearing a red suit and hat. Various mementos were shared among the brothers and sisters.

"Aunt Olevia, would you like a keepsake?" Johnson asked.

"No. My heart is full of memories that I can take out any time and enjoy. Besides, my things will soon be divided among survivors."

She did not speak in a mournful way—more as a matter of fact. After everyone had gone home, Aunt Olevia stayed two more days with me until my husband and father-in-law came down in a pickup truck to take home some things I wanted. During those two days of just us, we had time to talk. And I had the once-in-a-lifetime opportunity to get to know my Aunt Olevia. After getting to know her, I was and am even more flattered to be her namesake.

****

Returning to that 1957 sizzling summer, we soon accepted that even an exceptional fan did not create a cool house. So, when any company came, we spent a lot of Sunday summer afternoons sitting under the big sycamore tree in our front yard. The adults sat in chairs. We kids sat on the ground, mostly listening, and sometimes we watched a locust exit its shell or a butcher bird hang its prey on the fence.

On such an afternoon, my oldest half-brother, Johnson, and his family came by to sit a spell. His visit provided an even more important lesson, or maybe it just confirmed a fact of my life. However it might be characterized, it made my world feel more secure.

I still find it fascinating that I had a half-brother born in 1918, only eight years younger than my mom. Johnson served as a bit of an idol to the rest of us, as he was the one who did well. He had been in the military, so he told stories of the many foreign places where he served in World War II. He seemed a step or two above anyone else we knew in terms of worldliness and money.

We thought of him as rich; he lived in an upscale house and had paid for the aluminum siding that Daddy ordered for our house. He and his wife, Viola, had four children—Carolyn, Linda, Jimmy, and Bill—and he owned a lumber company in Rayne, Louisiana.

Rayne is known as the frog capital of the world. I say that here because it is one of the few mildly interesting things one could say about Rayne. Another of those few worth mentioning is St. Joseph's Cemetery.

St. Joseph's Cemetery is listed in *Ripley's Believe it or Not* as the only U.S. cemetery facing north to south. This unique cemetery did not originally lie contrary to the east-west tradition. It became an oddity after the construction crew failed to realize their mistake when transporting the graves five miles north as the town moved closer to the railroad. The story suggests that the discovery, made after they completed the job, lent itself more to contacting *Ripley's Believe It or Not* than it did to correcting it.

Let's get back to my June afternoon tale.

The sun had begun its descent into the western sky, and Daddy had that fidgety look that alerted most visitors to call it a day. Just at that moment, Johnson spoke, and his words settled each of us back into our places.

"Dad, these kids are young."

"What kids?" Daddy replied quickly. I knew he was stalling for time. I could tell by his stare into space and the rolling of his cheek between his thumb and forefinger that he had hopes of figuring out what Johnson would say before he said it.

Johnson went on, "Olevia and John. I can provide for them and give them advantages that may not be available here in Tioga."

Daddy continued to stare into the distance, as still as the leaves on the sycamore under which he sat. Johnny and I squirmed as if on pins and needles, wondering what would come next. To tell the truth, I felt stuck in a quandary as I tried to decide what to say if asked for my opinion. I'm not sure why it even occurred to me that my opinion might be on the table. It was not, as no one inquired.

Johnson looked at the sky, perhaps searching for words to fill the deafening silence. Then he leaned forward and continued, "Dad, I'm not saying you can't raise these kids. But look at your age. You're sixty-two years old, and Johnny here isn't even twelve. And Olevia's just getting into her teenage years. I'm thinking about you, Dad—and the kids."

Daddy continued to just sit and stare as if looking far into the future. Though he stayed motionless, I sensed the wheels spinning in his mind as he weighed options.

Viola tried her hand at helping Johnson get his point across. I knew that was a mistake.

"Mr. Yeager, Olevia and John need a mother. They need stability. They need—"

Daddy cut her off right there. He did not take kindly to women getting involved in conversations between men, but Viola was either unaware or didn't care.

"Viola, these kids have a mother," he said. "Mary may be dead, but she is still their mother, and we have stables out back."

He made a point of not understanding the mother reference to stability.

John and I looked at each other with a grin while Johnson tried to get the conversation back on track.

"Dad, just think about it a bit. You don't need to answer right now. Why don't you let the kids come home with us for the summer? Then, you can decide what is best."

Daddy stood up from his chair and looped his thumbs into his bib overalls, as he so often did. Then, he looked Johnson straight in the eye.

"Johnson, I know you grew up in the Masonic Orphan's Home. I was too young, and I couldn't manage four boys. I lost that time with you and your brothers. Nobody is taking these two." He started toward the front porch and then turned. "But if they want to go home with you for the summer, it's okay."

John and I stood stone still. *Should we go? Should we stay?*

We pushed the decision further down the road when I answered, "Can we think about it?"

Johnson agreed.

In the meantime, my world immediately became a safer place to live, one where my dad cared about me and my younger brother. He wasn't just stuck with us but rather wanted us. I now knew my older brother was willing to change his life and that of his family to make a better one for me and John. The words and the offer created more peace of mind and real security than a life preserver for a drowning man. Knowing of a backup plan—albeit not to be used because my dad loved me too much—made my world a safer, happier, and more secure place.

CHAPTER 38

HURRICANE AUDREY

OK Allen Bridge.

On June 27, 1957, Hurricane Audrey blew into South Louisiana. Packing winds up to 150 miles per hour, it swept across the bayou with a storm surge of twelve feet.

The town of Cameron sat squarely in the eye. Hundreds of homes, along with their residents, were washed away. Hurricane Audrey claimed the lives of over five hundred Louisianans. In the days following the initial onslaught, its milder form wreaked havoc north to the Canadian border with eighty-mile-per-hour winds bending—and too often breaking—whatever obstacles found in Audrey's path. To this day, Audrey remains the earliest recorded category-four storm to form in the Atlantic. Indeed, it is the strongest storm ever to occur in June.

Nothing in anyone's experience prepared South Louisiana for the upcoming devastation. Later, we learned that over forty thousand people were left homeless, and many bodies would not be found until months later. Survivors told stories of tying themselves to treetops, of children swept from their arms, of watching neighbors die from the bites of poisonous snakes and believing the end of the world had come.

As a tribute to the enormous loss of life, property, and livestock, authorities retired Audrey as a hurricane name.

As life will have it, people in the hurricane's path had been going about their daily lives with little concern for what lay ahead, which is likely the case before most catastrophes.

John and I were among those people. My first and only experience at a Baptist Girls Auxiliary Camp, somewhere near Lafayette, also became my first experience in surviving a hurricane.

Following Johnson's June visit to our Tioga home and his offer that we visit him and his family in Rayne, John and I decided it might be fun. Well, to be honest, I had to talk John into going with me. My campaign began shortly after Johnson left our house. We sat on the back porch alone, quietly discussing the events of the day. I sought out John's opinion of Johnson's offer, Daddy's response, and the possibility of going to Rayne for a little while.

"Were you surprised to hear Johnson say he wanted us to live with them?"

John laughed. "I was, but I sure am glad Daddy said 'no'! I like Carolyn and Linda okay, but I don't think I wanna live with 'em."

"I know! And Bill's so spoiled. Everybody must rush over every time he opens his mouth." I joined in with John's laughter.

"I think Jim's okay, but he never wants to do anything. Did you see him when I asked if he wanted to ride Kate with me? I think he shivered!"

More laughs as we realized we agreed on the main issue.

"But what would you think about going down just for a week or so?" I asked.

"Not interested," he rushed to answer. I had barely finished the question.

"Why?"

"Viola. You know she's got all kinds of rules. Here, we can do anything we want to."

"Well, that may be true, but we can't do much here by ourselves. At Johnson's, there's swimming and movies and picnics and things to see. We might even get to see that cemetery that's all messed up."

"We've visited them a lot, and we've never done any of that stuff."

"That's because we have never spent the night! We've only just gone, ate dinner, and come back home."

John, of course, had an answer for every positive I came up with. Finally, I had to play my ace in the hole.

"Please, please, John. I would do it for you, and I really, really want to go."

He nodded, finally agreeing. I sensed the agreement was on the surface only, but I knew he would keep his promise.

You might say I felt wired as if electric current flowed in my veins and gratitude lit a candle in my heart.

****

We called Johnson the next morning. We spoke to Viola and asked if she could come get us. We held the phone between us so we could both hear.

"Well, I can't, and your brother's busy. Maybe—"

Before she could say another word, John broke in. "That's okay, Viola. It was just an idea Olevia had."

Viola quickly moved to correct the situation. "No, John. I mean, we can't come to get you until the weekend. Johnson will be there Saturday."

My excitement grew daily, and John seemed resigned to his fate when we arrived in Rayne on June 8. The first week went well. It included a picnic, a movie or two, and (best of all) no chores. On the following Sunday, we accompanied the family to church, where there was talk of a GA (Girls Auxiliary) Camp planned near Lafayette. I overheard Viola talking to one of the Sunday school teachers.

"I know Carolyn and Linda are signed up for the GA Camp beginning June 23. But I'm not sure what to do about Olevia. She's with us for the summer, and I don't want her to feel left out."

The lady replied, "Well, add her name to the group. How old is she?"

"She'll be fourteen this coming November, and that's a little too old for Carolyn and Linda's group."

"So. There's a thirteen to fifteen group."

"She wouldn't know anyone, and I'm not sure she would be comfortable there."

I was beginning to get a bit concerned as I eavesdropped, but I felt drawn to every word like a bee to honey.

The teacher continued, "We can pull a few strings and get her into the same group with Carolyn. Do you think she'll mind being the oldest in the group?"

"No, that's perfect! Add her name, and I'll talk to her tonight."

****

That night, I explained it all to John. "Listen, I'm going with Carolyn to GA Camp."

"When?"

"Oh, it's not until June 23. We've got a lot of time, and I'll only be gone for a week. You don't mind, do you?"

"Nope." He walked away.

I knew his feelings were hurt, but I hoped he would get over it quickly.

The next morning, Monday, after breakfast, Johnson had gone to work. Viola was cleaning the kitchen when John walked through with his bag of clothes.

Viola looked up and asked, "Where are you going, Johnny?"

"Home."

"Well, you can't go home right now. Johnson's at work. Go put your stuff up, and maybe he can take you home this weekend."

"I don't need him to take me. I'm going to walk."

"John, you can't walk. It's over a hundred miles from here to Tioga. Put your stuff up, and we'll go to the swimming pool this afternoon. It's open now."

Carolyn, Linda, and I sat at the kitchen table playing cards. I became frightened as I watched the drama unfold. I knew my brother. I knew he never wanted to be here, and he only came because I had begged him. I added my pleadings to Viola's.

"Please don't go home, John. Just stay one more day."

Viola dialed the phone, and John didn't even turn around or speak as he walked out the back door. Johnson arrived home in a matter of minutes, and Johnny sat in our living room in Tioga in less than two hours.

I know because he called me as soon as he got there.

"Johnson picked me up before I even got to the highway. He sure was mad, Olevia. We drove so fast. When are you coming home?"

"I don't know," I responded. "I think I'll stay until the Fourth of July. Carolyn said they always have fireworks and stuff."

"We can have firecrackers here." His voice cracked, reeking with sadness, like a kid sent to time out for a misdeed he didn't feel he committed.

"We'll see."

****

Every day that week, we wrote letters to each other, but I did not immediately go home.

On the afternoon of June 23, I arrived at GA Camp where Carolyn, Linda, and I settled into our cabin. The Cabin Leader assigned bunks and set out the rudimentary rules of camp.

I still shudder remembering that first night. I found myself alone by virtue of my social ignorance. My cabinmates enjoyed a camaraderie that seemed mysterious, invincible, and equally uninteresting to me. The camp songs, the unspoken rules about hidden candy, giggling over last year's camp exploits, and other such things seemed silly and childish to me. The nine o'clock lights out announcement came like a reprieve from the warden—or so I thought.

No such luck; turning out the lights equaled raising the curtain on Act Two. The room burst alive with whispering, sharing hidden goodies, giggling, and all sorts of girl-talk— some of which seemed puzzling to me. I survived and slept soundly until we were rousted from bed at seven o'clock on Monday morning.

Of that day, I remember breakfast, lunch, and dinner with lots of unwelcome, organized activities scattered among them. My ambition became to make it through the week and never, ever attend another camp—GA or otherwise. By nightfall, the skies were overcast, and my thoughts ran toward wondering if maybe it would rain so we could avoid some of the scheduled tortures. If I never have to throw another dart in hopes of hitting a paper with a Bible verse to be read aloud to the group, it will be too soon. I didn't mind reading the verse, but hitting the target became my nemesis.

Monday night through Tuesday night proved a rerun, but by Wednesday morning, the weather began taking on a more sinister look. Counselors did not seem overly concerned in the morning, but by afternoon, radios were in evidence; they began to listen closely to weather forecasts.

Following dinner, the Camp Director told us to return to our cabins and remain there until instructed otherwise. Camp suddenly became interesting to me. I smile now, recalling how my attitude changed so swiftly.

Bad weather did not scare me. I had lived through a tornado or two—wind, rain, and lightning spawned more fascination than fear. I took a wicked pleasure in watching not only my cabinmates, but also my counselor, become more and more frightened by the elements. I had no concept of the ferociousness that fueled Hurricane Audrey. About midnight, we awoke to strong winds, howling like crazed wolves. The thunder boomed and made the building shake, punctuated by lightning strikes and rain so thick it seemed like a solid, opaque sheet.

Fear grew contagious and amplified. Some of the younger girls began to cry. The lights suddenly went out, but we all had flashlights, and the counselor had some candles to burn.

Our counselor had transported four girls from Lake Charles, and she felt a particular responsibility for them in addition to her assigned cabin. According to some of the forecasts, Lake Charles appeared to be a likely hurricane target, though we did not yet know Audrey carried a category four designation.

Around one o'clock in the morning, the counselor told us she was leaving to take her charges home. She cautioned us not to leave the cabin under any circumstances but to wait until a replacement counselor arrived. Her departure added to the growing hysteria among the younger campers—eleven and twelve-year-old girls. That gave me an opportunity to be accepted as a real cabinmate—indeed, the leader. Some girls were crying, some were praying, and some just sat stone still as if made of concrete.

One thought lodged itself in my mind: *This will be my last day at GA camp—at least one thing to thank God for.*

My niece, Carolyn, nearly thirteen years old, was the next senior member of our group. She had taken piano lessons. And, at my brother's, she often played hymns while we sang. She became our cabin song leader. Without any real plan and no piano, she and I began singing "When the Morning Comes."

Trials dark on every hand and we cannot understand.
All the ways God would lead us to that blessed Promised Land.
But He will guide us with His eye, and we will follow 'til we die.
We will understand it better, by and by.
When the morning comes, when the saints of God are gathered home
We will tell the story of how we've overcome
We will understand it better, by and by.

Being a faithful Baptist church attendee for as long as I could remember, I had heard that song many times before.

I knew it by memory, but on that day, the words really meant something to me. I caught the eye of Gloria, one of our cabinmates. She was probably eleven or twelve, but a tiny little girl that could have passed for nine. Her hair had been in pigtails and now just had stray rubber bands in a mass of hair. Tears streaked her face, and she held a sucker in her mouth that reminded me of a pacifier. If someone needed a picture of a sad little orphan girl trying to look brave, Gloria would have filled the bill.

I smiled and nodded in her direction as we continued singing. Carolyn followed suit with both of us moving a little closer in.

Oft our cherished plans have failed; disappointments have prevailed.
And we've wandered in the darkness, heavy hearted and alone;
But we are trusting in the Lord and, according to His word,
We will understand it better, by and by.
When the morning comes, when the saints of God are gathered home
We will tell the story of how we've overcome.
We will understand it better, by and by.

Without invitation, all the kids started to sing with us. The winds continued to rage. We heard trees hit the roof. Intermittent flashes of lightning lit the night like fireworks. The sound of falling trees and the crackling of electricity as the electric poles fell added an almost demonic edge to the storm.

Temptations, hidden snares often take us unawares.
And our hearts are made to bleed for some thoughtless word or deed.
And we wonder why the test when we try to do our best.
But we will understand it better, by and by.
When the morning comes, when the saints of God are gathered home
We will tell the story of how we've overcome

We will understand it better, by and by.

The fear subsided as we sang; a couple of girls found hidden candy stashes. One by one, they suggested their own favorite hymn. Gloria suggested we sing, "He's Got the Whole World in His Hands." Her clear, little voice stood out as she rocked side to side and added every attendant hand gesture she had learned in Bible school. But it was "When the Morning Comes" that provided the glue, and we seamlessly became a united group.

As daylight came, we tried to see what damage had been done. We were alone but not afraid anymore. The rain still fell, but the winds had let up some. A fallen tree prevented our opening the cabin's front door, but we forced the back one open a few inches. The winds raged with less intensity, and the viciousness of the rain had lessened as well. Trees were leveled and electrical wires were everywhere. We decided against going to the breakfast hall.

Everyone pooled the remainder of their goody stashes, and the fear transformed into more of a feeling of adventure as we imagined being stranded for days. We became Tom Sawyers and Huck Finns as we thought about how our parents would be worrying. We pictured them forgiving us for all past misdeeds.

GA Camp had become fun at the least expected moment. We shared stories of other adventures we'd had. One girl told how she had gotten lost in a department store and how a policeman found her.

"How did you get lost?" someone asked.

"It was in Baton Rouge! They have giant stores."

"Still, how can you get lost if your mother is with you?"

"Well, really, I just hid in a dressing room for a joke. I was only six! I didn't think my mother would panic. Boy, was she mad when the policeman returned me to her."

We all laughed at that. And so it went, story after story.

Sometime before noon, probably eleven or so, we heard the chainsaws outside. Within minutes, a man opened our door. He looked surprised to find us alone.

Raising his eyebrows and cocking his head to one side, he asked, "Where's your counselor?"

As I had now assumed a place almost of authority among my cabinmates, I answered, "She had to go home to take some girls back to Lake Charles."

He mumbled sarcastically under his breath. "Smart lady. Head into the storm in the middle of the night and leave a cabin full of kids behind. Somebody's going to hear about this."

He loaded us into the back of his pick-up and took us to the cafeteria.

I soon found out that I had been wrong about having spent my last day at GA Camp. Parents were not allowed in for almost two more days. We slept on the tables. And, until power was restored, we ate PB&Js and fruit. Flooded roads and debris covered the ground, made traveling by car not only difficult but heavily restricted.

Viola managed to be one of the first to arrive in a borrowed vehicle with four-wheel drive.

****

Back in Rayne, Johnson received a government assignment to transport building materials and relief aid to the closed areas of the state. At night, he related stories of the stench from decaying livestock, of seeing families sitting on piles of rubble that had been their homes, of the fear of snakes washed inland, and of bodies pulled from the water and stacked for transport.

Meanwhile, back in Tioga, my dad, John, and Mrs. Curry had experienced the same hurricane, though much of its fury ended a hundred or so miles south. As soon as I reached Johnson's, I called John.

"Hey, John. Are you okay? Is the house blown away?"

"We're okay. Daddy didn't even miss work."

"What?"

"Well, we were watching the weather on Channel 5 at twelve o'clock. The sky was getting black, and the weatherman said Hurricane Audrey would probably hit Alexandria at three that afternoon. That's when Daddy said 'I'll be climbing on the engine about that time. With this weather, I better get on out of here.' He went to work!" John said with an incredulous tone.

I could hardly believe it either. "What did you do?"

"It looked like nighttime. I got scared. I went to Mrs. Curry's. I tried to run, and I couldn't see because of the rain. The wind blew so hard, I couldn't go in a straight line. So, I headed for the cattle gap and let the wind blow me to Mrs. Curry's." He chuckled.

"Is Mrs. Curry, okay? Did her roof blow off? Is the wash house still there?"

"No, the roof didn't blow off. But her favorite Chinaberry tree, the really big one, blew over. Her house shook like a washing machine on a spin cycle. We sat in her sewing room, and she kept telling me jokes. I wasn't scared. Really, Olevia, I wasn't." His voice let me know he tried to be brave.

By seven o'clock the night of June 29, Audrey had become a skeleton of her former self, and the world John and I occupied began returning to normal. John said he got home by midnight on the day the storm hit, and Daddy brought him a hamburger and French fries from Billips

Cafe. He told me Daddy had been very brave to go to work in a hurricane.

"Guess what? Daddy almost fell into the Red River. He said the wind blew so hard that the car nearly fell off the O. K. Allen Bridge. He said part of the time his car went down the road sideways, and he just held on because there were no other cars around him. I guess nobody else took a drive during a hurricane."

We both laughed at the picture formed in our minds. Only Daddy would drive fifteen miles in a hurricane to get to work where no one else showed up.

"John, I'm coming home. I'm going to ask Johnson to bring me tomorrow."

"Okay. I kinda miss you!"

Again, we laughed, and I suddenly became excited and anxious to get back to Tioga.

My trip home with Johnson allowed time for Johnson to talk, and I happily became a rapt audience. He talked about the hurricane and how it affected South Louisiana, his lumber business, and his customers. He pointed out damage along the road and explained how he did not know if the area could or would recover.

About halfway home, he pulled into a Dairy Queen. I got a pineapple malt, and we sat to talk. I don't remember what he had, but I do remember the conversation—and I appreciated how quietly and kindly he spoke.

"I know what it is to be orphaned. I was only eight when my mom died, and Daddy put the four of us into the Masonic home. I was the oldest with a six, a five, and a three-year-old brother. I understand his decision, but I want you to know you can make your own decision."

"I could never leave Johnny or Daddy. I feel as if they need me, or maybe I just need them," I tried to explain.

"I can guarantee you college, opportunities, and a home where you will be loved and supported."

"I know, and I appreciate it. But my home is in Tioga with Daddy and John. We are our family now, and I think that is where Mama wants me to be."

He smiled slightly, put the car in gear, and started driving home. When we arrived, he helped me unload my suitcase and gave me a hug. As he prepared to drive away, he leaned out of the window to say, "If you ever need me, you know where I am."

Over the years, there were times that I've needed him, and he always answered with compassion and love.

CHAPTER 39

ANOTHER BEND IN THE ROAD

"Hey, John," I called. "Your math book is on the desk. Are you ready yet?"

"Almost," Johnny replied from the kitchen. "I'm just checking to see if there are any more of those cinnamon rolls."

"Hurry! It's already 6:30, and the bus will be here soon."

"Coming," he replied.

Tuesday morning, October 8, 1957, and we were almost ready to walk out the door when John decided he wanted his blue jean jacket. The weather temperature hovered at sixty to sixty-five degrees, a little chilly, but the sun was shining.

"C'mon, John!" I yelled as I stood in the doorway.

He raced up, and we opened the screen door to leave.

Our bus typically arrived around seven, and Daddy usually remained in his room until after we left. That morning, he sat in a living room rocking chair and hadn't said a word. He looked a little uncomfortable but not enough to cause real concern.

Just as the screen door closed behind us, Daddy called out, "Olevia!" with a desperate sound to his voice.

We both turned and rushed back inside. Eighteen days from now, October 26, 1957, would mark one year since my mother's death. It had been a quiet year, at least where my dad was concerned. He now lived almost exclusively in an airtight cocoon created by his grief and penetrated at home only by written notes left on the pink pad next to the telephone.

But this morning, Daddy's voice sounded different, sort of ominous. We both ran in.

"What's wrong, Daddy?"

"Hand me that clock."

I did so, and it dropped to the floor.

Daddy put his hand on his chest and spoke again. "Olevia, I have some indigestion this morning. I need a Coke, so I can burp."

"We don't have any!"

I began to grow frightened, and Johnny stood and stared, unmoving.

"I know that. Go to Merritt's Grocery and get a couple of Cokes. Tell Mr. Belgard to put it on my bill."

Merritt's was only about a mile and a half away. Even at thirteen, I had been driving for well over a year and would be fourteen in just over a month. In Louisiana, a driver's license is available at age fifteen, only a little over a year away. I grabbed the car keys and ran out the door, leaving Johnny to manage whatever might come next.

No traffic between my house and Merritt's made the trip easy. I stopped our 1954 Henry J almost on the store's steps, left the door open, and ran up onto the porch. A locked door stood between me and the Cokes. I banged on it as hard as I could. In seconds, Mr. Belgard opened it slightly.

"We're closed."

"My daddy's sick. I need two Cokes."

"Come back in fifteen minutes. We'll open at seven o'clock, like every other day. You know that."

"I really need them, Mr. Belgard."

"Then come back in fifteen minutes. I'll have them ready." He chuckled slightly as he closed the door.

I know he believed me to be just another teenager from high school across the street trying to get in early. Still, I'm not sure I ever really forgave him for not helping me that morning. One lifelong result is my tendency to trust most calls for help. Occasionally, my trust is misplaced. But much more often, it is not.

I jumped back into the car and flew home as quickly as possible. Then, I ran up the steps and into the living room where Daddy lay on the floor. A foreboding sort of groaning escaped from his mouth, and Johnny was on the phone attempting to give directions to our rural home to an ambulance service. My heart raced as I tried to maintain control.

"Hang up, John. We'll take him ourselves!"

John hung up the phone. Somehow, we managed to walk Daddy out to the car. I have no memory of how we stood him up; I just know we did.

Not thinking clearly, we helped him sit up in the front seat between the two of us and started off to Alexandria's Baptist Hospital, which was about twelve miles away. At this time of day, the route had developed the going-to-work traffic and, while rush hour did not involve many vehicles, it did provide my first time to share the road with more than a few. I found the two-lane blacktop to be a challenge—almost completely restricted to no passing zones due to the curves.

Added to that, Daddy's pain caused him to make efforts to speed up our car. Intermittently, he would step on top of my foot on the accelerator, and I would have to cross the double-yellow lines to avoid hitting the car in front of us. The braking and swerving were immediately followed by another swerve back into my lane as I managed to remove his foot from mine. In my mind, I can still hear and see the horns honking, people trying to avoid an accident, and Johnny trying to hold Daddy up. All the while, Daddy moaned, and Johnny gave instructions to me.

"Watch that car! Slow down. Can we put Daddy in the backseat? Do you see that car coming out of Fort Bulow?"

I just drove without reply and, once we arrived on Upper Third Street, I parked a block away. Shaking and on the verge of tears, I yelled at Johnny, who now seemed frozen in place.

"Johnny, pay attention. We gotta get Daddy to the emergency entrance."

He jumped into action, but before he could get out of the car, Daddy roused a bit.

Looking out the window, he murmured, "I can't walk. Need ambulance entrance."

Doors slammed and, without a cautionary look, I veered into traffic. Brakes squealed and horns honked. Looking back, it is difficult to imagine how we were not hit, but we weren't. In seconds, we careened into the ambulance entrance.

As John and I jumped from the car, two men—paramedics or orderlies, I assume—immediately removed Daddy to a stretcher. We ran inside and were pointed toward a business office. At the check-in desk, a woman asked us to have a seat.

She asked for all the particulars—name, age, date of birth, etc.—and we provided everything we knew until we got to the health insurance. At a glance, I saw Daddy still lying on a stretcher outside the office. I could not only feel my heart beating, I heard it like a rhythm pounding on a drum.

"Daddy has insurance! He's a railroad engineer and has insurance. He has good insurance," I said, breathless.

"Honey, calm down and take a deep breath."

I thought, *Easy for you to say. Your dad's not dying while lying on a stretcher outside the window.*

"Really, lady, he has good insurance!" I tried once more.

"Do you have an ID card or some proof?"

Tears were welling up in my eyes. Johnny now stood beside the window staring at Daddy and the lack of activity surrounding him. He must have been thinking much as I was: *'God, fix it. We can't lose Daddy.'*

"He works for the Missouri Pacific Railroad. Can't you call somebody?" I almost shouted, and tears escaped my eyes.

Again, the woman tried to reassure me. "Of course, honey. We can call the next of kin. Give me a phone number for your mother."

"We are the next of kin. Please help him. I can go home and get insurance information. But, please, help him now." I was frantic like a caged animal trying to escape this trap where nothing made sense, and every turn was a wall.

As if she heard not a word I said, she repeated the same request. "I need an ID card or some proof of his insurance."

Suddenly, I remembered Mr. Curry worked for the railroad, and I grabbed the phone on the woman's desk and dialed Mrs. Curry. I explained the situation to her and handed the phone to the admitting clerk. Within just a minute or so, she stepped outside to give instructions, and paramedics or orderlies whisked Daddy away.

When she returned, John had sat down with me, and we occupied the same chairs where she had left us. She again requested we call the next of kin. I told the same story—we were next of kin.

It did not seem to register with her. She said, "You two may have a seat over there until someone comes to help."

John and I sat down in the waiting area. For what seemed like hours, we didn't speak, and no one spoke to us.

Finally, Johnny said, "Olevia, do you think we should call Aunt Denie?"

Aunt Denie lived in Pasadena, Texas and had come to our house on multiple occasions during Mama's illness and immediately after her death. She often stayed with us for a month or more at a time. I agreed but thought we should wait a while longer until someone gave us an update on Daddy's condition.

Neither of us said what we were thinking: *Is Daddy going to die?* We continued to sit, silently praying for some sort of divine intervention.

It seemed as if hours had passed when the admitting clerk came over to us. A glimmer of compassion appeared in her eyes as she sat down beside me.

"Honey, your daddy's in the ICU wing, and there's nothing you can do right now. I think you should go home."

"Okay."

"How are you going to get there?" She raised her eyebrows.

"Drive. The same way we got here."

I stood up to leave, and Johnny quickly followed. Before we could exit and before the admitting clerk had recovered enough to react, I saw my half-brother, Johnson. He lived about a hundred miles south of Alex, and seeing him walk through the emergency entrance was a godsend. We weren't alone, and I knew everything would be okay. The relief was as indescribable as a rainbow during sunset while a peaceful rain fell. As it turned out, Mrs. Curry had called Johnson immediately after my phone call, and he wasted no time in getting to the hospital.

"Hey, kids. Ya'll okay?"

"Yeah," I answered for both of us. "They said Daddy's in ICU and stable. We were about to go home."

"Do you want me to take you?"

"No. We drove here, and we need to take the car home. But I wish you would stay here with Daddy. They don't want to tell us much, and I bet they'd talk to you."

He agreed and admonished us to be careful.

Before we left the hospital, we called Aunt Denie collect. She said she would catch a bus in the morning.

We had a much calmer drive home than the earlier one to the hospital. With very little traffic and no conversation, we sat alone with our thoughts. Like a tumbleweed caught in a breeze, I did what the situation demanded, unable to think or reason. John stared out the window as he dealt with his own fears.

Before we turned into our driveway, I saw Mrs. Curry standing on her porch, and I chose her driveway instead. Her arms formed a protective shield around us as she led us into the house.

"Your daddy's going to be okay. Let's put on a pot of coffee."

"Mrs. Curry, I'm so scared," I admitted.

"So am I, Olevia. Johnson will sort things out. He called me to let me know you were on your way here."

John and I slumped at the kitchen table, but the shock prevented any tears. Mrs. Curry scurried around, making coffee, baking biscuits, frying bacon, and talking nonstop. Slowly, the lethargy gave way to terror and finally to acceptance of another challenge. Mrs. Curry's chatter and warm kitchen helped make things seem manageable, like sitting around a warm fire after walking a mile through a snowstorm.

Daddy remained hospitalized for four weeks—the first three weeks of which I spent nearly as much time there as he did. Johnny went back to school, but I couldn't yet. Being there in his room or down the hall in the ICU waiting area gave me a purpose for being anything. Johnson came up as often as he could and sometimes spent the night with Daddy and me.

Every day, Mrs. Curry brought Johnny and Aunt Denie to the hospital for evening visiting hours. Small events gave structure to the days, such as orderlies changing out the oxygen tanks with great fanfare and noise or Johnson slipping my shoes off and covering me with a blanket when he thought I slept. Every morning, we also had ten o'clock phone calls home to update Aunt Denie.

Those phone calls organized my thoughts and led me, step by step, through Daddy's steady improvement. They gave me a feeling of control in a world out of control.

Returning to school resembled putting back on comfortable shoes after having worn a size too small for too long. Someone else was in charge, and I only had to learn whatever landed in front of me. I encountered one problem, barely six days after returning—report cards.

I had missed so much of the six weeks that every teacher allowed me to take the six-week test and receive that grade for the entire grading period. I studied as much as I could, but with its sines and cosines, algebra escaped my grasp. Being in honors algebra did not help because of the amount of material covered in a brief time. Besides, I never understood why I was in any honors math class; it's never been my forte!

My grade was passing, but barely. With a deep breath and a determined smile, I entered Daddy's hospital room.

"We got our report cards today, Daddy, and I need you to sign mine."

"Let's have a look at it." Daddy had improved to the point he almost looked like his old self, sitting up in bed.

"I did pretty good in everything except algebra."

"Let me see it."

I handed it over, and the change in Daddy made me think another heart attack might be in store. Daddy failed to understand the reason for any grade less than an A or maybe a B.

"Olevia, what's wrong with you? You don't have anything to do but go to school and study. There's no excuse for a D in algebra. Did you forget your name is Yeager?"

"No, sir. I made A's and B's in everything else." Tears blurred my vision.

Just in time to prevent an all-out sobbing, his comment brought the memory of Mama's response on so many occasions. When Daddy used the name Yeager as a tool for discipline, she would follow up later with: *That and a nickel will get you a cup of coffee*, always accompanied by a chuckle. In my mind, I heard her whisper, "It's okay," and my tears quickly dried. As if she stood next to me, she turned a difficult situation into an internal smile. I grasped the matchbox in my pocket with a warm rush of gratitude.

Daddy continued to voice his concern. He scowled. "This here says D is below average. Are you below average? Yeager's are above average."

"No, sir. I'll bring it up next time."

"See that you do. Get me my pen over there, and I'll sign this."

****

He saw an A in algebra on the next report card. But to this day, I don't really understand sines and cosines.

Daddy experienced a full recovery, and he said the doctors told him that his grief had brought on the heart attack. According to him, their advice was to get out more and be with people. Whether that is true or not, I do not know.

I do know he took those instructions to heart as soon as he got home, wherever they may have come from. Being sixty-two years old, widowed twice, with two teenagers in the house, could depress anyone, but things were about to change.

For the first three weeks of his recuperation at home, I served as chauffeur, and he found someplace to be taken every day.

On one trip, we picked up Aunt Grace before going to Pineville. Every visit to Aunt Grace's house began the same way. The snarling, black, and vicious-appearing dog growled, barked, and tried to get at us through the fence. The animal backed up the claim made by the Bad Dog sign on the gate. Despite the obvious, Aunt Grace stood on the porch and yelled. Her speech reminded me of a thirty-three-rpm record played at a forty-five-rpm speed.

"Come on in. He won't bite. Don't worry. The dog won't bite. Come on in."

Daddy yelled back, "Grace, tie up that dog. I just had a heart attack and can't go running up to your porch."

She laughed and corralled the dog so we could get into the house. Once inside, Aunt Grace's next vocal blast was as predictable as her welcome speech.

"I'm out of coffee. Do you want coffee? You don't want coffee. I'm out of coffee." Never pausing to catch her breath, she continued, "You don't want coffee, do you? Roderick forgot to bring coffee home last night. Just used the last of our coffee this morning. I'm glad you don't want coffee."

No one ever visited Aunt Grace expecting to be served coffee unless they brought it with them. Her family and friends amused each other mimicking her opening litany.

The rapid-fire staccato and predictability of performance served as entertainment in our community. She wasn't a laughingstock, just one of many unique individuals forming the fiber of our town, such as two Miss Clarks, twin carrot-topped postmistresses, the hairdresser who sang while she shampooed, and the man who found it necessary to be saved every night of the church revival meeting.

At the first break, Daddy assured her we did not want coffee and had come to see if she wanted to go with us to Piggly Wiggly. Without a moment's hesitation, she grabbed her purse and led the way to the door before we even sat down. Daddy smiled as we followed her out to the car; he clearly enjoyed her company.

We were just inside Pineville city limits and within the speed limit when a police car appeared in the rear-view mirror. The patrolman signaled us to the shoulder of the road. I sat at the wheel with Daddy in the front seat and Aunt Grace in the back.

"How old are you?" he asked.

I told him fourteen, and at the same time, Daddy said fifteen.

"Just how old are you?" he asked again.

This time, I said fifteen, while Daddy said fourteen.

Aunt Grace took over. "Well, she's fourteen, but almost fifteen. You know, her Daddy had a heart attack, not able to drive. I could drive. Well, really, I can't drive. But, if I could drive, I would drive. Can't drive though, so she's driving. She knows how to drive. She's almost fifteen, but she's really fourteen. Wish I could drive. Isn't this a pretty day? Really a pretty day to be driving. Maybe I'll ask Roderick to teach me. Does your wife drive? Driving's nice. Good day for a drive. Don't you think it's a nice day to drive? Wish I could drive. Then I would be driving."

The policeman stood like a statue, appearing to be almost in a trance as he watched her mouth move.

Aunt Grace paused for breath, and he immediately took advantage of the small break in her vocal performance. He had lost interest in winning the battle as soon as Aunt Grace entered the skirmish.

"Looks as if you folks have everything under control. But, young lady, if you don't have your permit, it's better not to be driving in Pineville."

"Sir—"

"It's okay today," the policeman interrupted. "Just remember what I said."

He turned and walked back to his patrol car, relieved to exit the situation. Daddy's deep guttural laugh, along with the giggle coming from the backseat, was the first I had heard in over a year—one more signal of the beginning of a new day.

Within weeks—as soon as he was released to drive— Daddy began to date, and life became even more interesting. Our first stepmother showed up less than a year later.

CHAPTER 40

A TEACHER MAKES A DIFFERENCE

After an extraordinary summer, Labor Day arrived a bit early in 1957. The next day, September 3, I officially became a high school freshman and felt much like a fish out of water.

My classes were still populated with the same kids I had first met in 1948 when beginning school. The only change on campus involved the move to (what we called) The Big Building, located near the railroad tracks.

Arriving at school, I immediately searched for Merilyn. She and I whispered to each other as we sized up the group.

"Are those boys playing with knives over there?" I asked.

"Looks like it to me! I think they call it 'Mumbly-Peg'"

"What? That sounds crazy! It looks as if even Jerry Ingram has a pocketknife on his belt." I gasped.

"I think the object may be to put a stick or something in the middle of a circle and then everyone tries to hit the stick with their knife."

That sounded ridiculous to me, and we both began laughing. "I guess girls get straight skirts and bras, while the boys get pocketknives and cigarettes."

Another shared burst of laughter erupted.

The high school area consisted of a two-story building surrounded by a gymnasium and an auditorium. It had a designated area for boys to smoke, called The Dumps—just across the railroad tracks from Merritt's Grocery. The distance from the grammar school and junior high was nominal in length, but the atmosphere felt as foreign as speaking in tongues while sitting in a synagogue.

Students and their circumstances changed when they walked through those doors. Among the youngest in my class, and with no hierarchy yet established, I hadn't yet quite determined where I fit in. The most popular students were still the most popular, and several of them were half of a couple (kids going steady).

Other than the one occasion I confused for a date when a boy's mother drove both of us to a movie and picked us up, I had no dating experience. Now, looking around, I could see that one afternoon occurrence did not remotely resemble a date!

Thank God for Merilyn, who spoke again and pointed to a blonde coming down the hall. "Hey, there's Charlene. Who's that guy with her?"

"Don Whiddon. He's two grades ahead of us. I heard they started going together this summer," I explained.

Having joined our school last year, Merilyn hadn't had an opportunity to meet any upperclassmen.

"I see Sara Terrell. She's not with anybody." Merilyn waved at her. "Hey, Sara, come over here."

Sara waved and started in our direction. When she got closer, she called out, "Have ya'll seen Sharon Barton?"

Sharon stood right behind her and tapped her on the shoulder. Sara nearly jumped out of her skin.

Norma Brown came up next to join us. Both Sara and Norma were redheads—the only two we had in our class before Merilyn moved to town and created the threesome.

Merilyn glanced around. "You guys don't even have any redheaded upperclassmen. At least none that I've seen." She locked arms with Norma and Sara. "I guess we really are special."

Everybody laughed. Slowly, our group morphed into pretty much the same group as we had the previous year: the popular girls, those who belonged, by virtue of good grades, and those who had a close relationship outside of school, such as Merilyn and me.

Dating did not appear on my Things-to-Do list, as I had adopted the same rules Merilyn had—no dating until age sixteen. An easy rule to follow and to hide behind when necessary—not that anyone had asked. To me, school served as more of an escape from reality rather than any social setting.

Merilyn's and my friendship remained as strong as ever, but for this year, our boy time consisted of little more than pointing and talking. We shared our Home Economics class, but no others. Socializing quickly became limited to lunch, after school, and on weekends.

I liked studying and learning, and that resulted in good grades through junior high. I found myself in two Advanced Placement settings: English/Literature and Algebra One. Unfamiliar with AP classes, I had no idea what to expect. To the best of my memory, Advanced Placement classes were not available until high school.

I shared my AP English class with eighteen other students, rather than the normal thirty to thirty-five. We had a different curriculum from the standard one.

Shakespeare's plays and Edgar Allan Poe's works became the staples of our first semester. Grammar, punctuation, and English basics were presented and learned via writing projects. I loved my English class and still remember so many specific happenings in that setting. The one most worth sharing changed both my high school experience and my life.

The first semester, almost completed, concluded with studying Poe's "The Raven." I had no preconceptions about the poem and no real knowledge of the author's history. To me, Edgar Allan Poe was a guy who authored scary stories. I don't recall having read anything he had written before I read "The Raven." It came as news to me that Lenore represented grief and loss, and it touched me on a deep level. Our six-week exam to close out our first semester consisted of drafting a story-poem based on feelings, thoughts, or ideas aroused by our study of this poem.

Mrs. Higdon's rules were firm and inflexible, especially those regarding major assignments. They included loss of points for not following the guidelines as well as loss of points for turning in an assignment late. And an assignment not completed on time could result in a zero.

That afternoon, I sat on my bed preparing to write something. But I had difficulty getting my head around what I wanted to say. I decided to forget the rules and write whatever popped into my head. I wrote about being on a Ferris wheel, reaching the very top, and being stopped there. I talked about the feeling of not knowing if I could ever move forward again and how being trapped in the unknown caused nausea as I rocked back and forth. I named my work "The Ferris Wheel" and wrote it in the required story-poem style.

The next morning as I gathered my books for school, I reread my poem. I decided it did not follow the rules and would be embarrassing to turn in. I left it lying on my bed. English class typically began my day on a high note; this day was not typical. All the way to school, I thought about what to tell Mrs. Higdon. In my house, grades were more than just important, they were a reflection on our family name. I knew I had earned a zero.

Daddy would not be happy, and he hadn't completely recovered from a heart attack experienced earlier in the semester. Unfortunately for me, he had seen a D in algebra on the report card earned during that tumultuous time. I began to think of some lies that might work in my favor if I told them just right.

As I entered the hallway to go to my locker, I saw Mrs. Higdon opening her classroom door. Like making a plea deal, if you arrive first, you've got a better chance of success.

So, I called out. "Mrs. Higdon!"

"Yes, Olevia. What's going on this morning?"

Her kindness destroyed my courage to lie.

"I made a bad mistake last night, and I am so sorry."

"What?" She looked truly concerned.

"I didn't follow the rules in writing the story/poem. I'm sorry."

"Did you do the work at all?" Her concern now had an edge of annoyance.

"Sorta. I just wrote my feelings, and they are all mixed up."

"Well, turn in your paper, and we'll take a look at it."

"I can't. I didn't even bring it to school today."

"Well, bring it tomorrow," she said as she walked into her classroom.

Then another strange thing happened.

On an average day, after everyone took their seats, Mrs. Higdon would ask us to come forward one at a time to put our assigned papers on her desk. My last name, Yeager, meant I occupied the last seat in the last row of every classroom since first grade. My lack of a completed assignment would be magnified to the entire class.

Her next words were the sheriff's posse arriving in time to stop the execution.

She announced, "Class, we have a lot to get to today. So, please leave your story/poems on my desk when class is over. We will discuss them tomorrow. Now, let's get out our books and turn to..."

With a sigh of relief, I made a vow to never be in an unprepared position again.

That night, I took another look at my paper and found myself no less unhappy with it than I had been the night before. My best efforts could not create any coherent document I believed relative to "The Raven" or its message. I eventually gave up and decided one low grade would not kill me. I'd turn in the paper as originally written and prepare to face whatever the consequences were.

Fast forward to class the next morning. I arrived early, as usual, and rushed into Mrs. Higdon's room before any classmates were there. Mrs. Higdon sat at her desk reading the exam papers. I left mine in the stack with the others from the day before, and I left quickly as she nodded in my direction.

When the bell rang, I tried to walk in as nonchalantly as possible before sitting down at my desk. I knew Mrs. Higdon was an honest critic of our work, and she never hesitated to point out our errors as well as our successes. Amidst the shuffle and sound of chairs scraping as everyone found their seats, I wondered if my classmates could see the apprehension on my face. I felt concern building in my chest like pressure in a teapot about to boil. I waited for the fallout to begin.

"Good morning, ladies and gentlemen."

Mrs. Higdon occasionally addressed us in that manner. To the best of my memory, she was the only teacher who did so. Those terms had a positive effect on me and probably every other student. I sat up a little straighter.

"I read your papers, and I am pleased. I found each one well done, and we are going to enjoy discussing them today. Olevia's was the last one I read, so let's begin with it."

My chest tightened as she read the entire one-page paper aloud.

"Okay, do we have any comments?"

No one said a word, raised a hand, or made any move toward evaluating what I had written. I am sure my classmates had no idea what my poem meant and did not see any relationship between it and "The Raven." Indeed, that's where I stood. I liked my poem, but I did not understand how it related to "The Raven." I felt like an actress who had forgotten her lines while the spotlight directed on her made certain no one missed her error.

Mrs. Higdon continued. "Have any of you ever been on a Ferris wheel?"

A dozen hands shot up. I slid down a little in my seat.

"Great! Let's start with you, Carol. Did the wheel stop and leave you dangling at the top?"

"Yes! And it was sorta scary."

"What about you, Ralph? What's your experience?"

"I went on one, once, in Shreveport. I don't remember if it stopped or not."

Someone else said, "It had to stop to let people on and off."

Everybody laughed, including Mrs. Higdon. She continued to work her way around the room, getting everyone involved. My heart returned to a regular pace. Once the discussion concluded, Mrs. Higdon held up my paper while she explained what it meant to her.

"I want you to listen carefully, class. There is a lot to be learned here." She smiled as she glanced from face to face.

I looked around as well to see all eighteen of my classmates as attentive as if we were discussing "The Raven," and I guess we were. I relaxed and began enjoying the class as much as I did every day.

Mrs. Higdon continued to talk as she leaned against the front of her desk. She scanned every face, and the students looked eager to hear what she had to say.

"Imagine yourself on the tallest Ferris wheel at the Shreveport State Fair. Are you with me there yet?"

"Yes ma'am," we answered in unison.

As I looked around the room, I saw Carol Nalley had her eyes closed. I decided to try it myself.

"Let that feeling of uncertainty and loss of control sink in. Being at the mercy of the world around us is what Olevia is talking about here. It's also what Poe is describing in his poem. Can you feel a relationship to those emotions?"

We nodded, and she went on. "When the Ferris wheel starts to turn again, we remember we are never alone. That journey from no control to peace relates well to Poe's emotions as expressed in "The Raven."

She paused for a moment. "Okay, let's move on." She picked up the next paper.

****

That was, perhaps, the first time Mrs. Higdon had a significant impact on my life. It became only the first of many. She stood in the shadows so many times during those high school years, lending an encouraging or cautionary word—whatever the situation required.

I could not know then that Mrs. Gladys Higdon, who taught that English class, would one day be instrumental in my move to Dallas. Teachers change lives. The good ones change lives for the better and are irreplaceable.

CHAPTER 41

Daddy's Social Life Heats Up

Daddy enjoyed Aunt Grace's company, but that was all she was—company. He searched for more. He wanted a wife, and Tioga didn't have an abundance of widow women interested in non-church-going widowers. Still, he managed to find a few. As a Mason, some Eastern Stars made the list. The first one in my memory made a lasting impression on me.

Via the pink pad by the telephone, Daddy notified us that he planned to bring home someone to share supper on Saturday. Our job consisted of cleaning the house and being scarce. The house got a lick and promise, and I stood at the ironing board with a blouse when I heard Daddy coming up the front steps. Grabbing the blouse, I headed down the hallway.

"Come in, Gertrude."

As soon as I heard the name, a shiver ran up my spine as I hid in the hallway. Gertrude—the name itself felt unfriendly.

"Thank you, John."

"Looks like the kids are down at Mrs. Curry's. No matter, you and I will fix us a bite to eat. Ellis gave me a mess of crappie this morning. How's fried fish sound?"

"I like fried fish-- if you have some light bread. Crappie is bad for bones." She used the Southern term—light bread for white bread, as opposed to cornbread. I continued to listen thinking maybe she wouldn't be so bad.

"I have light bread and a bottle of vinegar. How about fried potatoes and onions to go with them?"

Vinegar served as another antidote for swallowing fish bones. Both light bread and vinegar were always on the table when we ate fish and, more than once, someone drank a half-cup of vinegar followed by a slice of bread just in case a fish bone had been ingested.

"Good," she replied.

From my spy-spot behind the hot water heater, I got a good look at Gertrude. I saw a rotund woman; her gray hair rolled around some sort of hair rat and circled her head to look like a weird headband. Her short-sleeved, pastel-striped dress, heavy stockings, and black old lady high heels created a dastardly persona. Her face had the appearance of an un-ironed shirt, a mass of wrinkles combined with a sneer. Cinderella's wicked stepmother could not hold a candle to Gertrude.

A multi-compartment, large, black purse hung from her arm, and her make-up did not do her any favors, being too thick for my taste. The rose lips created a ghostlike look and added an almost tangible eerie feeling. My mind raced as I wondered what my dad could possibly see in that woman.

Her voice resembled chalk scraped on a blackboard, especially when she noticed the iron had been left on.

"John, this iron's on. Has it been on all day?"

"Olevia must have left it on."

Gertrude began a tirade enviable by the Wicked Witch of the North. "You gotta watch teenagers! They don't care about anything but that loud music. I can't abide it, myself. People let their kids run wild. Those ducktails or whatever those greasy boy hairdos are called disgust me. Have you seen what they call the Stroll dance? Everywhere you look, Elvis Presley is wiggling, and girls are screaming. Feels like end times to me."

On second thought, I hoped this visit would be her one and only time in our house!

The Diamonds had just released their new record, *The Stroll*, and Elvis' *Jailhouse Rock* movie played at the Paramount Theater downtown. Adults in our community and all over the U.S. were afraid of Elvis Presley's influence on young people. On his Ed Sullivan Show television appearances, the cameras did not drop below his waist. His gyrations were too sexual for a family television audience.

At a 1957 Los Angeles concert, the vice squad filmed him to ensure he wasn't gyrating too much. In our town, and in most of the South, his music failed to pass the test as white music. As it has likely been since the beginning of time, older people were afraid of change and anyone who didn't look like them. Young people flocked to his music and every other rock 'n' roller as a way of rebellion and freedom. Rock and roll became the Sunday sermon topic. And, while Tioga Baptist had never sanctioned dancing, it was now a mortal sin.

Merilyn and I saw *Jailhouse Rock* twice. *American Bandstand* did not broadcast via our window to the world, but we knew it existed. We waited impatiently to have access in our own homes to Dick Clark, the latest dance, and the record of the week.

But again, I have wandered off the subject and the current enemy I secretively observed—Gertrude. The man I saw standing next to her did not seem like my dad.

He reached over, turned the iron off, without a word. That was unlike him, and it struck me as almost scary. They went on into the kitchen, and I sneaked out the back door and down the hill to Mrs. Curry's house. I was eager to share the details of the first in what would become a lengthy line of Daddy's adventures in search of a woman.

"Mrs. Curry!" I yelled as I ran through the door, not bothering to knock. She stood in the kitchen, where she always seemed to be.

"Slow down and sit down." She laughed. "What's on your mind?"

I shared Gertrude with her, using the same description I've relayed here. She began to laugh.

"You're getting a front row seat, aren't you? I'm glad you're sharing it with me."

We both laughed as I settled in. Her words had the effect of opening a hot oven on a cold morning and letting the heat spread over you as you pulled out the hot biscuits ready to eat.

As I embellished my story even more, she made dinner for us. Mr. Curry and George were not at home, and we had a fun time roasting Gertrude while we ate. The combination of fried pork chops, rice, gravy, sliced tomatoes, and camaraderie replaced all my fears with peace.

****

Gertrude turned out to be the first in a series of short-term encounters—a date or two—with none of them satisfactory to me or to Daddy. Although Daddy never inquired as to my evaluation of any of these women, thus far, his decisions satisfied me.

****

Next step, Daddy enrolled in a lonely-hearts club, nationally publishing his picture and story. But before he received any responses, he found a so-called live-in housekeeper named Mrs. Doty. A little easier on the eyes than Gertrude, Mrs. Doty was a skinny, wiry, and asthmatic woman, likely about forty-five years old. Daddy moved her and her belongings into Henry's room.

Mrs. Doty's presence felt more like a shadow than a person, both in looks and movements. She did not inspire any immediate feelings of love or dislike in either Johnny or me. Her disposition did lend itself to becoming the object of some practical jokes.

We took advantage of her alleged allergy to dry dog food and her request that it be stored in the dairy barn. On breezy nights, John and I carried the fifty-pound bag from the barn to place it on two saw horses—the top rolled down to expose the contents—under her opened bedroom window.

Our intent and success in proving her lack of any allergy symptoms, and confirming her cantankerous personality, served as an empty victory because it went unacknowledged. So, we searched for other ideas.

John and his best friend, Chester Cassell, conceived and carried out the best joke of all. From my spot as a spectator, I watched the event unfold in our living room.

Mrs. Doty radiated excitement in anticipation of her out-of-state sister's visit. For two days, she cleaned every inch of the house and implored us to be on our best behavior. Finally, the Saturday of the sister's expected arrival came, and Mrs. Doty arose with the chickens to put the final touches on the housecleaning.

Chester and John sat in the living room, as they so often did, talking about squirrel hunting and other subjects of no interest to me. Still, being nosy, I sat at the dining table, close enough to hear, but far enough away to be ignored.

About two o'clock that afternoon, Mrs. Doty entered the living room looking as if she wanted to make an important announcement. The boys stopped talking and turned to look at her.

"Boys, my sister will be here about three-thirty, so I'm going to get a bath and get dressed. I suspect she'll call me from the bus station. If she calls while I'm in the tub, please answer the phone and take a message for me."

"Yes'm," both boys answered. Their expressions showed me the wheels in their brains were turning.

"Chester, wanna play a joke on her?" John's grin was contagious, and my ears perked up.

"Yeah. What?"

In those days, phone numbers consisted of four digits. Ours was four, nine, six, five. And we had a private line. A particular number combination, when dialed with the receiver off the hook, produced a ring on our phone when the receiver was replaced. As I recall, the combination was nine, one, nine, one, but I cannot swear to that.

"Let's make the phone ring."

"For what?" Chester questioned.

"You'll see," John answered. "We need to wait a while."

John and Chester gave Mrs. Doty ample time to be completely involved in her bath before John dialed the magic number. They quickly resumed their seats to wait, and it did not take long. About the fourth ring, Mrs. Doty flew into the living room, holding a guest towel to cover her rake-like physique. She resembled a poorly dressed scarecrow.

"Scuse me, boys," she said as she answered the phone only to hear a dial tone. "Oh, I must have missed her. Why didn't ya'll answer the phone?" She knitted her brows and huffed, distraught.

"It wasn't ringing, Mrs. Doty."

"Wasn't ringing?"

"No, ma'am."

"Oh. I guess I'm just a little over-excited today. Ya'll will answer it if it rings, won't you?"

"Uh-huh."

They repeated this prank twice more, and each time managed to keep straight faces until Mrs. Doty left the room. Once, they had to go to the front porch to muffle the noise of their laughter. In exasperation, Mrs. Doty got out of the tub, dressed, and sat down next to the phone to wait for it to ring. She acted as patient as a spider awaiting her prey.

The phone didn't ring, and her sister arrived in a cab to find her still sitting there.

About three months passed before Daddy helped her pack her things into the car, and they left. He returned alone, and neither John nor I ever asked about her whereabouts.

****

Within weeks, Daddy began bringing in stacks of mail—not from the mailbox in front of the house but from his private Tioga Post Office box number one, two, three.

His membership in the national lonely-hearts club paid off in stacks of letters. Oftentimes, he sat at his desk, sorting the responses. He reread some and stacked some for storage in his locked trunk. He kept a few out, with pictures on top, for further consideration. By snooping around, I determined several letters came from the same address in Moultrie, Georgia. However, he never shared any information with us about any inquiry.

Since he recovered from his heart attack, he always was busy. Even when not at work, he had some unusual projects going on at home. His work shifts changed at the drop of a hat, as did his days off. So, I suppose his being at home on a Tuesday morning should not have seemed unusual. Still, it intrigued John and me as we watched from the front porch.

John said, "What do you think Daddy's doing out there in the side yard?"

I shrugged. "Looks to me as if he is diggin' a grave. That hole's about eight by four foot, and it's hard to tell how deep."

In 1959, Daddy believed we were old enough to manage our own lives to a far greater degree than our friends were allowed. He also felt no need to share any of his plans beyond the basics. We found his antics more amusing than peculiar or concerning.

John asked, "Did you see the pick-up load of gravel he brought in? I think he's going to plant something."

His imagination apparently did not run as wild as mine! "I just hope it's not one of us." I smiled, but I'm not sure I felt totally at ease.

For the best part of the week, we watched the side yard activity. And, Friday morning, it seemed to be culminating as Daddy unloaded three rose bushes from his pickup truck.

The grave had been carefully prepared—with a layer of rock, a layer of soil, another layer of rock, and so on—for the three rose bushes to be strategically placed. He finished off the flowerbed with the remainder of the topsoil and returned his tools to the shed in the back.

Within minutes, he took his place in his rocking chair on the front porch. As always, when Daddy had something momentous to say, he rubbed his cheek between his index finger and thumb and stared out across the pasture to the gravel road about three hundred yards in front of us. He appeared to wait for inspiration and then suddenly spoke.

Small talk did not occupy a place in our conversations. If we asked a question, he may or may not answer. If he had something to say, we listened. We listened, not out of fear or his demanding that we do so but because we were genuinely interested. Today, the stare and the cheek rubbing loomed more earthshaking than typical. The tension in the air was palpable, much like the calm just before a tornado struck. He addressed us by name in an almost formal tone.

"Olevia. John. I will be gone for a few days, and you two need to take care of things around here. Feed Kate. Queenie will be okay just grazing, but Kate's old."

Queenie and Kate were two of our Jinnys. Daddy was partial to Kate, using her for plowing and, sometimes, just for conversation. He went on with the instructions.

"Be sure the calf gets his bucket twice a day. The eggs need to be gathered, and don't forget to feed the chickens. I know you'll take care of the dogs. Make sure you keep the house clean. If you need anything, go to Mrs. Curry's, but I'm sure you'll be fine."

"How long are you gonna be gone, Daddy?" I asked.

"Well, I don't know, exactly. It's a long trip. Maybe a week. Maybe a little longer. Anyway, I'll bring you a surprise."

With that, he got up and went into the house. John and I sat staring at each other for a minute or so. John spoke first.

"Do you think he's coming back?"

"Of course he is! I wonder where he's going?"

"A surprise for us. He said, 'Surprise.' What do you think that means?" John wondered.

We sat for a couple more minutes, each of us lost in our own web of doubt and confusion. Maybe he would not leave at all. Maybe he wanted to start a new life. A twilight zone settled in where everything blurred, and nothing made sense. Eventually, we wandered off in separate directions to whatever the rest of the day held.

****

I woke up the next morning in time to see the rocks flying as Daddy's pickup truck roared down the driveway. I ran into John's room.

"Daddy's gone!" I shouted but barely slowed down as I hurried to dress to go to Mrs. Curry's house. The sun had not yet become visible over the horizon, but that didn't stop me from banging on her door until she answered it.

"Hey, Mrs. Curry. Did I wake you?"

I had, but she just smiled. "Come on in. I'll get us some coffee going. Why are you up so early this morning?" She led the way to the kitchen.

"Daddy's gone! Did he tell you or Mr. Curry where he's going?"

"Gone? What do you mean 'gone?'"

"He left this morning, early, in his truck. He told us not to expect him for a few days, maybe a week. But we don't know where he went."

When the kettle whistled to indicate it was time to pour the boiling water into the coffee pot to drip, Mrs. Curry set out the coffee cups, sugar, and cream. I sat at the kitchen table in the chair that had become my comfort zone in so many ways.

****

Every school day since Mama's passing, I stopped at Mrs. Curry's for coffee before I caught the bus in the mornings. Another daily stop on most afternoons for a Coke or lemonade before I went up the hill closed out my day. Mrs. Curry listened to all my teenage woes and accomplishments. She listened without judgment but rather with a silver lining or a pat on the back—whichever made me feel better. As I sat there that morning, I remembered another day I ran to her because of something Daddy said.

I don't remember what he said, I only remember running away.

Running away is using the term in its loosest sense to describe my adventure. Angry with Daddy, I ran to Mrs. Curry's and told her I wanted to live there. She said that would be fine. On the second day of my stay, Daddy showed up for coffee. I hid out in the kitchen until Mrs. Curry encouraged me to serve his coffee.

When I walked into the living room, Daddy displayed no surprise; indeed, he sounded like the 'everyday daddy.'

"Well, Olevia, I've been missing you and wondered where you were. Are you living here now?"

"No, Daddy. I'm thinking about going home today."

"Okay. That sounds good. You know, Johnny misses you."

He finished his coffee and left.

Mrs. Curry knew my daddy well, and she helped me understand him better. Mrs. Curry had been my mom's best friend; now she was mine.

****

I smiled as I recalled how clever she had been to call Daddy over. But on this specific morning, as we sipped our coffee, she seemed as puzzled as I.

"You sure he said a week?"

"Yes, ma'am, maybe longer."

"Well, I don't know, but I'm sure everything will be okay. Your daddy will be back. Maybe he has some business to take care of. I don't know, but I do know he'll be back."

Her confidence turned my concern into an enjoy-the-adventure state of mind.

The subject turned to more mundane topics. School. Friends. Clothes. Boys. The stuff teenaged girls of my time— perhaps of all time—liked to talk about.

An hour or so later, I walked up the hill toward home, thinking again about Daddy's surprise for us. John stood on the porch, his hands in his pockets—a definite sign he knew something I didn't.

"What, John? Did Daddy call you? Did he leave a note?" I yelled out before I got to the porch. "Hurry up! What do you know?" My breath came in gasps as I filled with impatience.

John spoke with no urgency, as he enjoyed being the one who knew.

"He woke me before he left this morning, and I know what our surprise is. He told me!"

"Why didn't you tell me?"

"You ran in and out of my room too fast."

"What is it? What is it?" "

"You'll never guess. Wanna try?"

He enjoyed his temporary superiority as he stood there looking as devious as the cat who ate the canary.

"Please! You know you're gonna tell me. So, tell me now!"

"Okay. If you are gonna cry about it, I'll tell you. A biscuit maker!"

"A *what?*"

"Those were his exact words 'I am going to get us a biscuit maker.'"

"What does that mean? A biscuit maker?"

Exactly one week later, my dad drove up the driveway with a new mail-order bride by his side. We met our first stepmother—Thelma from Moultrie, Georgia!

I couldn't wait to get to Mrs. Curry's to tell her everything.

CHAPTER 42

THELMA FROM MOULTRIE, GEORGIA

Merilyn and I sat on my front porch talking about this and that, punctuated by friendly silences while we enjoyed the breeze.

After a long pause, Merilyn asked, "Do ya think your daddy's coming home?"

"Yeah, why?"

"I don't know. Seems like he's been gone a long time."

"He said a week or so, and it's a week today. I wish I knew where he went."

Merilyn smiled. "You know what my mama thinks?"

"What?"

"Well, I heard her talking to Mrs. Rice while getting her hair cut, and she said the lonely-hearts club provided a hint and the answer."

"How did she know about that?" I bristled a bit. "I only told you!"

"And I guess I told my mom." She looked apologetic and incredulous at the same time. "I didn't know it was a secret!"

"Merilyn, anytime I tell you something, it's a secret unless I say it's not!" That sounded so silly that we both immediately laughed.

"I'm sorry." She gave me a sweet, apologetic smile. "Do you want to know what I heard?"

"Yeah. What?"

"Mom thinks your dad went to get himself a new wife."

"Well, I hope he does bring a new wife. I'd love some help around here and some good cooking."

At that opportune time, Daddy's pickup turned in the driveway, and a woman was easily seen sharing the front seat—sitting toward the middle.

"There's your daddy, and he's not by himself!" Merilyn shouted as if she had won the lottery.

Suddenly, my desire for a stepmother melted. I felt like I had fallen into a bucket of ice as a shiver ran up my back.

She added, "I guess I need to go home."

"Why?"

Daddy pulled up to the front gate, and I immediately needed a friend.

"Mom told me to come straight home if your Daddy came in today. She said ya'll have a lot to talk about, and I'd be in the way."

"Don't leave." I grabbed her hand, almost in desperation.

"Okay, but I'm not staying long." She sat back down beside me.

Daddy got out of the truck and walked to Thelma's side. Almost as soon as she hit the ground, Daddy lifted their suitcases out of the truck bed.

I whispered to Merilyn, "I wonder where they got married? Or if they're married?"

Before she could respond, a just-under-five-foot-tall Thelma emerged around the end of the truck. She carried a cocker spaniel under one arm and a caged parakeet in her other hand.

I didn't believe my eyes at first, but it began to sink in when Daddy called out, "Olevia, come help Thelma with these things."

As if hypnotized, I didn't move. I stared.

Merilyn punched my shoulder. "Let's go help 'em."

Thelma reminded me of Sponge Bob Square Pants. Height and width mirrored each other, and her smile went from ear to ear.

"Honey, come here. Which one of you is Olevia?"

"That's me," I responded in a monotone voice.

"Let me hug you. I've heard so much about you."

I seriously doubted that but smiled and leaned in for the hug she offered. Merilyn carried the bird cage, and the dog ran around the front yard.

Then Thelma pushed me gently, squeezed my shoulder, and stepped back to look me up and down. I felt like used furniture or a stack of wrinkled clothes on the last day of a garage sale. Her next comment added to that image in my mind.

"I bet you and I can share some clothes."

Strangely, the memory that immediately came to my mind included a school bus driver, Bert Smith. Once, when he helped me onto the bus following an ankle sprain, he asked me what I weighed. I proudly answered, "100 pounds." I did not consider myself fat.

His exact response: "Oh, just like a sack of feed."

Although I knew Mr. Smith to be a kind man and that he intended no offense, at fourteen years old, I chose to hear it as an unkind remark. I remained crushed for weeks. I tried to wear things that made me look thinner—no straight skirts, gathered only, etc.

I mentioned it to no one, not even Mrs. Curry. I thought I had forgotten that incident and the feeling of being an ugly duckling who couldn't fit in until this woman stood in front of me making her appraisal.

Thelma, who must have weighed nearly two hundred pounds or more, suggested sharing clothes with me! I turned in time to see Merilyn's wink and smile. If she had not been there, I may have burst into tears. Just one of the hundreds of times my friend had come to my rescue. I managed to smile as I stepped back to take a long look at Thelma as if I might be interested in sharing clothes.

Merilyn continued the farce. "And you like striped skirts, don't you?"

To avoid a giggle, I turned my back to grab a bag of things Daddy had put on the ground.

Thelma's short hair clung to her head in tight curls; they appeared to be pin curls from the night before that had not yet been combed out. Her vertically striped skirt hung to mid-calf, and a white short-sleeved blouse topped off the outfit. Her feet sported black, lace-up shoes, and her stockings ended somewhere under her dress.

Daddy finally had something to say and not about sharing clothes, thank God. "Hey, Red." He acknowledged Merilyn with a grin. "Good to see ya."

She responded, "How are you, Mr. Yeager?"

"Oh, I'm alright. It was a long haul home, but we made it." He turned toward me and continued, "Where's Johnny? I want him to meet Thelma."

"I don't know. He might be over at Chester's."

"Have ya'll taken care of everything since I've been gone?" he asked as he glanced around the fields.

"Yessir."

He put his arm around Thelma. "Well, Olevia, this is our new biscuit maker! We got married in Mississippi. This lady is officially Thelma Yeager."

Thelma held out her hand on which she wore a pretty diamond ring.

"That's gorgeous!" I remarked in my pretend-friendly voice. "Merilyn, look at this ring."

Merilyn stepped up to take a look. "That's nice! Mrs. Yeager."

I cringed at hearing her called 'Mrs. Yeager'—at least, inwardly—but kept the fake smile going. Thelma beamed as if she had just been crowned homecoming queen.

"Thanks so much, girls. Olevia, your daddy is a wonderful man."

As if I had stepped out of my body, the scene had become one of a fake setting filled with fake people that I could only observe. Just like fake fruit, there was no flavor, scent, or texture. Everything felt flat.

I wondered when Daddy had bought that ring. Typically, any jewelry Daddy purchased came from only one Alexandria jeweler—C A Schnack Jewelers, also known as the official railroad watch jeweler. I guessed Daddy likely took the ring with him since most of his jewelry purchases were made on time—the common term for financed.

"Come on. Let's get inside." Daddy opened the front door and carried in the suitcases. Thelma had the birdcage. The dog ran between his and Thelma's legs to get into the living room as well. I recognized having a dog in the house would be a temporary situation. Then I thought, *What do I know? Daddy's become a mystery to me.*

Merilyn and I stayed on the front porch rather than follow them. Emotionally, I continued to occupy a different reality than I saw surrounding me. Or, I should say unreality. As if in a house of mirrors, every direction offered no escape, just more of the same. Merilyn did not know what else to do, so she sat on the steps. I joined her, and we listened as Daddy became a tour guide, showing Thelma around.

"And this here's our bedroom. Notice that nice chifforobe for you to put our clothes in."

She threw him a properly appreciative glance and asked, "And a closet? Where's our closet?" Her face shifted from an ear-to-ear smile to a minor frown.

"We don't have a separate closet, but there's a nice, long rack in the washroom where all the clothes hang. Come this way." He led her through my room toward the washroom.

Merilyn and I moved toward the screen door to listen as long as possible.

As they walked through my room, Thelma noticed my closet. "John, what about this small closet here?"

"No. Too small. Your clothes would be full of wrinkles and need to be ironed every time you wore something. Come this way. You'll like this better."

They were then out of earshot, and Merilyn started to leave. Then she turned, looked at me, and tilted her head. "Wanna come home with me? You could spend the night."

"Not a bad idea, but I don't think I better. I need to be here when John comes home. I'm going down to Mrs. Curry's for a while though, so I'll walk with you to the road." I yelled through the door, "Daddy, I'm going to Mrs. Curry's for a little while."

I have no idea if he answered or not.

I hoped Mrs. Curry could offer something I needed and wanted. I didn't know what that something was—peace, comfort, direction, or maybe normalcy? But I knew the best chance of finding it would occur at Mrs. Curry's kitchen table.

****

Time moved on. John and I worked our way toward a workable relationship with Thelma. She did make biscuits— not nearly as good as my mama's, but that was a high bar to meet. She kept the house clean and put meals on the table.

John asked her one day, "Can you make squirrel and dumplings?"

"My word, Johnny! You don't eat those things, do you?"

"Yes, ma'am, and they're really good when fried. Do ya want me to kill and clean a couple for you?"

"No! Sometimes I'll make some chicken and dumplings."

Thelma acted friendly and made overtures to me, which I ignored. She complained that I spent too much time at Mrs. Curry's and forbade me to go at night. I ignored that rule as well. One night, she sent John to frighten me on the way home. She told him to make me feel unsafe walking at night up our long, dark driveway.

He went along with her plan, to a certain extent, by sitting under the oak tree located about halfway between the houses. At almost a trot, I hurried home to get there that night and be in bed before Daddy arrived from work at midnight.

John called out, "Hey, Olevia."

I nearly jumped out of my skin when he yelled. I turned to stare at him.

He chuckled. "Thelma sent me to scare you, so act scared when you go into the house."

I replied, "Well, won't be much of an act."

We laughed and walked home together.

I can't say why, but I disliked Thelma from day one. I don't think the sharing clothes remark created all the angst, but it didn't help. I ignored her and did not attempt to ease her plight in any way.

Six weeks later, she disappeared. I have no firsthand knowledge of what happened, but I did see the aftermath. As I got off the school bus one afternoon, I saw Daddy's truck in front of the house—which seemed out of place, as he should have been at work. Rather than make my regular stop at Mrs. Curry's, I ran up the hill.

Daddy sat on a rocking chair in the living room, staring at the wall. The phone lay in the middle of his desk with the wires pulled from the wall. No evidence of a cocker spaniel or a parakeet was apparent.

"Hey, Daddy. Where's Thelma?" I tried to sound nonchalant.

"Gone." He sighed and continued to rock without looking up.

"Gone where?"

"Home, I guess. I'll call the phone company tomorrow. Put on some coffee." He then got up and moved to the front porch.

The story, which I later learned from Mrs. Curry, involved an argument between Daddy and Thelma about some phone call inviting her daughter to come visit (Daddy said to live with us). Daddy pulled the cord from the wall, told her to pack her stuff, and took her to the bus station. On the way, they dropped off the dog and the parakeet at Mrs. Curry's house, both of which remained with Mrs. Curry for the rest of their natural lives.

For all practical purposes, the marriage concluded in less than two months, but not officially. Under Louisiana law, one year of separation of bed and board is required before a divorce is granted. That meant there might be a year of dates, but no new stepmother for a minimum of one year.

I hadn't known that before this break-up. My education began to include legalities that would maybe better prepare me for our next stepmother.

Funny how once Thelma exited our lives, it almost felt like going back to normal. Or maybe, I no longer had a clear idea as to what normal really was!

CHAPTER 43

DADDY BREAKS IN A CAR

During the twelve months Daddy waited for the divorce from Thelma from Moultrie, Georgia, he never slowed down in his new busy-bee approach to life. As luck would have it, his siblings planned a reunion in Richardson, Texas. Uncharacteristically, he decided to go and take Johnny with him.

****

Daddy had a long-term reputation with cars among our family, our friends, and his co-workers. He and his fireman, Mr. Jeansonne, rode to work together every afternoon. Mrs. Jeansonne shared with Mama the stories she heard from her husband with his heavy Cajun accent.

You will have to imagine it here because my knowledge of Cajun French is limited to such things as "Suck the head and eat the tail"—the proper way to eat crawfish. "Ç'est bon" means "that is good," and is used regularly when eating Cajun cuisine. "Laissez les bons temps rouler" means "Let the good times roll" and refers to Louisiana life in general.

I remember one day Mama and Mrs. Jeansonne, who fortunately did not have a heavy Cajun accent, sat drinking coffee and swapping stories at the kitchen table. I listened in from the living room.

"Mary, John scares my man to death when he drives. He told me John waits for traffic before he pulls out on

Highway 165. He just likes to see if he can beat it." She chuckled.

"I know. John's got a thing about him, especially if he sees a Volkswagen. They're not allowed to pass him! Something about the Germans and the war. Sometimes I'm afraid for the kids to ride with him."

Even though they were both expressing fear at Daddy's driving ability, they also laughed as if telling jokes. That led me to believe they were not truly afraid of any consequences for Daddy's unusual approach to driving, but they were rather amused by it.

Mrs. Jeansonne went on. "Harry Lee said his daddy told him Mr. Yeager's nickname is 'Women and Children Yeager' down at the roundhouse. He said Mr. Yeager approaches every railroad crossing saying, 'Don't slow down unless you see women and children.'"

Mama laughed and nodded, surely recognizing the truth of the statement. I chuckled to myself, knowing it too. Early in their marriage, Mama had relinquished all driving privileges after just one lesson at the wheel with Daddy in the passenger seat. She told the story to Mrs. Jeansonne, and I remember it well! In fact, over the years, I heard it many times.

Mama and Daddy had not been married long when Daddy decided to see if she could drive well enough to use the Model A Ford he had. At a 'T' in the road, Daddy yelled mixed instructions that landed the car almost in a creek and Mama in a lot of hot water.

"Mary, look what you've done!!!"

To use Mama's words for his reaction: "He looked like he might have a stroke at any moment. His face could have been a blank stop sign; it appeared to be red enough to bleed. I could see my marriage in the burn pit with the rest of the trash!" She always laughed following that explanation, but I heard it years after it happened. Actually, she said, "I'm sorry."

"Whatcha drive into this ditch for?" Daddy had no comprehension of his behavior as at least part of the problem.

"I don't know. I got confused." Mom answered.

"Well, that's the reason women should not be behind the wheel. They get confused too easily. We could have been killed."

"This is a pretty shallow ditch, John, and I wasn't going fast." Her patience became thin, and she climbed out of the car.

Daddy climbed out right behind her, still instructing her in the dangers of confused driving. "It's the same principle whether you're going fast or not. You must pay attention to what you're doing at all times. Women don't have the focusing ability of men."

This spiel told from the distance of time also brought laughter to anyone present and familiar with Daddy's driving reputation.

The argument began while they sat in the car with people slowing to look. Some even slowed to offer help. Once they exited the vehicle, offers of assistance began in earnest.

Mr. Pardue, one of the wanna-be rescuers, called out, "Mr. Yeager, is everything alright? Do you need some help?"

"No, everything is not alright," Daddy snapped. "You can see my car's in the ditch!"

Mama stood quietly by as Mr. Pardue, knowing my dad as well as he did, took no offense at either Daddy's tone or remark. Rather, he quietly began to solve the problem.

"I've got a chain in the back of my truck. Let's see if we can pull it out."

They removed it from the ditch, and the episode ended with handshaking, laughter, and pats on the back between Mr. Pardue and Daddy. Mama got back into the car without comment but with a bit of annoyance that could be easily read on her face and heard in her tone.

This memorable story of her last driving day (until she taught me to drive at eleven years old) became a family tradition in retelling. Every time I heard it, I found it amusing and a glimpse not only into my parents' personalities but into their relationship as well.

****

Over the years, we had a lot of cars, beginning with an A-Model Ford that craved water, not the same one Mama had wrecked. However, it couldn't have been a new one either since they stopped manufacturing in 1931.

A trip to Rayne included multiple stops at roadside ditches where Daddy dipped water for the radiator. The torn seats bloomed cotton with a propensity to cling to the occupants' clothing, particularly on a Sunday morning, just one of the reasons why we arranged Sunday morning rides to church with Mr. Davis, a deacon who lived not far away. Hannah and I both had our first driving experiences in an A-model, though mine was up and down the driveway only—more like driving a toy car.

Daddy replaced the A-model with a tiny, brand-spanking-new 1950 Henry J. John, and I sprinted out to the gate when we saw the tiny, tan car enter the driveway. Cars were Daddy's business, and the rest of us rode in whatever he provided—no questions asked. Hannah helped Daddy keep the roads hot with this vehicle for a couple of years until Daddy wrecked it in a serious, non-fatal, one-car accident. Only minor injuries were involved, but the car was a no-go. He had hit a tree when swerving to avoid another vehicle.

The police brought him home bandaged up with broken ribs and a bruised ego. Accustomed to his driving challenges, Mama barely looked up when he came up on the porch.

"Miss?" The policeman tilted his head toward Daddy with a chuckle. "Does this belong to you?"

"Yessir, that's my husband."

Johnny and I stayed silent and stared.

Daddy grimaced and snarled at the same time while the police officer helped him up the steps. "Mary, I need a heating pad—now."

****

That car accident resulted in a bent frame—according to Daddy, a fatal flaw in any car—and a new 1954 Willys for the family. It was a two-toned green color. The lime green topped by an even paler green gave the car a faded-box look, as if it had been left in the weather too long. The used-car appearance intensified over the next several years, and John and I celebrated the pink 1959 Studebaker Lark Daddy bought to replace it three years after Mama died.

As luck would have it, or maybe as Daddy intended it, his sister planned a family reunion at her home in Richardson, Texas the same weekend he picked up the car.

Johnny can provide firsthand knowledge of the trip, and he takes the story from here.

****

Excited is a mild word for what I felt that Saturday morning Daddy woke me up to go with him to pick up our right-off-the-showroom-floor 1959 Studebaker Lark. We strolled into the garage area, not wanting to look overeager or too impressed, and there it sat—a shiny salmon-colored car.

"Why'd you buy a pink car, Daddy?"

"Well, I gave that a lot of thought, son. There's a lot of dirt out where we live, and I drive on many gravel roads. When you start hosing off a car, trying to get all that dirt off, it's hard on the paint job. This here cantaloupe color won't show dirt. You don't have to wash it as much, and the paint job lasts longer. I'm going to drive this car a long time."

The salesman came out about that time, and he and Daddy visited for a while. I listened to their small talk and watched where he left the Willis. They found where the owner's manual was—nothing that seemed too important to me. About five minutes elapsed before the salesman got to what I wanted to hear.

"Your Studebaker is ready to go, Mr. Yeager." He handed Daddy the keys and headed back into the showroom.

I hopped right in, and Daddy had his door almost closed when he stopped short. He pointed to a black guy sweeping up on the other side of the garage.

"Just a minute, Johnny. I'm gonna talk to that guy over there."

We walked over to him. It's possible that Daddy thought the man was a mechanic because he stood in a garage.

"You know anything about this car, boy?"

The guy stopped sweeping and leaned on his broom.

"Yessir."

"What's the cruising speed?"

The guy stared at the car for ten seconds or more, got off his broom, sauntered over to it, moseyed around it, and examined it from all angles. He pondered for several minutes before replying. "Well, that car'll cruise on up to a hun'erd miles an hour."

Butterflies took over my stomach because Daddy knew there were a lot of good roads between Alexandria and Richardson—maybe perfect for checking the cruising speed.

Dad seemed eager to query the man further, and I noted the glint in his eye. "This thing's brand new. How do you suggest a man break it in?"

The guy mulled that question a while, taking his cap off, rubbing his head, and scratching above his eyes. He could not have looked more serious if he had been asked if he wanted to quit his job and go with us.

"Well, sir, you don't want to start out driving at a set speed or nothin'. Like you wouldn't want to take off on some long trip right away."

"That's exactly what me and my boy are about to do. Should I keep my old car for that?"

"Oh, no sir!" The guy answered quickly for fear he had just ruined a sale. "The main thing ya gotta remember is you never want to drive a new car at the same speed for very long—leastways not until you get about a thousand miles on it. When you're breakin' in a new one, you need to race it on up to seventy or eighty miles an hour and then drop back slow."

"So, it's okay to take a long trip if I follow the break-in rules—up to seventy or eighty and then drop back slow?"

"Yessir. If you do that, the engine'll set just right, and it'll give you good service for a long time."

Daddy shook hands with the man and thanked him before we both got back in the car and headed home. At Upper Third Street, I held on when we shot out like a bullet; high speed scared me, and Daddy at the wheel doubled the fear. Seat belts were not yet invented and, as a small child, I used to lay down on the back floorboard when Daddy drove. But I knew that wouldn't go over well at fourteen years old. So, I held on tight to the side of the seat.

We immediately slowed down to about ten miles per hour and crept along for a couple of minutes before Daddy hit the gas again. We shot out like round two of a repeating weapon. Daddy let his foot off the gas until we were down to about ten or twelve miles per hour. All of that happened before we got to the last red light to turn towards Tioga. Things didn't change once we turned; we had bursts of speed followed by creeping along all the way home.

I'm sure I had a ghostlike appearance by now, white as a sheet and slightly nauseous. Daddy ignored my condition as he carefully explained the necessity of following the instructions of an expert.

"You ask somebody who knows. If they know and they tell you, then you ought to do the way they tell you. If somebody asked me about a diesel engine, I would tell 'em about that engine because that's what I know. That man's business is cars, and we are going to follow his instructions. I need to get a lot of service out of this car."

I thought, *That man's business is sweeping,* but I kept my mouth shut and my eyes closed. I wanted to avoid any conversation that might cause Daddy to take his eyes off the road.

When I went to bed that night, the excitement of making the Texas trip had dampened a lot. I began to regret all my bragging to Olevia about getting to go when she had to stay home. But there was no going back now.

By three o'clock the next morning, Daddy and I were headed to Richardson. All the way—all 365 miles—Daddy drove as he had the day before. Going eighty miles or better an hour, we would hurtle past seven or eight cars and pull in front of them where Daddy let the car roll to a near stop.

Highway Eighty was the main highway, but it remained two lanes at a time except for the passing lanes that had been constructed in several areas. The passing lanes were approached by Daddy as non-consequential and utilized only if they happened to show up at the right time.

Initially, people who waited for a passing lane stared at us as they eased by our slowing car thinking we might be having car trouble. About the time all of them were again in front of us, Daddy would push the accelerator to the floor, and off we flew to begin the process anew. All the time, Daddy talked nonstop about breaking in a car right and how he knew what to do.

My ears poised to hear a police siren, and my eyes searched for a police car and maybe some relief. Neither occurred. The only result of this bizarre action came other drivers who rolled down their windows to shout and shake their fists at us. Daddy paid no attention to them or even acknowledged their actions. I held on tight when he hit the accelerator, tried to stay in my seat, and kept my eyes shut.

The outskirts of Richardson were a welcome sight, but I could tell the Texas off-freeway streets made Daddy nervous. If he had a straight shot, he felt in control. But the minute he exited at the Richardson sign, his death grip on the steering wheel increased. He glanced furtively in every direction as if something might sneak up on us. I considered the change in his approach to driving as an answer to my prayer, and I sat up confidently.

There happened to be a guy standing on the side of the road and Daddy stopped to ask for directions. That first attempt to find Aunt Nowata's house failed, as we seemed to almost drive in circles. The next several attempts for directions were equally unsuccessful. Everyone professed to know exactly how to get to the address Daddy showed them, but we couldn't find it.

After about ninety minutes of goose-chasing, we saw the right street sign. I breathed another sigh of relief. Once my stomach settled, I knew I would be hungry, and I longed for a few hours of sitting still.

All the aunts and uncles I knew were there, except Uncle James, who had died a few years back. The remaining ones looked tickled to see us. Everybody came to the car to welcome us. Uncle Jake put his arm around Daddy's shoulders and took him over to a wine table.

"Johnny, you look a little frazzled," he said. "Why don't you try this? This is a real dry wine."

Daddy sort of rinsed it around in his mouth and agreed with Uncle Jake's assessment of pretty dry.

"We have some sweet wine over here. Try a little glass of this. A glass of wine is good for you, and it settles your nerves."

I wished I could have one but kept that idea to myself.

Daddy took a swig, pronounced it too sweet, and asked for a cup of coffee. Aunt Nowata brought one and told us to sit down because dinner would be ready in just a little while.

"No, Wataw (my dad's name for her), we don't have time to eat. We must get back to the house."

Aunt Mary chimed in. "John, you don't want to leave yet. You just got here! It's too far to drive not to spend the night. Frank, come over and talk to John. He's getting ready to leave already."

"Mary, I know what I need to do," Daddy answered a bit curtly. "The boy and I have cows and horses and chickens to feed. You can't just go off and leave them for days at a time."

Aunt Denie and I talked together while Aunt Olevia tried her hand at convincing Daddy to stay. I knew his made-up mind rarely changed just because he was wrong. Aunt Olevia met her match this time.

Daddy talked to everybody. We probably stayed an hour or two before he told me, "Get in the car, boy. It's time to go."

Aunt Nowata carried out a big platter of meat as Daddy started the engine.

"Daddy, why couldn't we stay to eat? I'm hungry."

"Son, these people don't know about responsibilities. We've got animals depending on us. You want to keep your dogs, don't ya?"

"Yes, sir, but I sure want to eat too."

"Well, we'll get something on the way home. Now, help me look out for Highway 75 South."

For a few short minutes, I thought the trip home would be a more pleasant experience. Not so. Once we found the highway we needed, the same rhythm as the one coming— fast, slow, fast, slow—began. As we crossed the Louisiana state line, Daddy slowed down and turned into a beer joint.

"Are we through breaking in the car yet, Daddy?" My tone and my expression must have resembled the starving man with a chance of food.

Daddy chuckled a bit under his breath. "No, son. You heard the man tell us a thousand miles is the break-in mileage, and we are just a little over five hundred. Get out. I want to show you something here.

We went into the bar, and we each climbed on a stool.

"Bring this boy a Grapette and a hamburger."

"All we have is Coke or Pepsi," the bartender responded.

"Well, bring him a Coke and hamburger. Bring me a Falstaff, and I think I'll have a hamburger, too."

That hamburger tasted good, and I ate it quick. Daddy ate his pretty fast too. I had only started to drink my Coke when I noticed Daddy turn his beer up, and it disappeared in two or three swallows. I wasn't even half through with my Coke, when Daddy got off his stool and motioned me to follow him.

"Come on. I want to show you something."

They had a little dance hall attached to the bar.

"You've heard me talk about those knock-em down, drag-em out places?"

"Yes, sir."

"This is one of those. You see in there where we had our drinks?"

"Yeah."

"That's where they knock-em down, and this is where they drag-em out. Well, let's go. We need to be heading for home."

"You reckon I could get my Coke off the bar?"

"No, you are not allowed to bring drinks out of the bar. We'll have to leave it. Let's get on out to the car."

We got in the car. He pulled into a gas station next door, where he allowed me to run in to buy a Coke while he filled the gas tank. I also got some cheese crackers. The next stop would be home, and I passed ready to get there. I couldn't even remember why I wanted to go on this trip! I made up my mind that, once out of this car, I would not ride in it again until Daddy completed the break-in process and was not planning any long trips.

We turned into our driveway in the wee hours of the morning.

Traveling with Daddy is one of the things that made me a homebody. Relaxed trips did not occur when Daddy drove. And as soon as we left home, he started talking about getting back. So many times, I wondered why we were going when coming home pleased him most.

I never asked.

CHAPTER 44

ELDERBERRY WINE

By the summer of 1958, John and I had grown fairly accustomed to our lives. We were close to each other but traveled on sort of parallel paths. For the most part, we each explored our own ways and enjoyed our individual adventures. Occasionally, our exploits closed in on one another, and we would share a moment or two. Such was our wine-making experience.

****

The only obvious alcohol in our house consisted of a fifth of Four Roses Whiskey. Daddy displayed that bottle conspicuously on the living room mantel as some sort of independence badge at every deacon's or preacher's visit. Although Daddy rarely drank, he kept whiskey in the house for three purposes: to set on the mantle when any clergy visited, to use medicinally, and to make Christmas Eggnog.

In my mind's eye, I can still see him and Mama sitting beside each other in our living room rocking chairs, each with a bowl and an egg whip in their laps. Mama relished her assigned goal—egg whites in stiff, fluffy peaks—while Daddy managed the yolks. Daddy's responsibility included well-beaten yolks with one tablespoon of whiskey per yolk.

I am not certain what else the recipe called for, but their team effort produced the best eggnog I've ever tasted, then or now. The pleasant taste multiplied in the presence of the easy back and forth between Mama and Daddy when the first tasting took place. The conversations such as shown below occurred every year I remember until Mama's health failed. They discussed whose expertise served the higher purpose in producing the delicate balance in taste and product consistency.

"Mary, you did a good job on these egg whites, but I'm not sure the sugar's just right. How much did you add?"

"Same amount as always! It could be that whiskey. Did you remember it is only ONE tablespoon per egg?"

He countered with, "Did you use the heavy cream from Sally's milk? Jersey cows produce the best milk, and Sally's can't be beat."

"How many years have we been doing this together?" Mama reminisced with a smile as she poured each of them a cup of the finished product. "Let's call Ellis and Novie to come up for a taste."

Daddy never failed to give Mama a squeeze as they agreed and shared a chuckle. That's the moment I knew Christmas had arrived in our house and hearts.

****

This short journey down alcohol memory lane must include Dr. Tichenor's Antiseptic and Hadacol. These medications were the first solutions applied to almost any illness occurring in our house. Physical injuries, such as stepping on a nail, required a coal oil treatment, but those were rare. More often, the ailments consisted of tonsillitis, a bad cold, or maybe a minor virus.

Dr. Tichenor's was—and probably still is—seventy percent alcohol. It came into play as both a preventative and a cure for sore throats, colds, coughs, and any other flu-like malady. John and I grew up with tonsils intact when everyone else seemed to undergo a tonsillectomy before reaching the age of ten.

Personally, I am surprised our tonsils still existed after the onslaught of Dr. Tichenor's. When suffering from a targeted illness, we drank a half an ounce in one large gulp. I felt sure our tonsils were eliminated by the extreme alcohol burn Dr. Tichenor's provided.

If there were a fever accompanying our sore throat, we had the pleasure of a hot toddy between antiseptic burns. I loved hot toddies—still do—a jigger of whiskey, a cup of warm water, lemon juice, and a teaspoon of honey. Sometimes Mama sprinkled a bit of ground cinnamon on top as she warmed it on the stove. The aroma wafted through the whole house. My illness began to disappear as I inhaled the sweet air the preparation created. Indeed, writing about it returns me to the scene, the taste and feeling of how loved and safe I felt in those days.

Hadacol does not share any feel-good memories. It looked and tasted like medicine, and it smelled awful. Dudley J. LeBlanc, a fellow Louisianan, invented and marketed Hadacol. When he ran for governor in 1952, his campaign primarily consisted of the claim that anyone who could convince people to buy and consume Hadacol could bring industry to Louisiana. He lost that election, but not Daddy's devotion to Hadacol.

While he had taken small doses of the offensive solution since it appeared on the market, Daddy's dedication to Hadacol became more apparent after his 1957 heart attack. His daily morning breakfast, even before coffee, became two well-beaten, raw eggs in eight ounces of milk along with a quarter cup of Hadacol, drank quickly. Once, as I watched him prepare this awful concoction, I asked, "Daddy, why do you drink that awful stuff?"

"Well, it's a constitutional treatment." He poured it into a glass.

"How do you know it works? Just smelling it makes me sick to my stomach."

"Every medicine cannot taste good. It's not made to taste good. It's made to ward off germs and strengthen the immune system." He then downed the entire glassful of nasty liquid in two or three swallows.

He instructed John and me to take one teaspoon with a glass of milk every Saturday. I avoided my dosage whenever possible—any time Daddy was not home and/or not present. It tasted terrible and seemed to work as a laxative. John also rarely took his dosage.

We would be careful to pour a little Hadacol down the drain every Saturday morning, just in case Daddy checked the bottle. I don't know if he checked it or not, but he never questioned us about it.

****

For reasons I no longer remember, John decided we should make some wine. Almost overnight, the thought of drinking homemade wine became pervasive and all-consuming for him. His enthusiasm spread quickly to me during one of our at-home-alone-talks—an apt proof of how little was going on in Tioga to entertain teenagers.

John had no recipe for, nor firsthand knowledge of, winemaking. Why he thought I might know something about it is a mystery to me.

"Olevia, have you seen how the elderberries down by the trestle are getting ripe?"

I threw him an enthusiastic grin. "Yeah, I thought we might pick some and see if Mrs. Curry would make some elderberry jelly or jam. What do you think?"

"Jelly or jam. Why?"

"I just thought she may like to. She makes good jelly."

Looking very serious, he stared at me for a minute as if I had grown a new head. "She's got plums, blackberries, Mayhaws, and watermelon rinds. Why would she want elderberries?"

I didn't take kindly to his tone or his attitude and assumed some attitude for myself. I stood up and, with hands on my hips, growled, "You probably don't even know that elderberries are poisonous unless cooked. You'll get sick if you eat them raw!"

Before I could make my dramatic exit, he stood up, put his hands on his hips in imitation of me, and started to laugh. To avoid being laughed at, I joined in the laugh and sat back down. We sat there for a couple of minutes; the frost melted, and our conversation ran free again.

"Olevia, do you know anybody who has ever made wine?"

"No, why?" *This could get interesting.* "What are you talking about?"

"What about Uncle John? Did he ever make wine?"

Uncle John was a black man who had lived in our washhouse before we moved to the big house on the hill. He often went blackberry picking, and he sometimes took us along when we were much younger kids. Once Mama had enough blackberries for a cobbler or two, he kept the rest. If Mama commented about the leftover berries, Uncle John's response always included a reference to wine and thinnin' the blood. Still, I had never seen any actual winemaking set up and probably would not have recognized it if I had.

With wrinkled brow, I answered, "I don't think Uncle John made wine. Why are you being so mysterious?"

"Well, that's a puzzle! I wonder where he got the wine that I know he drank." He shook his head and seemed to be deep in thought as he stared at the ground.

Losing patience, my annoyance came through clearly when I grumbled, "Okay, I don't know anything about Uncle John's drinking or winemaking habits, and I'm losing interest in this twenty-questions game. What are you talking about?"

We were sitting beside each other on the edge of the back porch. I prepared again to make an exit in a huff when John answered in a matter-of-fact tone, "I think we should make some wine."

That piqued my interest and served to sit me back down. "For what?"

"Well, didn't the doctor often say Mama oughta drink a little glass of wine every day? I think it'd be good for us to have some wine in the house."

Don't be misled here. My brother wasn't concerned about my health, his health, or anyone else's health. His plan to involve me in what I should have recognized as an unwise undertaking worked like magic. In hindsight, it seems almost unreasonable that I went along with such a harebrained scheme or that he came up with it. I guess you had to be there! It sounded exciting and new, something to do and share.

It was *All Over but the Shoutin'* as they say, when I became a fellow conspirator. I was all in, no turning back. The rocket had left the launch pad, and the adventure began.

"I think wine is made with berries or grapes or apples or something." I tilted my head as I tried to remember any possible nugget I knew about wine. "Maybe we could get a recipe. I'll ask Mrs. Curry what she knows about making wine."

John cautioned, "Don't tell her why you want to know."

I did talk to Mrs. Curry and kept our secret while I got a bit of elementary advice regarding winemaking. Mrs. Curry originally hailed from Fort Smith, Arkansas. At least, Fort

Smith was the nearest town, as she and her family lived in the Ozark hills. Her brother, Adolf, occasionally visited Mrs. Curry, as did her dad, Mr. Weaver, and her sister, Ruby. All of them bragged about moonshine, at various times, as well as about winemaking carefully hidden from the revenuers. I asked Mrs. Curry to tell me stories she could remember, and I stored away every tidbit of information gleaned. I eagerly shared it with John as I learned it.

In a matter of days, John's enthusiasm almost paled in comparison to mine. Once onboard, I wanted to be captain of the ship while John swabbed the decks. That idea had no chance of survival, but I did inhabit a partnership position.

"John, the dewberries, and blackberries are already gone. What are we going to use?"

"You mean for the wine?"

"What else would I be talking about?" I grinned as I recognized his pleasure in having an involved co-conspirator. "What about elderberries? Didn't you suggest that before?"

We were now both getting high on our plan, and it felt a bit like old times when everything was a joint adventure.

"You know, I didn't suggest elderberries for wine. Be serious!" He knit his brows. "You said they were poisonous."

"Oh, okay, but that's only if eaten raw. People might make elderberry wine. The trestle bushes are covered with berries, and they'll be completely ripe soon. We could wait for the muscadines? There's a lot of those in the woods too, and they'll be ripe by mid-August."

He winked, and his head tilted in the way that used to make me laugh when he was about five years old. "Sometimes you're such a scaredy-cat. If elderberries were poisonous, elderberry wine would not exist."

"I'm not sure it does!"

"Of course, it does, and we're going to make some." His words weighed heavy with finality, as irreversible as a wax seal on an envelope.

"But the berries are not completely ripe yet," he added in recognition of my concern and clearly indicating he stood on the fence as to at what point elderberries became safe to consume.

"In that case, we may have to add more extra sugar. We need a big bucket to cook them in. I know for a fact that cooked elderberries are safe to eat."

His enthusiastic nod reminded me of a dog jumping for an offered treat. I had to slow him down a little. "We can't cook 'em in the house. Daddy'd probably find out."

"I know." He squared his shoulders. "I'm cookin' 'em in the barn. I've already made a place."

"What else have you done? How're we going to get the rest of the stuff we need? I don't have any money, and I'm pretty sure we'll need more sugar than we have in the kitchen."

"I don't know. I do know we don't need sugar until we have berries. Come with me."

We went to the barn where John had stashed four gallon-sized ribbon cane syrup cans with the handy handle on top. Without giving it another thought, we each carried two and started to walk the railroad tracks toward the trestle and the woods. We filled out the first two cans quickly— twice over, in fact.

Elderberries begin as white, pleasant-smelling flowers on small trees. They then become hard, green balls about the size of an English pea. Finally, they ripen into small, deep-purple berries. The small, hard berries we carried were somewhere between the early green and the ripe purple. They did not encourage consumption, and neither of us were brave enough to taste one. Our berry gathering did not occur with any finesse; thus, the buckets included a lot of the bush as well as the berries. Stems, leaves, and even a few flowers well past their prime evened out our four gallons of elderberries.

Now, I took the side of the poisonous berries and solicited assurance from John.

"Are you sure these berries are not poisonous?"

"Yeah, I'm sure. I never heard of anybody dyin' from eating elderberries. Have you?"

"No, but—

"Besides, you're the one who said they cannot be poisonous after being cooked. Olevia, don't make everything a big deal!"

I followed his lead and moved on to the nitty-gritty challenges of winemaking. "You know, John, it's gonna take a lot of sugar to make these berries sweet."

John nodded. "I have an idea!"

"What?"

John leaned forward, his eyes round and his face full of viral excitement, just waiting to be spread.

"Let's put all of our berries in a number three washtub and cover them with water."

"We don't have money to buy a washtub," I interrupted with a deflated voice.

"And we don't need to buy one." John's tone grew vocally animated, and his eyes shined with the sheer joy of our project.

"Do you already have one?"

"Not exactly, but Daddy has some. There's one under every hydrant. One won't be missed."

The next phase of winemaking began in earnest. The inside of the barn idea seemed a bit dangerous to me, and John acquiesced to our setting up for berry cooking behind the barn. We scheduled all berry cooking for after three in the afternoon, when Daddy's whereabouts were known. His work hours gave us a three to eleven o'clock window with an hour left to be sure we were safe in the house before he turned into the driveway at midnight. Of course, my evenings with Mrs. Curry were not interrupted for our winemaking duties, as that would have been far too suspicious.

Getting enough sugar presented the next largest obstacle. After considerable discussion, we decided to simply order it. Before Mama's death, she regularly had groceries delivered to our door. Since her death, Daddy had taken to dropping me off at Piggly Wiggly in Pineville to grocery shop with a ten-dollar check.

Still, we had no reason to believe Mr. Belgard would not deliver groceries to our house if we called. In the past, Mama just signed the ticket, and Daddy paid the bill at the end of the month. That extended our current need to problem solve for at least thirty days. By mutual agreement, John made the call, using his most grown-up voice.

The manager answered, "Hello, Allen speaking."

"This is John Yeager. I need to get a delivery made."

"What do you need, Mr. Yeager? Otis Belgard is about to leave for his morning run, but I can get him to add your order on his truck before he goes "

"I need twenty-five pounds of sugar, six lemons, and a cake of yeast."

"Okay. Otis will get that out to you today."

I still do not understand why he did not question that order. Of course, my dad could sometimes be unusual, and people accepted it.

John quickly replied, "Make that after three. My boy'll be home to receive the delivery. You'll take his signature, won't you?"

"Oh sure; I'll alert Otis. That's Johnny you're talking about, right?"

"Yeah, that's the one."

It's a mystery to me why Mr. Allen believed John was Daddy or if he really did. Still, the delivery arrived, and we questioned it no further.

We squeezed the six lemons over the boiling berries and dropped the yeast cake in. Twenty-five pounds of sugar seemed to be overkill, so we started the brew with only ten pounds. We took turns between watching and stirring the pot and gathering sticks and stuff to keep the flame going. We added berries, water, and sugar, and we boiled the concoction until well after sunset. Then we extinguished the fire, covered our brew with two towels, and left it to ferment.

The next morning, as soon as we could do so without arousing alarm, we went out to check on the status of our wine. It looked awful. A sort of waxy build-up covered the top, and the whole mess was sticky. It looked more like a jam-making attempt gone awry. We still had ten pounds of sugar left. With Daddy safely at work, we decided to add more water and do a bit more cooking that afternoon.

In the end, we spent several days adding water and cooking; we even went back to the store for another cake of yeast and a couple of lemons. However, after having invested two weeks into creating this culinary disaster, we began to lose interest.

John's birthday was August 29th, and school started on September 2. Periodically, during that time window, we dropped by the washtub to take a look. Once maggots began to squirm in the jellylike substance, we emptied the container and closed the door on our ineptness at winemaking.

We thought the story had ended. We marveled at our ability to operate under the radar with no repercussions from having the sugar delivered. In our youthful ignorance, we assumed Daddy just paid the bill, no questions asked. After all, he was an old man, and we were young and crafty! It seemed reasonable to think we had outsmarted him; that is, it seemed so until early October. As we got off the bus at the end of our long driveway, I noticed Daddy's car sat in front of the gate. Being almost four-thirty in the afternoon, he should have been at work long ago.

"Hey, John. Look at that! Daddy's home. I wonder what's going on."

"I don't know. I hope he's not sick or something."

"Well, it looks as if he's sitting in the rocking chair on the front porch. Uh-oh, he's standing up."

We walked up the hill. Although it crossed my mind a couple of times to stop at Mrs. Curry's, I sensed going home held priority today. Daddy stood in the middle of the porch when we started up the steps; he looked directly at John.

"John, why'd you buy twenty-five pounds of sugar?" His voice sounded level and calm like he was just curious.

"Sugar? Daddy, I haven't bought any sugar."

Thinking back, I'm pretty sure Johnny was not lying—at least not at the beginning. Over two months had passed since our winemaking fiasco. Buying that sugar had left his mind.

"Don't lie to me, boy! You bought twenty-five pounds of sugar and had it delivered to this house." Daddy's voice became louder and more agitated.

"Oh, yeah. I remember. Mr. Belgard brought it. How did you find out?"

"WHY?" Daddy fairly screamed, and we both noticeably flinched.

"I don't know, Daddy."

"You don't know why you had Mr. Belgard bring twenty-five pounds of sugar to this house?"

"No, sir."

"Are you crazy or what, boy?"

"No, sir."

At this point, I hoped John would stick to his story of amnesia. I remained completely mute as I edged toward the front door. I knew Daddy would not hit John—he was the baby after all—and if he could just keep a straight face, we might both be home free.

"I don't know why you're lying, boy, but you are. What trouble could you get into with twenty-five pounds of sugar? It makes no sense to me. What bothers me most is you charged it to me."

Daddy looked flustered, a little sad, and suddenly very old.

I felt some sympathy for him and tried to offer a solution by saying, "Daddy, maybe we could pay for it."

Daddy ignored me and continued to talk to John. "You know, boy, I've never been late paying my bill at Merritt's. Today, Mr. Allen called me to see why I hadn't been in to pay my August bill. Do you know how that made me feel?"

"No, sir."

Daddy's voice escalated as he described Mr. Allen's call as if it were from a collection agency and we were all headed to debtors' prison. "I'm asking you a question—do you know how that made me feel?"

"No, sir."

"My credit's my good name, and you took a chance with it. Why'd you do that, son?"

"I don't know, Daddy."

What a relief to hear boy replaced by son—a good omen that Daddy was coming to terms with the situation. Maybe we would all live through it.

I made one more attempt to offer a solution. "Daddy, we want to pay the bill. Please?"

Daddy continued to look past me and directly at John. John, bless his heart, took all the heat, leaving me scot-free.

"John, YOU are going to pay this bill. YOU are going to pay it twice—once because you owe it and once because you lied. Until you get it paid, you are not allowed to go anywhere but school. I don't want to see that Cassell boy over here either."

"Daddy, I don't have any money. How can I pay the bill?"

"Well, sounds like you've got some thinking to do, don't ya?" With that, Daddy turned around and walked into the house.

John called after him, "How much is the bill, Daddy?"

"You just keep paying me until I tell you to stop."

Over the next day or so, we determined that the sugar was forty-two cents per five pounds, the lemons were a nickel a piece, and that yeast cost thirteen cents per cake. $2.96 times two. All added together to include the extra yeast cake and lemons equaled $5.92.

During the school year, Daddy gave us each a dollar every Monday, and our discretionary fund amounted to fifty cents of that dollar. I usually used mine for a canteen treat after lunch, and John's was more apt to end up in the pinball machine in Billups' Cafe. Because neither of us wanted to give up all our spending money, we agreed on twenty-five cents each as our weekly payment. John gave Daddy the fifty cents from his allowance, and I reimbursed him with a quarter of my fund. I know he also collected and redeemed empty Coke bottles for additional funds, but those were destined for pinball machines, not Daddy's pockets.

After a couple of weeks, John and I came and went pretty much as we pleased. His friend, Chester, again became a welcome guest. But restitution payments remained the same, with no slack anywhere. Although we knew we were paid up at the end of twelve weeks, we dared not mention it to Daddy. He accepted the fifty cents for two more weeks, taking the last payment on the Monday after school resumed following the Christmas break.

On January 5, 1959, our debt could bear the stamp of paid in full! And a couple of important lessons were learned. One: don't take chances with other people's money, and two: John and I could depend on each other, no matter what.

CHAPTER 45

JOHN DRIVES THE TRAIN

Daddy's crew.

Johnny remained aloof from Daddy's women—stepmothers, housekeepers, and dates. He concentrated on traveling in his own world—a day-by-day trudge through sometimes a daydream, sometimes a nightmare, and sometimes boredom interrupted by singular extraordinary events.

The day Daddy shared his everyday job of driving the train highlighted one of the most special and unforgettable events. The story below shares a look into John's life from his own memory.

****

My Daddy was fifty years old when I was born and sixty-one when my mama died. He grew up as a country boy using a horse and buggy for transportation. His dad was a blacksmith. In those days, the U.S. Cavalry still chased Geronimo, and only the elite had automobiles. Here in 1958, he'd been widowed twice, married multiple times, and recovered from a heart attack before I had reached my thirteenth birthday.

Without Mama to temper his decisions or soften his ways, he did the best he could. He went to work every day on the three o'clock switch engine turn and came home about midnight. Many nights, he brought me a Billips Café hamburger and fries. He would come into my room and shake me awake to say, "I got ya' a hamburger and French fries."

I'm betting manna from heaven was no more welcomed by the Jews or tasted any better than a Billips hamburger at midnight. On those special nights, I wolfed mine down, visited with Daddy a little bit, and went back to bed. We communicated mainly via notes written on rough, pink tablets of paper he brought home from work. That worked pretty well, and I had become used to the routine.

Then, unexpectedly, he bid on another job!

At that time, railroad workers were governed by a bid system, allowing the man with the most seniority to have the job he most wanted. Daddy wanted the Lake Charles turn, and he got it. His job required driving a passenger train to Lake Charles—about a hundred or so miles southeast of Alexandria, and then deadheading back. One Thursday, as we sat on the front porch together, out of the blue, he said something for which I was totally unprepared.

"Son, would you like to make the run to Lake Charles tomorrow and ride up in the engine?"

If the president had invited me to visit the White House, I would have been no more shocked than I was by Daddy's surprise invitation. My heart beat so loudly I imagined he could hear it.

I gasped, "I surely would like to go, Daddy."

"Alright. Tomorrow, when I get up for work, you'll need to get up too."

I went to bed happy that night, and I tossed and turned until the first light. By five in the morning, we headed for the roundhouse, a trip during which I said not a word because the mood was too good to disturb. Upon arrival, I scrambled out of the car and stood quietly, awaiting further instructions.

Daddy pointed to the engine and indicated with his head I needed to climb up the ladder. Mr. Cole, the fireman, a young skinny guy who seemed to be covered in smiles, occupied what I called the passenger seat. He had a face that clearly expressed, "I like you and I hope you like me." I did.

Daddy climbed up behind me, and Mr. Cole said, "Hey, Uncle Johnny. I see you brought us some help today."

"Yeah. I brought him down here to see if he could give us a hand."

I explored with my eyes, and a sign stating 'Danger, 5,000 Volts' immediately grabbed my attention. I recognized volts as something to do with electricity but couldn't make the connection to a diesel engine. Mr. Cole's smile gave me the confidence I needed to give in to my curiosity.

"Daddy, why do you need electricity to run a diesel engine?"

"Well, son, this engine ain't nothin' but a big old generator. The generator runs on diesel, and the electricity runs the wheels. It's called a diesel engine because diesel runs the generator. It's dangerous. Don't open that door. Now, you need to get right back here and sit on that stool."

He motioned to a cubbyhole directly behind him. "No need for everybody to see you riding up here in the engine."

"Yes, sir." I hunkered down behind Daddy and stayed out of sight.

"What do you think the superintendent would say, Uncle Johnny, if he saw you with your boy on here?"

"I'll tell you what, Cole. I'm prepared to sacrifice the rest of my years on this job. I've been here almost forty years, and if he wanted to fire me for this, he could. This experience is worth that to this boy. I bid on this shift so I could take him with me to Lake Charles."

I listened to every word Daddy spoke and felt like my ears grew bigger hearing them. I'd always figured Daddy sort of owned the engine, the way he loved it and talked about it. I wondered who this superintendent was who could fire my daddy, but I stayed quiet and slunk down even lower to be sure I wasn't the cause of any trouble. I kept my eyes peeled and ears open. I watched Daddy shove a lever up, hit another lever that caused a bell to ring, and finally pull a rope hanging from the ceiling to blow the whistle. Hearing that bell ringing, that lonesome whistle blowing, boy, I was in hog heaven!

I wanted to stand next to Daddy, and I tried not to squirm too much in that cubbyhole. With his hand on the throttle, Daddy looked down those tracks as if in charge of the world. Pride bubbled in my chest like fizzy soda. The wheels hit the tracks—click, click, click. Every now and then, Daddy hit the whistle while he and Mr. Cole made small talk. The clicking got faster and faster—clickety, click, clickety, click. The engine swayed from side to side, like a rocking chair, as speed increased.

As we left town, Daddy motioned me out of my cubbyhole.

"Come on up here, boy. You're going to have to do some work."

I wondered what kind of work I could do on an engine, but I felt ready to try anything. I clambered up to stand next to him while he gave me instructions.

"Any time you see a road or a highway crossing these tracks, flip this lever right here so the bell will ring; then pull this string here. Pull it as hard as you can, a couple of times, because that's the whistle. Engineers are required by law to do these things at every crossing. If there's a car coming, the driver will know we're coming and stop his car. We don't want anyone to get hurt."

I gave him a vigorous nod, beaming brightly at his faith in me. Boy, I liked that job. I thought, *I've found a job I can do. Maybe if I do it well, I'll be invited on more trips with Daddy.*

By the time we left Alexandria that train was barreling down the tracks with the engine swaying from side to side. I noticed the lever Daddy was pushing had eight notches on it.

I pointed at it. "What's that lever for, Daddy?"

"Well, that tells us how fast we're going, like a speedometer on the car. We started out at one, and you can see we're at four now. If we get to eight, we might be flying." He chuckled.

I kept a close eye on the lever. I disliked speed in a car, but somehow it seemed all right here in the engine. When it reached six, the engine quit swaying and began to go up and down. It felt good to me, but Mr. Cole's smile looked strained.

"Uncle Johnny, you don't think there's anybody out here today checking speed, do you?"

"Oh no. I'm watching. I don't know why they worry so much about it. You know, Cole, I started out on a steam engine. They had sorry tracks, sorry crossties, and they let us run just as fast and as far as we wanted to go. Now, we've got the best tracks, the best crossties, the best railroad beds, and they want us to hold back to sixty-five miles per hour. I think we'll stretch this thing out a little bit; and then, just outside of Lake Charles, I'll cut her back some. The orders say we have a passenger train facing us, and we're going to have to get on a side track anyway."

He pulled out his watch, and at the same time, Mr. Cole pulled his own out. "It's 9:16, and we ought to hit Lake Charles at 11:19."

When railroad men expressed time, it was never 11:15 or ten o'clock. It had to be something real precise, like 11:59 or 10:18.

Engines were not radio-equipped, so pocket watches carried by the engineers scheduled everything. All engineers were required to have their watches checked for accuracy by railroad officials once a month. At each check, the official provided a current Health Certificate to be carried with the watch and available for random checks by supervisors.

Daddy enjoyed getting his watch checked. George Alexander, the official who typically checked it, always found it within four or five seconds of the exact railroad time. Railroad men wore their watches with more pride than a five-star general.

"Cole, does your watch match mine?"

"Yes, sir."

"Then we're okay." Daddy's confident look and Mr. Cole's one foot resting on the dash eliminated any fears I had. Daddy continued to explain the engine to me.

"Son, you see this pedal down here that I have my foot on?"

"Yeah, I see it. What's that—another gas pedal?"

"No, this is the dead man. I've got my foot on this pedal. If I were to fall dead, my foot would come off it. The engine would slow to a stop to prevent a runaway engine."

That sounded cold to me. I didn't like the sound of dead man because I surely did not want anything to happen to Daddy—not on account of that engine but because we sort of needed him at home.

"You know, I'm feeling pretty good, and my foot is getting tired of holding down this dead man pedal. Hey, Cole, hand me my dead man stick."

Mr. Cole handed him a stick someone had whittled out to fit the space. Daddy braced it under the dash onto the dead man pedal. Relaxed, he took his foot off. Then, we moved on. We'd see a crossing, and I'd put the bell on and hit the whistle. We were out in the middle of nowhere when Daddy saw something near the tracks a way in front of us.

"Look at that up ahead. What do you see?" he asked Cole.

"Looks like three little black boys playing, maybe six, seven years old. They look pretty small and they're awfully close to the tracks."

"That's what I'm thinking." He turned in my direction. "Son, this ain't no street crossing, but you never know what kids will do. Hit that bell. Give four or five shorts and two or three longs on the horn."

"I can do that." I was living in high cotton!

Just before we got into good sight of those boys, Daddy leaned way over. I flipped the bell and hit the whistle. When they looked up, they could see only me driving the engine. They pointed, laughed, and waved at me. A grin covered my face when I waved back. That's a memory etched in my mind forever!

Out of their sight, Daddy settled back in his seat and began to slow the train. He and Mr. Cole pulled out their watches and verified the time for each other.

"We're going to have to get on the side track here; we have one coming through," Daddy explained to me.

The switchman leaped off the slowing train and trotted over to throw the switch—a big lever that looks something like a bow tie until it's thrown. When thrown, it goes crosswise the track and eases the train off to the side. I bet we hadn't been there a minute when the other train came barreling toward us.

"Before this train comes by you need to get back in that cubbyhole, son."

I did. I heard the other train just a whoosing; it sounded close enough to touch. Daddy hit the whistle with a couple of shorts and gave the other engineer a deliberate wave. The train gone, the switchman threw the switch back, and we eased onto the main track with our string of passenger cars. It felt like the wheels were slipping as if on ice.

"Is something wrong with the engine, Daddy?"

"Nah, son. See how we're going up a little hill here?"

"Yessir."

"Our driver wheels on this engine are steel, and the tracks are steel. When you're pulling a hill like this with this kind of load, it's hard to get traction. See, this other little lever up here?"

"Yessir."

"That's sand. Flip that lever toward the door."

I flipped it and felt the engine wheels start to catch—to pull instead of slip.

"You just put sand on the rails for me. That gives us traction. Once we get our momentum again, you can turn it off."

It wasn't long before the up and down replaced the side-to-side swaying and Daddy told me to cut off the sand. Mr. Cole's face betrayed his worries about our speed, his brows knit tight.

"I hope there's not an inspector hiding out back there. If there is, he may say something. What do you think, Uncle John?"

Daddy replied, "No. I looked around and checked all the pastures. No inspector around there." He sounded a bit impatient with Mr. Cole, and I decided to ask another question; I think he knew how his answers impressed me.

"Daddy, if there were somebody wondering how fast you were going, how could he tell for sure?"

He pulled out his watch. "Look at your watch and count how many telephone poles the engine passes in one minute. You divide the result by the right number, and you have the speed of the train. But these are good tracks; they're not like they used to be."

I nodded, glad to have the equation for figuring out speed. I thought, *It's so cool to know that. I can't wait to tell Chester.*

He went through that story again with Mr. Cole about checking everywhere for a speed trap, and Mr. Cole seemed placated.

"Oh, yeah, Uncle Johnny, I know you know what you're doing."

"Cole, do you know who they call when water goes over the tracks on that Monroe run?"

"No."

"They call me. You've seen that steam engine down at the roundhouse?"

"Yeah, I've seen it, but I've never seen it being used," Cole replied.

"You can't run one of these diesels in high water. They'll short out and won't go. When they must make a run and there's water on the tracks, they use a steam engine, and they call me to drive it. When I get back on a steam engine, it'll go through water above the cowcatcher. I'm about the only one left to run a steam engine."

I felt good again, so proud of my daddy, my chest almost burst. I knew my daddy could do just about anything when it came to railroading. We rolled on in, and Daddy ordered me back in the cubbyhole when we got into Lake Charles. He pulled out his watch.

"I'm right on time. Cole, you know, I'm the only hogshead who can stay this close to schedule every time."

Railroad engineers were called hogsheads, and Daddy liked to talk about himself a little bit. Mr. Cole laughed and, since I occupied the cubbyhole where I couldn't be seen, I grinned too. Daddy told me to keep my seat until he signaled me to come out.

He and Mr. Cole got off, and I hoped Daddy would return soon because the engine was running. Directly, Daddy crawled up the ladder and motioned me to come on down. As I climbed down the ladder, he asked me if I was hungry. I was.

"Let's go get us a hamburger."

"Don't you have to turn off the train first?"

"Nah. The crew taking us home will take care of that."

We walked into a nearby café where everybody knew him. The waitresses, the cashier, everybody spoke to him, calling, "Hey, Uncle Johnny."

He waved and said hello to everybody, individually shaking hands. Those striped overalls with his long-sleeved white shirt and that railroad cap created a vision for me that put Superman to shame.

It seemed as if everyone there asked about me.

One lady asked, "Uncle Johnny, who's this young man?"

"Oh, I had to bring some help with me this time. This Lake Charles turn can be a tough run. This is my boy, Johnny, Jr."

Everyone laughed, and a couple of them rubbed me on the head. A couple of the waitresses hugged and kissed me. I liked it, but the attention embarrassed me too. Being friendly seemed the name of the day in that café. Daddy bought a hamburger for each of us and got me a Grapette. We ate and talked. It was good.

"Well, we have about half an hour or an hour to kill. We need to get back to the roundhouse because I gotta talk to the hogshead who is going to take the train back since we are deadheading."

That meant the engineer who brought the train in would ride in a passenger car on the trip back. Daddy walked up to the assigned engineer, and they stepped off out of my earshot. I watched every move. The engineer pointed to a guy standing over at the ticket window, and Daddy walked over to him. I heard that guy talking to Daddy.

"Hey, Uncle Johnny. Did you bring that one in?"

"Yeah. I brought it in. Are you the conductor going back?"

"Yeah. I'll be punching the tickets."

Daddy touched him on the shoulder, and they walked away to where I couldn't hear their conversation. Before long, they headed back my way.

"So, this is the help you have?"

"Yeah. This is it. We're deadheading back on your train."

The conductor tousled my hair and goosed me around a little bit. He was a heavyset man, maybe in his early fifties, with a paunchy tummy and a triple chin. He did not have that starched and ironed look of my daddy, and I sorta resented his acting superior—though that might have been a figment of my imagination.

Forty-five minutes later, Daddy and I got on the train and found seats up front.

"Is the conductor the boss?" I asked.

"Oh, no. They argue about that a lot of times, but everybody knows the man who has the throttle is the boss. Now, if you asked him, he would probably say he is the boss, but his job is just to tend to these passengers."

The train pulled out, and we headed toward Alexandria. I noticed the passenger cars didn't sway back and forth and then go up and down like the engine did when Daddy and I were at the throttle; they just kept swaying from side to side. Daddy pulled out his watch, counted the telephone poles, and moaned and groaned about how these new hogsheads drove.

"You know, son, I don't know how these new boys even pass an examination."

"What do you mean?"

"Well, they drag along on these fine tracks. They got fine railroad beds and the best crossties, yet they act like they're afraid to run the engine."

"Did you take an examination to run the train?"

"Yes, sir, I did. Passed with flying colors, too. Hogsheads today have the best equipment in the world, and they don't know what to do with it. When all we had were steam engines, the railroad bosses stayed outta our business. They let us do our jobs, and the engineer ran the show. Now, you gotta watch for some inspector, some supervisor, somebody who don't know nothin' but wants to tell you ever'thing. You know the railroad's gonna make me retire when I'm seventy, and I've forgotten more about running these trains than these young fellas ever learned."

"Why would they make you retire if you don't want to?"

He sorta laughed and looked far away.

"Well, it's the union contract. Seventy seemed a lot further away when I voted for it." He stared out the window, and we rode along quietly for a while. Then he started in again on the railroad.

Finally, we got back to Alexandria and pulled into the station. The conductor got off and put down the step. I started to run off because we were in the first seat, but Daddy held me back.

"Let the passengers go first. They're paying, and we're just deadheading."

We stood back and let everybody off before we got off. When we stepped down, the conductor turned my cap sideways.

"I sure enjoyed meeting your help, Uncle Johnny."

"I sure appreciate what you did." Daddy smiled.

I couldn't figure out anything he did but sit back there in the back of the car with his hands folded on his stomach looking as if he were half asleep. We walked out to the car, got in, and headed back to Tioga. Daddy seemed too quiet, driving with the window down and his elbow resting on the ledge.

He rolled his cheek in one hand and drove with the other, an obvious signal to me of serious thinking. I got a little jumpy when he did that, but I never asked if anything was wrong. My reticence in doing so likely came from knowing I didn't want to know the answer.

"You know, son, I've told you there are rules to live by."

"Yes, sir."

"Well, every now and then, you see a rule that needs to be broken to make somebody else happy or help somebody. Do you know what I mean?"

"No, sir. Do you mean I can break the rules sometimes if somebody else wants me to?"

He answered as if I had not even spoken.

"If breaking a rule doesn't hurt anybody, then it might need to be broken. It is hard to tell those kinds of rules, but they are out there. When you get older and have your judgment, you'll know every now and then there's a rule that needs to be broken. I broke a rule today."

"You did!"

"Yeah. I broke one today."

"What rule was that, Daddy?"

"Did you have fun?"

"I had a lot of fun. I wanna to go every time!"

"You can't go every time, but I am glad you had fun."

"What rule did you break today, Daddy?"

"Oh, I don't know."

He dropped the subject as we pulled into Billips——about a mile and a half from the house—where he ordered a cup of coffee for him and a Grapette for me. He motioned the enormous waitress over to our table.

"Ruby, take a look at this boy's hair. Ain't it pretty?"

Cowlicks going in every direction covered my head and, to my chagrin, my hair seemed to be a source of amusement to my entire family. I ducked down a bit and looked off as if I hadn't even heard him.

"Well, yes, sir. Mr. Yeager, that boy does have some pretty hair. Mine used to be that color."

Daddy laughed, and she did too as she took a seat at the table with us. They shared some small talk while he finished his coffee, and we went on home.

Indeed, a day to remember, and I'll never forget it. I learned a lot and, maybe most importantly, how much my Daddy loved me.

CHAPTER 46

SEPARATE BUT EQUAL

By the summer of 1958, John and I had grown fairly. As a white girl growing up in rural Central Louisiana in the late 1940s and 1950s, racism surrounded me. I, like many others my age, lived in my own world, oblivious to any racial inequities. I rarely saw black people at all, even though an entire community lived just across the railroad tracks from Merritt's Grocery. Silk Stocking Lane was their main road, and I personally knew no one who had even driven or walked down that road.

Oh, I might see a black person walking down the road toward the Tioga bus to Alex or even in front of my house on their way to a job. And certainly, I observed black people riding in the back of the city bus.

Segregated schools were the norm, and the same rules applied to businesses, local parks, and amusements.

Not being of the economic standing to have servants or housekeepers, other than having a black lady (whose name I never knew) who came to our house to help a few times during Mama's illness, I had little reason to personally know any black person.

In parks and public buildings, drinking fountains were clearly marked white or black to separate the races, even when getting a drink of water in a public place. All public buildings had at least two entrances, each with racially specific signs. And I assumed black people did not go out to eat, as I had never seen one in a restaurant. That did not seem odd to me since my family ate in restaurants maybe once every couple of years—other than at the local Billups café/service station establishment.

Interaction between the races rarely occurred in my daily life. I did have a rare experience when I was twelve and visiting Missouri by train. I observed black people in the same environment as whites and interacting with each other. That experience did not leave a deep enough impression to cause me to compare circumstances once I returned home. Segregation stood as the law of my rural Louisiana area and, as embarrassing as it is to admit, I was blind to the reality or effects of the discrimination.

Everything seemed good to me.

By the mid-1950s, rumors abounded about racial unrest. The stories included talk of freedom riders and other troublemakers coming in from up north, creating problems for both the whites and the black people in our paradise of camaraderie.

Our one available television station, Channel 5—our Window to the World—provided access to both national and local news. I later discovered that window often closed with a window shade in the form of repeats of old *Perry Mason* episodes or other such one-hour dramas. These were inserted to save us from the real-world drama, and, as explained by some, to save our Negroes from unnecessary upset.

As a rural teenager, I wore a safe white blanket of racism to protect me from news of the racial discord occurring all over our country.

Of course, a little news sneaked past the barriers, and a version of the truth seeped through to us from our parents. I proudly wore my "Separate but Equal" armband to school. Somehow, it made sense to me. Who would not want to be with their own kind if everything were equal? I felt neither animosity nor superiority toward black people, but rather a separateness.

Then came November 15, 1958—a Saturday, and a special one for me. Four days earlier, I celebrated my fifteenth birthday, got my driver's license, and acquired a job as a salesclerk at Kresge's Five and Dime in Alexandria. My shift included Saturdays and any school holidays from November 15 until January 15 (i.e., the Christmas holiday period through gift returns).

Any paycheck represented an upgrade in my finances. That one-dollar allowance didn't go far, and I wanted some independence. A job at any level excited me and offered all sorts of imagined possibilities.

I dressed early that Saturday, and, unfortunately, my newly-acquired driver's license did not prevent me from walking the almost three miles to the only Alexandria bus stop in Tioga—actually, Paradise—on Shreveport Highway 71. The walk allowed me to think about my upcoming day. With a pleasant temperature and my excitement off the charts, the gravel road seemed a yellow brick path to success.

Fifty cents per hour would be mine, from 9:00 a.m. until 5:30 p.m., and my supervisor would assign my hours. The bus rides cost twenty-five cents each way, and I brought a sandwich with me for lunch. I was walking in high cotton, feeling ten-foot-tall and bulletproof!

The seven o'clock bus reached my stop directly across the main street in front of Kresge's at 8:30 a.m. I darted across the street, having been taught by my dad that on time equated to fifteen minutes late.

My previous Saturday's brief orientation allowed me to be somewhat familiar with the layout. Two cash registers and two salesclerks occupied each counter. The salesclerks faced opposite directions to better serve the customers.

A supervisor, assigned to each area, spent whatever time necessary at the beginning of each shift to be certain every newly hired salesclerk understood their responsibilities and how to accomplish them. Once the supervisors felt comfortable, the salesclerks fell under the jurisdiction of eight floorwalkers. They wandered around the store all day watching for any situation outside of the norm and particularly observing the salesclerks' interactions with the customers.

Upon entering through the Employees Only door, I immediately saw Miss Gautier, the woman who had hired me and provided the orientation the Saturday before. I hurried over.

"Good morning, Miss Gautier. I'm Olevia. Do you remember me from last week? Today's my first day." I beamed and gushed at the same time, as if I'd been named Employee of the Month.

Miss Gautier smiled. "Of course, I remember you. I hope your enthusiasm lasts!" She chuckled quietly as she led me through the first steps of the day.

"Okay. All salesclerks must lock their purses, wallets, and any other belongings in this locker. You can check them out at noon, if necessary. And, of course, when you leave tonight."

"I brought my lunch. Do I put it in here too?"

"We have an employee breakroom with a refrigerator. If you would rather leave it there, you may."

"Yes, ma'am. I would rather leave it there."

She reviewed the chalkboard of instructions with me. I learned where to hang my jacket and how to note my arrival as well as any break times taken. On the list of assigned counters, I looked for the one posted next to my name. Miss Gautier explained that clerks were paid in cash at the end of each day worked.

When she pointed out the Cash Drawer Assignments Desk, I felt like the luckiest girl in Tioga. —a job, a cash drawer to be managed by me and I was just eight hours from picking up my first pay envelope *Lordy, I'm walking on air*.

Miss Gautier walked with me to my register. As we approached the counter, I noticed baby-to-toddler clothing occupied half of it and the other half contained costume jewelry.

I mused, "I wonder why jewelry and baby clothes are on the same counter."

"That's done for the sake of our salesclerks and to keep the customers more evenly divided."

"What?"

"If you're shopping for jewelry, you're less likely to be shopping for baby clothes. So, you shop at one end of the counter and check out with that salesclerk. Otherwise, it's likely that one of you would have the longer lines and be less familiar with the merchandise," Miss Gautier explained.

"Let's take a look at your register." She led me to the baby clothes end.

She took the cash drawer out of my hands and showed me how to turn the cash key once I inserted it into the cash register. The cash key was on a lanyard hung around my neck to avoid losing it.

Next, I counted the bills in each drawer section and confirmed the change slots. By the time I completed a couple of no-sale practices, my first customer stood ready to buy a toddler shirt and some tiny matching shorts.

I rang up the dollar and quarter plus tax, careful to include plenty of "Yes ma'ams." I pointed out the receipt in the bag and went the extra mile to tell the customer she would need the receipt if something did not fit. I added, "Thanks for shopping Kresge's, and please come back again."

"Olevia, that was very well done!" My supervisor almost sounded surprised. "And I noticed you double-checked your change and closed the drawer while you counted it out to the customer."

I smiled.

Miss Gautier went on to say, "No problems here. It's a payday weekend, and Christmas is coming. I suspect you'll be busy today. If you find yourself becoming overwhelmed, don't worry. One of the floorwalkers will notice and come to your rescue."

"Yes, ma'am. I can do it." I gave her my most eager grin and set to work.

****

Things rolled along quite well. I succeeded in trading out cash drawers with my lunchtime replacement and managed handling increasingly numerous customers. About mid-afternoon, my area became crowded. I decided to ask my customers to help me to help them.

"Ladies, would you mind lining up from the cash register out? I want to be sure everyone gets the right service. It's my first day." I smiled and indicated where to start the line.

Without hesitation, my customers cooperated, and I fairly blossomed in confidence in my ability to manage anything. Customers moved in and out quickly. All left with a smile and most with an encouraging word to me. As I finished with each customer, I would call out, "Next."

The line moved quickly, and I kept smiling.

A young woman walked up with a small child of maybe three or four years old. I didn't notice she was a black lady until she laid her purchases on the counter, and I looked up. This information had zero effect on me. But, as if out of the atmosphere, a floorwalker materialized beside me.

The floorwalker moved in as silently as Casper the Ghost. Lost in my job, I jumped when I realized she and another salesclerk were standing behind me. She leaned into me and said in a loud whisper, "Finish this sale and cash out your register."

I made no reply as I suddenly felt a cold shiver up my back. I intuitively knew my job was in peril. I finished that sale with the same courtesy as every other one—maybe a little more, as I wanted to impress the obviously angry person standing beside me. I removed my cash drawer and, before I could put the key around my neck, the Wicked Witch of spoke again.

"Give that to me, Miss, and follow me."

"Yes, ma'am. Where are we going?" I handed the key over and awaited instructions.

"Just follow me, and you'll find out." An ominous cloud of darkness radiated from this woman.

"Yes, ma'am," I replied as I followed her into a storage room. She closed the door and stood in front of it. I stood a little distance away to avoid any bad karma she might be emitting. I truly feared this woman.

"Olevia, do you know what you did wrong?" she barked.

"No, ma'am. I was careful to smile and say 'yes, ma'am' and 'thank you for your business.' I counted the change and closed my cash drawer before giving it to the customer." Perplexed and frightened, tears began to gather.

"Okay, Olevia. I don't think you purposely broke the rules, and I'm going to give you another chance."

Her voice and demeanor seemed to soften, at least a little, and it crossed my mind that maybe she thought she saw something that she didn't. She gave me my cash drawer and drawer key, and I immediately put the key around my neck. In confusion, I thought I might even get an apology!

She sat down and motioned me to have a seat as she reiterated, "Do you have any idea of what you did wrong?"

"No, ma'am. What did I do? I didn't do it on purpose, and I know I can fix it. I love this job."

Although still confused, I could see some compassion hidden in her eyes trying to make a breakthrough.

She began her explanation. "The last customer you waited on was a Negro, but she was not the last customer."

"Oh, did she break in line? I didn't see it. I'll be more careful to watch the line."

"That's not exactly what I'm saying."

"Okay." I took a deep breath as I listened to her continue to teach me how to serve my customers.

"When white customers are waiting for service, black customers must wait until all white customers are served. We still encourage them to come in through the side doors, but we can't do much about that anymore." She slowed to take a breath and close her eyes for a second or two.

I took another breath myself; it felt as though I had entered an adjacent reality. I must have looked as bewildered as I felt because the floorwalker went on to explain my Biblical duty to Negroes.

"The thing you forgot, Olevia, is that we—the white race—are burdened by superiority. It's our responsibility to help the Negroes stay in their place. It's all there in the Bible."

"But she waited her turn?" I simply did not understand the logic. I had no idea what part of the Bible she referred to, even though I mentally ran through the Ten Commandments. I did not have to wait long before the floorwalker cleared up everything for me.

"When we treat Negroes in ways that make them feel equal to their superiors, they get uppity. When a Negro gets uppity, it is neither good for them nor for us. And we cannot have it in this store. Do you understand?"

A little edge returned to her voice, but I still saw some empathy in her eyes because she saw me as uninformed and teachable rather than ignoring the rules.

"I guess so." I looked at the floor. I did not understand, but I wanted my job. The best option appeared to be acquiescence. I thought I would figure it out later.

To be sure I understood, she added, "And 'yes' and 'no' are adequate for the Negroes. Save your 'ma'ams' and 'sirs' for your white customers."

"Yes, ma'am."

Back at my register, I finished out the day, picked up my pay envelope, and went home a bit deflated. My enthusiasm was as gone as yesterday's breeze. The experience lodged in my mind. And, at that moment, I became more observant of my surroundings.

****

As soon as I got home, I mentioned the Bible reference to my dad as I came up the steps. He got up from his rocking chair, went into his desk, and came back with a small six-by-six-inch book, maybe half an inch thick. He handed me the book and sat back down in his rocking chair as I sat down in the remaining one.

"Your boss is right. The Noah's Ark story explains it all."

"I still don't understand. Why should any customer be treated differently from another customer?"

"You'll understand when you read that book. The Bible sets out the relationship between Negroes and whites. It's only a few pages and easy to understand." He rocked his chair and fell silent.

"Okay, but can you just tell me how Noah's Ark relates to black people?"

I then heard a story I had never heard before—not in my house or anywhere else—but one apparently believed and endorsed by most of the adults in my world.

Daddy continued, "You remember how Noah got drunk after the flood receded?"

"Yes, sir, I think so."

"Do you remember that one of his sons laughed at his drunkenness?"

"I'm not sure. Mostly what I remember are the animals and two-by-two."

"Well, let me tell you the rest of the story!"

He sounded like Paul Harvey for just a moment, and it made me smile. However, there was nothing funny about this story, and it became instantly clear Daddy accepted it as gospel.

"Have you heard of the 'Curse of Ham?'" he asked.

"No, sir."

"Well, Ham, Noah's son, saw his father naked, laughed at his drunkenness, and mocked him in front of his brothers. When Noah awoke, he banished his son and all the son's descendants to another land. He declared their skin would turn to black and they would be servants forever."

"Do you really believe that is the truth, Daddy?"

In a somber voice, he replied, "Olevia, it's in the Bible. The Bible is a book of truth." At that, he got up and walked into the house.

I looked down at the book I had in my hand. The title was *Curse of Ham*. The story seemed so fantastical to me that I never read the book. I simply returned it to Daddy's desk. I don't know where it is today, but I know it still occupied a drawer there when Daddy died.

The events of November 15, 1958, awakened my curiosity and began to pierce that comfortable, white blanket of racism. My first thought was, *I'm not a racist; I'm a believer in separate but equal.*

I started to explore exactly what that meant, and I discovered separate but equal did not exist then and never did. I was frightened, angered, and sad as I became aware of the unbelievably racist community in which I lived. My neighbors, the adults in my life, and my friends were all good people who I feared shared a belief I could not accept.

Although my thinking changed, it did not strengthen my backbone. I became a lukewarm activist. Lukewarm activists are usually cowards who do not overtly contribute to correcting injustices but silently cheer for the underdog. I took a few small steps to let people know where I stood— things such as sitting in the back of the bus as I rode to town. Of course, rarely anyone on the bus knew me, and I likely made the black people in the back of the bus uncomfortable.

As another small act of defiance, I crossed the road to face any black person heading in my direction. The accepted rule was: If a white person is walking on one side of the road and a black person is walking toward them, the black person must cross to the other side of the road. This may be hard to believe, but any time that had happened to me up until then, I assumed they were being polite. I had no idea it was required! Of course, my attempts at showing equal acceptance via breaking this rule again probably caused more discomfort than help toward changing the situation.

I stopped wearing my Separate but Equal armband and *thought* about replacing it with one reading The Little Rock Nine but didn't. I excused myself by believing most of my friends would not know who The Little Rock Nine were. Most of my friends were apolitical and operated in the world that they lived in without complaint or awareness of racial injustice.

Little Rock's news was a year old, anyway, having originated when Little Rock's Central High School became integrated in September 1957. I didn't know that until I began to research. To this day, I don't really know when Tioga High School became an integrated place of learning. I do know it was still a segregated facility when I graduated in 1961.

Perhaps I could have helped, but I didn't.

****

I showed up for work at Kresge's the following Saturday and worked every hour allotted to me until January 15, 1959. I provided cashier service to my customers based on their place in line, and I used "yes, ma'am" and "no, ma'am" without reference to race.

During the remainder of my sixty-day tenure, no one in authority at Kresge's reminded me of the white race's burden of superiority. I don't know why. Maybe the wheels of change were slowly grinding forward? Maybe it was a management change? Maybe one overzealous floorwalker mentioned it initially, and it was not a widely held rule in the store? Though, I doubt that. Maybe the circumstances were such that a good worker could be allowed some leniency? I don't know.

I am grateful for the experience because it not only opened my eyes to the reality of racism, but it also taught me to look beyond the surface in every life situation. Don't take for granted that the norm is the right way or that the common belief is the truth. I learned to study in search of my own truth.

I am especially grateful that, after the floorwalker's tirade, I was still allowed to be me in the face of what the floorwalker warned. I became stronger and more confident.

And, as always, I felt my mama's hand on my shoulder and heard her voice in my mind, saying, *Do what you know is right and have compassion and patience for those who do not yet know. Be an example.*

****

As I reread this chapter, I remembered Uncle John, the black man who lived in the washhouse behind our little house. He was kind to Johnny and me. He took us blackberry picking and did anything Mama or Daddy asked of him. And yet, when writing this chapter, I tried to think of black people I interacted with, and he didn't even cross my mind—until about the fourth reread. That is how invisible black people were to me, while I stayed safely wrapped in my blanket of racism. This memory, coming so late in my writing of this chapter, is way more telling than I wish it were.

CHAPTER 47

THELMA FROM VIDALIA, LOUISIANA

Suse, me, Peg, Daddy, Thelma, and Merilyn.

By the summer of 1958, John and I had grown fairly Daddy's one-year separation of bed and board with Thelma from Moultrie, Georgia came to an end. Still in search of companionship, he began bringing in stacks of envelopes from his personal Tioga Post Office mailbox. This time around, John and I knew the routine and watched carefully as he sorted and selected the ones to which he would reply.

At one of our breakfast coffees, I shared the situation with Mrs. Curry. I thought we would enjoy a laugh and share imagination as to the expected results. Not so! To say I was surprised is a shadow of the emotion felt when Mrs. Curry spoke.

"You know, I think I might have an answer for Mr. Yeager's search." She threw me a conspiratorial smile.

"What? I think Daddy's looking for a wife!" I could not imagine how she could—or would want to—become involved in that pursuit.

Mrs. Curry smiled again and chuckled a bit as she replied, "I know, honey, and I may know someone he'd like to meet."

"Who?" I thought I knew everyone Mrs. Curry knew and none of them fit the bill.

"I talked to Lovey yesterday, and she mentioned a new friend of hers who's a widow."

Lovey, Mrs. Curry's sister, lived in Vidalia, Louisiana. I had met her a few times. Vidalia was about seventy-five miles northeast of Alex, almost on the Mississippi border. Other than its location, I knew little about Vidalia.

Mrs. Curry continued, "I think Lovey said the woman's name is Thelma."

"Well, Daddy apparently likes that name!"

We both chuckled as Mrs. Curry took the biscuits out of the oven. The heavenly smell made my mouth water, and I got the butter out of the fridge and syrup from the cupboard. She poured fresh cups of coffee, and we settled in for a cozy chat.

Such a scene never failed to bring back fond memories of days gone by when Mama and I shared hot biscuits in our own kitchen. The feeling of peace, comfort, and safety replaced all fears, doubts, or anxiety. The fresh-baked fragrance provided a congenial contentment I find difficult to describe. I settled in to hear more about a potential stepmother as Mrs. Curry continued to talk.

"I'll have to get more details on the woman, but I can tell you what I know now," she offered. "Lovey said she had recently moved to Vidalia from Natchez. I don't know if she's living there permanently, but she attended Lovey's church last Sunday." Mrs. Curry's brow wrinkled as if thinking hard about what she said to make sure I had the right story.

It made no sense to me, and my brow wrinkled too. "Why do you think Daddy would want to meet her? Neither you nor he really know anything about her."

This comment turned the concerned brow into laugh wrinkles. She replied, "And how much does he know about those lonely heart responders?"

"I guess you've got a point." I grinned. "Still, I don't think Daddy wants you, or anybody, to get involved in his love life."

"You let me worry about that." She smiled. "Now, dear, tell me what's going on in your teenage world."

She listened to me ramble on about my teenage concerns as we shared breakfast and a moment. During those times of sharing, I felt at home as if she were my second mom; perhaps she was.

****

A week or so passed without any further discussion of Lovey or her friend, and the next step caught me almost as unawares as it did Daddy. On a Saturday afternoon, Lovey came to town. Along with the Curry's, Lovey and her husband, Curtis, sat under the crepe myrtle trees in Mrs. Curry's front yard. Merilyn and I were also visiting with them—more as spectators than anything else. Looking up the hill, I saw Daddy walking out to his car.

"Looks like Daddy's going somewhere. I wonder where?" This was an inside joke Merilyn, and I shared, knowing he would be on his way to the post office.

Mrs. Curry took over the conversation, saying, "Ellis, why don't you walk over to the fence-break and flag him down? See if he wants to come over for coffee. Tell him Lovey and Curtis are here and want to say 'hello.'"

Merilyn and I looked at each other. I had shared with her my earlier stepmother conversation with Mrs. Curry. Now, the curtain rose on Act One—the spinning of the web and the fly being attracted. Indeed, it may have gotten underway a bit earlier when Mrs. Curry invited Lovey for a visit. The day became more interesting, like a rock tossed into still waters, making ripples extending across the lake.

Daddy did stop in. After saying hello to everyone, he settled in with coffee and a piece of Mrs. Curry's spice cake. I continued to observe the plot thicken as if watching a film or a fly dancing around the edge of the spider's web.

"Whatcha doin' out this afternoon?" Curtis began. "It's certainly a pleasant day for a ride." He grinned. "That's what Lovey and I were doin' when we decided to head on up here for some of Novie's hospitality."

Polite chuckles and smiles lit up all around as Daddy answered, "Oh, I'm runnin' up to Merritt's to pick up a few things, and I need to stop by the post office. I didn't get there yesterday."

Merilyn and I shared a knowing glance.

Mr. Curry then added a little honey to the web when he said, "Johnny, Novie told me you're getting mail from women all over the country. I guess it can be nice to be a widower; the market's worldwide."

The comment contained no disrespect, and everyone laughed. Merilyn and I tuned in even closer as Lovey added to the intrigue. "Well, Mr. Yeager, why are you going so far away to find companionship? Aren't Louisiana women good enough for you?"

"Oh, Lovey, I just don't know any widow women here who don't seem off-limits for some reason. Maybe because they knew Mary, or they want me to go to church every time the doors open, or they're not interested or something. It hasn't worked locally." He smiled, ate the last bite of spice cake, and drained his coffee cup. "That sure was good cake, Novie. I remember when Mary would bake and how much I enjoyed coming home to that smell of something sweet when I opened the door. She made the best blackberry cobbler I ever tasted."

"That's the truth," Mrs. Curry replied. "Let me have your plate. Do you want another piece?"

"No, I gotta get on up to Merritts, but I appreciate ya." He started to stand up, but Lovey put her hand on his arm. "Why don't you at least have another cup of coffee? I might have a story you'd like to hear."

He sat back down, and Merilyn and I glanced at each other and winked. The fly had touched the web with no thought of what lay ahead.

Everybody sat there silently until Mrs. Curry came back with the fresh coffee. Sorta felt like an intermission in our play; Act Two of *The Spider and The Fly* would commence shortly. Mrs. Curry brought the pot and refilled all the cups before she sat down. Mr. Curry got a second piece of cake, though I hadn't heard him ask for it.

Daddy said, "What's your story, Lovey?" He leaned back in his chair.

"Well, Mr. Yeager, I don't want to get into your business, but I met a widow lady—"

"And I don't want anybody in my business, Lovey," Daddy cut her off. "I know you mean well, but I don't like it and don't need it."

He sounded stern to me, but none of the adults seemed to notice. Instead, they added more honey to the web.

Mr. Curry added his two cents with a tilt of the head. "Johnny, what have ya got to lose? You don't even have to meet this woman, but you could listen to Lovey. It might be fate, and it might be fun."

I had never heard Mr. Curry say something even remotely similar in tone or words. It startled me, and I think Daddy felt surprised too.

"Okay, let's hear it," he said with resignation. The fly listened and became more tangled in a carefully woven web with every word spoken.

Lovey began her sales pitch by saying, "A funny thing, her name is Thelma. Wasn't Thelma the name of that mistake a year or so ago?"

Daddy nodded but said nothing, and she went on to describe Thelma in detail and explain how she had gotten to know her.

Act Two was well underway. Daddy seemed enthralled, and I knew the fly had lost the battle.

****

In the summer of 1960, Act Three played out when Thelma Smith became Thelma Yeager. John and I referred to her as Thelma 2. She was an attractive, petite, dark-haired, and spirited woman about forty-five years old, which was the same age as Mama when she died and twenty years younger than Daddy.

I cannot remember her wearing anything other than shirt-waist dresses with full skirts. In many ways, she reminded me of Mama. She wore glasses that were much like Mama's and exhibited an unfeigned warmth for teenagers. She approached her step-mothering with enthusiasm and tried to create the normalcy of a two-parent family. The new atmosphere felt good, and I welcomed her as she became the woman-in-charge of the house. She showed up at every school function involving parents or me, and she became a coffee mate for Mrs. Curry.

Still, John and I simply tolerated her. We weren't rude; we just avoided becoming emotionally involved with her. We accepted her presence in our lives, not as a conscious decision, but rather just as a matter of fact.

At age sixteen, John quit school and moved to California with my sister. I lived with my friend Sara and her family for a few months following my senior year in high school but returned home before moving to Texas.

****

Thelma 2 still lived in our house when I boarded the train to Dallas in August of 1962. She had moved out before my first visit home in December of the same year. I never heard or asked about the details, although I did receive a short letter from Thelma once she returned to Vidalia.

This time, Daddy did not file for divorce until August 1964, when he began his final search for Mama's replacement. He met and began dating Mrs. Gibson, a widow who lived in Tioga and who seemed to check all the boxes for him. Louisiana law and Daddy's death from a sudden heart attack on May 30, 1965, prevented another marriage.

Daddy planned for the future and lived in the present until the last night of his life. On that night, he had dinner with Mrs. Gibson to tell her that I and his sixteen-month-old grandson would be visiting the next day. He asked her to come over so they could announce their engagement together to me.

As I entered the driveway the next afternoon expecting to meet a third stepmother-to-be, Mrs. Curry came to the fence-break and flagged me down to tell me my dad was found dead that morning in his bathroom.

I felt like my heart sunk down to my toes, and my ears buzzed like live wires with the shock of that news. Mrs. Curry reacted to my sudden disbelief and reached over to put a hand on my shoulder as if to steady me. I did not feel dizzy, but perhaps my mind did!

I need to believe he reunited with my mom, and I know he no longer suffered from loneliness.

CHAPTER 48

EIGHT SATURDAYS SWEEPING

The year 1958 slowly morphed into 1959. My birthday had come and gone while John and I continued to move in our separate circles. Too often, we had no knowledge of each other's paths. Fortunately, I had Mrs. Curry, along with a slew of teachers, to help me navigate any troubled waters.

On the November morning of the tale below, I had been oblivious to both the story and the fact that John enjoyed the same solace and direction in his relationship with our Grandpa Williams. My mom's dad was the only living biological grandparent we had, and we knew him well. Johnny had a special and exclusive relationship with him, of which I did not become completely aware until many years later. Over the years, John has shared with me several important and poignant stories emanating from that relationship. One such story is told below from his perspective.

****

John's Story:
Something was wrong. Grandpa could tell by the way I rode my horse, tilted my head, and slumped my shoulders. Still, he didn't hurry me, but he moved with the deliberateness born of experience. I didn't know that then, while lost amid the whirlwind I called my life.

"Hey, boy. Out early for a ride, ain't cha?" he called out as I rode up to his front gate on my horse shortly after daylight.

Grandpa sat on the porch of a house that could have been an Appalachian transplant, but Grandpa bore little resemblance to a hillbilly. A Louisiana Cajun to the bone with a touch of Choctaw Indian running through his veins and a profile reminiscent of the buffalo nickel deftly describes my grandpa.

As a young man, he worked for the state highway department. His obituary said he was a Motor Patrol Operator. I have no idea as to the duties involved. In my memory, it seemed he always turned out to be at home— planting tomatoes, raising a pig or two, and sometimes crawling into his 1946 Ford half-ton pick-up to haul Grandma to church on Sunday mornings or Wednesday nights.

Lately, he sat on the front porch most of the time and watched the driveway for visitors He once said, "When you work, everybody knows your name. When you retire, they even forget where you live."

Grandpa, born in 1885, lived in the woods about ten miles from my dad's and ten thousand miles from my generation. Running water and indoor plumbing were new to his house, but he still savored a cool, clear drink hand-drawn from the well out back.

Every morning, regardless of the season or the occasion, he donned starched but faded overalls, a long-sleeved shirt, black brogans, and a wide-brimmed felt hat. He fathered nine daughters and two sons. Two of his daughters—one was my mom—died before he did. Susan, his other daughter, had died, along with his first wife, in 1923. I think, typhoid fever had proved their death sentence.

He lived a simple life, now peopled mostly with memories and hampered by the agonies of age.

Several years before his time was up on this side, we rode together to the cemetery to view his tombstone.

Already selected, set, it waited for the date of his death, which didn't occur until May of 1968. He chose to be first to see what others would see soon enough. When I questioned the lack of an epitaph, he said, "Your name says it all."

I thought about that as Grandpa stood to his full six feet and lifted his hat for the familiar three-fingered scalp-scratch.

"Whatcha doing out on a day like this, boy? Rained all night."

Things weren't right, and Grandpa knew it. The firmly clinched-in-the-corner-of-his-mouth pipe added to both his character and his control. He slowed conversations and cleared his mind by cleaning that pipe, tapping the bowl on his hand before tamping down the fresh tobacco.

Once lit, he stared in the distance, inhaled, and exhaled two long drags before speaking. No one spoke while Grandpa considered his thoughts. I hung on every word he said and on every word he didn't say. On chilly winter mornings, we often occupied matching rocking chairs, side by side, sipping hot coffee and staring into the fireplace together. A lot of communication took place during those periods of silence.

That day, as I prepared to dismount from my horse, I heard him say, "Grace, pour this boy a cup of coffee. He's wet to the skin." He instinctively knew I needed more than silence that morning.

He spoke over his shoulder to Grandma as he walked toward me. Arthritis was evident in his gait, but the anguish and pain of his years disappeared when I saw my reflection in his eyes. He chuckled quietly as he reached for Buck's bridle, and I slid down. The gnarl of his knuckles and the calluses on his hands felt as soft as lambs' wool when his arm draped over my shoulder.

"Boy, it's good to see you ary time, but especially on a morning like this one."

I spoke without hesitation. "Grandpa, I'm in trouble."

"Trouble? What kind of trouble?" No change in tone, approach, or anything—just Grandpa ready to sit a spell.

The air dripped the way south Louisiana air often does on cool November mornings. Clouds dragged along the treetops, occasionally resting in the valleys surrounding the creeks, the bayous, and especially near the Red River. Had it been a cloudless morning, the sun would have peeked over the horizon long before I reached Grandpa's house, but not today. The chinquapin trees bordering the quarter-mile driveway created eerie shadows, adding a chill to the near-darkness. I avoided Grandpa's eyes.

"I messed up, and I can't tell Daddy." I glanced at him with pleading eyes as I stood next to Buck.

"Well, you can tell me," he said. "But first, lead Buck around to the barn. Looks like this might be more than a one-cup visit."

I didn't have to imagine the twinkle in his eyes; I saw it. It felt like a wall to slow the disaster, as well as an arrow for the trouble I had created for myself.

I had turned thirteen the previous August and had come to depend on Grandpa to clear the cobwebs of my teenage world. Mama had been gone over two years, and Daddy, at sixty-three, seemed to me to be unsuited to single parenting for a 1950's teenager. Funny how a man ten years his senior could be so much more in tune with me—not my world, but with me. I unsaddled Buck and left him to run the pasture or stand in the barn, his choice.

Grandma handed me a cup of coffee as I passed through the kitchen. "You okay, Johnny?" she asked.

"Yeah."

I found Grandpa seated in a straight-backed chair on the porch, coffee cup in one hand and the bowl of his pipe in the other. I sat in a chair beside him and looked at the floor.

"Now, tell me, Johnny, what's the matter?"

My tears spilled as he spoke.

"C'mon, can't be that bad," he said. "We're both on this side of the pearly gates this morning, so whatever it is, we still got time to fix it." He smiled, adding to my misery.

He's going to be so disappointed. How could I let this man down? Those thoughts tore at my mind as I answered, "I don't know, this time, Grandpa."

"Let's find out together."

I heard my heart pounding more than felt it, and the words tumbled out without explanation. "I stole stuff!"

"Stole stuff? What? Where? Why? When?"

Any appearance of amusement disappeared from Grandpa's manner. Stealing almost rated up there with murder and could not be easily explained- and certainly not accepted- in my family.

"Thirty dollars at The Eggerton's."

The "why" created a more difficult challenge. Grandpa leaned his chair against the wall and studied something far out in the distance as he took a deep drag on his pipe. I sat mute, hating the quiet but afraid of what would come. After an interminable silence, Grandpa spoke again.

"I can't think of no *good* reason to steal, Johnny. Can you?"

"No, sir," I answered while trying to prevent any sobs.

More silence, more heart pounding, and more wishing the ground would swallow me.

Chester Cassell, a teenage buddy, and I enjoyed pinball in Billips, a local hamburger joint. On November 14, 1958, the machines owned our dollar in less than ten minutes, and we backed our way toward Pineville, raising our thumbs in hopes of a ride. As we passed Eggerton's Grocery, a larcenous idea surfaced, and a little discussion fleshed it out. Eggerton's operated on a two-man system with Ms. Eggerton running the front and her butcher in the back at the meat counter.

The Saturday before, we had talked about how easy it would be to take advantage of this set-up. The store closed at exactly six every evening, and Ms. Eggerton spent the last half an hour in the back helping her butcher clean the display case. Broke and at loose ends on a Friday night, we put our fantasy to work.

I called out to Ms. Eggerton as we entered the door. She was a sweet, old widow who always had time for any teenagers who dropped by. She asked about our parents, school—normal small talk—and then suggested we let her know if we found something we wanted. She returned to the back, and Chester stood at the door obstructing her view of the register.

As they talked, I hit the No Sale key and held the drawer to prevent the loud ring. While facing the other room and my back to the register, I slid my hand into the cash drawer and withdrew two bills. With the drawer safely closed again and the money stuffed in my jeans, I used the escape ruse, saying, "It's almost six o'clock, Chester. Your mom'll be wondering about us."

At a safe distance from the store, I pulled the bills from my pocket. I had twenty and ten—thirty dollars.

Chester froze. "Johnny, you can go to the pen for stealing that much money!"

I blanched. I just wanted some fun, not serious trouble. The money had to be returned, though we weren't sure how. We raced back to the store and walked in as nonchalantly as possible. I dropped and found thirty dollars on the floor.

I called out to Ms. Eggerton, "Look what I found!"

She came out of the back, holding her broom. "Whatcha got, Johnny?"

"We just walked in here and found this on your floor." I held up the twenty and ten. "Who was your last customer? I didn't see this money when we were here a few minutes ago. Did you, Chester?"

He confirmed that he did not see it, as I handed it to Ms. Eggerton.

Seemingly out of nowhere, the butcher appeared and spoke up. "Good job, Johnny boy. That must have fallen out of my apron pocket when I was sweeping in here." He made a big show of checking his pockets and said, "It's my lucky day. Glad you boys found it."

Ms. Eggerton rewarded my honesty with a beef jerky stick.

Hearing this story returned a hint of amusement to Grandpa's eyes, but it didn't extend to his voice. "So, you're tellin' me you stole thirty dollars, and the butcher stole the same thirty dollars?"

"Yes, sir."

"What do you think we oughta do?" Grandpa asked.

"I don't know."

"Well, let's get some breakfast, and we'll take a ride over to the Eggerton's."

The biscuit and eggs didn't go down easily, but I made it through. A few minutes after nine, Grandpa stood near the Eggerton's door as I told my story to Ms. Eggerton. Her expression said it seemed as unreal to her as it sounded to me. The butcher's steely eyes cut through me from the back room, but he said nothing.

Grandpa laid his arm on my shoulder and capped off my narrative.

"Well, Ms. Eggerton, Johnny here is mighty sorry for his part in this, and he wants to make it up to ya. Don't ya, Johnny?"

"Yes, sir."

"Have ya got any chores he could do for ya?"

"Why, Mr. Williams, I do." Her spell seemed to be broken, but I wondered if she had really understood what I said. She didn't move toward her butcher, just homed in on me.

"A shop like this always has work to be done. Sweeping, taking out garbage, cleaning windows, and straightening merchandise."

I grimaced a bit but said not a word.

She continued, "Johnny, I bet you could do every one of those jobs. Of course, I don't want you to skip any school. How about on Saturdays?"

And that's why I spent eight Saturdays sweeping the Eggerton Grocery store, taking out the garbage, cleaning the windows, and straightening the merchandise.

I did find a silver lining: getting to spend the Saturday rides to work with Grandpa in his rattling pickup. He didn't talk much during these rides, but the caring he generated felt as overwhelming as a tidal wave. I felt safe.

The butcher kept his job, and I don't know what Ms. Eggerton may have said to him or if he paid the money back. I carefully maintained a safe distance between us. Perhaps his punishment included spending his Saturdays with me.

Something so wrong became so right with a little time and love. I am still amazed by that experience.

****

It often occurs to me that Grandpa truly was John's Mrs. Curry, and I'm grateful for that. Mama loved her dad so much, and I saw a lot of her in him. Maybe that should be said in reverse, but my sight cleared only after her passing, and the evidence of her continued love blossomed through him.

CHAPTER 49

HIGH SCHOOL CHALLENGES —NOT MY FINEST HOURS

From September 2, 1957, my first day in the ninth grade, until May 30, 1961, when I graduated from high school, I fought periods of fear and enjoyed excitement. I felt lonely and simultaneously full of expectations—all the commonplace emotions for teens in my world. I suspect those same highs and lows have been a rite of passage for teenagers since caveman days.

Nowadays, many of those ups and downs arise from different challenges (as well as privileges), and different approaches are utilized to reach the same results—maturity.

A couple of my many emotional challenges may be worth sharing for an insight into a generation or so ago.

****

In the late fifties and early sixties, Tioga teens were not automatic recipients of cars to go with their driver's licenses, but the licenses themselves became the badge of independence. Using my driver's license, Merilyn and I pushed our rebellion to the limit.

My fifteenth birthday fell on a Tuesday in 1958. True to his promise, Daddy went with me to Colfax's State Highway Department. I got my license and had my first encounter with a dirty, old man on the same day.

The Department of Public Safety office, manned by two people, a guy and a woman, opened its doors at eight o'clock that morning. Daddy and I were among the first people there; in fact, we were the only applicants there that morning. Trips to the DMV were not the agonizing events they are today involving long lines, appointments, or a half a day to accomplish any task.

While Daddy explained the purpose of our visit to the officer on duty, the woman directed me to a table to take the written exam—a chore I quickly completed, but I remained seated as Daddy continued to chat with the DPS officer.

"You know, Red, Olevia's fifteenth birthday occurred just this week, but she's been driving a while. I think you'll find she's a pretty good driver."

"I'm sure I will, Mr. Yeager. Does she take after her daddy?" He laughed but did not get even a smile from Daddy in return.

A bit of silence ensued, and Daddy stared out into space. I had the feeling he waffled between taking me and storming out or putting up with the poor joke so I could get licensed. Fortunately for me, the latter option won.

I watched the guy for a while and didn't like the looks of him, especially his oily hair, which was about an inch too long for adults of that day. An older man, probably in his fifties, he had a seedy look about him. His uniform lacked any evidence of pride in his job and didn't present his wife— if there was one—in a good light. Though clean, it lacked a starched and ironed look, and no badge provided a look of authority.

The scuffed shoes and the hint of dirt under his fingernails screamed, *I just don't care about this job or what you think!*

Of course, we were in Colfax, a town not exactly known as the crown jewel of central Louisiana. That day, such things didn't matter; I wanted my driver's license. He and

Daddy resumed conversation and even shared a chuckle or two; that was good enough for me. I took my completed test to the woman at the desk.

"Hey, Red, she's finished the written part. You gonna take her out to drive?" she called over to the officer.

"Yeah." He looked at me. "What's your name again?"

"Olevia Yeager."

"No need to be so formal. I just need your first name, Olevia. Let's get in your Daddy's car so you can show me what you can do."

His appearance, voice, attitude, and even his odor made me uneasy, but the desire for a driver's license far outweighed any safety concerns. Besides, he didn't seem dangerous, just repugnant.

I heard my heart beating and wondered if he could too. My hands shook as I slid under the wheel and reached for the ignition.

He laughed in a way that reminded me of a cat playing with a mouse. "What's the matter, Olevia? I don't bite."

"Yes, sir." I gave my best smile while trying to look relaxed, adult, and in control.

"It's just us now. Relax. Back the car out here. Pull around that corner and down the alley."

Down the alley! echoed in my brain while I did my best to remain calm. "Yes, sir," I answered. Not only did my voice tremble but so did my entire body.

Red enjoyed my discomfort, as evidenced by his amused expression coupled with periodic chuckling. "How long you been driving, Olevia?"

"Since I was thirteen, sir."

He moved over next to me on the bench seat, and his breath reeked of teeth needing dental work. His leg touched mine, and I visibly shivered.

"I gotta sit pretty close here, honey. You don't mind, do ya?" His sneer had the look of a fox circling the chicken house and brought to my mind a picture of the Big Bad Wolf as he stalked Little Red Riding Hood.

Not waiting for answer, he went on, "Never know when I might need to grab the wheel." His sneer mutated into an ominous, almost whispered voice as he added, "Of course, you're experienced, aren't you, Olevia? Now, make a right on that first street."

"Yes, sir." I looked straight ahead and used the proper hand signal for a right turn.

"That was good, Olevia. Let's try for a left one."

I wished he would quit saying my name. I'm not sure I know how to explain what it felt like, but it sounded more like a tool than a form of address. He used it to remind me who had control and the power between us. I firmly reminded myself of my goal—to get my driver's license—and offered another polite answer.

"Isn't that next street a one-way, going the wrong way for a left turn?" I used a fake smile to soften my response and, at the same time, to point out my attentiveness to driving.

"Good catch, Olevia," he responded. "Take the next street that allows a left turn." His words were accompanied by both an uncomfortable snicker and contempt of my remark.

"Yes, sir."

We drove around for about fifteen or twenty minutes, his leg constantly rubbing on mine as he continued to make inappropriate comments to enhance his pleasure. After what felt like eons, he directed me back to the office. As I removed the keys from the ignition and opened the door, he leaned over from the passenger seat he had reclaimed immediately before I turned into the driveway.

"Hey, Olevia."

I turned to face him as I prepared to get out of the car.

He smirked. "You want me to favor you a little?" With that, he reached up and pinched my right breast.

I leaped from the car as he continued to chortle, clearly savoring his power over me. I stood mute in the office next to my dad before the officer even reached the front door.

I considered sharing my experience with Daddy. I knew if I did, it would not go well for Red. Regrettably, I also realized it would not go well for me in that I would not leave that office as a licensed driver. That driver's license represented a win to me, and I moved it to the front of my mind.

Red came in smiling directly at Daddy. There was no sign of fear, even though we both knew what had happened. Evidently, we also mentally concurred that silence created the fastest route to a driver's license.

"Well, sir, she's one excited little girl. Isn't she, Mr. Yeager?"

"How'd she do? Didn't hit any curbs, did she?"

They both chuckled. "Naw. She did really good. I'm giving her a ninety-five on the driving portion. Ester, how'd she do on the written test?"

"Missed one question, Red."

"Well, it looks like Louisiana has another licensed driver."

He shook hands with Daddy as if I were not in the room. They shared a bit more small talk and moved on to his desk. Ester prepared my temporary license and handed it to me.

To seal my victory with license in hand, I glanced at the officer as I walked out the door. My attempt to show I won failed miserably as the guy winked at me and went back to his paperwork.

Since that day, I've regretted not telling Daddy what I experienced. If I had, maybe some other teenager would have been spared the humiliation. Maybe self-absorption allowed me to file it away and not mention it to anyone for many years. The experience of reaching my goal, even with powerlessness and humiliation, has never left me. Sometimes, the only person who needs to know who won is you.

****

My license gave Merilyn and me the independence we wanted. Ways to borrow the car from Daddy became a regular topic of conversation. Wednesday nights were good during the summer. Using our pretense of going to Girls' Auxiliary at church, we won the battle often. I dropped him off for work at the roundhouse at two-thirty in the afternoon for his three o'clock shift. The next stop was Merilyn's, and we each wore skirts with shorts underneath.

Once in the car, our first maneuver involved a run through the Tioga Baptist Church parking lot. We easily convinced ourselves we were then absolved from the lie we told our parents. There were nights we went to church first, including any night Merilyn's mother decided to attend the Women's Auxiliary meeting!

On the way to my house, we made a quick stop at Merritts to pick up a pack of Salem cigarettes to share for the evening.

My house served as the last stop before the fun began. We ditched our skirts and checked our make-up before packing the remainder of the night with as much adventure as possible in whatever hours we had left before eleven o'clock—more accurately, ten o'clock, as it took a while to prep us and the car for picking up Daddy. We rolled all the windows down and sprayed lots of hairspray to cover the cigarette smell in the car. And, most times, we went by my house to change back into our skirts with fresh blouses.

During the school term, our exploits in my car were limited to Saturday afternoons and nights. Sara Terrell, as well as some of our other friends, got their parents' cars on Friday nights and Sunday afternoons. But, for Merilyn and me, our Saturdays provided the most fun.

Camp Livingston, an abandoned military base, often got our attention when we drove around aimlessly, enjoying the freedom of being free. On one such afternoon, we met Clarence Bruce driving what had been his parents' car, a 1955 Oldsmobile. The car, customized to all hand controls, allowed him as a polio paraplegic to drive it. He pulled up beside us, and we stopped.

"Hey, Clarence. Whatcha ya doing?"

"Hey. Testing out this car. Whatcha ya'll doing?"

As the driver, I answered for us. "We're just driving around. How fast will your car go?"

"I don't know. What about yours?"

"I don't know either, but I bet it'll beat yours. My daddy drives pretty fast."

"Bet not. Wanta find out?"

"Yeah. How much?"

"A dollar."

Merilyn and I determined we had a dollar between us and accepted the bet. We lined up the cars side by side, and the race was on.

Clarence set the rules. "Okay, Olevia, let's count to ten, race to that pine tree there, and see who wins."

"Okay."

To decrease any wind resistance, we rolled up the windows while Clarence and I watched each other count off in unison.

"One, two, three, four, five, six, seven, eight, nine, ten!"

I floored the accelerator, and our Studebaker Lark felt as if it was taking flight, much like a flock of seagulls riding high-octane ocean breezes. The speedometer registered slightly over ninety-seven miles per hour as we passed the designated pine tree. I doubt Richard Petty ever became more excited in a race than I did that day. Clarence's car crossed the finish line first, but the fun of the competition offset any disappointment in losing.

We pulled up next to each other, facing in opposite directions, and rolled down the windows. I handed Clarence a handful of change.

He smiled. "Wanna try again?"

"No, we're probably going down to the Palms Drive-in in a little while."

****

We all—in true teenage fashion—felt invincible behind the wheel, and I recall taking more chances than reasonable. On a day we were headed to our favorite hangout, the Palms Drive-in on Upper Third, I found myself creeping along behind some old guy. As we were leaving Lee Heights and approaching the bridge/hill just before Mary Hill Road, I decided to pass the old codger.

I pulled out and pressed the accelerator. When even with him, I glanced over. Mr. Powell, a friend of Daddy's occupied the driver's seat; he slowed his car and waved frantically for me to pull in front of him. Merilyn yelled as I looked up to see a car coming head on. We fishtailed in front of Mr. Powell, avoiding, by inches, an accident that could have killed us all.

Rather than showing gratitude, I hoped this incident could be mine and Mr. Powell's secret. I gave him a conspiratorial glance with my finger held up to my closed lips, indicating "Shh…." If Daddy had known the chances we took in his car, I would have spent a lot more time walking.

Thank God for Guardian Angels. I'm sure I must have worn out more than a few!

****

We considered The Palms Drive-in our own little den of iniquity where the carhops determined the legal drinking age as being tall enough to see over the steering wheel. Complementing our pack of Salems, Merilyn and I ordered a Tom Collins, a Vodka Collins, or my favorite, a Sloe Gin Fizz.

The evils of drinking and driving or cigarette smoking were topics rarely discussed outside of church, and no one blamed liquor for accidents or any other trouble teens experienced. Contrary to today's community where parents are often the fall guys, teens were typically blamed for any trouble they instigated or in which they were involved.

I carefully hid both my drinking and smoking from Daddy because I knew he was too old to understand how grown up I had become. I also did not care to hear his routine reaction to any ill behavior exhibited: "Your name is Yeager, and you did that!"

A blemish on the entire Yeager Clan was too much to bear! I never got drunk—I had to pick up Daddy before eleven! One drink combined with cigarettes proved adulthood or, at the very least, gave the appearance of climbing the mountain toward grown up.

Once at the Palms, we searched for a spot near a car with a couple of guys in it. Ordinarily, England Air Force Base guys were readily available. As we parked, we fantasized about our futures, our eyes roaming among the current patrons. Most nights, we lured a couple into our car to talk and flirt or vice versa. Despite the fact we never dated any of the guys we met, we perpetually believed that imagined date lingered immediately around the corner.

In my mind, Bernie Goheen filled the bill as the perfect guy, and I made a play for him.

"Where are you from, Bernie?"

"Indiana."

"Wow, I've never been to Indiana. Tell me about the town where you lived."

"Indianapolis."

"Oh, wow! Isn't that where the Indy 500 runs in May every year?"

"Yes. That's about all Indianapolis has going for it."

Someone else in the car chimed in, "Bernie, did your sergeant get transferred last weekend? The one you didn't like?"

And the conversation wandered around the car without any control from me. Our entire relationship consisted of either me sitting in his car or him sitting in mine, along with three or four other people. Sometimes, our Palm Drive-in group would spread among two or three other vehicles, and we migrated from one to another.

Necking amounted to nothing more than a mind trip for me; yet my vivid imagination assured me Bernie could be in my life forever. I waited for that Sleeping Beauty kiss that would begin a fairy tale life.

The first Saturday night he didn't show up, the fantasy began to disintegrate. He wasn't there again the next Saturday, and I decided to query a couple of his buddies.

Approaching the nearest one, I asked, "Where's Bernie tonight?"

"Home on leave."

"Indiana?"

"Yes."

"When will he be back?"

"He won't be. Transferred to North Carolina."

The wicked witch of the government had obviously ruined my life, and even Merilyn lost patience with my distress on the way home.

"God, Olevia, you only sat with the guy about eight times. Did you think you were going to marry him?"

Her expression showed me she found my reaction to his transfer to be ridiculous and entirely out of proportion to the situation.

"I thought he liked me."

Merilyn merely shook her head, and we had no further conversation on the way home.

Sunday, I skipped church and arrived at Mrs. Curry's still feeling teary-eyed. I saw her and her Pentecostal sister, Lovey, working in the front yard like busy beavers, getting things together for a big family fish fry.

As I walked up, Lovey asked, "What's the matter, Olevia? Are you fighting with your Daddy again?"

"No. My boyfriend left me."

Mrs. Curry looked up surprised. "Your boyfriend? I didn't know you had a boyfriend."

"Well, I did. Bernie Goheen. He's in the Air Force, and I thought he liked me."

"When did you meet him? Where did you meet him?"

"About two months ago at the Palms Drive-in."

Mrs. Curry's knitted brow indicated her displeasure at the mention of the Palms.

"You need to stay away from the Palms," she stressed one more time. "What made you think he was your boyfriend?"

"Well, we talked to each other every Saturday night, and he almost kissed me the last time. I didn't even know it would have been a goodbye kiss!" I tried to keep my composure, subtly squaring my shoulders.

Mrs. Curry smiled and winked at Lovey. With that bun in her hair, no make-up, and dress mid-calf, Lovey looked old. She sat down in a torn lawn chair under a watermelon-red crepe myrtle tree, portraying the exact antithesis to anyone I ever wanted to become. She smiled and commented, "Sit down here beside me, honey. You and I both have heart trouble. Yours is the kind you'll get over pretty fast." She chuckled.

I almost felt sorry for her, convinced she had never experienced love. But, as she predicted, I recovered and found a new target: the Junior Class President, Gene Byrd. He and I were the same age, but not in the same grade level. As a senior, I outranked him at school.

****

Gene's popularity grew by virtue of his James Dean persona. James Dean, one of my favorite movie stars, died in a car wreck in 1955—before I or most of my friends even knew he existed—but by 1960, he shared a spot with Elvis as one of our idols. Gene's blond, perfectly coifed crewcut and defiant, blue eyes added to his overall allure. A tall, thin guy, he always left his shirt unbuttoned to the fourth button, exposing a large necklace. And, when not in class, a cigarette dangled from the corner of his lips.

He became our local James Dean—at least in my mind. Admiring Gene represented a safe rebellion, and his Junior Class did just that in the voting booth. The teachers and our principal, Mr. Aiken, worried about our future and our heroes. As I remember, Gene's name even made its way into some Sunday school lessons.

In my book, Gene occupied first place as the best-looking guy in school, and only a duck tail could have made him more perfect. We started to occasionally talk to each other, and I took his asking me for help with his homework as a compliment and a way to express personal interest in me.

One day, as I corrected his English homework, he startled me, saying, "Olevia, I'm joining the Army."

"Why?"

"I hate this place, and my parents think it would be good for me."

"When are you leaving?"

"Next weekend. I'll go to Fort Ord, California first."

"Will you write to me?"

"Sure. Give me your address."

So, every day of his basic training, I wrote to Gene and probably received about five letters in return. Ferlin Husky's rendition of "On the Wings of a Dove" remained number one for ten weeks, and we chose it as our song, ignoring the fact it was a country gospel tune. Every time the record played, I assumed the dreamy-eyed, lost-in-teenage-jail-look of a girl who couldn't see past a good-looking, sexy guy.

When the day came for Gene to come home from basic training, I fairly danced through my classes. As sure as eggs are eggs, I visualized his marriage proposal preceding our happily ever after. Nothing else mattered that Friday.

Mrs. Higdon, my English teacher, took a special interest in me, as I have mentioned before, and I liked her. She approached me at my locker and said, "Hey, got plans this weekend? How's everything going for you?"

"Everything's great, Mrs. Higdon. It's Friday, and I have a date."

"With whom?" she asked as if she didn't already know, and it didn't occur to me then that she did.

"Gene Byrd. He's home from Boot Camp."

"You know, Olevia, we get to make a lot of choices in our lives. Sometimes people make choices that affect their future when they are only thinking about today. Nothing important is as simple as it looks."

It didn't even occur to me that Mrs. Higdon referenced Gene when she spoke to me at my locker. I had no idea what the woman meant and didn't care to find out. I just wanted to catch the bus home to prepare for my date.

I said, "Yes, ma'am." Then, I waved and flew out of there like Cinderella toward the Prince Charming of my dreams.

Gene picked me up at Mrs. Curry's because Daddy wasn't home. As often as possible, I tried to avoid the whole "this is my stepmother, Thelma," introduction. The dark side of twilight marked the Chinaberry tree's shadows when Gene walked up the porch steps wearing his military uniform and looking like my answer to a way out of every day and a way into the fairy tale fantasy I dreamed of.

"Mrs. Curry, Gene's here. We're going now."

"Just a minute, Olevia. Hello Gene. Where are you taking Olevia tonight?"

"We're going to a movie, ma'am. I'll have her back by eleven-thirty."

"What movie are you going to see?"

"I don't know what's playing." He smiled at me, and I could hear the unspoken *it doesn't matter anyway.*

"I'll be home on time, Mrs. Curry," I said before glancing at my Prince Charming. "Let's go, Gene."

We were no sooner in the car, than he reached for my hand. "Let's go to the Pines Drive-in so we can talk."

"Okay. What's playing there?"

"I don't know what's playing. I just know who's playing—us."

So funny, so smart, so suave, so not-Tioga High School. I slid across the seat as he bought our tickets, and soon his car occupied a space in one of the back rows. My head lay on his chest, and his arm draped comfortably on my shoulders as he shared with me how much he liked the army and what he wanted to do next.

He described his drill sergeant and how he made the army work for him by pretending to be who they wanted him to be. The last light of the sun disappeared, the movie previews finished, and both Gene and the movie moved to the main attraction. He leaned over the seat, making sure he mashed me a little, and uncovered a case of beer in the back seat.

"You want a beer?"

"Isn't it hot?"

"Yeah, but it's still good."

"No, I don't think I want any."

"Are you sure?"

"I don't like to smell it or drink it." To be sure he didn't think me prudish, I added, "I do like Sloe Gin Fizzes and Vodka Collins."

"You oughta try a beer. Beer relaxes you. I'm already feeling relaxed. We want to enjoy ourselves, don't we?" He threw me a teasing grin.

"Yeah. I'm enjoying myself now. I'm so glad you're home. Are you going to let me wear your necklace?"

"Probably. I think I'll have a beer right now."

He downed three before the movie reached halfway, and he hadn't even asked me if I wanted some popcorn or a Coke. Things weren't going as I planned; more as if I'd planned a picnic on the rainiest day of the year. His hands were busy trying to undo my bra, and his beer breath did not have the effect he may have hoped for. Smelling it made me slightly nauseous, and I felt more than a little nervous.

Disappointment bloomed in my heart like a bouquet of rotten flowers, and my reactions to his overtures were obvious.

"What's the matter?" he asked.

"Nothing. Can't we just talk some? You've been gone a long time, and I've missed you."

"Are you afraid because we aren't married?"

"Afraid of what?"

"Me. You know I love you, don't you?"

"No."

"Is that what's wrong? I do love you."

Like a lightning strike, I knew Gene Byrd did not love me, and I didn't even like him.

"I was going to ask you to marry me tonight," he added.

"You were?"

"Yes, but now I'm not so sure. I don't know if you really love me."

"Oh."

"Olevia, I love you. Will you marry me?"

"No."

Like flipping a light switch, his tone changed. He moved to his side of the car and spoke in a matter-of-fact tone. "Okay. I think I'll ask Linda Thornhill. I'll take you home now, okay?"

"Yes."

By nine o'clock, Mrs. Curry and I were playing Rook at her kitchen table, and Gene Byrd evaporated from my mind.

****

For twelve years, my teachers and I got along well, with two conspicuous exceptions: Melba Humphries and Doris

Robert, bookkeeping and home economics. Ms. Humphries—single, young, and attractive—had a reputation among the female students as favoring the boys, and I resented their getting more attention for less work.

On one occasion, having finished my semester test, I prepared to leave the room. Mickey Urban handed me a dime and whispered, "Get me a candy bar at the gym before it closes."

Ms. Humphries picked up on it, assumed we were sharing answers, and requested that I go to the principal's office immediately; she issued no reprimand whatsoever to Mickey. With my test completed and lying face down on my desk, I had nothing to lose. I took Mickey's money and walked out the door where I passed Mr. Aiken in the hallway.

"Hey, Olevia," he called. "Where are you going?"

"I've finished my six weeks bookkeeping test."

"So, where are you going now?"

"To the gym to get a couple of candy bars from the vending machine before it's locked up for the day."

"Is that all?" he asked.

"Ms. Humphries told me to go to your office because she thought I was cheating. I wasn't."

My anxiety level increased substantially; I had never been sent to the principal's office since I started school.

He didn't smile, but his caring expression was non-threatening when he responded. "Go home. I'll talk to Ms. Humphries later."

I had no further run-ins with Ms. Humphries, and this incident did not surface again.

The Ms. Robert confrontation resulted from my own inappropriate behavior, but nevertheless, I resented her for it. As a junior in high school, all girls were required to take Home Economics, where both sewing and cooking were taught. In conjunction with these classes, all students were assigned, in pairs, to cleaning days to keep the kitchen area clean.

My cleaning partner for the day, Ruby Ates, and I were deep into our chores when I discovered a small can with four slices of pineapple inside. Canned pineapple, a delicacy at our house, never appeared on our grocery list. I suppose I could have purchased a can when Daddy dropped me off at Piggly Wiggly, but it never occurred to me to do so. Something primal took over at the sight of that can of pineapple, and I just had to have it.

"Hey, Ruby, look. Here's a can of pineapple."

"So."

"So, do you like pineapple?"

"Yeah, I guess so. Why?"

"I am going to eat this pineapple."

"You better not, Olevia. We'll get in trouble."

"Ms. Robert probably won't even miss it. She'll be too busy talking about the Pellagra she thinks my family has."

We both laughed at that. My sister, my brother, and my dad had dry skin almost to the point of flaking if not regularly oiled. My dad wore long-sleeved shirts, even on the hottest days, to protect his arms from the sun. Both he and my sister applied tubs of lotion to all exposed parts. During a class discussion of menus and the need for variety in vegetables, Ms. Robert brought up my sister, asking, "Olevia, your sister, Hannah, has a skin disease, doesn't she?"

"No, ma'am. I don't think so."

"Yes, honey, I believe she does. She was in my class, and I remember her skin as very scaly. It seemed to be flaking off."

"She has dry skin. That's all. She eats lots of vegetables."

"Pellagra is what it looked like to me. Anyway, what I'm trying to say is we need balanced diets to have good skin and teeth."

As soon as I got out of that class, Merilyn and I went to the World Book Encyclopedia in the library to look up Pellagra and found it to be some sort of potentially fatal skin disease caused by an inadequate diet. No one in my family suffered from Pellagra; three members simply had dry skin!

The next day, I told all the girls in Home Economics how ill-informed Ms. Roberts was, and Pellagra became an underlying joke in our class. Just mentioning the word somehow justified stealing a can of pineapple, and we savored every bite.

The next day, the flavor had faded when Ms. Robert showed up for class.

"Before we begin today, class, I'm afraid I have some bad news."

We sat stick-still, thinking something terrible must have happened to one of our classmates or maybe one of our teachers. Ms. Robert looked as solemn as an undertaker meeting the family of the deceased. The silence in the room made my ears ache to hear the tragedy she would soon report.

"Someone has stolen a can of pineapple."

Oh, God. What now? The thought flashed through my mind like a neon sign.

"You know, class, stealing is a sin. When you steal, you don't just break a Tioga High School rule, you don't just break a Louisiana State law, you don't just break a United States of America law, you break God's law."

My mind raced. I took a four-slice can of pineapple, not the charity drive proceeds! The class remained completely quiet, but eyes were beginning to wander in hopes of locating the guilty party. Ruby Ates and I looked directly at each other as Ms. Robert continued her sermon on the evils of stealing.

"It starts small—a little lie, a little theft—and soon lying and stealing become a way of life." As she wandered up and down in front of the class, I thought of *Elmer Gantry*, a film starring Burt Lancaster that was currently playing at the Paramount.

"Whoever stole from this class thought only about themselves. They didn't consider any effect their actions might have on the whole class."

Although Ms. Robert sought to describe the thieves as some sort of Bonnie and Clyde personas, I wondered if there had been some bigger theft. Maybe someone pilfered a case of pineapple or the petty cash from her desk drawer—some theft of which I had no knowledge. How much of an adverse effect could a single four-slice can of pineapple have on twenty-five girls?

Ms. Robert's quiet but emphatic tirade continued. "I can't let this breach of conduct, this sin, go unpunished. I don't want to punish twenty-five girls for the action of maybe one or two, but I cannot make that choice lightly. The guilty girl must make the choice. I'm going to give you a few minutes to think about the situation. Let's just close our eyes and consider our own consciences."

After several minutes, she called out, "If you stole the pineapple, raise your hand. Your classmates won't know. Just you and I will know, and we can work out your punishment."

If you have ever stood in a revival meeting with your eyes closed while singing "Just as I Am," and the preacher asks, "If you are a sinner and ready to admit it, raise your hand," then you have an idea of what I experienced in that moment.

Many thoughts went through my mind, the least of which considered what punishment might be in store.

Oh, I hope Ruby keeps her hand down. I told her yesterday that I would take the blame, and I will. But not now, not in front of the whole class. It was a four-slice can of pineapple, for God's sake. Why's Ms. Robert making it the Brinks Robbery? I sighed. *Is it another sin to pray not to get caught for the first sin?*

I prayed hard as we sat, supposedly with eyes closed. My squints discovered my classmates doing the same thing—not praying but squinting. They all wanted to know who the thief was, all but Ruby, whose eyes were tightly closed and whose hand remained by her side.

After what seemed hours, Ms. Robert said, "Okay, class, the guilty girl has chosen to punish all of you. Remember, it's not me who is assigning the extra homework, but one of your classmates who stole from you—yes, from you—and now she's choosing to punish you for her sin."

An audible groan emerged from the class as a unit, and I almost faltered in my resolve to remain quiet.

Just in time to prevent that mistake, Ms. Robert relented, saying, "Okay, girls, to be as fair as possible, I'm going to give the thief one more chance to come forward. I will stay in this building for half an hour after class lets out. If the guilty girl confesses during that time, the rest of the class will go unpunished. We'll talk about it tomorrow. For now, get out your Simplicity pattern book."

I agonized and fought with my conscience for the balance of that class. As unacceptable as I knew stealing to be—even a four-slice can of pineapple—I directed my anger at Ms. Robert's overreaction. I seesawed between thinking *I'll never tell* and how unfair not confessing would be to the rest of the class. In the end, my conscience won, and I confessed.

Ruby went with me, and Ms. Robert looked a bit surprised to see both of us. She expressed more compassion than I expected as she assigned my punishment—to clean the refrigerator from top to bottom. Ruby attempted to join in the guilt, but Ms. Robert's questioning verified Ruby served more as a witness to my misdeed than a participant. My prayers were answered to the extent that the discussion of the theft ended in the confessional.

No one ever brought the subject up in class, and Ms. Robert did not mention it.

****

Being a teenager is not easy, and neither is being their teacher, their parent, or anyone with authority. Through luck, prayer, and the goodness of lots of people, I made it through high school unscathed, with a better-than-average education and a reinforced moral guide. That quiet little voice of conscience became amplified through my mom's earlier teaching as well as her heavenly concern for me.

The match cover I still carried in my purse also helped. It became as ingrained and pronounced as rings in an ancient oak tree.

CHAPTER 50
GROWING UP WITH HENRY

Henry.

While I worked my way through high school, learning to be a teenager, learning to cook, and simply learning to live a life without Mama, Johnny did the same in his world. We had a couple of years between stepmothers, and this story took place in that vacuum.

While I remained lost in my own teenaged black hole where life was all about me, John and I became disconnected from one another—at least on a social level. The tale told here came as news to me when Johnny shared it many years later. To set the stage, a cursory introduction to Henry is in order.

Henry, the youngest of our half-brothers, never married, lived in Alexandria, and worked for Roy O. Martin Lumber Company. On most weekends, he would be a fixture at our house. At three years of age, he lost his own mom, Pearl, Daddy's first wife, when she died in childbirth. He grew up with his three older brothers in the Alexandria Masonic Orphan's Home. He served in the military during World War II, came home, and got a job. Some people said he never really recovered from his childhood trauma. I can't vouch for the truth of that, but I do know he did his best to live an independent life.

I'm going to let Johnny take it from here.

****

Henry's influence on my life was negligible until Mama died. Oh, he came over on the weekends for as long as I can remember. He mopped floors, fed our cows, or did whatever chore Mama or Daddy requested. Most Saturday mornings, he brought funny books—as I called comic books back then—to Olevia and me. He sometimes played rummy or Crazy Eights with us.

Oftentimes, when I mowed the lawn, he came out to take over when he saw Daddy coming up the driveway. One day, as Daddy got out of the car, Henry turned off the lawn mower and wiped his brow with a rag he kept in his pocket for that purpose.

"Boy, Daddy, it's hot out here today."

"It sure is! You might want to hose yourself off or get a glass of cold water. Don't wanna be getting heat stroke. I sure do appreciate you doing this mowing."

"Okay," he replied and headed for the hose out back with a smile on his face and a bounce in his step. I'm not sure why that didn't make me angry, except Daddy and I both knew who really mowed the lawn. It seemed right to allow Henry to take the credit.

Other times, he lay on the bed in a back room (referred to as Henry's room since the day we moved into that house). I slept there as well. A missing pillow would cause Henry to hold his head at an odd angle while he lay there and called Mama, saying things like, "Mary, could you bring me a pillow back here? Mine's missing."

As long as she was physically able, she did so and made no complaints about it. Those were just a couple of his peculiarities, but you get the picture. He was an odd fellow but goodhearted. Despite his being a regular part of our household, he had little, if any, impact on my everyday life until Mama died.

After that awful day in October, Henry still came out on weekends, but his visits took on a new meaning for me. They added a level of excitement and a way to fill empty hours within a whole new world still under construction.

He smoked Lucky Strikes and made them readily available to me if I asked, although I had not yet hit my twelfth birthday. He taught me to play stud poker and shoot craps using the Monopoly game dice. He gave me money and won it back. I relished gambling in a house where Daddy prohibited even playing Solitaire on Sundays. Of course, we concealed our games from Daddy and from Olevia for fear she may tell Daddy. The secret rebellion made the games more fun, and I felt more powerful.

Daddy allowed me to spend an occasional night with Henry at his hotel—a boarding house at Ninth and Beauregard in Alexandria. His room had a big closet, a double bed, and a place for him to wash his hands. A long string from the lightbulb tied to the bedstead allowed Henry to turn the light off or on without getting up. He shared the bathroom down the hall with other boarders.

When Daddy granted my begged-for permission, I hitchhiked to the Majestic Café and met Henry. The Majestic Café, a favorite haunt of Henry's, became one of mine as well. Think of a poor man's *Cheers* in the late fifties—a friendly place where your secrets stay and caring for each other is palpable.

A middle-aged Cajun lady ran the place. Her black hair stood out as the kind that screamed: "This came out of a bottle; I was gray yesterday." The first time Henry introduced me as his little brother, I had an experience I've never forgotten.

She smiled from ear to ear and pulled me toward her. "Whatcha say your name is?" she asked as she roughly hugged me to her large bosom.

"Johnny," I answered.

"Well, Johnny, I'm glad to meet you!" She hugged me again, and I glowed crimson as I grinned. She pushed me back and eyed me up and down. "We'll be good friends." The acceptance in her voice radiated down to my toes.

Any time we were in the same room, she treated me as if I were the stars and the moon. Her hugs and kisses felt like cool water to a thirsty soul, and I needed that human touch. Yet I cannot recall her name—just her compassion.

Our routine, Henry's and mine, never changed. We ate a hamburger at the Majestic; sometimes Henry would pay cash, and sometimes he would say, "Fix this up where I can sign it."

That always reminded me of Mama calling in groceries to be delivered from Merritt's store. She'd say something like, "Put that on John's bill and send a copy with the groceries. I'll sign it for you."

After the hamburger, we ambled over to the finance company for Henry to make his weekly five-dollar payment on whatever loan he had going. The next stop was the liquor store for a pint of Jim Beam whiskey, and then it was back to the café.

Our eyes searched the room for a table with at least one vacant chair. Once seated, Henry opened two Cokes and set out two glasses. I soon learned the vacant chair became a cover if the cops showed up. On more than one occasion, the chair served its purpose when some member of the police force darkened the door. Henry knew all of them by name but always referred to each one as officer. Henry liked to be first in acknowledging the cop's presence.

That night was no different. Knowing how the encounter would work, I smiled to myself when the policeman walked in.

"Hey, officer," Henry called out with a grin. "What's happening in your neck of the woods?"

"Not much, Henry. Who's this you got here?"

"This here's my little brother, Johnny. He came out for the weekend."

The two glasses remained on the table, while I innocently sucked on a Coke—which is what I did most of the time anyway. The appearance of getting away with something fueled my excitement. The officer acknowledged me, patted me on the shoulder, and made the same joke he made every time.

"Well, Johnny, you look like a good boy. Watch yourself with Henry. Don't you let him teach you any of his bad habits."

Everybody laughed and, after wandering around the room for a few minutes, the officer left. Following a couple of drinks, Henry bought three rolls of nickels to play the twenty-five-hole pinball machine—a great gambling game. The more nickels in, the better the odds of winning. Henry put on quite a show pecking the buttons, slapping the sides, and talking the balls into whatever slot he wanted. He gave the impression of a windup toy drummer wound a little too tight but fun to watch.

"Watch this, Johnny."

Henry danced from one foot to the other, lifted the machine with his knee, and hit the buttons. Watching a mob of kangaroos chasing an ostrich could not have been more fascinating to me—and I'm guessing, to anyone else, since they all stood around watching.

I stood next to him during his performance and leaned over to ask, "What'd you do that for?"

"That's how you get more options and more features. I have a better chance to win now."

That lucky Saturday, the words were just out of his mouth when he won six hundred games; we strode over to the cash register as if we were million-dollar lottery winners. The cashier flipped a switch, and the games clicked off while Henry danced in time with the clicks.

The whole café stood and cheered, and the barmaid deposited the thirty dollars in his hand, five dollars at a time. We both stared at the stack of fives. Henry folded five of them for his pocket and handed one to me.

"Let's go, Johnny. Here's your five."

"Thanks, Henry." I beamed in appreciation. "Where are we going?"

"Over to the liquor store. Drinks are getting short around here, and I need some smokes too."

"Could I have a pack of cigarettes of my own?"

"Sure, we got the money tonight!" He tussled my head and laughed. We were not just walking in high cotton; we were rolling in it. I felt as rich as I had ever felt before—or since—with those five dollars in my pocket. Maybe that's when I first learned: *it is not the amount of money, but with whom you share it that makes all the difference.*

Outside of the liquor store, Henry divided up our goods—a pint and pack for him and a pack for me. If they had brought out the green jacket from the Master's tournament when we walked back into the Majestic, Henry would have looked comfortable wearing it. He sort of pranced when he walked, smiling at everybody. He counted the money he had left. We sat down at a table with a group of guys.

While talking to his buddies, Henry morphed into somebody I hardly recognized. I wondered which Henry was the counterfeit one: the one who came to our house on weekends or the one sitting with me that night. Maybe, neither. More likely, just two sides of the same coin.

Fourteen-year-old boys were scarce in the Majestic Café, and I basked in the attention Henry's cronies gave me. My sex education began at the Majestic Café. They asked me things to see me blush and, when I did, they hollered, slapped me on the back, and laughed until they were in danger of falling off their chairs.

"Hey, Johnny, when's the last time you kissed your girlfriend?"

"I don't have a girlfriend."

"Well, you ought to, a good-looking boy like you. Maybe Henry can help you find one."

"I don't have any money." I shrugged.

They whooped and hollered, and my face reddened. Henry danced with a woman, and she asked me to dance. Tioga boys from Kingsville Baptist aren't supposed to know how to dance, but it looked easy enough to me. "Window Up Above," a newly recorded George Jones song, played on the jukebox, and my head rested on her chest. I was happier than a possum up a pant leg. One thing is for sure, I knew my buddies in Tioga would be jealous if they only knew or if I could tell them. Of course, I couldn't; it would get back to Daddy and might create a problem.

Back at our table, an old crone called Gimme-A-Nickel hit Henry up for a nickel. He gave her two; after all, we were in the money that night. Gimme-A-Nickel's smile—just before she kissed Henry's cheek—looked like a chainsaw that had just been cranked. She held up the biggest pair of red panties I'd ever seen and showed them off to everybody at the table.

"Look what my boyfriend just bought me."

Henry asked, "What did you do to get those?"

Everybody roared as she threw them over his head; he buzzed his lips and clowned around with her. Soon, she moved to the next table and the next victim. Henry patted my shoulder and said he'd be back in a few minutes. "Hey, guys, can you keep an eye on my little brother?" he asked.

One of the guys at the table answered, "Sure, we're not going anywhere." He put his hand on my shoulder and suggested, "Let's put a couple of nickels in that machine over there."

I readily agreed, and the two of us had a pretty good time, although I think I used most of my five dollars. Henry had left with my earlier dance partner, stayed gone about an hour, and then returned alone.

"Johnny, it's about time we get on back to the hotel."

"Where did you go with that woman?"

"It don't matter, Johnny. I'll get you a woman when you get older. For now, you know Daddy would want you to be in bed at this hour."

He tousled my hair again. We laughed, and I hoped when he got me a woman it wouldn't be Gimme-A-Nickel. Back home, life continued as usual. I rode my horse with my friends, fed the chickens and cows, talked to Olevia when she showed up, and waited for the next opportunity to play grown-up.

Henry was as good of a brother to me as he knew how to be. He loved me and was truly a blessing to my life. My interactions with Henry provided a little hot sauce to an otherwise bland meal.

CHAPTER 51
John Leaves Home

"Bye, John. I love you. Please write. Don't forget to write every day," I yelled. I waved until I could no longer see the car or the dust that followed it.

John leaned out the back window to return my waves. I tried to smile as the car slowly disappeared. He was entering a new world. Like a wave withdrawing from the shore and dissolving into the sea, he was leaving me so he could be his own person.

I briefly wondered if I could survive without knowing where he was and what he was doing. Then it occurred to me, I didn't know that now. Like a giant mudslide oozing down the mountain, a bit of a chasm had developed between us in the last year or so. It moved so slowly, we both just stayed in front of it and ignored any possible final outcomes.

"Don't worry, Olevia," he shouted just before the car moved out of earshot. "I'll be fine. I'll send you a picture of California." He looked happy and excited to go through the next door to face whatever would come.

As I turned around, my tears fell to the point that I could not see. I knew John made his best choice, but my heart ached when I imagined a life in Tioga with only my stepmother and dad. It would be hard knowing that John didn't live there too. Thelma put her arm around my shoulder as we walked up the steps and back into the empty house.

"Olevia. You know this is best, and it's not as if Johnny is running away somewhere. He's going to California with his sister and her whole family. Your senior year in school is coming up, and you have things to do. Everything's going to be fine."

Intellectually, I knew she was right. But in my emotional teenage jail, I didn't even like her for saying it, much less accept any comfort from hearing it. I could only imagine John's absence from my life as the darkest cave where no glimmer of hope, light, or laughter could enter.

****

I recall most of how it unfolded, though there are some gaps in my memory, perhaps due to the trauma of what I felt was a sudden change.

John quit school at sixteen despite my best efforts to keep him there. He wanted to join the military. In fact, he did enlist in Alexandria and made it all the way to Shreveport before a large, burly sergeant inquired one more time as to his age. The truth escaped, and John boarded a bus back home before he could even get used to being gone.

After that escapade, only a few more weeks of summer days had dragged by before Hannah alerted us to a change in her life. We were all sitting on the front porch, just before sundown, drinking iced tea and talking about nothing. During a short break in the conversation, Hannah got everyone's attention with an announcement.

"Robert has been assigned to temporary duty."

Daddy asked, "What does that mean?"

"He leaves this week in route to Suisun City, California. We're not sure how long he will be there. I'll join him in a week or so."

"If it's temporary duty, why do you have to go at all?" Daddy asked while the rest of us remained quiet.

"Well, from Suisun City, he'll be sent to Misawa, Japan for his next hitch. We'll be there for two or three years."

"It sounds like you're saying you and your family are going to be gone for a long while. Is that what I'm hearing?"

Before Hannah could answer, John interrupted. "Daddy, I'm not going back to school. I hate it. Can I go with Hannah? As soon as I'm seventeen—and that's not long, just a month or so—I can join the army out there. All you will have to do is sign for me. I want to go to California. Please?"

So, in a matter of seconds, I learned both my sister and my brother would be leaving my immediate world in a few weeks. Some sort of alternate reality took over, and I could not see clearly through the fog that surrounded my mind. I could deal with Hannah and her family leaving because I had done it before. But John? No way. I sat mute and stared.

Daddy assumed his chin-between-the-forefinger-and-thumb pose as he looked out across the pasture. He gave serious thought to John's question, but not one of us had any real idea as to what he was thinking. I felt torn between wanting John's emancipation from Tioga and not wanting him to leave me there. The tug of war in my mind seemed to ebb and flow like the confluence of two rivers where I couldn't decide which offered the least chance of drowning.

The quiet had never felt more silent than it did in that gaping hole between the question and the answer. Outside of a jack braying in the pasture and the squeak of Daddy's rocking chair, we heard no sound, and we made none.

Daddy leaned back to seemingly allow room for his announcement. "Johnny, you belong in school. You know that don't you?"

His quiet but serious tone came unexpected to me. Typically, he told us what we could and couldn't do; now he sounded almost conversational.

"Yes, sir. But I don't like it. I don't like the teachers. I don't like anything about it, and I don't want to go." John frowned. "Please, Daddy, let me go with Hannah to California," he pleaded.

****

He had quit going to school a few weeks before the end of the last school term, just before summer break. He left home every morning as if going to school. Then he returned after Daddy came in from work and the school bus ran. To my knowledge, Daddy remained unaware of his status, but sometimes I wonder if he did know and chose to allow John to find his way.

Scholastically, John wasn't doing nearly as well as he could in school, and he knew he was failing Algebra.

I went to see his teacher in search of a solution.

"Mr. Dossman, if John fails Algebra, I know he'll quit school. Can you please let him pass? What grade does he have?"

"He has a 68, Olevia. He has already failed the class. I'm not here to *give* passing grades. I'm here to reveal the grades my students earn."

"But, Mr. Dossman, Merilyn Haydel had that exact average the last six weeks, and you let her pass with a D. Why can't you do that for John? He'll quit school if you don't! I'll work with him for the next six weeks."

"You don't know what John will do, and the case with Merilyn is completely different. She tried. She studied. She did her homework. She did her best. John is a smart student who does not care and does none of those things." His brows wrinkled as he peered at me, adding, "There are consequences, Olevia."

"But—"

"No more conversation," Mr. Dossman answered with finality, and he ushered me out of his classroom. Brows knit, he repeated, "There are consequences."

****

John failed. He quit, and now we sat on our front porch waiting to see how the next chapter in our lives would begin. The breeze in my hair felt like winds of change. I watched the leaves fluttering on the Sycamore tree out front and sensed a similar movement in my own mind. I did not feel comfortable with sudden change; the anticipation heightened my sense of feeling no ground beneath my feet and a lack of a billowing parachute to save the landing.

Then, Daddy shattered the silence in one short sentence: "You can go, son."

And, at that point, I became temporarily deaf and blind to anything happening around me.

****

If any of us said another word, I don't remember it. Now, as I sit to write about this pivotal moment, I wonder. What did John do first? What did he say? What was Hannah's response? Did she check with Robert to ask what his thoughts were? Did Daddy chat with John to offer advice? I doubt it, but I don't know. Did Thelma voice any opinion? Who helped John get ready to walk out of our Tioga life?

This must be what amnesia feels like. There's a hole in my memory, and nothing over the years has allowed me to explore those missing hours.

From hearing my father say, "You can go, son," to standing in the driveway, days later, waving at John, there continues to be an empty space of nothing. A huge black hole lingers.

When he left, I wavered between being happier for him than I was sad for me, and I felt as if I could barely breathe. The decision was too much for one day as if an entire ocean had rolled over my heart.

But life goes on, and emotional bonds cannot be broken. John and I are all that are left now from our fifties and sixties Tioga family. We live near each other and talk regularly. I am blessed by my brother and thankful for the relationship we shared as kids and the one we continue to share. I love him more than I can express.

CHAPTER 52

A THREE-HOUR PARTY

Tioga High School, even though a small rural school, had an excellent reputation for statewide scholastic ratings and extraordinary teachers. This made me proud of my school and my education. We had ninety-seven students in our graduating class, and the vast majority of them were the same kids who had entered school together on the day after Labor Day in 1949.

One boy, Carl Van Veckhovan, whose transfer from Alaska occurred in the fourth grade, remained a transfer student in all natives' minds. Carl's status was duly noted under his cap and gown graduation picture in *The Tribesman*. Just one example of how difficult piercing the armor surrounding our cabal could be.

****

As graduation day approached, excitement filled every nook and cranny of our high school. Personally, apprehension seemed more the name of the game as I felt my internal barometric pressure machine forecast an approaching hurricane. As a good student, my name landed near the top of my class, academically, and near the bottom, socially.

Other than three especially close friends (Merilyn, Charlene, and Sara), my interaction with the larger girlfriend group had remained limited to a couple of slumber parties and school-organized activities. While lying in the grass and looking up at the clouds, I thought about the upcoming ceremony. I found my mind wandering through various avenues of my life and contemplating the state of things important to me prior to the pressure of the pivotal graduation moment.

Boyfriends were mostly classmates who needed help with their homework, and we sat on the school steps or in the library. Any dates were double dates with friends or because the entire class participated in an extra-curricular activity. In those instances, we were matched up boy-girl for whatever games were to be played.

I dressed okay. My dad supported us adequately on his Missouri Pacific Railroad engineer's salary. I had a driver's license—no car, just a license. My job on the weekends and holidays at Kresge's Five and Dime in Alexandria added to my spending money. Having a car would be nice, but it was not mandatory. On work days, I walked three miles to the bus unless rain prevented it. In those cases, either Daddy or Mrs. Curry drove me.

After I grew weary of cloud gazing, I got up and went inside. My mind naturally drifted toward the state of our home. We lived in a house with unfinished wood floors, no curtains or blinds on the windows, and sparsely filled with furniture. Still, my life pleased me, and I looked forward to attending the newly established Louisiana State University at Alexandria Junior College, actually located in Lafayette.

****

During those weeks before graduation, everywhere you turned, someone talked about their party or the get-together in the works to mark this important date in their lives. Those parties and celebrations caused me to wonder where I fit into the graduation atmosphere.

Then, as so often has happened to me, a fairy godmother showed up to wave her magic wand.

My English teacher, Miss Higdon, stopped me in the hallway on a Monday morning. "Olevia, come with me for a minute. I need to talk to you."

Only Miss Higdon could do that without frightening me. Over the years, we had become friends, and she often spoke to me privately about something personal in my life—a hoped-for boyfriend, a planned activity, or whatever. She had become a sort of mentor. I followed her down the hallway, curious but not concerned.

Once in her classroom, she closed the door and took her chair at her desk. I sat down on one of the vacant student desks.

She continued, "Your cousin would like to host an afternoon Coke Party for you at her home."

Well, that was an out-of-the-blue surprise. "What cousin? Maybe my Aunt Grace? She's not a cousin."

The only cousins I knew came from my mom's family. I had met many of Daddy's siblings and their children, but they didn't live anywhere close and certainly were not likely to be planning any parties for me.

"No," she said. "Your dad's cousin. I ran into Scott Yeager's wife, Winona, and your name came up. She asked about having a little graduation party for you."

"Are you sure she was talking about me? I don't remember ever having met her."

****

I knew she existed but could not fathom why she would be interested in my life. I felt as if another one of those parallel worlds had occurred or maybe I was hallucinating. I could not imagine Winona Yeager even knowing my name, much less being aware of my high school graduation.

Lying on my bed after getting home from school one afternoon, I tried to recall what I knew about her and her family. The Scott Yeagers were the rich Yeagers—at least, as seen by me. Daddy occasionally visited with them— typically about some family tree thing. He and C. Scott Yeager, Sr. were first cousins, but his visits were not necessarily just social. They were both involved in the Yeager Family Tree compilation. When Daddy visited, he went alone to their house. None of them, to my knowledge, had ever visited our house. They lived in Ball, Louisiana, just a few miles up the Monroe Highway, but a million miles from our lifestyle.

I had seen their homes—huge estate-like houses (think Tara). They had two-story white frames with large pillars in the front situated under magnolia trees and surrounded by camellias and what we called cashmere bouquet bushes (also known as gardenias). The street on which they lived bore the name Yeager Drive and still does so today.

The elder C. Scott was an attorney and 'land investor'— whatever that means. I had heard the term when my dad described him to someone, but I had not been curious enough to inquire as to its meaning. C. Scott Jr. became an architect, and he had twin younger brothers, John Moore Yeager and William Martin Yeager. William died young, at age thirty-four, in 1954. I don't know from what. John became a medical doctor in Alexandria, but, again, I don't know that for a fact. I never looked for his office and had little to no interest in what went on in their family.

While I didn't know much about any of them, aside from the basic family tree, I had heard all the wives devoted themselves to making their communities better. Since I didn't live in their community or move in their social circles,

I had no idea what they did to accomplish that goal. Their kids went to private schools in Alexandria, and I never met any of them.

****

Mrs. Higdon continued. "Yes, Olevia, we were talking about you. What would you think about a small Coke party for the Saturday before the Baccalaureate Service on Sunday?"

I knitted my brows, trying to make some sense out of this conversation.

"That's not going to be a very good day. Lots of people are having graduation parties that Saturday. Who's going to come, anyway?" The idea of someone I did not know giving me a Coke Party did not compute in my brain.

"We plan to invite every senior girl and your stepmother. The party will be at Winona's house at around two in the afternoon. Snacks and Cokes will be served, we'll have a little music, and you girls can just have fun. It will be over before five, so no Saturday night parties will be affected."

I nodded.

She smiled. "By the way, are you going to a Saturday night party?"

"No. On graduation night, I plan to go bowling at the new bowling alley on MacArthur Drive. Just four or five of us girls are going."

Her response amplified the party as a done deal. Apparently, the last piece to be nailed down turned out to be me. Much as Cinderella sat on the hearth while her stepsisters went out, I planned to ignore the party scene. And just like Cinderella, the magic wand waved.

"So, what do you think about a small celebration for you?" She tilted her head and waited for an answer.

I suddenly felt I would be letting her down in some way if I said no. "I guess it's okay. I can come, and I'll ask Thelma."

"Don't worry about Thelma. I'll talk to your stepmother."

"What about everybody else? Do I need to send invitations or what?" I had not listened to all the graduation party chitchat surrounding me at school and had no idea how one would be put together.

"No, I'll take care of everything. Your job is to show up on time." She chuckled and squeezed my shoulder as she got up to prepare for her class. I glided from the room—pretty sure my feet never touched the floor as I tried to make sense of the world around me.

****

I did not sleep well waiting for Saturday to come, more from fear than anticipation. I understood every girl in my graduation class got an invitation, but believing they would show up required a lot of imagination. No one at school even mentioned it to me. I brought it up to Merilyn, and she appeared oblivious to the whole thing. My excitement turned into a let's-just-get-it-over-with feeling.

Daddy drove Thelma and me to C. Scott's house. I wore my best gathered skirt, blouse, and penny loafers. While Daddy drove up what seemed, at the time, to be a long driveway (but what I now know is not), I fretted inwardly as to whether anyone would come. Well, I thought my best friends might feel obligated to show up, though not one had mentioned it to me all week. I certainly didn't bring it up.

There were girls in my class that I had rarely, if ever, spoken to beyond hello or some classroom discussion. Being academically blessed and a member of the BETA

Club, along with my Tioga Baptist Church attendance with the girls who lived on the right side of the tracks, gave me access to the popular girls' clique despite being socially challenged.

If their parents knew about the party, they would probably insist those girls show up. However, I had classmates who were not in my group or any group of which I was aware. Most attended Kingsville Baptist Church and lived lives of which I had no knowledge. I could not imagine why they would come to my party.

Like a condemned man walking that last mile, I approached the front porch with trepidation. I took a deep breath and reached for the doorbell while Thelma stood beside me wearing her sunflower-like smile. Before I touched the doorbell, a lovely lady appeared and welcomed me in as if I were a regular visitor to her gorgeous home.

"Look here, girls. Olevia's here!" Then she turned to my stepmother. "And you must be Thelma? I'm Winona. So nice to meet you. Come on in and get comfortable."

"Comfortable" did not describe the slight nausea I felt or the desire to run away that throbbed in my brain. Thelma's hand on my shoulder gave me the confidence and courage to smile. I look back now with thanks for Thelma, not just on that day, but on other occasions when she made my life more manageable by just showing up.

The house, at least the part I could see, seemed to be filled with girls. Some even had their moms with them! They stood and clapped as if I were a celebrity. The scene caused me to think of the frog kissed by the princess and transformed into a prince. I must have been dreaming because I did not recognize myself in the person being celebrated.

Winona stepped over to a nearby table to pick up a scrapbook. "Here, Olevia. You have so many friends! I want you to have each of them write a note about today in this scrapbook. We are all so proud of you and your accomplishments."

I seriously wondered, *What accomplishments? I graduated from high school, not Harvard.*

****

As with every important event in my life, a memory of my mom flashed by. Her presence became palpable, and I heard her voice in my mind, saying, *I'm proud of you.* For the past week, I had been thinking a lot about her and how concerned she would be if she were still here. She knew about my tendency to fall into a sad place in my mind, and the week had been difficult. I still carried the match cover given to me just days before she crossed over. The words were worn off but remain forever etched in my mind: *Be good. Love, Mama.*

I put on my best smile, entered the main room, and began the teenage hugging routine. I thought it silly that girls hugged each other when they met even if they had just been together hours before. Today, it felt right, and I felt treasured.

I finally found my voice. "Wow! Thanks, everybody. This is such a surprise. I love everybody," I gushed.

All the girls laughed.

Mrs. Higdon stepped in. "We have the snacks set out, and the Coke bar is ready. Why don't you choose some music? Put some records on the Victrola." She took a smiling Thelma's arm, and they went to some other room.

The snacks included those little sandwiches with no crust, cut into fours. Chicken salad, tuna salad, pimento cheese, and I don't know what else. There were bowls of fruit and nuts, chips of every kind, and the Coke bar—I had never seen one like it before nor have I seen one since.

The set-up looked like a real bar, but the drinks consisted of Coke, Pepsi, Dr. Pepper, and Seven-Up. An ice machine was readily available, and there was even a bowl of peanuts to put into our Pepsis or Dr. Peppers if we liked. Finally, a container of warmed Dr. Pepper with cinnamon sticks and orange slices floating on top graced the end of the table.

The wonderful smell of cinnamon engulfed the room. There were fancy stemmed glasses, beautiful China cups, and a gorgeous crystal ladle lay beside the ornate punch bowl. The whole scene felt both special and every day at the same time; it felt like family, and I was grateful.

The afternoon proved memorable. I received presents, and we all laughed, danced to records, wrote in my new scrapbook, and planned the rest of our lives—all the things high school girls did in the late '50s and early '60s.

****

For many years, I often thought of that party and the kindness of Mrs. Higdon and Mrs. Yeager. I never saw Mrs. Yeager again. The afternoon activities may have been a part of her improve-the-community projects by throwing a party for the less fortunate, but her motives were unimportant to me then and still are. The memory lives on.

****

In 2011, while attending my 50-year high school reunion in Alexandria, that long-ago party afternoon came up in conversation. Not every member of my graduating class attended that reunion, but most of my friends were there. Quite a few of the classmates whom I couldn't really call close friends and some I barely remember but had graduated with me were also there.

One of those people, Joann Belgard—now Joann Barnes—attended. I heard her talking about politics with one of the guys, John Kirkland, and recognized her name by the tag she wore. It turned out we shared a lot of political views. As the conversation broke up, I walked over to her.

"Hey, Joann, I wish I could think as fast on my feet as you! Congrats on winning that one! In high school, John always won—probably because he was good-looking."

We both laughed as she examined my name tag.

She said, "Olevia?" with a question in her voice.

"Yeah. Though now I go by Ann."

Without hesitation, she hugged me, and when she stepped away, the tears in her eyes surprised me. I was glad to see her, but it certainly did not bring tears to my eyes.

I thought of her as one of those very shy girls whom I rarely, if ever, spoke to in high school. Her family consisted of seven children living with her parents in a two-bedroom house on Pardue Road, not far from my house, but eons away from how I lived in terms of freedom, space, thinking, and lifestyle.

She said, just above a whisper, "I apologize for tearing up. Do you remember your graduation party?"

"The Coke Party? Yeah. Why?"

"Your party was the only party to which I received an invitation or attended in all of high school. I remember everything—from getting the invitation, to getting dressed, to walking into your cousin's mansion." Animation, pleasure, and emotion filled her voice as she went on. "That one afternoon made a lifetime impression on me. In some ways, I believe it changed how I saw my future. I can't explain it, but I can say thank you now."

Now, guess who had tears in their eyes! We hugged again, smiled, and found a table to take a short trip down memory lane. Then, for an hour or more, we sipped drinks and shared information about our current lives, our families, and our careers.

I found out she lived up the road, in McKinney, Texas—about twenty minutes from where I currently live. We are now close friends and remain in regular contact with each other. It's amazing how a single afternoon might shape a lifetime and fructify a friendship decades later.

****

A random act of kindness counts double when no one asks for credit but allows their deed to speak for itself in terms of results in making the world a better place to live.

I can't remember sending a thank you note to either Winona or Miss Higdon, though I am certain Thelma did so on my behalf—at least to Winona. I have no idea of the results of any of Winona's other possible improve-the-neighborhood projects, but this one improved the world in ways she could not have imagined.

These unexpected angels' blessings extended not only to me on that day, but to others and far beyond.

CHAPTER 53

LIVING WITH THE TERRELL FAMILY

I graduated from Tioga High School in May of 1961 and was among the top ten in my class, an honor limited by our class size of ninety-seven. Except for Merilyn, Carl Van Veckhoven, Carroll Hammack, and maybe two more, we had all been together since first grade.

Two of our fellow students had died along the way. Carol Kaye Wren sat directly in front of me in every class we shared from first grade until her death at age sixteen. She fell at the skating rink, and the hospital x-rays revealed a brain tumor that ultimately snuffed out her life. Even in her absence, Carol Kaye's picture headed up the senior class photos in *The Tribesman*.

In the seventh grade, a boy classmate whose name I've forgotten died with leukemia—a death sentence diagnosis in 1955. He had been a transfer student and did not command a spot in our graduation annual.

Carol Nalley, another friend, gave up her right to the Valedictorian honor by marrying before graduation. In the early sixties, the children of the fifties were not yet ready to publicly protest anything. So, Carroll Hammack, the scholastic runner-up, received public recognition for first place results, while Carol sat. To her credit, she was selected as Miss Scholastic. It is important to note, in many households she earned admiration by early achievement of her *true* purpose in life—finding a husband.

The graduating class sat in order of our scholastic achievements. Our school did not field a football team, though we did boast a better-than-average basketball squad, an okay baseball team, and an outstanding music program. The scholarships awarded that year were largely academic, and I took advantage of a small one offered by LSU-A in Lafayette.

Ultimately, it paid for three semesters—summer, fall, spring—at Louisiana State University at Alexandria. I had foolishly anticipated financial help from Daddy but found that coffer bare. I attempted to alter the result via many debates about the value of educating girls. Some of those disagreements grew louder than others, as Daddy attempted to save me from making a mistake!

I recall one in particular:

"You don't need to go to college, Olevia. There are plenty of good boys around here. You'll find one and get married. I'm not giving you a bunch of money to waste on college."

"Daddy, you let Hannah go to business school. Why can't I go to college?"

"If you want to go to business school, maybe I can help you. Hannah works hard. I'm not sure you'll put in the work. You need to find a man to take care of you."

"I don't want to be taken care of. I don't want to go to business school. I don't want to be a secretary. I want to be a teacher. I want to go to college." My pleas fell on deaf ears.

"Well, if you want to take care of yourself, that's your choice. I'm not paying for it."

I cried buckets of tears. Thelma, the stepmother du jour, sympathized with me, but neither of us influenced Daddy to give an inch. LSU-A, a two-year community college, would give me time to figure out the rest. With a normal seventeen-year-old's alacrity for any new experience, I quickly moved on from Daddy's displeasure and eagerly awaited the September opening day.

****

Several wheeled Tioga students attended LSU-A, and I immediately established a system of rides with one group in the mornings and another in the afternoons. My part-time job at Life of Georgia Insurance Company in Alexandria and Mr. Azemar, my boss, required I be at work by one in the afternoon, every day. From there, I caught the Tioga bus home at five.

Although an adequate arrangement, it was cumbersome, and I longed for my own transportation. I pictured a '57 Chevy convertible but would have been happy with used '51 Henry J.

Meanwhile, Sara Terrell severely injured some nerves in her right hand in a one-car accident, and she decided to take a semester off from Louisiana College in Pineville. A solution to my transportation problem appeared out of the blue (as almost every problem's solution has come to me in my life) when Mrs. Terrell invited me to live with them for a while.

Mr. Terrell sweetened the pot by offering to pay all my college expenses with no repayment required, so long as I graduated. Had I been a more astute and sagacious person, I would have recognized and been astounded by this blessing. I wasn't. To me, it represented an immediate but only interim answer to my situation.

I moved in and, within just days, Mr. Terrell handed me the keys to a car for my and Sara's exclusive use. The conservative-looking sedan (I don't even remember the make or model) was not the '57 Chevy or T-Bird of my dreams, but it was reliable, comfortable, available, and free.

Sara and I had been close high school friends and enjoyed each other's company living together; still, there were some minor adjustments to be made.

My family considered the Terrells (Luther and Effie) to be well-to-do. Mr. Terrell worked as an oil company field inspector, and Mrs. Terrell taught the second grade. Both were active in church. Mr. Terrell was a deacon, while Mrs. Terrell taught Sunday school. From my limited perspective, Sara, as an only child, had it made.

I recall visiting her bedroom for the first time. The royal Princess Mary would not have expected a more fairyland bedroom. Every shade of purple, the color of the moment for Sara, found its way into the décor—the curtains, the bedspread, the pillow covers, and everywhere. A four-poster canopy bed occupied center stage with a pair of purple, fuzzy slippers beside it on the purple throw rug. The hardwood floors sported a shiny finish, and the sun sparkled through two large windows. Her room included a walk-in closet filled with just her things, and a vanity table with a padded stool in front of the mirror completed the dream room.

My look in the mirror did not get the response of fairy tales, the fairest of them all, but rather it reflected my feeling in awe of where I stood as wide-eyed as I would be viewing the Grand Canyon or Mount Everest.

Just outside the bedroom door sat a baby grand piano. It graced the left side of a large living room that included a fireplace and a stereo system. The living room opened into the dining area with a sort of breakfast nook on one end. Barstools stood next to the counter. Just to the left and down the hallway was the main bathroom. This part of the house belonged almost solely to Sara and me.

As I put my things in the assigned dresser drawers, I wondered why I breathed the air of *Alice in Wonderland,* allowing me to share this fantasy filled with so much more than I had experienced or expected. I lifted to heaven a silent prayer of thanksgiving.

Her mom and dad shared the den, their bedroom, bath, and study as their living quarters. We all shared the kitchen, from which Mrs. Terrell's cooking expertise ensured never-ending good aromas wafting through the house.

The first time I noticed it, Sara sat on the piano stool, attempting some one-handed pieces. I nudged her and asked, "What's that I smell?"

She sniffed. "I don't know, but Mother's baking today. I think she's taking something to someone. I'm not sure who."

I grinned. "I'm going in there to check it out."

A delicious fragrance filled the air, one that immediately caused me to close my eyes, inhale deeply, and utter, "Ahhhhh." It competed with my favorite baking smell—homemade bread—and maybe even beat it by a length or two.

I jostled myself up and rushed to the kitchen. "What are you baking?" I took in a big sniff. "It certainly smells good!"

"Peach pies and peach cobblers." Sara's mom beamed at me. "Luther brought in an entire bushel of peaches this morning, and I'm not in the mood to can."

"What are you going to do with these pies?"

"Thought I would take most of them to church tomorrow to add to shut-in's baskets. Gonna freeze a couple for us."

"Oh great." I grinned, then knitted my brows. "Are shut-ins just people who are sick?"

"No. Shut-ins are those folks who are ill or otherwise providentially hindered from attending church."

I changed the subject back to cobblers! "What about today? Are we going to eat one today?" I must have sounded truly concerned or very hungry.

Mrs. Terrell chuckled. "Yes, indeed, Olevia. We'll have one for dessert tonight with dinner. You can top it with ice cream."

I breathed a sigh of foretaste knowing supper was just hours away.

Mr. Terrell cultivated a large garden and had a peach orchard and a huge strawberry patch. I knew whatever vegetable adorned our table every night would be freshly harvested and perfectly cooked.

Flashbacks to my mama's kitchen came tumbling back as I remembered the hot biscuits on a cold winter morning and the blackberry cobblers stuffed with June dewberries. I could almost taste them one more time and again felt Mama's presence as if she had entered the room.

Both Mr. Terrell and Mrs. Terrell indulged me when it came to eating. I loved the strawberries. Mr. Terrell often invited me to assist him in picking a small bucket for breakfast with cereal or just with milk.

On a cooler afternoon, Mrs. Terrell made spiced tea, hot chocolate, or fudge. When our friends came over, she once heated Dr. Pepper and served it in China cups with orange slices floating on top. The cups sat on flowered napkins beside cinnamon sticks to be used for stirring the hot beverage. She added a large platter of homemade cookies to the table while we planned our next adventure.

****

This heaven seemed too much and too good to last, and I feared making some terrible mistake resulting in my eviction. What I considered my first close call happened a few weeks after moving in.

Sara had these wonderful slippers—fuzzy inside and out. They looked rich to me, something to be handled with care. I thought my world might end on the day I found one of them in the washing machine! In a rare moment of helpfulness, I had gathered all the dirty clothes in our area and put them in the washing machine. My heart hit my throat as I unloaded the washer and discovered one of those pricey, upscale slippers transformed into a drenched, shrunken blob.

A calmer, more rational person than I would have stopped with the damage done and faced the consequences. Rather, I envisioned a completely restored slipper by popping it into a dryer set on high. Sara's size-four shoe emerged from the dryer a size-two lump covered with knots. Now, the situation seemed too extreme to report. I enjoyed living with Sara and did not wish to be found out as the source of her slipper's demise.

Again, I trotted down the path least likely to lead to a good solution—I hid the slipper. That very night, Sara mentioned her slippers.

"Have you seen my other slipper, Olevia?" she asked while I sat at the vanity table.

"Did you look under the bed?" I answered innocently.

"Yeah. Only one was there. Mother, have you seen my other slipper?"

"I haven't been in your room in the last day or so. No, I haven't seen your slipper. It must be there somewhere." Mrs. Terrell stopped vacuuming the living room and came into our bedroom. Together, they scoured the bedroom from top to bottom with no luck in finding the slipper.

Sara always called her mom Mother—another sure sign of the rich and famous. Still, she called her father Dad, and that sounded sort of like me.

Anyway, the search for the slipper went on for about a week before her mom discovered it in their dirty clothes hamper. She brought it into our room.

"Sara, look what I found. It looks like it has been in the washing machine. Why didn't you just tell me it was ruined?"

"Mother, I didn't put it in the washing machine. I don't know what happened to it. Why do you always think everything's my fault?" She tossed her an indignant frown.

"Well, something happened to it. What do you think it could have been if you didn't put it in the washing machine?"

"I don't know, but it's not my fault. I didn't put it in the washing machine," Sara repeated with an emphatic tone and raised brow. She glanced in my direction but said nothing.

I just sat idly by. No one seriously considered me to be the culprit or even questioned me about the ruined slipper. Maybe they didn't expect me to be helpful enough to load the washing machine or dumb enough to put the slipper in the dryer.

I could tell Sara's honest denials were digging her ditch deeper, as her mother became more annoyed. The perceived deceit got under her skin. Time for me to face the music.

"I did it, Mrs. Terrell. I ruined Sara's slipper." By this time, I was crying.

Mrs. Terrell's compassionate nature immediately came through. Her voice dripped forgiveness for me. "Well, Olevia, it's nothing to cry about. We'll just have to get Sara some new slippers. It does bother me that you did not tell me what happened or when it happened."

"I'm sorry."

Sara glared at me as I sat under a shower of Mrs. Terrell's forgiveness.

"Sara, I am sorry for the misplaced blame." She said this as a matter of fact and with compassion, even touching Sara's shoulder to emphasize her apology.

She then turned to me and went on to explain how to avoid such a tragedy in the future. She put her arm around my shoulders. "Next time, you need to separate the clothes more carefully. And never, ever put anything nylon in the dryer, especially not when it is set on high!"

A great weight lifted from my shoulders, replaced by a cape of love. By the time evening rolled around, Sara had blown off the misdeed as well, and we were securely locked back in our friendship.

****

Still, I didn't hear the message clearly. Oh, I learned how to properly do the wash, but I still felt more like a guest than a roommate, setting the scene for the next drama.

Sara had a fingernail care kit containing a cuticle stick, clippers, a fingernail file, something to push the cuticles back with, and all sorts of little instruments the likes of which I had never seen much less used. Had I asked to use this kit, Sara would have agreed immediately. There is no reasonable explanation as to why I waited until she was not at home to experiment with the tools—except maybe to hide my lack of familiarity with the kit and my fear of losing space in that gorgeous bedroom.

Sitting in the purple paradise alone, I decided to do my fingernails and carefully opened her fingernail kit. I filed, trimmed my cuticles, and properly prepared my nails for painting. Then I selected the perfect color from Sara's many bottles of polish.

Dried polish had firmly attached the lid to the bottle. Had I been the wise fairy godmother instead of one of the awful stepsisters, I would have simply chosen another color. Instead, I sought convenience when I reached for the cuticle tool, leading to another dilemma when the handle fell off. Proceeding with the same ill-thought-out approach that had worked so poorly with slippers, I used clear fingernail polish to reattach the handle. I then placed all the tools back in the case, put the case in the drawer, and wore an innocent expression on my face.

****

Saturday morning, Sara decided to do her nails! To delay the inevitable, I reached to remove the shoddily repaired tool. "Sara, do you ever use this? It doesn't look like it would be very useful."

"That's to push back your cuticles. If you don't push them back, they will grow on your fingernails. I use it every time I do my nails. Let me have it." She reached for the tool.

"Your cuticles look like they are already pushed back. I thought you would use a cuticle stick for that anyway. Why don't you use a cuticle stick?" I asked as I handed one to her.

"Sometimes I use both. Give it to me."

"It might not be good to use it every time. Do you think maybe you should use it only when your cuticles are grown out?"

"Olevia, what's wrong with you? Give me my cuticle remover." Her tone had become such that I realized she had become more than just annoyed.

I had run out of options, so I just handed it over. It looked as if she had barely touched her finger with the tool before it fell into two pieces.

Then, in what had become my go-to reaction, tears flowed.

She knitted her brows, confused. "What happened? What did you do?" She now sounded puzzled. Not angry, just puzzled.

"I'm sorry. I used your nail kit without asking, and that tool just broke. I'm sorry."

"Well, I'm not mad at you. Sometimes, I don't understand you!" She sounded exasperated as she shrugged her shoulders.

I didn't know why she wasn't mad with me. I think, unconsciously, I felt angry with her just for having things like that and for not being mad.

By the time the tears and apologies were over, I got the message loud and clear: these people were not going to throw me out. So, I relaxed into being me again. Being me did not necessarily mean a good thing, but a more comfortable role for both Sara and me. We became co-conspirators in annoying her parents, particularly her father—her mother was a saint.

****

In the early sixties, young people were frightening to Mr. Terrell, and we exploited that fear. Whether our music, our dancing—any dancing— or our lack of respect for authority, everything looked to Mr. Terrell like a banner of self-destruction and the highway to hell. He fought hard to save us while we battled to prove that not only could we not be saved, but we were eager to occupy that figuratively described handbasket to hell.

Though we were not directly involved, a typical skirmish in that battle to save teenage souls had occurred on high school graduation night when the Tioga Baptist preacher led a delegation—including Mr. Terrell—to spy on the kids who dared to organize a senior class dance. Sara and I were not part of that group, but we lined up solidly in their defense.

At church on the Sunday morning before, Dr. Brown had again outlined the evils of dancing and asked for a show of hands from the graduates who would be going to the student-organized party. We both clearly raised our hands. I don't know for sure; Sara may have attended. I had no intentions of going—just covering my bases so everyone knew where I stood.

Dr. Brown subsequently reminded us that there would be deacons at the party, of which Mr. Terrell was one, to observe any dancing that might occur.

The party, scheduled at the Tioga Community Center, allowed anyone to come and go, but I feel sure Dr. Brown's warnings significantly increased attendance.

It seems strange now that I never asked Sara if she went to that party. On graduation night, I still lived at home. Daddy let me have the car, and Merilyn and I went bowling. Thinking back, there were a couple of other girls with us, but I cannot remember who they were.

****

Mr. Terrell displayed kindness to me, appearing to care about me and my future. I know he wanted what was best for both of us, but our behavior totally mystified him.

Looking back, I am glad there were a few occasions I did thank him for his efforts—usually when we shared a bowl of strawberries shortly after sun-up. But those times were far outweighed by my mischievousness.

The Terrell's lived in Ball, about five miles north of Tioga and twelve miles north of Alexandria. Ward Ten's dry area—no liquor allowed—included Ball. We found that Hocus Spocus, a liquor store in Alex, had a delivery service, which we utilized for the sole purpose of embarrassing her dad. An occasional peach brandy bottle in the mailbox provided enough powder to create an explosion. Attempts to change his convinced position that rock and roll was the devil's music and Elvis Presley was the devil's tool were as fruitless as trying to teach a pig to talk. Moreover, his concern ensured that we would play it loud, long, and late.

Mrs. Terrell came to our defense, on that count, so we added fuel to the fire by inviting Jerry Ford over under the pretense of studying.

Sara's hand had healed enough for her to return to school, and Jerry attended LSU-A. He arrived at the door near dark, carrying books and forty-five rpm records. Less than an hour had passed before the books were put away and music was blaring.

None of us danced, but we encouraged Mr. Terrell to believe we did. Chubby Checker's latest hits, which included a re-release of his version of the "The Twist" had regained and held the number one spot on all the charts in 1962. "Let's Twist Again," "The Peppermint Twist," and "The Oliver Twist" were accompanied not only with The Twist, but other dances as well: The Fly, The Hully Gully, The Popeye, The Jerk, The Locomotion, to name a few. The confines of a deacon's living room inhibited any real wildness we might have aspired to, but we reveled in the rebellion of just listening to the music.

The Venetian blinds were tightly closed, and the lights were low, but we knew Mr. Terrell prowled the front yard for a glimpse of silhouettes in the window. The next day, we were admonished and warned about the lifetime consequences of our behavior.

We smoked, stayed up all night, sneaked in peach brandy, and drove too fast. Through it all, Mr. Terrell remained my bank as necessary. My job paid for gas, make-up, and the little extras. The Terrell's paid for this last summer semester at school and my clothes, and they supplied room and board. I even had nylons bought from Wellans; it was my first experience with saying, "Just put it on the account" anywhere but Merritt's store.

Despite being given every opportunity—maybe it was just too easy—I moved back home during the late summer, before the fall semester began. I worked full-time, rode the bus each way, and often stopped at Merilyn's. She attended college in Natchitoches, but her grades were not great, and she considered not going back in the fall.

****

We spent the summer doing what we had done in high school—borrowing the car, driving around, meeting Air Force guys at The Palms, and fantasizing about our futures including apartments, husbands, kids, and more.

Indeed, Sara met her Air Force husband-to-be, Richard Blackburn, at The Palms. Merilyn and I had small parts in her wedding festivities and wondered when our big day would come.

Then, one day, my phone rang, and Miss Higdon offered me a way out of dreaming to full awareness.

She asked me over to her house, saying there was something she wanted to discuss. I had never been summoned to her home before. In fact, I had to look for it, but I arrived in less than fifteen minutes. Little did I know my life's path had approached a fork in the road—an exciting one.

As I've said before, I've never felt far from my mom's direction and care. My guardian angels always show up at the right time to lead me in the direction meant for me.

Those angels take many forms including friends and their parents, teachers, neighbors, relatives, and even people who came into my life for the briefest of times. Those saviors, aided by that small, quiet voice in my heart, continue to provide me with a blessed and joyous life.

Life is good, and I am thankful.

CHAPTER 54

LEAVING TIOGA IS ON MY MIND

When the phone rang shortly after noon on a Sunday, I had no idea it was the bell announcing the next round in my life.

The weather lacked its normal suffocating heat usually associated with mid-to-late summer. I now worked full-time, and Sunday afternoons were often filled with getting ready for the week. I sat on the porch polishing my shoes in preparation for Monday morning. In no particular hurry, I put down the shoe and headed inside to answer the phone.

"Hello?"

"Hello. This is Gladys Higdon, and I'm calling Olevia. Is she there?"

"Yes, ma'am. This is me."

"This is I," she automatically corrected my grammar.

"Sorry. Miss Higdon. This is I."

She laughed. "You know we teachers never stop teaching."

I laughed as well, but a bit uneasily, wondering about the purpose of her call.

She continued, "I would like for you to come by this afternoon. I have something to discuss with you."

Without hesitation, I answered, "Yes, ma'am. I can be there in a few minutes. Is anything wrong?"

"No, honey. I'd just like to visit with you for a few minutes."

We hung up, and my mind danced in all directions, going down a dozen rabbit holes as I considered every reason I could think of—even obscure ones—to cause Miss.

Higdon's mysterious summons. The first stop required getting permission from Daddy to use his car.

"Where are you going in the middle of day?" His knitted brow and lack of any smile confirmed his suspicion of my motives.

"Miss Higdon just called me. She asked me to come by her house."

"Why would she do that?" He sounded incredulous.

"I don't know. It must be important because she wants to see me in person today." A bit of attitude now grew visible and audible in my response. I tilted my head in an unspoken challenge.

"That doesn't make much sense to me. You do understand I can call Gladys to verify your story?"

"Do you think I'm lying?" My tone relayed that I could not believe my ears. I stood with my hands on my hips and a look of dismay on my face.

"No. You can use the car, but remember I talk to Gladys more often than you might think."

His ominous voice caused no fear because, contrary to other times when I finagled myself into a borrowed car, today I stood on solid ground. In fifteen minutes, I knocked on Miss Higdon's door and, at twenty, we sat in her living room chatting.

She served me a Coke. Once the pleasantries were done, she asked, "Olevia, are you going back to school in the fall?"

I hadn't expected to be questioned about my future and wasn't sure what to say. I shrugged and replied, "I don't know, Miss Higdon. I'm doing pretty good at my job. I believe there is room for growth there."

"Have you ever thought about leaving Tioga?"

That thought made my brain freeze, and I remained silent a moment, feeling like a stunned rabbit when a big dog walks by. I considered her question and tilted my head.

She repeated, "As I asked, do you plan to stay here in Tioga, go back to school, or what?"

"Well, I'm not going to live at home. I'm thinking about getting an apartment in Alexandria. I can't afford it yet, but I may ask Merilyn to move in with me. I don't think she's going back to school."

She continued, "Did you know I go to Dallas once a month to see a doctor?"

I thought she had changed the subject. Though bewildered, I tried to stay focused on her question. "No, ma'am. Are you ill?"

She blew off my question with a sharp retort. "That's not pertinent to our conversation."

I began to wonder if she was in the beginnings of some sort of weird Alzheimer's. The only way forward appeared to be allowing her to control the conversation. I nodded and listened.

"In Dallas, I visit the Maxfield Clinic. On my last visit, Dr. Jack, my physician and a partner in the clinic, mentioned a job opportunity available in their office."

"Really?" I had no idea what the proper response should be, so I traveled carefully. "Are you taking the job?" In my wildest dreams, I could not imagine that to be the situation, but I was traveling in an unknown territory. It occurred to me that she might ask me to stay in her house while she was gone. She had never been married and had no children, so that thought made sense on some level.

She absolutely guffawed. "No, I'm not moving to Dallas or taking any new jobs."

She stopped to catch her breath, and I filled the gap with another question. "Are you suggesting I should move to Dallas?"

"If I were, would you consider it?" Her face grew suddenly serious.

In shock, I sat and stared like a deer in headlights.

She continued, "Dr. Jack said they're looking for a good x-ray typist. You could do that, couldn't you?"

"I don't know. I type sixty words a minute. I'm not familiar with medical terms, but I'm sure I could learn." I sighed. "I'm confused!" Mentally, I wandered in a House of Mirrors looking for the one right path, and my disorientation must have shown on my face.

Miss Higdon's expression suddenly changed to one of compassion and understanding. She smiled one of those smiles where the love shows through.

"I'm sorry. I'm excited about this opportunity for you, and I'm just rattling on. Let's slow down a minute." She paused with a half-smile. "Take a deep breath."

I did, and I felt more relaxed now that I could see Miss Higdon still mentally lived in our world. I smiled back as she continued.

"This is an opportunity to get a job and a brand-new start in a completely new place. You should think about it. A job is not promised, but I can confidently promise you an interview if you're interested."

Finally, we were on the same page, and my mind quickly slipped onto the stage of her imagined world.

"Okay, an interview can't hurt anything, and it might be fun."

"I'll call Dr. Jack to set it up for you."

"Remember, I work every day, so a Saturday interview would work best. And I don't know how I'll get there," I replied.

"One thing at a time. I'll get an interview set, and then I'll call you."

I floated out of her house and into my car on a cloud of anything-can-happen-now. I drove on automatic pilot to Merilyn's while my mind raced past the interview and all the way to living in Dallas. I visualized my apartment, my independence, and a whole new person occupying my body.

I left the car's motor running when I dashed to Merilyn's door, loudly calling, "Merilyn!"

Probably noting the urgency in my voice, she ran to the door and asked, "What's wrong? Are you okay?"

"I'm better than okay. Come take a ride with me."

"Mom," she yelled, "I'm going for a ride with Olevia. I'll be back in a little while."

I don't think she waited for an answer. We exited her driveway as if it were the yellow brick road to riches. We drove around and dreamed for almost an hour. We envisioned ourselves in Dallas, on our own, meeting our future husbands. At the very outside tip of reality, I talked about making enough money to go to SMU. You can see how far a young woman's fantasy can grow with the least amount of impetus.

This heady stuff and our overly optimistic approach resembled Voltaire's Pangloss' take on the world. We feared nothing, had no misgivings, and held absolute faith in our success.

I dropped Merilyn off at her home while I still occupied my cloud of possibilities. Once I arrived home, Daddy quickly turned that cloud into a thunderstorm. He sat on the porch waiting for me, and the interrogation began before I topped the steps.

"Where have you been?"

"Miss Higdon's. Let me tell you—"

"You have not been at Gladys' for two hours!"

"No. After I left her house, I ran by the McCarty's for a little while."

"What for? You told me you were going to Miss Higdon's."

"I did go to Miss Higdon's, Daddy. Merilyn and I took a ride afterward. Why are you so angry?"

"Well, I called Gladys, and she told me you had left an hour earlier. I don't like your lying."

"I'm sorry. I didn't mean—"

"And Gladys told me you were talking to her about a job in Dallas?"

"Yes, sir. But I don't even have an interview set up yet."

"Don't bother with an interview. You're not going anywhere."

Obviously, now was not the time to discuss interviews. "Okay." I handed Daddy the car keys and went into the house. My excitement had bloomed and wilted in less than three hours, as ephemeral as swamp grass.

****

Two days passed, and I had almost totally recovered from my adventure in dreamland and reacclimated to living in Tioga when the magic wand reappeared. Miss Higdon called.

"The interview's set for a week from last Saturday."

"Are you saying it's set for THIS Saturday?"

"Yes, you have three days to get ready."

I felt like I'd received a call from Dialing for Dollars, or a sweepstakes win. "I'm so excited! What time? Where? How am I going to get there? Thank you. Thank you."

Mrs. Higdon chuckled. "Slow down, Olevia. Remember, I told you this is an interview only—not the promise of a job. You must earn that on your own."

"I know. I'm delighted and nervous at the same time. Thank you so much. I'll ask Daddy to get me a pass on the train, but I'm not sure he'll be onboard with the interview."

"Well, the interview is at two o'clock on Saturday afternoon."

"I'll talk to Daddy tonight when he gets home."

"Okay. Let me know how it goes."

I met him at the door when he came in from work—not the best approach! I temporarily forgot that Mama never brought up bad news until Daddy sat down with his coffee. Thelma did the same, but I hadn't even discussed my plan with her, so she had no chance to caution me.

"Daddy, I have a job interview in Dallas next Saturday. It's with Miss Higdon's doctor. Will you get me a pass to ride the train?" I didn't breathe from start to finish, and Daddy looked stunned.

"What are you talking about? You have a job here. Why would you want to go running off to Dallas?"

"I want to go. It's just an interview. And I'm eighteen, so there's no reason to stay here."

Daddy had told us kids for as long as I could remember that his contract ended when we reached age eighteen. After that, we were on our own, and it seemed like a good time to play that card.

"I don't think you know what you want. I'm not going to be a part of you making the biggest mistake of your life."

Thelma had wandered out on the porch by now with two cups of coffee in hand. "Here's your coffee, John. What's going on out here?"

"Olevia thinks she wants to go to Dallas. Better put, she's not thinking."

"I am too!" The frustration and determination sounded in my voice and, surprisingly, Daddy took notice. His eyes widened.

"Tell you what, Olevia. I'll call Gladys to see what this is all about."

"Okay. It's only an interview. I don't even know if I'll get the job." The wise choice seemed to be to not push and let him check it out in his own time. When he came in from work the next day, he called me out on the porch.

"I talked to Gladys, and this is only an interview in Dallas. That may work as good practice for future interviews. I ordered you a straight-through pass for Saturday, and it should be ready tomorrow."

On the inside, I jumped for joy; on the outside, I remained calm, cool, and collected. "Okay. I appreciate that. Thank you." I went into the house and immediately dialed Merilyn's number.

"Merilyn, I'm going to Dallas for the job interview!"

"Wow. It came through?"

"Yes, and Daddy ordered me a straight-through, roundtrip pass. The interview is this coming Saturday."

****

I've often wondered why he ordered the pass for me. Maybe he never thought I'd get the job. Maybe he thought I'd never leave. Maybe he thought it was no more than a day's adventure. Maybe he thought I would be afraid when I saw a big city. I don't know what he thought. Maybe he thought it might be the right thing for me. Maybe my guardian angel influenced his decision. It doesn't really matter, because I had no doubt I would be in Dallas on Saturday at two o'clock.

CHAPTER 55

THE INTERVIEW

The sun was creeping over the horizon in tangerine hues when Daddy dropped me off at the Alexandria Railroad Depot.

"Olevia, please be careful." His melancholy voice caused me to reconsider the interview for a few seconds as I closed the car door. Going home crossed my mind too. I didn't do either.

"I will, Daddy. I'm going to ride the train directly to Dallas, catch a cab, and go to the interview. I'll be back home before I'm missed." I tried to laugh to add a bit of humor to the moment.

His flat response seemed as distant as a long, lonesome train whistle from the past. He gazed straight ahead. "I wonder what your mama would think?" I didn't see any tears, but his voice sounded so melancholy that I almost cried.

"She would be proud of me," I said with the confidence of an Olympian athlete who is facing, with trepidation, the first unknown opponent. "I know she would," I added for emphasis and maybe to convince myself as well.

With no change of expression, the pensiveness in his voice felt palpable. "I'm sure she would be too. Make her proud, and don't forget your name is Yeager. That's all anybody really has, their name and their character."

"Yes, sir," I replied and hurried out of the car and into the depot before he made me cry.

Once on the train, a long, boring trip ensued with only two stops between Alex and Dallas. People got on, off, and went to the dining car. Kids whined. I got lost in the book I had brought to read, and time passed faster.

Reality returned when the conductor shouted, "Next stop, Dallas. Arrival within a half-hour. Prepare to disembark the train in an orderly and brisk manner. A group of passengers are waiting to board."

I closed my book and sat straight up in my seat. My butterflies returned. We were a few miles southeast of the depot. I can't explain why, but staring out the windows at the clear blue skies and the scenery changes eased my mind. Anticipation replaced foreboding. A roller-coaster does not have more ups and downs than my psyche experienced from climbing out of bed that morning to stepping into a new world that afternoon. The highs and lows created an emotional merry-go-round, moving quickly, but going in circles.

As I stepped off the train, I reached into my pocket to touch the faded matchbook cover to remind myself I was not alone. I had an address but little else other than optimism and my mom in my heart to face whatever might happen. I took a deep breath and said a short prayer as I entered the depot.

Once in the depot, I rushed to look for a cab stand—my first experience doing so alone. I hoped I looked like a native when I waved to the next cab in line. It pulled up, and I hopped confidently into the backseat.

"Where to?" The driver glanced into the rear-view mirror.

"Oh, I'm sorry. I need to get to the Maxfield Clinic."

"And where's that?"

"On Oak Lawn, I think."

"In Oak Cliff or on Oak Lawn? I need an address." He sounded gruff to me, but then maybe that's the way taxi drivers sounded in Dallas. I had nothing to compare it with.

Any fantasy of looking adept in the city environment evaporated as I rummaged around in my purse to find the address again. "2711 Oak Lawn Avenue."

During the ride, my nervousness expressed itself in conversation. I told the driver all about my day, my interview, and my hopes for moving to Dallas someday.

"I'm here to see Dr. Jack Maxfield about a job. Do you know anything about that clinic?"

"Not really, other than it is a cancer clinic. I think they have some new methods, radiation or something."

"Well, I know somebody who is a patient." I said this as if it were some sort of badge of honor. "She said they have a nuclear medicine program of some sort and famous patients."

"Really? Like who?" the cab driver asked, though I don't think he had a lot of interest in my answer.

"Movie stars, for one. I don't know which ones. She also said Dr. Edward Teller is a patient there."

"Umm. That's interesting. Looks like we're here."

Once we arrived, I paid the fare AND remembered to add a tip! The driver smiled and wished me luck.

I met a receptionist, Emily, at the front desk and explained that I had an interview appointment. She led me to a small room with just a desk and a couple of chairs.

"Have a seat here, and I'll let Dr. J.R., and Dr. Jack know you are here."

"Thanks."

The room included a small window, and I walked over to look outside. It opened over a well-manicured courtyard with some benches and flowering bushes. A few people sat around. When Dr. J.R. entered, I was still standing at the window. I had been examining people in the courtyard, assigning a category to each: patient or family member of the patient. Lost in my daydream, I didn't hear or see him until I turned around.

"Ooohh!" I almost jumped out of my skin. He had a surgical gown on, complemented by cowboy boots and a wide-brimmed hat. His serious look was offset by his chuckle and reply.

"You must be Olevia. Gladys has told me a lot about you. She seems to think you're special."

Not knowing how to reply, my answer lost any appearance of sophistication. "That's nice. I think she's special, too."

When he laughed, I joined in. All the tension left the room like a soft landing from a second-story window. He asked me a few routine questions about my current job and what kind of grades I earned in school. Then, he left as fast as he had appeared. Dr. Jack took his place. He wore normal surgeon's attire without the cowboy accessories. He introduced himself as he handed me an application form.

"I'd like for you to complete this app for me. But, before you do that, I'm curious about your motive for wanting to move to Dallas. Do you have a job in Alexandria?"

"Yes, sir. At Life of Georgia Insurance Agency. I didn't even know anything about this job until Miss Higdon told me."

"So, why do you want to move? Are you thinking of coming alone? Are you leaving any trouble at home?"

"My best friend may move with me and, no, there's no trouble at home." I purposely avoided answering his first question because I didn't know how to answer it. I simply wanted to move because it felt right, but how do you tell someone that without sounding like a fool? I needed some time to think.

I took the app, and he excused himself, adding, "J.R. will be back in a minute." And, poof, he disappeared.

I sat at the desk to complete the form.

Before you could say "Jack Robinson," Dr. J.R. returned. This time, he sat down and pulled up a chair. "Tell me why you want this job."

I answered as truthfully as I could. "It's an opportunity brought to me by my favorite high school teacher, and it feels right."

He nodded his head and sat silently for a minute or so. "How confident are you that you can do the job?"

"Well, I don't know exactly what it is yet, but I learn fast and am smart. I know I can do anything I want to."

"How sure are you that you won't be here a month or two and get homesick?"

"I am not sure at all, but I'm not a quitter. I'll do my best and, if it doesn't work out, I'll make my departure as smooth as possible."

"Finish those papers. Jack will be back soon, and we'll decide where we go from here."

"Yes, sir."

I completed the task, then I reviewed my answers half a dozen times and finally sat quietly thinking about the decision I had to make. In my optimistic approach, I believed the job was mine to take or leave. I consciously listed the pros and cons and weighed each one. The pros far outweighed the cons!

Dr. J.R. and Dr. Jack came back together. This time, Dr. J.R. had removed his surgical gown and wore a sports jacket sporting a large, diamond stickpin—so large it stood out. Dr. Jack perused the completed app and asked if I had any questions.

I said, "No," but in my head the questions echoed:

- How much would I be paid?
- Are there nearby apartments?
- What are the hours?

In the state I was in—the state of euphoria—these seemed trivial and mundane considerations. (*Oh, to be young again!*)

Dr. J.R. took the lead. "Okay, Olevia, this job is strictly a beginner position, a dictaton typist in the x-ray department. You will transcribe tapes recorded by Jack and me following patients' visits, surgeries, and so forth." He sat back on his stool, crossed his arms, and smiled slightly. "Do you want this job?"

"Yes. I must give notice to my boss at home. I think I can be here in two weeks." No pauses between statements, as I wanted to end the interview and get to a phone.

"Okay. He handed me a book of medical terms and continued. "This is a big decision—not to be taken lightly. Think about it on the way home and call me on Monday to give me your conclusion." He then turned to Dr. Jack. "Do you have time to take Olevia to the train depot?"

"Sure. My schedule's clear for the rest of the afternoon. Gimme twenty minutes, Olevia, and I'll see you in the lobby."

"Yes, sir." I floated into the lobby and spent a few minutes chatting with the receptionist.

"Your name is Emily, right?"

"Yes, and yours is Olevia? Are you our new employee?"

"I'll be back in two weeks. I've never seen a doctor wearing a cowboy hat and cowboy boots. Does Dr. J.R. always wear those? I just have to ask!"

She laughed. "Yes, he does, and people always ask. He's got quite a history. Check him and the Maxfields out in your library encyclopedias."

"Really?"

"Yes," she answered just as Dr. Jack walked through the door.

As I gathered my things, she whispered, "He's a lifelong, honorary Texas Ranger. Very proud of it."

"I'll see you soon." I smiled, gathered my things, and walked out with Dr. Jack.

I remember nothing about the shared ride to the depot except for the brief goodbye. I said, "Thanks a lot. See you in two weeks." Inwardly, I had moved on and needed a telephone. I practically ran for the first available booth in the depot to place my collect call.

"I got the job!" I squealed.

"You got the job?" Merilyn shrieked.

"Yes, I got the job! Wanna move to Dallas in a couple of weeks?"

I could hear Mrs. McCarty in the background. "Did I hear you accept a collect call?"

Merilyn ignored her question and answered mine.

"Yeah, but I gotta hang up now. Mom's going to have a cat fit when she gets this bill."

"See you tomorrow."

****

My train arrived in Alex in the wee hours of the morning, and I took a cab to Tioga. I had no idea this could be considered unusual or dangerous. Later that same morning, I learned from Mrs. Curry that no one took cabs to Tioga in the middle of the night.

"Olevia, what were you thinking?"

"That I wanted to get home?" I laughed, not realizing her concern was real.

"It's just dangerous. Please tell me you'll be more careful in Dallas."

"Sure. Let me tell you what I'm going to do."

Coffee brewed, and the smells escaping from the oven reminded me I had not actually eaten the day before. "What's cooking?"

"I'm warming a cinnamon roll for myself. Ellis and George are off fishing this weekend and won't be in until late afternoon." As she took another Danish from the fridge and reached for a second coffee cup, she spoke again. "I'm serious, Olevia, about your safety. Dallas is a big city, and I worry you might feel safer than you are."

"Oh, Mrs. Curry! You know I'm always careful. Do you have any bacon or sausage? I'll cook it." My tone, slight grin, and wink made the comment glibber than I meant it to be.

She simply sighed, put some sausage on the stove, sat down across the table, and prepared to listen as she always did.

****

When talking with Mrs. Curry, I consistently occupied the chair used by my mom for so many years. Oftentimes, I felt I naturally channeled my mom and continued to have her presence at every challenge and triumph. As we chatted, a divine-like peace settled over my heart like a warm jacket on a chilly morning.

CHAPTER 56

CATCHING THE FREEDOM TRAIN

On a beautiful September Sunday in 1962, around noon, I stood in the Alexandria Railroad Depot. My best friend, Merilyn Haydel, and her family stood beside me. Sleep had been evasive the night before—maybe for several nights before—for both Merilyn and me (and likely her family as well). Nonetheless, I felt good. The weather was pleasant, a little cooler than expected, and more like the beginning of something than the end of a life chapter.

****

Two weeks earlier, at first light on the Sunday after accepting a job in Dallas, I shared my story over coffee and sweet rolls with Mrs. Curry.

"Olevia, are you sure this is what you want to do? There's no rush in your leaving. You know you are always welcome to stay with me any time you want a break from home."

"That's not it. I don't want a break or need a break. It's more like I want a life of my own, and I'm not sure I know how to get that in Tioga."

"Aren't you just a little afraid of taking off to some big city?"

The twinkle in her eye and the tilt of her head made the question amusing, and I laughed. She didn't, so I recognized her concern as real.

I answered soberly. "To be honest, I don't know if I am or not. I'm a little nervous, but I'm excited too. And Uncle

J.T. and Aunt Cly are there, and I know they would be my safety net if I needed one. And I'm not going by myself. Merilyn's going with me. And I have a job."

She looked resigned to the situation when she spoke again. "One thing about it, I know once you've made up your mind, you'll succeed at anything you want." She got up to get the sizzling sausage off the stove and pour two new cups of coffee.

The conversation with Mrs. Curry had its usual calming effect and enabled me to find myself in the jumble my brain had become. I left her house knowing my life flowed in the direction designed for me before I landed here on earth.

That same day, I walked to Merilyn's and arrived at a perfect time to be invited to Sunday dinner. Marilyn's grandparents and her mother, as well as her stepfather and two of her three sisters, were there. She and I managed to help with dinner without really helping. We set the table and poured the tea. Mostly, we avoided being in earshot of anyone else while we talked.

Finally, we all sat around the table. Once the blessing had been completed, I startled everyone by announcing, a bit louder than necessary, "Guess what?"

Alarmed, everyone stared at me.

Mrs. McCarty asked, "What?"

"I'm moving to Dallas! I've got a job there."

One could have heard a pin drop. It seemed as if forks stopped in midair like hummingbirds. I could have just grown a second head and not attracted more shocked faces.

Finally, Mrs. McCarty broke the silence. "Well, this is a surprise. Dallas, huh?" She cocked her head to one side. "What kind of job have you got over there?"

Though everyone's trance seemed to crack, they continued to look at me as they ate.

"I'm going to be an x-ray typist."

"That's wonderful! Did you have to go to Dallas to get the job?"

"Yes. That's where I was when I called Merilyn yesterday. I'm sorry about the collect call."

"That's okay. If your boss here is looking for a replacement, I would love to talk to him. I need something less physical than this nurse's aide job."

Before I could answer, Merilyn dropped her bombshell at a lower volume. Just above a whisper, she mumbled, "I'm going with her!"

The atmosphere changed again, drastically, as if a cloud had covered the sun. Again, Mrs. McCarty spoke first, staring at Merilyn. "You're what?" No one seemed congratulatory any longer, and everyone began to talk at once.

"Where are ya'll gonna stay?"

I answered, "We don't know yet, but I have an uncle there. I plan to call him."

"Merilyn, what are you going to do for money?"

"I'm going to get a job."

"Well, you won't have one on the day you arrive. What are you going to do until you get a paycheck?"

"I'm going to get a job really fast!"

Mr. McCarty spoke up, asking, "Olevia, does your uncle live close to where you're going to work?"

"I don't know. I've never been to his house. Besides, if we stay with him, we'll only be there for a few days. We're going to get an apartment. I'll figure out how to get to work. Maybe a bus."

Both Merilyn and I fielded questions for several minutes when I glanced at her grandmother, who had stopped eating. She looked pale and overwrought as she studied us.

Visibly shaking and in her most whiney, old lady voice, she said, "Dallas is a wild and woolly town. What are you two going to do when you find that out?"

Everyone turned in our direction to hear the response. Merilyn's younger sisters, Cheryl and Jan, were trying not to giggle as they thoroughly enjoyed the show.

Without hesitating, I answered, "Just be wild and woolly, I guess." I know I sounded cocky and impudent.

Looking back now, I regret my lack of both respect for an elderly lady and bad judgment in making a joke of her concern.

Merilyn and I provided the only laughter that resulted from my poor attempt at humor. Her grandmother slammed her chair against the wall, grabbed her walker, and left the table. My flippant reply ended the conversation for that day. Merilyn and I completed our meals quickly and did the dishes as some sort of penance. Then I walked home.

Later that night, I shared my good news with Daddy; I foolishly thought he might share some tidbit of my enthusiasm. Proof of my unrealistic optimism, I even asked him for passes for BOTH Merilyn and me. Youthful exuberance led me confidently down the wrong lane to a dead end.

"No. I'm not getting passes for either of you because you're not going."

"Yes, I am, Daddy. Some way, somehow, I will go to Dallas in two weeks. You can't stop me."

"Well, get there by yourself. I'm not going to be a part of this mistake."

****

On Monday, I alerted Mr. Azemar to my impending departure.

"Olevia," he said. "I congratulate you on your new job. Before you leave here, can you help me find your replacement? Do you have anyone in mind?"

"No, sir. I thought you would just put an ad in the *Town Talk*, right?"

"Well, you know the job and what we need here. I'm going to depend on you to send me some applicants."

"Okay. I'll check around. Thank you."

I called Merilyn. "Hey. Mr. Azemar said he would be willing to talk to anybody I recommend for taking my place. Do you really think your mom is interested?"

"I think so." She then called her mom to the phone.

"Hey, Mrs. McCarty. This is Olevia. Are you interested in interviewing for my job?"

"I am. I can type. I've worked in office clerical positions before. I'm already bonded, too, since I sometimes work in a patient's home. I know I could do it!" She sounded genuinely excited.

"Okay. I'll talk to Mr. Azemar. Is there any day that works best for you?"

"No. Since I'm working in the hospital right down the street from your office, I can come at almost any time."

"Great. I'll let you know."

Mr. Azemar agreed to have Mrs. McCarty try out for the job; subsequently, she worked there for twenty years.

****

That very night, I began to pack everything I thought I needed to begin life in a new environment. I owned one large suitcase and an overnight kit. Both were unused graduation gifts from Johnson that I had believed to be superfluous to my lifestyle. And, as it so often does, it occurred to me that my mom continued to watch over me and guide me through every life change. I smiled and silently said, *Thank you.*

For the two weeks until showtime, I spent my non-working hours either on the phone with Merilyn or at her house. Her parents calmed down, accepted the inevitable, and agreed to give her one hundred dollars as seed money. Once Merilyn spent the hundred dollars, she would be on her own. That sounded to us like a generous start. Combined with my last check, we felt almost rich.

Daddy remained adamant in his refusal to get a pass for either of us. Merilyn's parents bought her train ticket, and I waited. The Thursday before we were to leave on Sunday, I fired one more volley—the last one in my arsenal.

"Daddy, I leave Sunday at noon. Are you coming to the depot?"

He dodged the question, saying, "You should not be going to Dallas."

"Why don't you want me to be happy? You have Thelma. John's at Fort Ord in California. Hannah's in Japan. Why can't I go to Dallas?"

"Because you're making a mistake. You don't know anything about being in a city, especially about being alone in a big city. You belong here. Look around you. You could find a good husband. I can't let you go off like that. Your mama would turn over in her grave if she knew what you're doing."

I resented him playing the Mama card and trying to use it to change my mind.

"I have a job there, and if you won't give me a pass, then I'll figure out something else to do. I want to go, and I'm going."

I could see defeat in his eyes as he turned and walked from the room.

On Saturday night, I called Uncle J.T. "Guess what? I'm moving to Dallas."

"What? When?" His voice revealed his surprise as if he had just opened a Jack-in-the-Box.

"Tomorrow. My best girlfriend's coming with me."

"How're you getting here?"

"We're coming on the train, but I don't know where we're going to stay tomorrow night."

"You'll stay with us. Why are you moving to Dallas?"

"I have a job there. We're going to get an apartment, first thing."

"What time will you arrive?"

"I'm not sure yet. Depends on whether Daddy gets me a pass and, if he does, what kind. I'll need your exact address, so we can catch a cab to your house."

"You are not catching a cab! I'm your uncle, and I'll pick you up." He sounded pleased and protective.

"Wow! Thanks. That's super." I grinned to myself. "I'll call in the morning and let you know what time our train's scheduled to arrive.

By seven the next morning, Merilyn and I were on the phone planning how to get to the depot. Daddy left for work without a word, and I checked all the obvious places to see if he had left me a pass. I didn't find one. Thelma watched me as I looked around.

"Thelma, did Daddy say anything about leaving me a pass?"

"No, honey. He just said you're not going to Dallas."

"Well, he's wrong there. Tell him I'm gone when he gets home."

"Honey, are you sure this is what you want?"

"Yes. I am."

I gave her a little hug and told her I would miss her. "Why don't we have one last cup of coffee together before the McCarty's get here?"

I sat down at the table, and Thelma poured us each a cup.

"You know, honey, I care about you, and I'm concerned about this move you're making. Have you really thought it through? There's still time to change your mind."

"Everybody but me, Merilyn, and Mrs. Higdon seems to think I can't take care of myself!" The frustration in my voice came through loud and clear, like a fog horn in a storm.

"It's not that so much as it will be lonely around here without you."

Now, I knew she was scraping the bottom of the barrel for convincing arguments, and maybe she did have a legitimate concern for my welfare. We rarely spent time together and missing me would not be high on things changed by my absence.

I smiled, drank the last sip of coffee, and gave her one more little squeeze. "Mrs. Curry's always just down the hill with conversation readily available."

She chuckled. "I guess you're right. I think I hear the McCarty's car coming up the hill."

I slid my large suitcase toward the front door and picked up the smaller one. Mr. McCarty rushed to my rescue and carried both to the car.

****

That's how I came to be standing in the Alexandria Railroad Depot counting my money. It would be close, but I could buy myself a ticket and still have enough money to live on until I got my first Dallas paycheck. I hadn't purchased the ticket yet; I wanted to hold on to my money as long as possible. The clock continued to tick toward zero hour as I counted my funds one last time.

I looked up to see Daddy across the station. He appeared to be looking for someone, shifting his gaze this way and that with narrowed eyes. I knew he must be on his lunch break from work down at the roundhouse. My heart raced a bit, realizing he had decided to come see me off.

"Merilyn, I'll be right back. There's Daddy!"

I half-ran, waving and calling, "Over here, Daddy."

He waved back and picked up his pace a bit. When we met, he behaved as if I should have expected his arrival.

"Olevia, you left this lying on my desk this morning." He handed me a train pass. "I thought you might need it today. And here's fifty bucks as emergency funds."

What came to my mind first was the story of the three Hebrew children thrown in the fiery furnace and rescued without even the smell of smoke. Daddy saved the day. And, in my heart, I felt the part of those three kids doomed and saved in the blink of an eye.

Tears blurred my vision as I gave him a grateful hug. "Thank you."

He gently pushed me back and, with a smile and a twinkle in his eyes, said, "If you need anything, don't call. Write. Postage is cheaper."

I smiled back, and we shared one more heartfelt hug.

"I gotta go, Daddy. Looks like the train's about to board." I ran to catch up with Merilyn, who headed for the train and looked around for me simultaneously. I got there in time for a few more hugs, goodbye kisses, and tears as we left the McCarty's.

Merilyn and I shed tears of joy without any regret or reticence to leave. We were eager to board the train and begin our new lives! It seemed like electricity coursed through my veins providing a shining, golden light toward the future.

When settled into our seats, I remembered I had promised J.T. I would call him to let him know our arrival time. I nudged Merilyn, who seemed detached from reality, alternating between staring out the window and fixating on people sharing our car. A deer in headlights came to my mind.

"I forgot to call my uncle this morning!"

Her voice sounded strange and seemed to originate in a parallel world. "Well, you can call him when we get there."

"You're right. I can." And I breathed the first breath of real independence. We felt thirsty to drink in every nuance of our new autonomy, and the watering hole waited right around the corner.

The feeling of real freedom cannot be expressed in words. I know there are different levels and different sources of freedom based on every individual's situation and goals. However, I have come to learn that every level arrives with the exhale of fear and the inhale of knowing, *It's up to me.*

Thus began a lifetime of adventures.

CHAPTER 57

DALLAS ARRIVAL

Our train pulled into the Dallas Railroad Depot at 10:10 p.m. Even though we did not have straight-through tickets and stopped at every little town between Alex and Dallas, it seemed only minutes had passed since we had boarded ten hours before. At the same time, it could have been years. I felt as though we had passed through Einstein-Rosen's wormhole to a parallel universe completely unknown to us.

Merilyn and I soaked up every facet of our train trip from what we saw out the windows to the two-dollar ham sandwiches from the dining car. The scenery hypnotized us until darkness fell, and then the lights from the villages and small towns became our entertainment.

We didn't know when the Dallas buses ran. We didn't know where Jay and Cly lived. We had no idea as to where we might find an apartment, and Merilyn would be shopping in the dark when looking for a job. Those things did not affect our plan, as there was no plan. Thinking about all that, I told myself, *No problem, we got this!*

We stumbled off the train, lugging two huge suitcases and two overnight kits. We barely avoided falling when going down the steps. The distance between our climbing off the train and getting into the actual depot looked significantly further than I had anticipated. Having been given the choice of checking our bags into the baggage car when we left, we had chosen not to. We were among the last ones to board the train in Alex and, at the time, keeping our bags with us seemed a good idea. The train wasn't crowded, and we enjoyed sharing four front seats in our car.

That decision became less attractive as we stepped into our new lives.

"Gosh, Merilyn, it's a long walk just to get into the depot!"

"Why didn't you know that?" She frowned. "You were here two weeks ago." She sounded irked.

"Well, I wasn't checking out the landscape." I felt as if I had been pushed out of a plane on my first jump and introduced as the instructor! Unfamiliar with the equipment, the destination, and still expected to manage the fall.

Would you believe wheeled suitcases had not yet made the scene in 1962? At least, not for us, and our bags were packed to capacity. Our spirits immediately brightened when we spotted a nice-looking young man standing near the depot door. Using our best smiles and come hither looks, we nodded at him. He returned our smiles and, in the blink of an eye, stood beside us.

"Hello, ladies. Do you need some help with that luggage?"

The parachute had landed safely!

"Yes. Thank you so much," I said with a bright smile as he loaded our baggage onto his cart.

"Where to, ladies? Do you need a cab?"

"Not yet. Is that a gift shop over there?" Merilyn pointed across the building once we were inside.

"Yes. It is," our angel answered.

"Let's go over there for a few minutes." She looked at me, and I nodded.

We gave our helper instructions to follow us to the gift shop, where we profusely thanked him again as he removed our luggage. As we began looking about, I noticed he stood and stared at us from the front door.

"Merilyn," I whispered. "Do you see that guy staring at us?"

"What?" she replied as she continued to rummage through all displayed souvenirs.

"Never mind. He's gone now."

The lady standing beside me spoke up. "Honey, I think he was waiting for his tip."

"Oh. Thank you." I blushed.

My thoughts were spinning. *This Dallas environment's going to provide a new education on many more levels than envisioned. Can't imagine a guy offering to help me and then expecting to be paid. Apparently, he's not our angel, just a guy doing his job.*

I flipped through the postcards looking for one to send to Daddy. Merilyn continued to browse through everything else. About twenty minutes into our gift shop event, a tap on my shoulder got my immediate attention.

I spun around and then smiled. "Jay! When did you get here?"

"Well, Olevia, this is the third train I've met today." The irritation in his voice was outvoted by the kindness in his smile.

"Why? I told you we would probably be in around ten or so, didn't I?" At that moment, I remembered again the promised call I had forgotten.

"No, you didn't."

"Oh, I'm so sorry. Today has been a whirlwind! I forgot."

"No problem to me, but Your Aunt Cly is a basket of nerves and has been all day. We called your dad, but he had not come in from work yet. Thelma answered but knew only that you had left on a train sometime today. Cly just knew you and your friend would be scared to death, alone at night in a big city."

I thought, *Why? Nothing looks dangerous around here.* But I knew that was better left unsaid. I called and waved to

Merilyn, who stood across the shop busily talking to someone.

She looked over and waved. "Be right there."

"Well, what was that all about?" I asked as she strolled up to Jay and me. She'd taken her good time, leaving me to make small talk while feeling guilty about the missed phone call.

"Oh, I was telling my new friend about that guy who helped us with our luggage and then stood around staring at us. She thinks he might have been a baggage person who helps people with their luggage and will even get a cab for them. She said they make their money through tips. I told her we didn't give him one, and she replied, "No wonder he was staring!"" Merilyn chuckled as she continued. "My friend did ask if we were new in town and cautioned that we should be careful."

Jay broke into our conversation. "Hi. I'm Jay, and you must be Merilyn?"

"Yes, sir."

"Okay, let's get your bags, and we'll head home."

When we loaded the car and took our seats, my first thought was that I wanted a cigarette. I smoked, as did Merilyn, Jay, and Cly. No adults in Louisiana, except for Mrs. Curry, knew we smoked. My dad allowed no one to smoke in our house, not even Henry or visitors. Well, not exactly no one. Mrs. Curry brought her own ashtray and completely ignored Daddy's feigned coughs or the raising of his eyebrows and the windows. Once, he set up a fan behind her to blow the smoke through the open door. She thanked him for the extra breeze, saying it felt good on a summer day. Her sincerity sounded so real that he felt obligated to respond, "You're welcome." She and Mama laughed many times over coffee, reliving that incident and so many others. Had it been anyone other than Mrs. Curry, they would have been asked to leave, but she had the right charm to handle Daddy.

Merilyn and I never smoked in the company of any adults, but we were in Dallas now.

"Jay, do you mind if I smoke in your car?"

Jay had a cigarette in his hand already. "No, honey. That's okay. Why don't you two tell me about your trip?"

We took turns telling him everything up to and including our untipped porter. By the time we finished a rather embellished recounting of the day, he pulled into his East Dallas driveway.

"Jay, is there a bus close by that I can catch to get to work? And Merilyn's going to be job hunting, so she'll need to ride the bus as well." I began my questioning before I even got out of the car.

"I'll get you a bus schedule. You can catch it just two blocks away. But, for tomorrow, I've taken the day off to take you to work and make certain everything's in order."

"Okay," I answered as I walked to the porch to greet Cly, who stood almost wringing her hands while watching Jay struggle with our suitcases. Their five-year-old son, Jimmy, asked us repeatedly, "Why are you spending the night?"

Apparently, he was not interested in an answer, and we quit giving him one after his fifth inquiry.

My thought was, *Why aren't you in bed?* Another one of those thoughts best not shared with others!

Following the hugs and welcomes, Cly sat us down to inquire about our immediate plans. "Olevia, do you have to be at work tomorrow?"

"Yes, ma'am."

"What time?"

"I think eight o'clock."

"How are you going to get there?"

"Jay said he scheduled tomorrow off to take me. We'll work something else out after that."

"Well, he certainly has the PTO needed to do that."

I had no idea what PTO meant, and I didn't ask that night.

Clydell pointed out the bathroom and our bedroom—a converted den. The couch extended into a double bed, and it looked like a great place to be.

"You girls need to get to bed. It's after midnight. Olevia, if you're going to be at work by eight in the morning, you need to be up by six, so we'll have time for breakfast and to chat a few minutes before you leave."

"Okay." The thought of crawling between clean sheets gave a feeling as pleasant as a cold glass of sweet tea on a hot July afternoon. We closed our door, got into our pajamas, and collapsed into bed.

Without intention, probably because we were exhausted from a rough two weeks with little sleep, we began to laugh. The harder we tried to control our laughter, even with pillows over our heads, the more uncontrollable it became.

Cly must have thought we were crying and trying to muffle our sobs. She knocked on the door. "Olevia, are you all okay? I know it's hard to be in a strange house so far from home, but you'll be okay. It's normal to be homesick. Can I do anything?"

Funny how, for just a moment, her voice reminded me of Mama's.

Merilyn and I managed to get the giggles under control.

"We're okay, Aunt Clydell. We'll see you in the morning."

Only the most naïve, unworldly, and immature adventurers could have been so blasé in facing unknown challenges and dangers as well as delights of a completely new reality. Without fear, we became Cinderellas leaving the hearth behind to enter the mansion's ballroom.

The next morning would come early, and I eagerly awaited the sunrise on whatever the day would bring. The one thing I knew for certain, then and now, is that I am never alone.

About the Author

Ann Mullen has enjoyed writing throughout her life. From journals to vacation memories, she's writing it all down. Ann has a number of articles published in various magazines, and several columns in small newspapers for advertisement of state parks and their volunteer projects. Upon becoming semi-retired, Mullen dove straight into her passion and has writing projects in the works, including booklets of commentary and philosophy, and a group effort titled *12 New Christmas Stories*. Ann's favorite phrase is one of her own, "Writing does not make my living, but it does make my living worthwhile." Ann can be reached at annmullen1943@gmail.com.